Marxism and Urban Culture

Marxism and Urban Culture

Edited by Benjamin Fraser

Foreword by Andy Merrifield

LEXINGTON BOOKS
Lanham • Boulder • New York • Toronto • Plymouth, UK

Published by Lexington Books
A wholly owned subsidiary of Rowman & Littlefield
4501 Forbes Boulevard, Suite 200, Lanham, Maryland 20706
www.rowman.com

10 Thornbury Road, Plymouth PL6 7PP, United Kingdom

British Library Cataloguing in Publication Information Available

Library of Congress Cataloging-in-Publication Data

Library of Congress Cataloging-in-Publication Data Available
ISBN 978-0-7391-9157-6 (cloth : alk. paper)
ISBN 978-0-7391-9158-3 (electronic)
ISBN 978-0-7391-9448-5 (pbk: alk. paper)

∞™ The paper used in this publication meets the minimum requirements of American
National Standard for Information Sciences Permanence of Paper for Printed Library
Materials, ANSI/NISO Z39.48-1992.

Printed in the United States of America

Contents

Acknowledgments

This book project is the product of extensive reflections on a central contradiction obscured by the triumphant and triumphalist discourse of interdisciplinarity—as it plays out in academic institutions, in peer-review processes, in scholarly association meetings, and in numerous (if not, necessarily, all) disciplinary contexts. Although this contradiction is not explicitly discussed in the present volume—and although the topic is surely worthy of sustained consideration—it has motivated the selection of chapters and the brief introduction. The contradiction is this: that at the same time that mention of the word "interdisciplinarity" hypnotizes university administrators, hiring departments, job-seekers, editors, and authors, and more, still, it is nonetheless disciplinary knowledge which continues to exercise hegemonic power over scholarly activity, broadly conceived. I will spare the reader the numerous and varied experiences which have led me to this conclusion.

Make no mistake: I want neither to tout interdisciplinarity as a panacea nor to dig my heels into the disciplinary landscape that continues to shape the production and reception of scholarly work. Instead, this book has been—from its conception to its final structure—an attempt to expose the dimensions of disciplinary specialization through both the juxtaposition and the cohabitation of different approaches in a single volume. My belief—foregrounded also in the recent formation of the *Journal of Urban Cultural Studies*—is that "the urban" provides a point of encounter where disciplinary specializations can be brought to dialogue with one another. I do not believe that they cannot be fully transcended. But seen together they may help us to understand how it is that disciplinary specialization is, *a la* Henri Lefebvre, a form of alienation. In this sense, Marxian scholarship, clearly—though it should not necessarily be so—has been no exception to the rule that scholarly writing has tended to fragment a totality into relatively autonomous, manageable areas of expertise.

In this light, I would like to take the time to thank those colleagues whose scholarship has been particularly valuable in thinking through disciplinary specialization by working across Hispanic Studies and Urban Studies specifically: Malcolm Alan Compitello, Susan Larson, Araceli Masterson-Algar, Stephen Vilaseca, Monica Degen, Rebecca Haidt, Amanda Holmes, Donald McNeill, Marcy Schwartz, Eugenia Afinoguénova, Edward Baker, Alberto Chamorro, Susan Divine, Matthew Feinberg, Daniel Frost, Leigh Mercer, Carlos Ramos, Nathan Richardson, and Nil Santiáñez. I owe thanks to countless others, of course, in Hispanic Studies and beyond, and to that end I would also like to thank those who have agreed to be on the editorial board of the *Journal of Urban Cultural Studies*. Thanks, too, to Adam David Morton for his encouragement of this book project, and particularly also Andy Merrifield, who graciously agreed to pen this book's foreword.

As always I thank Abby.

Foreword

Urbanism as World Culture and Here Comes Everybody

Andy Merrifield

One of the great wish-images of the *Communist Manifesto* is something Marx calls "world Literature." World literature, he says, is what everybody and anybody can read. We get it because we've somehow helped script it; it's a literature that's translatable and communicable—notwithstanding our native tongue. But it isn't tabloid trash Marx has in mind here; it isn't narrow-minded, trivial journalism, nothing provincial. Quite the opposite: it's the broadest of broadsheets, a global literature that hits the newsstands as samizdat, as popular agitprop. Invariably, this literature is a dialectical byproduct, an unintended good thing emerging from an intentional bad thing. It's a byproduct, Marx knew, of a bourgeoisie intent on business, tapping the world market, exploiting old-established national industries, downsizing these old industries and replacing them with dwindling workforces and new product lines. "In place of the old wants, satisfied by the production of the country, we find new wants," Marx says. "In place of the old local and national seclusion and self-sufficiency, we have intercourse in every direction, universal inter-dependence of nations."[1]

Marx is adamant that this process isn't only an earth-moving (and earth-shattering) act of material production; it's also an earth-moving and potentially earth-shattering act of "intellectual production." What's more, in his eyes, these "intellectual creations of individual nations" have the power to become "common property."[2] World literature becomes a new sort of commons, for Marx, a collective visual and written language, something we see today as an ever-emergent *world culture*, as use-values ordinary people everywhere continually have to fight for and struggle to hold on to, especially as human value systems melt into air and get converted into anti-human, hyper-inflated exchange-values. In the *Manifesto*, Marx sketches out the developmental forces of the mode of production, its historical and geographical mission, its need to urbanize itself, to create industrial cities, to move mountains, to dig canals, to connect everywhere, nestle everywhere, to do all of that because of its inexorable urge, because it, as a mode of production, had to. Within it all, Marx thought urbanization would create a physical and emotional proximity of workers, workers piled on top of one another, beside each other. Cosmopolitanism would thus be a kind of sharing, an awareness of common lived experience.

Before us and inside us, urbanism today is a truly cosmopolitan world culture, our very own world literature. It's the expansive realm, we might say, of *Here Comes Everybody*, of H.C.E.—Joyce's sigla from *Finnegans Wake*—the "normative letters of planet" urban, the social, political, and economic environment to which everybody is coming and which everybody is somehow shaping, even if always unevenly. H.C.E, says Joyce, represents a "manyfeast munificent," an archetypal image of our collective, desiring unconscious.[3] The dreamer is "more mob than man," Joyce jokes, "an imposing everybody he always indeed looked, constantly the same as and equal to himself and magnificently well worthy of any and all such universalization."[4] Perhaps, with a little imagination, we can read *Here Comes Everybody* as what global citizenship ought to be about, a citizenship conceived of as something urban, as something territorial, yet one in which urban territoriality is narrower and broader than both "city" and "nationality"; a citizen of the block, of the neighborhood, becomes a citizen of the world, a universal citizen rooted in place, encountering fellow citizens across the corridor and at the other end of the planet, sharing world music together, reading books in every language, watching world cinema, entering Twitter streams, and communing on Facebook.

World literature has morphed into world culture, and this world culture is now an urban arena in which a more advanced cosmopolitan citizenship emerges—might emerge—a *Here Comes Everybody* forever present during its own birth pangs. In this citizenship, *perception* replaces passport and *horizon* is almost as important as habitat; a perception and horizon simultaneously in place and in space, off-line somewhere local, and online somewhere planetary, somewhere virtual. If we want to call this perspective a newly formulated cognitive map in our heads, we can. What's important in this mapping is that it maps the totality, that it works when people see these two realms coming together, when perception and horizon conjoin, encounter one another, and give rise to a collective political awareness. Citizenship therein *reveals itself through the negation of distance and the reaching out to distance*, through an opening up and a drawing in, a passionate embrace. It's the point of convergence of both, a dialectic that's a structure of feeling and a way of seeing—feeling and seeing oneself on the same plane as one's planet. At the point of convergence, any singularity will be so powerful that no border patrols can ever prevent its rites of passage.

Official identity cards aren't necessary for citizens of the urban universe, for people who know they *live* somewhere yet *feel* they belong everywhere. Or who want to feel it. The conjoining of knowing and feeling is what engenders a sense of empathy whose nom de plume might really be citizenship itself. Urbanization makes this new sense of belonging possible, makes it both broader and narrower, even as it sometimes rips up the foundation of one's own dwelling space—dwelling in a narrow sense. This is the sort of dialectic that *Marxism and Urban Culture* is trying to work through, tries to look in the face, tarrying with the magical power of the negative, deriving something positive in the process. The assembled essays form a cultural contraflow that roams through historical time and global space, that bed themselves down in Hispanic studies as well as in political science, in Communication studies as well as International Relations, in Madrid as well as in Montreal, in Vienna as well as in Cairo, in Osaka as well as in Los Angeles and Guatemala City, on reel as well as in the real; it's a peripatetic grand narrative that concerns itself with art as well as protest, with representation as well as mobilization, sometimes in the street, occasionally unto death, but all times with an expressive desire—in Henri Lefebvre's words—"of *metamorphosing* the real."

In *The Urban Revolution*, Lefebvre uses a beautiful turn of phrase: "the urban consolidates" [*l'urbain rassemble*], he says.[5] The urban becomes urban because it creates its own definition, because, as complex web of social relations somehow hanging together, it engenders and expresses a specific kind of sociability. The urban is a bringer together, and the harbinger and transformer of everything in that coming together: capital and goods, people and information, activity and conflict, mass and underground media, confrontation and cooperation. The urban "de-structures and re-structures its elements," Lefebvre says. As a form, it concentrates and intensifies things, creates simultaneity and difference, difference where no awareness of difference existed; and what were once thought distinct and isolated become conscious of universality, of universality in their particularity. This is why Marx lobbies for its coming, for the becoming of urbanization. *The urban consolidates*: it is a particle and wave, a flow and thing, its own random uncertainty principle prevailing in everyday life.

More than a hundred and fifty years since the *Manifesto*, what gels people together doesn't only emerge from the workplace but from the dwelling space—"dwelling" in its broadest sense—dwelling as world culture beyond four walls. World culture forces our four walls open, enlarges their scope, widens their horizon, ensures that living space is now about *the totality of political and economic space in which one belongs.* Once, seemingly long ago, people went out into the world, discovered the world, often through the world of work; now it seems the world comes to people, discovers us, sometimes whether we like it or not. Nowadays, if people identify with other people it is because of something shared, because of something that cements us together, bonds us across frontiers and barriers. Arguably, the world of work is no longer where this bonding takes place for a lot of people.

Is it, then, urban-consciousness rather than class-consciousness that bonds? Yes and no. It's affinity that bonds, and the urban is the site though which this affinity takes hold, takes place: a staging, to be sure, but not a passive staging when the curtain goes up, when the drama actually commences. The urban, just as Marx said, somehow helps affinity and class-consciousness grow, helps it become aware of itself, aware that other affinities exist in the world, that affinities can encounter one another, become aware of one another, aware of one another as the 99 percent, in a social network connected by a certain tissuing, by a spider's webbing, by a planetary webbing, by common notions. Meanwhile, the urban lets people become collectively conscious of an enemy, collectively conscious of a desire to do something about that enemy, collectively conscious about wanting no truck with this enemy's game. This has to be what progressive global urban culture is now all about. This is what it can be about. It's the terrain and stake for any twenty-first-century Marxism, for a Marxist culture of the urban, for *Marxism and Urban Culture.*

—*Andy Merrifield, Cambridge, England, November 2013*

NOTES

1. Karl Marx and Friedrich Engels, *The Communist Manifesto* (Penguin Deluxe Edition, New York, 2011), 68.
2. Marx and Engels, *The Communist Manifesto*, 69.
3. James Joyce, *Finnegans Wake* (Penguin, New York, 1976), 261.
4. Joyce, *Finnegans Wake*, 32.
5. Henri Lefebvre, *The Urban Revolution* (University of Minnesota Press, Minneapolis, 2003), 174.

Introduction

What is Urban Culture?

Benjamin Fraser

To some it will seem that this introduction—and by extension this edited volume as a whole—sets out for itself a monumental task. Others may say that there is relatively little that is novel about the motivation behind *Marxism and Urban Culture*. The truth is, of course, somewhere in-between. All things considered, the perspective adopted will not depend on how one understands *Marxism*, on how one understands *urbanization*, on how one understands *culture* . . . but rather on *how one understands each of these three variables in relation to the others*.

Indeed, this book builds on the central premise of an entire tradition of scholarship in the subfield of urban Marxism, just as it expands upon the way in which culture and cultural production are engaged by that tradition. On the whole, its intent is to spark dialogue across the humanities and the social sciences. The form of an edited volume provides an advantage in this respect: it allows for the gradual emergence of an inherently uneven method, one perhaps attuned to the uneven geographical development of contemporary capitalism in specific urban locations. Individual chapters have not been subjected to a coherent formula; authors have been free to approach Marxism, to approach culture, in the way that has been most appropriate given their subjects and chosen cities. Nonetheless, from these necessarily idiosyncratic snapshots the reader will reach a vision—once again, their own, one inflected by their own interests—of urbanized society as a *totality*. These chapters—their cohabitation in a single volume; the disciplinary debates replicated in their implicit collisions with one another—provide an opportunity for the *active* reader to reconcile the fields of politics, economy, geography, history, culture, literature, film, cultural studies. Rather than present a unified theory, they uncover a variegated scholarly terrain. Rather than encourage simplicity, these chapters reveal complexity. Rather than provide an answer, they pose a question centered around not two but three terms.

MARXISM—THE URBAN—CULTURE . . . each of these three terms is unequivocally the subject of heated, substantial, and continuing debate. It is only possible to say otherwise if one is content to take the most narrow of views, and the increasingly interdisciplinary terrain of both the humanities and the social sciences has only made the limitations of such narrow views more apparent. It is clear that there has been much written on the subject of urban culture throughout the twentieth century—not all of it Marxist in nature, of course. From the point of view of disciplinary method, the scholarly landscape constituted by these writings is certainly an uneven one; that is, it is my position that, to date, there has been relatively little reconciliation of humanities and social science approaches to critiquing capital. The question driving social science approaches to urban culture has often been delimited by a method that, in practice if not also in theory, reduces artistic creations to being mere products enveloped in circuits of exchange. To ignore that culture seen in this light is indeed a commodity would be impossible—and I shall make no attempt to do so here. But this undeniable truth does not exhaust the nature of culture, nor does it exhaust the relevance of culture to a critique of urbanized capitalist society. In particular, it does not exhaust the potential of urban culture, but instead reveals its contradictory position in contemporary capitalist urbanization.

Henri Lefebvre once wrote that,

> For many Marxists, it seems that art is only a distraction, a form of entertainment, at best a superstructural form or a simple means of political efficacy. It is necessary to remind these people that great works of art deeply touch, even disturb, the roots of human existence. The highest mission of art is not simply to express, even less to reflect, the real, nor to substitute fictions for it. These functions are reductive; while they may be part of the function of art, they do not define its highest level. The highest mission of art is to *metamorphose* the real. (1988: 82–83, see also 2006)

From this point of view, urban culture cannot be solely a vehicle for capitalist accumulation. Simultaneously, that is, it may exercise a potentially disalienating role. If the question "What is urban culture?" has been answered many times with the response "It is but a commodity," it may be of help to remember the following dictum taken from the *Grundrisse*: "Frequently the only possible answer is a critique of the question, and the only possible solution is to negate the question" (Marx 1973: 127).[1] That is to say: we must think rather carefully, indeed, when formulating the question posed by this introduction. That question, evident in the subtitle appearing at the start of this brief essay, is "What is urban culture?"

A. ON THE QUESTION OF URBAN CULTURE

Before outlining the chapters of this book, and as a way of reformulating the question of urban culture—subjecting it to critique, negating its habitual bias, and exposing its inherent contradiction—I want to explore what, in my estimation, represents the most visible if not hegemonic Marxist approach to urban culture at the current time. Turning to Marxian geographer David Harvey—who is mentioned frequently throughout this book—we find a quick and appropriate way to broach the contradictions of culture in light of the aims of the present edited collection. It is clear that Harvey's "The Art of Rent"—the fourth chapter of what is, at the time of this writing, the critic's most recent book, *Rebel Cities* (2012: 89–112)—follows from his previous work. This would include, generally, his extension of Marxian thought into geographical territory via the urban phenomenon (by way of Henri Lefebvre, who is also frequently cited in this book's pages; see Harvey 2010, 2009, 2006, 2000, 1996, 1991, 1990, 1989). It would also include, specifically, earlier texts such as the very similar chapter of *Spaces of Capital* titled "The Art of Rent: Globalization and the Commodification of Culture" (Harvey 2001: 394–411).[2] In both publications, the spatial theorist discusses monopoly rents, cultural and symbolic capital, tourism, and the dynamic tension between the uniqueness and the marketability of culture. In the main text, he gives particular weight to the consequences of the latter; that is, the cultural homogenization which accompanies the successful marketing of unique commodities. It may be unnecessary to point out that urbanization broadly understood—(is there any other way to approach the urban?)—constitutes an implicit grounding for the entire piece. This is true even when he discusses the wine trade, and the urban also figures directly into his remarks on the way in which unique city locations are routinely traded upon by developers and speculators manipulating urban forms of capital.

What is so interesting, of course, is the way in which Harvey references urban culture (in both articles; see Harvey 2012, 2001). Evident here is the chosen method of the social scientist. This method is not an erroneous one by any means, but it is one that is, for lack of a better term, provisional or incomplete. (It is to this incompleteness that the present volume responds.) He writes,

> That culture has become a commodity of some sort is undeniable. Yet there is also a widespread belief that there is something so special about cultural products and events (be they in the arts, theater, music, cinema, architecture or more broadly in localized ways of life, heritage, collective memories and affective communities) as to set them apart from ordinary commodities like shirts and shoes. It may be, of course, that we set them apart simply because we cannot bear to think of them as anything other than different, existing on some higher plane of human creativity and meaning than that located in the

factories of mass production and consumption. Yet even when we strip away
all residues of wishful thinking (often backed by powerful ideologies) we are
still left with something very special about those products designated as "cultural." How, then, can the commodity status of so many of these phenomena
be reconciled with their special character? The relation between culture and
capital evidently calls for careful probing and nuanced scrutiny. (Harvey 2001:
394; rewritten with minor changes in 2012: 89–90)

Clearly, the forms of urban culture referenced by Harvey ("the arts, music,
theater, music, cinema [. . .]") are not engaged at the level of textual representation but are instead intended to be read as embodied cultural practices in
urban contexts (as Sharon Zukin [1995], for one, has also done quite compel-
lingly, for example). As elsewhere, here Harvey wants to discuss the cinema
hall, but not the cinema; music venues, but not the music itself; the theater-
going public, but not the staged performance; the art museum, but not the art
it holds. He wants, as he put it on another occasion, to interrogate "the ways
in which aesthetic and cultural trends get woven into the fabric of daily life"
of urbanized capitalism (1990: 347). Accordingly, however, his chosen
method (that of the social scientist) directs that he focus his attention on a
certain and constructed "scale" of analysis by leaving textual representation
out of the picture.[3]

Some may see this turn away from humanities texts as one properly
befitting a "cultural geography" or "cultural studies" approach (of this, too, I
am skeptical; cf. Williams 2007a). It should be noted that, to his credit,
Harvey has not shied away from "reading" humanities texts specifically in
some of his other writings. Therein, he has enjoyed more or less success,
depending on whether or not we are taking into account the perspective of
literary and filmic scholars (that is; see Harvey 1990, 1996, 2003, 2006)[4]. It
bears repeating that the social science approach to culture is undeniably
important if we are to interrogate the imbrication of humanities discourses at
the extra-textual scale (in contemporary circuits of exchange and accumulation). But the question remains, what of these humanities texts themselves
(novels, poetry, films . . .)? Have they also "a special character" that requires
"careful probing and nuanced scrutiny"? Or may we write them off as—
always, everywhere—pertaining to what might be called the alienating veneer of cultural phenomena under capitalism? May we reduce humanities
texts to being merely signs of distinction, tangible forms of the cultural and
symbolic capital discussed by Harvey? Or, as I believe—and as Harvey
would ultimately agree (cf. chapter 2, this volume)—is their relationship to
capital more complex?

Along with many others doing cultural studies work within the disciplinary structures of traditionally literary fields, I would argue that the "textual
culture" of the humanities is ultimately neither distinct nor distinguishable
from the nontextual urban culture that Harvey privileges in his analysis.

Interestingly, although Harvey's work is inspired by Marxian geographer Henri Lefebvre,[5] he has proven unable to reproduce the French urban philosopher's more capacious view of culture. In the article "Toward a Leftist Cultural Politics: Remarks Occasioned by the Centenary of Marx's Death" (published in English translation in 1988), Lefebvre wrote of the way in which aesthetics and culture are, in effect, one point of entry onto an entire world:

> It so happens that the word "culture" also evokes a magical image for me, that of Sleeping Beauty. She does not doze on flowers and on fragrant grass but on a thick mattress of texts, quotations, musical scores—and under a vast canopy of books, sociological, semiological, historical and philosophical theses. Then one day the Prince comes; he awakens her and everything around the forest comes to life along with her—poets poetizing, musicians musicking, cooks cooking, lovers loving, and so on. Singers? Songs? Yes, they are a part of culture, yet they must not be considered in isolation but within an ensemble that also includes dance, music, cartoon strips, television, and so forth. Moreover, culture is not merely a static palimpsest of texts, it is lived, active, which is what the fable of the wakened princess suggests to me. (Lefebvre 1988: 81–82)

Lest the reader think it was Lefebvre's intention to "move beyond texts," it is important to make clear that what he wanted to do was to fold texts back into everyday life; he wanted, not to consider them in isolation from cultural processes, but rather to adopt the more capacious view of culture to which I have just referred. His point is not that texts should be disregarded as static objects but rather that they should be seen as part of an ensemble of culture whose breadth is so seldom acknowledged by Marxists. The way Lefebvre framed urban space itself as a text (e.g., 1996) should thus be seen first and foremost as a way of blending humanities and social science concerns and of overcoming the limitations of disciplinary specialization. The place he found, in his oeuvre, for literature, poetry, and artistic work in general—as well as the "theory of the work of art" he elucidated in a foundational text still awaiting English translation (Lefebvre 2006 [1980])—demonstrates the inclusiveness of his capacious view of culture (cf. the way discussions of texts figure into Lefebvre 1991, 2005, 2006, 2007; also Fraser 2014).

We should not forget—Lefebvre did not forget—that the specialized role in society embodied by literary scholars, film scholars, art scholars in general, has long stemmed from (and has also reinforced) a pernicious bourgeois fragmentation of knowledge. The fragmented nature and fragmenting activity of knowledge was discussed explicitly and at length by Henri Lefebvre (1996, 2003), just as it was also implicit in the denunciation of bourgeois literary analysis launched by figures such as Raymond Williams (2007a, 2007b, 1975) and Fredric Jameson (1999, 1981).[6] But there is an essential contradiction at work here—one that can only be partially explained by the pendular swings that are taken to constitute the historical evolution of academic scholarship. The contradiction is this: that in rightly asserting the role of culture within Marxism and within Urban Studies (as the Marxist urban geographer himself admits, two areas that have erroneously been dominated by a myopic understanding of political economy that marginalizes Marxist and Urban approaches), David Harvey has *in practice* essentialized and disregarded textual culture.

I say in practice, because this view seems to be congruous neither with his understanding of Marxism nor with his point of view on culture in general. As should be obvious to any literary scholar—and as follows from a broad application of Marxian thought—humanities texts are not things in the simple sense any more than a building or a city is a thing. As Harvey makes clear in his discussion of urban culture, as Lefebvre made clear in his extensive work on the urban phenomenon, and as Marx made clear in his nuanced exploration of the commodity form, what appear to us as simple things are in fact social relations that hide the conditions of their (re)production. How strange it is, then, that for many Marxists—as Lefebvre succinctly notes—grasping urban culture by the root should mean emptying cultural texts of their artistic qualities, their structure, and thus their nuanced construction and their necessarily social meaning . . .? As if cultural texts were solely products! To take this view of humanities texts—without a more nuanced understanding of the commodity—is, of course, to affirm the logic of capital. Cultural texts are indeed products, they are indeed (more and more, perhaps) circulated as products in webs of exchange. But—as it is with other commodities—they are also more than products. Just as with other products, their seemingly hard borders in fact hide the social reality of their split essence—that is, their dual existence, positioned betwixt and between use and exchange value. While aesthetics and culture have clearly been co-opted by the urbanized process of capital accumulation there is an aspect of culture that resists commodification. By this I refer to the use value of humanities texts in the hands of some scholars. This is not to say that scholarship is itself a world of its own, free from the influence of capital. As illustrated by the debates surrounding the future of scholarly publishing—(the rise of pay-to-publish models affecting the humanities, for example, along with the corporatization of formerly independent journals not to mention the not-unproblematic rise of the "public humanities" and the digital humanities, none of which will be discussed here)—academic scholarship is more a part of capital accumulation than it has ever been. But the arts in general will always continue to have a use value to the degree that they help us to think more carefully through how capital operates.

Make no mistake, the appropriation of culture by capital is ongoing and perhaps, in an immediate sense, unpreventable. But it is also a dynamic and nuanced, uneven process. Moreover, the process of textual representation—alongside historical, geographical, anthropological analyses, that is—allows us to see capital in action and to envision how it is that material and immaterial forces interact in the continuous shaping of our urban worlds. That is, more important than dismissing culture as a mere tool of capital or, on the other hand, celebrating culture as an alternative utopian space—(whichever side one takes, would not this fragmented understanding reaffirm the spatializing alienations of capital?)—a nuanced approach to culture must seek to connect humanities and social science perspectives.

Here I find it helpful to turn to Henri Lefebvre—for the reason that it is in his work where we find a subtle yet persistent emphasis on the relationship between capitalist alienation and disciplinary knowledge, specifically. I have written on this at length elsewhere,[7] and here I will merely reproduce a quotation I feel to be crucial for the present project:

> Every specialized science cuts from the global phenomenon a "field," or "domain," which it illuminates in its own way. There is no point in choosing between segmentation and illumination. Moreover, each individual science is further fragmented into specialized subdisciplines. Sociology is divided up into political sociology, economic sociology, rural and urban sociology, and so forth. The fragmented and specialized sciences operate analytically: they are the result of an analysis and perform analyses of their own. In terms of the urban phenomenon considered as a whole, geography, demography, history, psychology, and sociology supply the results of an analytical procedure. Nor should we overlook the contributions of the biologist, doctor or psychiatrist, or those of the novelist or poet (. . .) Without the progressive and regressive movements (in time and space) of analysis, without the multiple divisions and fragmentations, it would be impossible to conceive of a science of the urban phenomenon. But such fragments do not constitute knowledge. (Lefebvre 2003: 48–49)

Here—as it is throughout his numerous works—Lefebvre seeks to work from fragmentary knowledge toward *totality* (a concept explored in greater depth in one of this volume's chapters and implicit in many more). In this process, the work of art plays a privileged role. That is, to return to the question of the "special" cultural commodity broached by Harvey earlier in this introduction: "Art is," as Marc James Léger has written in his own work on Lefebvre, "a specialised activity that resists specialisation" (2006: 151).

It is the relationship—or better said the tension—between specialization and totality which is key to understanding how capital, space, and culture intersect in the twenty-first century. The format of an edited volume is perhaps uniquely calibrated to explore this relationship, given the way in which different points of view and themes may be juxtaposed in a single text. The grouping together of numerous specialized points of view within a single if variegated framework may aid in identifying the consonant and discordant qualities of each chapter, and thus in reaching a notion of totality. It is not insignificant, then, that many publishers seem to be doing away with edited volumes—by all accounts, because they are not as profitable as "coherent" monographs; neither is it unrelated, of course, that the humanities are under increasing pressure as university education becomes instrumentalized (even as a peculiar invocation of "interdisciplinarity" has become the catch-phrase of an increasing number of institutions). In this context, this edited volume responds to the following two needs: (1) the need to acknowledge the tension between specialization and totality and also (2) the need to trace the struggle between capital and oppositional movements.[8] The way these questions are interrogated, of course, ultimately depends on which chapter of this book you are reading.

In the end, this volume responds to the need for humanities and social science scholars to collaborate and combine forces in understanding the various ways in which culture is influenced by urbanization and, in turn, influences urban spaces—urban spaces that are shaped by both material and immaterial forces. In the pages of these contributions, culture is approached from perspectives that are alternately filmic, literary, historical, anthropological, and of course political. Rather than being a drawback, this mixture of both humanities and social science perspectives is advantageous. Humanist Marxist scholars, for example, may certainly find some chapters more accessible than others, but they will also be pushed to explore the social science perspectives to which they are all too infrequently exposed. Social scientists may gravitate toward other specific chapters, but will be exposed also to the way that close readings of cultural texts align with their own urban-scaled analyses and critiques of capital. Thus although the individual chapters may have different objectives—and even though they may at times seem to be at cross-purposes in how they define culture—what all these perspectives share is a common drive to "urbanize" cultural studies and to rethink Marxian cultural critique in urban contexts.

The reader should keep in mind the radical spirit that underlies the quotation referenced earlier in this introduction. When Lefebvre writes that "The highest mission of art is to *metamorphose* the real," he is clearly building on Marx's insight that the world must be transformed and not merely interpreted. Nevertheless, it may be necessary to point out that this truth has a more nuanced meaning in the context of the French urban theorist's oeuvre. Both thinkers, that is, wanted to grasp society by the root, just as each wanted to expose the intimate and dynamic relationship between material and immaterial forces structuring (urban) modernity. But in addition to urbanizing Marx's thought, Lefebvre also vastly extended and elaborated upon the Marxian critique of alienation. Applying the latter to everyday life—applying it to the notion of disciplinary specialization, as intimated above—he also simultaneously pushed Marx's thought further and further into cultural terrain. It should come as no surprise, then, that a large number of this book's chapters reference his approach (along with that of Lefebvrian thinker David Harvey).

B. CHAPTER SUMMARIES

1. Mobilizing the Filmic City

The two chapters in Part I reconcile cities as represented on film and as constructed through discourses of urbanism and critical social practice. Chapter 1, Les Roberts's "The Archive City: Film as Critical Spatial Practice" reads Marxist thinker Henri Lefebvre's observation that film is an "incriminated medium"—allowing for, at best, only partial understandings of and engagements with the dialectics of urban space—against film's capacity to mobilize more critical understandings of the dynamic and multi-layered spatialities of cites and urban landscapes. Although in some respects, the moving image is complicit in the reduction of cities to spectacular and virtual spaces of representation—a process described as the "cinematization" of urban space—Roberts explores how archive film imagery may prompt re-evaluation and reimaginings of urban landscapes as spaces of "radical nostalgia," where past and present are brought into dialogue and tension. Demonstrating the ways that archive film can function as a form of spatial critique, the author draws on research conducted in Liverpool—and a cinematic project conducted and exhibited in Bologna—in order to sketch the outlines of "cinematic cartography" as a hitherto underdeveloped mode of critical urban practice. By mapping and engaging with the "archive city," film can offer a means by which the representational spaces of the past can be harnessed and mobilized as part of a wider Marxian politics of urban spatial practice.

Chapter 2, Malcolm Alan Compitello's "Capital, Mobility and Spatial Exclusion in Fernando León de Aranoa's *Barrio* (1998)," frames the director as one of a group of younger Spanish filmmakers whose artistic creations play into the urban process through their skillful thematization and visualization of the spatial inequity wrought by capital. *Barrio* is mediated by a cartographic imaginary that contests the uneven expansion of Spain's capital city and raises questions of transportation, mobility, and access to the city for all of its residents. Key sequences in the film are examined in light of Marxist geographer David Harvey's work, which infuses a spatial dimension into Marxist meta-theory and forges relationships between cultural products and the way they resist deleterious transformations in the built environment. Ultimately, the author's analysis of the film's visual structure lays bare the fate of those left behind or pushed aside by urban expansion precisely because they do not have the resources to keep up with the vertiginous pace of change.

2. The Human Senses in Urban Contexts

In the next two chapters, Benjamin Fraser takes on a pair of fiction films
using a Lefebvrian approach to the urban. Chapter 3, "Henri Lefebvre in
Strasbourg: The City as Use Value in José Luis Guerín's *Dans la ville de
Sylvie* (2007)," applies central tenets from the French theorist's reconfigured
Marxism—rhythmanalysis, (urban) use vs. (urban) exchange value, the right
to the city, and the notion of play as resistance—to the film's on-screen
presentation of the city. Strasbourg is a perfect fit for this approach given
Lefebvre's own personal and professional relationship with the French city,
which is also explored in the early part of the chapter. Culling insights from
The Right to the City (1968), *The Explosion* (1969), *The Urban Revolution*
(1970), *The Production of Space* (1974), and *Rhythmanalysis* (1992), Fraser
takes on key formal aspects of Guerín's purposely difficult and masterful
film. While it is largely devoid of dialogue, its use of naturally occurring (if
diegetic) sound, sets, editing, and shot composition foregrounds a Lefebvrian
vision of the urban that is defiantly at odds with the ideological content of
urbanism and planning as it has developed over the past two centuries.

Chapter 4, "Sensing Capital: Sight, Sound, and Touch in Esteban Sapir's
La antena (2007)" turns more toward Lefebvre's remarks on totality and its
apparent fragmentation through capitalist alienation. Here the urban environment represented in the film is not Buenos Aires per se, but rather a fictional
City XX that nonetheless recalls aspects of Argentina's turbulent twentieth
century. Sapir's persistent focus on the human senses throughout the film's
content and form provides an opportunity to reflect upon the resurgence of
what Andy Merrifield has called the "sensuous Marx," an opportunity which
Fraser siezes by linking this tradition to Lefebvre's *Critique of Everyday
Life*. Bringing previous scholarly work on the film together and subjecting it
to a unifying approach here serves as a way to explore the material and
conceptual alienations that accompany urban forms of capital. In the end, *La
antena* itself drives at just such a unifying discourse—one that similarly
strives to reconstitute the totality of modern urban life.

3. Cultures of Urban Protest

The chapters in this section mark the beginning of a gradual shift from the
production of cultural texts toward the notion of urban practice and resistance
as itself a cultural space of great relevance to enacting social change. Chapter
5, Marc James Léger and Cayley Sorochan's "Psychoprotest: Dérives of the
Quebec Maple Spring," turns to the student demonstrations that politically
transformed the experience of city space in Montreal, interrupted the downtown *quartier des spectacles* and elaborated a constituent media representation. Based upon an unlimited general strike against a proposed 75 percent

tuition increase, these mobilizations were unprecedented in scale, with more than 300,000 students and supporters turning out across the region. Aware of the newly defined stakes involved in the occupation of city streets, demonstrators and citizen supporters engaged in practices of mass psychogeography, civil disobedience, and direct action. The authors revisit the Situationist theory of the dérive as a means to account for the "return of history" to a city of festivals and a system of privatization.

In chapter 6, "The *Huelga de Dolores* and Guatemalan University Students' 'Happy and Wicked' Reproduction of Space, 1966–1969," Heather A. Vrana begins with a striking image: the moment in 1966 when, in a fleeting pause in state repression and forced disappearance, economics student Juan Luis Molina Loza dressed as Che Guevara and carried a cross bearing the phrase "The Latin American Revolution" through Guatemala's commercial center. Part of a venerable and distinctly Guatemalan university tradition, called the *Huelga de Dolores* ["Strike of Sorrows"], this annual event owed more to carnival than protest and included a costume parade, a theatrical revue, a newspaper, and various ludic bulletins in a hybrid of religious procession and political dissent. In this repetitive, ongoing, but singular moment, San Carlos students remade the social topography of urban Guatemala City, marking sites where protest, play, and empathetic memory could come together in a volatile union. Reading students' spatial practices alongside Henri Lefebvre's theories of spatial practice, this chapter elucidates how the Huelga challenged representations of space through students' bold anti-imperialist claims and the event's unusual temporality of a past-present exemplified in their refrain "*Somos los mismos*" ("We are the same"). Ultimately, *huelgueros* reappropriated the urban and placed it in the hands of student agronomists, economists, dentists, doctors, and engineers, thus constituting a new sensibility of spatial and temporal practice.

4. The Housing Question

The next two chapters take on the capitalist discourse of urban dwelling. Chapter 7, Jeff Hicks's "Residential Differentiation in the Vertical Cities of J. G. Ballard and Robert Silverberg" examines selected prose works by the novelists through the lens of Marxist urban theory in order to illustrate the piercing accuracy of the New Wave's critique of urban space. By the end of the 1960s, the utopian promise of the "Ville Radieuse"—Le Corbusier's ambitious Modernist vision of a harmonious future city dominated by glass-and-steel skyscrapers—had begun to come under heavy criticism in the work of science fiction's New Wave authors. In this context, the author explores the novelistic connection between isolated, self-contained living spaces and the residential differentiation and class segregation analyzed by Marxist urban theorists such as David Harvey, Edward Soja, and Mike Davis as characteristic of contemporary cities. Deploying Harvey's conceptions of a just distribution of income and apportionment of urban space, as outlined in his 1973 book *Social Justice and the City*, Ballard's and Silverberg's novels show how, even under seemingly ideal conditions, a utopian alternative to inequitable living standards simply is not possible under capitalist social relations.

In chapter 8, Kimberly DeFazio's "Red Vienna, Class and the Common" takes part in the contemporary debate over radical praxis (including *The Idea of Communism*, edited by Costas Douzinas and Slavoj Žižek, Jodi Dean's *The Communist Horizon*, and Michael Hardt and Antonio Negri's *Commonwealth*) by engaging what has come to be called "Red Vienna": the period between World War I and World War II when Vienna operated under the "municipal socialism" of the Austro-Marxists (e.g., Otto Bauer, Max Adler, and Karl Renner). The extensive housing projects (the *Gemeindebauten*) which have come to represent the hallmark of Red Vienna and its social programs and policies provide a particularly important opportunity to assess not only the theoretical and political assumptions underlying municipal socialist policies and their consequences but their legacy in the contemporary turn to the "common" and "communism." Ultimately, a rereading of Engels ("The Housing Question") prompts an argument for reconnecting culture to the relations of wage-labor and developing a transformative praxis for the twenty-first century.

5. Inter(nationalizing) the Urban

The two chapters in this final section explore the urban as an expression of (inter)national culture. Chapter 9, Brecht De Smet and Jelle Versieren's "Urban Culture as Passive Revolution: A Gramscian Sketch of the Combined Transitional Development of Rural and Urban Modern Culture in Europe and Egypt" employs a Gramscian approach to the analysis of social formations that distinguishes the conceptual abstract dialectic of capital and the real, fractured history of class struggle. In order to understand the dialectic of the universalization of commodity production and the concreteness of capitalist transition, the authors compare the historical trajectory of Western Europe with that of Egypt, using Gramsci's Italy as a microcosm of the uneven and combined nature of modernity. The authors first analyze the interplay between changing political regimes, articulations of modes of production, social structures, and cultural practices in the transition toward capitalism in Western Europe and Egypt before scrutinizing the classical Durkheimian or Weberian dichotomy between countryside and urbanity. Next, they descend from the macro-level to the concrete social world of city life and factory floors to take on the topics of proletarianization and new forms of production in the shaping of urban culture and finally they explore how the processes of the microphysics of power in the factories help to clarify the success and limitations of the succeeding cycles of passive revolutions.

In chapter 10, "The Urban Working-Class Culture of Riot in Osaka and L.A: Toward a Comparative History," a team of scholars comprised of Manuel Yang, Takeshi Haraguchi, and Kazuya Sakurada analyze various fundamental aspects of synchronous urban riots in Osaka and Los Angeles. These riots erupted in working-class districts that were products of industrial capitalist development in the half-century arc from its late nineteenth-century laissez-faire form to its post-World War II Keynesian permutation. A major source of this transformation was struggles of the industrial working class, whose self-definition spanned a wide gamut, from rickshaw drivers and professional gamblers to vagrants and waterfront workers, as shown by the 1903 Osaka riot, 1905 formation of the Industrial Workers of the World, and the trans-Pacific radical culture that they had forged. While these struggles—especially those of the waterfront workers, who later organized a "trans-Pacific strike" in the wake of the first Kamagasaki Riot—led capital to restructure itself to offer workers a social compact, it also restricted their class identity hierarchically according to the hegemony of the urban industrial factory, which marginalized day laborers, blacks, and lumpen-proletarians. When these latter members of the working class revolted, with their demand for civil rights and rioting during the 1960s, they attacked the city that had become a socialized factory and created a new militant lumpen-proletarian culture that connected Black Power on the West Coast with the *romusha* of Osaka. This signaled a historical return, albeit in a post-industrial context, to what E. P. Thompson called "class struggle without class," as social antagonisms no longer manageable by the Keynesian dictates of industrial labor spread among auto workers, prison inmates, and indigenous peoples, to which the ruling class responded with state terror, deindustrialization, financialization, and other neoliberal counteroffensives. The L.A. and Osaka Riots of the early 1990s demonstrated the further dissolution of a singular class identity and the generalized condition of class struggle, which have made it impossible for us to conceive either "city" or "culture" in a reified, fetishistic manner that mirrors the residual ideology of the ascendant era of urban industrial capitalism.

NOTES

1. It is significant that this point is made by Henri Bergson and by Jane Jacobs, in addition to Marx: "The truth is that in philosophy and even elsewhere it is a question of finding the problem and consequently of positing it, even more than of solving it" (Bergson 1934: 51); "Merely to think about cities and get somewhere, one of the main things to know is what kind of problem cities pose, for all problems cannot be thought about in the same way" (Jacobs 1992: 428). For a blended account of how these three perspectives can be fused in a pedagogical approach to the urban, see Fraser 2009.

2. This is chapter 18 of *Spaces of Capital* and begins by acknowledging that it was "Prepared for the Conference on Global and Local, held at the Tate Modern in London, February, 2001" (2001: 394).

3. On scale, see; Brenner 2004; Fraser 2011; Howitt 1993, 2003; Keil and Mahon 2009; Lefebvre 1996; 2003; Marston 2000.

4. His previous work illustrates, of course, that his approach to culture is not as nuanced as it might otherwise be (see, e.g., his perspective on *Bladerunner* as evident in Harvey 1990; or his discussion of prose works where discussion of content and its relationship to history eclipses discussion of structure, form and artistry, despite his intentions, Harvey 2003, 2006).

5. Lefebvre was cited prominently in Harvey's *Social Justice and the City* (2009 [1973]) —where the urban geographer asked the question "what insights and revelations do we gain through the use of Marx's method in the investigation of urban phenomena?" (2009: 302)—and figures also into Harvey's most recent book in the preface titled "Henri Lefebvre's Vision" (Harvey 2012: ix–xviii).

6. Interestingly, this is a fragmentation of knowledge that Lefebvre, for one, curiously contextualizes within the rise of modern urban planning as a bourgeois science in the nineteenth century (1996, 2003).

7. By this I mean to reference the inaugural editorial of the *Journal of Urban Cultural Studies* (Fraser 2014) and also the book ms. titled *Henri Lefebvre and the Humanities: Toward an Urban Cultural Studies* (in progress).

8. "The problem for capital is to find ways to co-opt, subsume, commodify and monetize such cultural differences and cultural commons just enough to be able to appropriate monopoly rents from them. . . . The problem for oppositional movements is to speak to this widespread appropriation of their cultural commons and to use the validation of particularity, uniqueness, authenticity, culture and aesthetic meanings in ways that open up new possibilities and alternatives" (see also Harvey 2001: 188–207).

BIBLIOGRAPHY

Bergson, Henri (1934), *The Creative Mind* (trans. M. L. Andison), New York: Citadel.

Brenner, Neil (2004), *New State Spaces: Urban Governance and the Rescaling of Statehood*, Oxford: Oxford University Press.

Fraser, Benjamin. (2009), "The 'Kind of Problem Cities Pose': Jane Jacobs at the Intersection of Philosophy, Pedagogy, and Urban Theory," *Teaching in Higher Education*, 14: 1, pp. 265–76.

———. (2011), *Henri Lefebvre and the Spanish Urban Experience*, Lewisburg, PA: Bucknell University Press.

———. (2014), "Inaugural editorial: Urban Culture Studies—A Manifesto," *Journal of Urban Cultural Studies*, 1: 1, pp. 3–17.

Harvey, David (1989), *The Urban Experience*, Baltimore: Johns Hopkins University Press.

———. (1990), *The Condition of Postmodernity*, Cambridge, Mass. and Oxford: Blackwell.

———. (1991), "Afterword," in H. Lefebvre, *The Production of Space* (trans. Donald Nicholson-Smith), Oxford: Blackwell, pp. 425–34.

———. (1996), *Justice, Nature and the Geography of Difference*, London: Blackwell.

———. (2000), *Spaces of Hope*, Berkeley: University of California Press.

———. (2001), *Spaces of Capital: Towards a Critical Geography*, New York: Routledge.

———. (2003), "City Future in City Past: Balzac's Cartographic Imaginary," in *After-images of the City*, Joan Ramon Resina and Dieter Ingenschay (eds.), Ithaca; London: Cornell University Press, pp. 23–48.

———. (2006), *Paris, Capital of Modernity*, London and New York: Routledge.

———. (2009), *Social Justice and the City*, Athens: University of Georgia Press.

———. (2010), *A Companion to Marx's Capital*, London; New York: Verso.

———. (2012), *Rebel Cities*, London; New York: Verso.

Howitt, Richard (1993), "'A World in a Grain of Sand': Towards a Reconceptualization of Geographical Scale," *Australian Geographer*, 241, pp. 33–44.

————. (2003), "Scale," in *A Companion to Political Geography*, John Agnew, Katharyne Mitchell and Gerard Toal (eds.), Oxford: Blackwell, pp. 138–57.

Jacobs, Jane (1992), *The Death and Life of Great American Cities*, New York: Vintage.

Jameson, Fredric (1981), *The Political Unconscious*, Ithaca: Cornell University Press.

————. (1999), *Postmodernism: Or, the Cultural Logic of Late Capitalism*, Durham: Duke University Press.

Keil, Roger and Rianne Mahon (eds.) (2009), *Leviathan Undone? Towards a Political Economy of Scale*, Vancouver; Toronto: UBC Press.

Lefebvre, Henri (1980), *La présence et l'absence: Contribution à la théorie des représentations*, Paris: Caterman.

————. (1988), "Toward a Leftist Cultural Politics: Remarks Occasioned by the Centenary of Marx's Death" (trans. David Reifman), in *Marxism and the Interpretation of Culture*, Lawrence Grossberg and Cary Nelson (eds.), Chicago: University of Illinois Press, pp. 75–88.

————. (1991), *The Production of Space* (trans. Donald Nicholson–Smith), Oxford: Blackwell.

————. (1996), "The Right to the City," in *Writings on Cities* (eds. and trans. E. Kofman and E. Lebas), Oxford: Blackwell: pp. 63–181.

————. (2003 [1970]), *The Urban Revolution* (trans. Robert Bononno), Minneapolis: University Minnesota Press.

————. (2005), *Critique of Everyday Life,* vol. 3 (trans. Gregory Elliott), London; New York: Verso.

————. (2006 [1980]), *La presencia la ausencia: Contribución a la teoría de las representaciones* (trans. Óscar Barahona and Uxoa Doyhamboure), México D.F.: Fondo de Cultura Económica.

————. (2007), *Everyday Life in the Modern World* (trans. Sacha Rabinovich, introd. Philip Wander), Eleventh paperback ed., New Brunswick and London: Transaction Publishers.

Léger, Marc James (2006), "Henri Lefebvre and the Moment of the Aesthetic," in *Marxism and the History of Art: From William Morris to the New Left*, Andrew Hemingway (ed.), London: Pluto Press, pp. 143–60.

Marston, Sallie (2000), "The Social Construction of Scale," *Progress in Human Geography* 24: 2, pp. 219–42.

Marx, Karl (1973), *Grundrisse*, Harmondsworth: Penguin.

Williams, Raymond (1975), *The Country and the City*, New York: Oxford University Press.

————. (1977), *Marxism and Literature*, Oxford: Oxford University Press.

————.(2007a), "The Future of Cultural Studies," in *Politics of Modernism: Against the New Conformists*, London; New York: Verso, pp. 151–62.

————. (2007b), "The Uses of Cultural Theory," in *Politics of Modernism: Against the New Conformists*, London; New York: Verso, pp. 163–76.

Zukin, Sharon (1995), *The Cultures of Cities*, Malden, MA; Oxford.

I

MOBILIZING THE FILMIC CITY

Chapter One

The Archive City

Film as Critical Spatial Practice

Les Roberts

The opening lines of Guy Debord's 1967 book *The Society of the Spectacle* declare that: "In societies dominated by modern conditions of production, life is presented as an immense accumulation of *spectacles*. Everything that was directly lived has receded into a representation. The images detached from every aspect of life merge into a common stream in which the unity of that life can no longer be recovered" (2004: 7). These words also appear, in spoken form, at the start of Debord's 1973 film of the same name. Accompanying the narration is a series of détourned film clips: a view of the Earth filmed from space; an astronaut moving around on the outside of a space vehicle; an exotic striptease performed on a Henri Rousseauesque studio set; a view shot from a railway platform of a train pulling into a station, followed by a pan up to two platform monitors on which passengers can be seen alighting the train; a busy street scene, also framed by monitors, this time from within the traffic control center of a bustling metropolis.

If commenting on the cinematic works of a critic and polemicist who decreed that "The cinema, too, has to be destroyed" (Levin 2002: 1; Noys 2007) highlights some of the necessary contradictions that underpin De-bord's thesis, these contradictions are nevertheless both germane and inci-dental to the wider arguments explored throughout this chapter. Thomas Levin remarks on "the almost clichéd move that points out the contradiction involved in a public denunciation and examination of the spectacle by means of the spectacle," a move which overlooks the otherwise contradictory capac-ity of filmmaking practices to refine a "critical anticinematic film aesthetic" (2002: 403). When more specifically applied to the role—or *place*—of mov-ing images in the production and consumption of everyday urban spaces, the

3

contradictory dynamics of cinema's "anticinematic" potential are, or at least should be, one of the foremost points of critical reflection and praxis. While the representational spaces of film are ever more deeply in hock to the rapacious demands of the global commodified spectacle, at the same time this needs to be offset by closer consideration of the critical role of moving image practices in staking out contested geographies and histories of urban space. One of the benchmarks by which to gauge the critical efficacy of film as a tool of spatial praxis is its capacity to revivify, and thus potentially reclaim, the lived spaces of urban "habiting" (Lefebvre 2003: 81), rather than merely furthering the dissolution of the "directly lived" into the "common flow" of virtual and immaterial accumulation.

Taking the random selection of moving images described above, we could quite readily map these across a far wider historical canvas of spectacular phantasmagoria (Pile 2005) to show the resonant affectivity of these détourned images from the vantage point of the today's global mediascapes. The footage of the astronaut, filmed from a camera situated above the subject and looking down on the Earth below, brings to mind the 2012 Red Bull Stratos, the official title of the twenty-four-mile-high space jump performed by Felix Baumgartner, which was sponsored by the multinational energy drinks company. The jump was watched live by an estimated 8 million viewers on Red Bull's YouTube Channel, the highest number of concurrent views ever on the video sharing site, a phenomenal marketing coup for a company whose brand status was, as a result, quite literally propelled to globally stratospheric proportions.[1] If in the digital world the cut to Debord's "long striptease" is analogous to that made possible by the click of a mouse, viewers in search of other onlin+e thrills could jump, almost in an instant, from Baumgartner's Red Bull spectacle to any one of the estimated 4–5 million pornographic websites that can be found on the Internet[2] (perhaps, in time, taking advantage of the more embodied simulatory experience offered by digital "spectacles" such as Google Glass[3]). Cut again to the railway station and we are transported back to the birth of cinema itself in the form of the Lumière brothers' *L'Arriveé d'un train en gare* (1895), one of the very first films projected publicly. While the projection of the Lumière film is said to have induced a state of panic among those not yet accustomed to seeing the cinematic spectacle of train hurtling toward them, in the détourned railway footage from half a century later it is the seamless (and otherwise unremarkable) transition to a scopic regime of automated surveillance and monitoring that is of note. Moving on from the train platform by way of a further cut, we arrive at the bank of monitors in the traffic control center. Although the use of closed-circuit television (CCTV) technologies was a relatively new innovation in 1960s systems of urban governance, another half century on and the pervasive reach of a "surveillance society" (Lyon 2002; Coleman 2004), not least in the UK, has brought with it the panoptic spatialities of a

scopic regime in which social space is rationalized, privatized, bureaucra-
tized, and subjected to evermore coercive mechanisms of power and control.
The UK has more CCTV than any country in the world, with more cameras
than the rest of Europe put together (Minton 2009: 47). The "common
stream" of which Debord speaks has become a veritable torrent of imagery
that irradiates every conceivable facet of modern industrial-capitalist society.

From a cursory glance at the first few minutes of Debord's anti-cinematic
cinematic thesis, it is not difficult therefore to extrapolate from its dissonant
aesthetics some of the ways in which the moving image has proved instrumental in the reduction of large swathes of socio-spatial living into the cor-
poratized fetishism of the commodified spectacle. However, while cinema
has helped to bring about the further consolidation of—to paraphrase Jameson (1991)—the spectacular logic of late capitalism, its complicity in wider
processes of virtual accumulation warrants consideration of a countervailing
spatial logic in which the idea of "accumulation" conveys a more progressive
and dialectical sense of *mobilization*. Reframed thus—and pushing the argument toward a more specific focus on the *urban*—accumulation here denotes
a *critical mass* of spatio-visual practices that go against the grain of the
consolidated flow of virtual, "centrifugal" (Dimendberg 2004) mediations
that cement the architectural infrastructure of the neoliberal urban spectacle.
Put interrogatively: to what extent might the accumulation of urban cinematic geographies be harnessed as a tool of critical spatial praxis?

Much as these preliminary discussions have honed in on issues of spatiality it is no less the importance of time that demands critical attention if the
question just posed is to be in any way adequately addressed. Films that
capture some aspect of a city—whether this be its architecture or transport,
key events, or the everyday practices of those who inhabit or "narrate" (de
Certeau 1984) its urban spaces—are irredeemably date-stamped. That is,
although the historical provenance of a specific film or slice of footage may
not be immediately obvious (particularly so in the case of "orphan" films and
home movies) the "inadvertent" archive quality of film (Brunsdon 2007:
213) means that landscapes as they may have appeared or been represented at
any given time potentially exist in correspondence with those captured, represented, or *lived* at other moments in the historical geography of the city.
The conceptual edifice of what I have elsewhere described as the "archive
city" (Roberts 2012a) is built upon the central premise that the representational spaces of the city are a dynamic and, at times, precarious assemblage
of multiple accretions and imbrications enfolded in and across space and
time. What or indeed *where* the archive city is or may be found, *how* its
spaces might be inhabited and engaged with, or *why* it is deemed important to
excavate, build upon, or in some cases demolish its various precincts, landmarks, boundaries, and byways are all questions underscored by the recognition that a city's cinematic geographies can productively play host to a poli-

tics and praxis of urban spatiality. Taken in the round, the archive city is therefore as much a composite and slightly ramshackle product of urban cultural *bricolage* as it is the residual accumulation of archival image-spaces that have become detached from everyday practice and propelled, like Red Bull's capsule, further into spatial abstraction.

In this chapter I set out the case for envisioning the archive city, and of archival film practices more generally, as a critical method of urban spatial analysis. I begin by outlining further the idea of the city as an urban spectacle and, by drawing on the work of Henri Lefebvre and others, critically examine the role of the moving image in the virtualization and "cinematization" of postmodern urban space. The chapter then goes on to consider two case studies that exemplify what mobilization of the archive city might look like in practice. The first of these is based on research conducted in the port city of Liverpool in the northwest of England as part of the University of Liverpool's *City in Film* and *Mapping the City in Film* projects. The second case study discusses the work of the National Family Film Archive based in Bologna, whose exhibition *Cinematic Bologna*, which ran from November 2012 to January 2013, drew on the archive's extensive collection of home movies to map the shifting postwar landscapes of the city. In both cases, archive film, and amateur film in particular, provide a productive point of entry to cinematic spaces of urban memory and everyday life. What these examples illustrate is the scope of archival film practices to create and *remap* spaces of critical reflection that nurture the production of alternative cultural and historical geographies of the city. To this end they contribute to a cultural politics of the urban that challenges ongoing processes of spectacularization by seeking to reconnect cinematic spaces of representation with the lived spaces and embedded urban landscapes from which, under neoliberalism, they have become increasingly detached and abstracted.

A. AN INCRIMINATED MEDIUM?

Despite the growing number of studies on film, space, and place that have emerged in recent years, particularly in relation to cities, critical analyses of the spatiality of film, or, as Doreen Massey has noted, "the relation between film and spatiality in general" (Lury and Massey 1999: 231) remain comparatively underdeveloped (Roberts and Hallam 2013). Unquestionably, this can partly be attributed to a hesitance or reluctance to venture beyond disciplinary comfort zones or to take up the theoretical cudgels more routinely wielded by, for example, critical geographers, urbanists, sociologists, or anthropologists. The contribution of perspectives drawn from critical spatial theory, and the work of Lefebvre in particular, can shed useful insights into the relationship between film and urban space that otherwise remain obscured (Roberts 2012a: 40–63). If the landscape of critical thinking in this area can itself be likened to a city, then, to quote from Ed Dimendberg's groundbreaking book *Film Noir and Urban Space*, researchers seeking to mine the rich veins of analysis that course along its busy streets and pavements, are, by way of preliminary orientation, adjured to "travel to the extra-cinematic precincts of geography, city planning, architectural theory, and urban and cultural history" (2004: 9).

Much of the recent studies into the relationship between the urban landscape and the moving image have, as the artist and architectural filmmaker Patrick Keiller remarks, been largely focused around the influences that the imageries of film and architecture have brought to bear on each other. While not dismissing these influences (although he does suggest they have been exaggerated), Keiller goes on to argue that much of these observations seem to miss the more obvious point, which is the extent to which cinematic space is so very unlike *actual* space as it is lived and experienced (2003: 382). The implications of this are historically significant when considered in light of dramatic changes to the built environment and social geography of cities that began in earnest in the 1960s, when the fault lines between "the abstractions of cultural representation and the actualities of lived experience" (Siegel 2003: 139) became increasingly apparent. With visual media and screen culture now even more firmly entrenched within the perceptual and experiential landscapes of city living, these contradictions and ruptures are at their most acute. Yet critically, the spatial significance of moving image culture, and the historical production of space that has influenced the imaging of cities, has attracted at best only a marginal level of analysis in film studies research. According to Siegel "present discursive practices surrounding the medium of film tend to exaggerate the decoding, deconstructing, and dissecting of the film text at the expense of those quotidian media creating experiences that elucidate and alter social space" (2003: 141).

A common fallacy that runs through many discussions of film, space, and place is that promulgated by references to "reel" and "real" geographies of film (AlSayyad 2006; Penz 2010). From a Lefebvrian perspective on film and urban spatiality, this reductive binarism both presupposes and sustains a dualistic "abyss" (Lefebvre 1991: 6) between symbolic/imaginary ("reel") and material/empirical spaces of film ("real" or "pro-filmic"). Putting aside for the moment Lefebvre's dismissal of film as an "incriminated medium," it is the dynamic and fluid imbrications (and contradictions) of different spatialities, whether these be filmic, embodied, cartographic, abstract, etc., that are the focus of analysis and critical spatial praxis. This dialectical approach, which epistemologically foregrounds the social and cultural *production* of urban space, provides the central theoretical underpinning of the "archive city," understood as both a set of socio-spatial practices and a simulacrum of reality from which everyday urban imaginaries and spaces of memory are dialectically construed. In order to get a better sense of how this "mobilized" model of urban spatiality might inform analyses of a city's archival spaces of memory, it is necessary to briefly rehearse Lefebvre's tripartite spatial structure of "Spatial Practices," "Representations of Space," and "Spaces of Representation," which he sets out in his seminal work *The Production of Space* (1991 [1974]).

Spatial practices, or "perceived space," define an understanding of space as a site and product of everyday social and economic reproduction, and constitute the ways in which space is perceived and utilized (e.g., forms of urban mobility, commuting, transport, geographies of leisure, commercial and industrial activities, policing and forms of urban regulation). In disciplinary terms this epistemological framing is most closely associated with the more empirically-focused spatial disciplines such as geography and urban planning.

Representations of space are the conceived spaces of rational, technocratic, and intellectual production. These include maps, designs, and other abstract representations of space produced by groups such as architects, planners, artists, philosophers, and mathematicians. For Lefebvre, this is the dominant space in society, and provides, as Ed Soja puts it, "a storehouse of epistemological power" (1996: 67).

Spaces of representation (or "representational spaces" as they are sometimes referred to) are the lived spaces of the social imaginary, and are associated with the symbols and icons that shape subjective understandings and experiences of space in the more phenomenological sense. As spaces *of* representation, these real-and-imagined spaces constitute "the dominated—and hence passively experienced—space which the imagination seeks to change and appropriate" (Lefebvre 1991: 39). Lived space is thus a site of resistance, openness, difference, and struggle. Spaces of representation are those most closely associated with forms of cultural practice, including film, performance, literature, and festivals. Again, in terms of disciplinary or methodological perspectives these lived and symbolic spaces are associated with ethnographic, semiotic, psychoanalytic, or psychogeographic modes of spatial enquiry.

This conceptual triad does not set out to epistemologically privilege one aspect of the production of space over another. Despite acknowledging the dominance of conceived space in the abstract spatialities of advanced capitalism, Lefebvre is concerned to explore the dialectical relationship between these three conceptualizations of space.

In the image-saturated landscapes of global consumer capitalism, the theoretical efficacy of perspectives such as those advanced by Lefebvre and others is becoming increasingly evident as scholars seek to venture beyond semiotic and representational frameworks of analysis, finding productive modes of engagement with the multivalent spatialities within which cultural

texts such as film are embedded. As Karen Wells suggests in relation to ·
visuality and urban space: "Lefebvre's triadic theory of the production of
space is a useful conceptual tool for thinking about the material and visual
cultures of cities in ways that do not simply reduce them to language" (2007:
143).

In positing the dynamic and layered nature of social space, Lefebvre
challenges one of the dominant conceptions of space in Western Enlighten-
ment thought as that of a container within which action and activity unfold.
Such a view is governed by what Lefebvre calls the "illusion of transparency" in which space is assumed to be open, luminous, and intelligible, an
assumption informed by the privileging of the visual and optic over other
senses. Viewed thus, visual cultures of cities mediated through photography
and film can be seen to compound the illusion of transparency and concomitant processes of geospatial abstraction: "Where there is error or illusion,"
Lefebvre suggests, "the image is more likely to secrete it and reinforce it than
to reveal it. No matter how "beautiful" they may be, such images belong to
an incriminated "medium"" (1991: 96–97).

Rogoff argues that "Lefebvre's negation of the illusion of transparency is
of the utmost importance to numerous endeavours in cultural studies and
cultural criticism" (2000: 24). By drawing attention to the spatial contradictions that are both revealed and obscured through different forms of cultural
production, Lefebvre's arguments throw down the gauntlet to filmmakers to
engage with questions of spatiality in ways that challenge the complicity of
moving image cultures in the abstraction and spectacularization of quotidian
urban space: "Wherever there is illusion, the optical and visual world plays
an integral and integrative, active and passive, part in it. It fetishizes abstraction and imposes it on the norm. . . . After its fashion, the image kills." (1991:
97)

Rather than reading this as a dismissal of film tout court, it is more
instructive to look upon this critique in terms of its capacity to incite and
problematize further the explicit nature of the relationship between the city
and the moving image, and thus to reposition questions of spatiality more
firmly at the epistemological center of debates on visual culture and the
urban experience. As a symptom of the fetishization of abstraction that is
endemic to multinational consumer capitalism, the cinematization of urban
space represents the further consolidation of the city-as-spectacle, but at the
same time it can encompasses a set of urban cultural practices that are critically bound up with a more progressive *bricolage* model of the city-as-
archive: the *archive city*.

B. CINEMATIZATION OF URBAN SPACE

The merit of arguments for and against the motion that cinema represents an "incriminated medium," to use Lefebvre's terminology, rests in large part on the extent to which it constitutes a representation of space or a space of representation/representational space. For Keiller, the spaces of cinema are among those Lefebvre identifies as representational spaces, and as such can exert an influence on architecture and the built environment. He goes on to suggest, however, that "cinema is only one of many such sources among which literature, for instance, might be thought at least as important" (2003: 382). Through its capacity to create alternative and utopian visions of what cities look and feel like when seen through the oblique lens of aesthetic practice, cinema certainly does exert an influence. In this respect Lefebvre's arguments do not hold much water (and the lack of any sustained critical analysis on film in his work does weaken his overall case in this area). Yet it is equally true to say that the spaces of cinema also count as representations of space insofar as these map the built environment in ways that often bear close comparison to the rational, Cartesian perspectives of the cartographer, architect, or urban designer. Moreover, as a set of industrial and economic practices (networks of distribution and exhibition, economic geographies of production and consumption, and so forth), not to mention the site-specific logistics of location filming, cinema practices also fall under what Lefebvre defines as spatial practices. Representing a constellation of practices and aesthetic/representational formations, cinema therefore encompasses a range of spatial modalities which, in analytical terms, are particularly well served by a Lefebvrian-based theory of spatial dialectics.

Arguing the case for a Lefebvrean analysis of the material and visual cultures of cities, Wells lists under the heading of representations of space— or what, after Barbara Bender, she refers to as "rhetorics of spatial practice" (2007: 138)—the following objects and practices: monuments, surveillance, town planning, and cinema (2007: 138–40). If we consider the example of Liverpool, the city that formed the case study from which ideas of the archive city were principally developed (Roberts 2012a), the symbolic importance of monuments and memorials is widely reflected across films of all genres shot in and around the city. The erection of statues and monuments to the great and the good (philanthropists, industrialists, civic leaders, military heroes, monarchs) has symbolically marked out areas of the city as spaces associated with power, wealth, nationhood, and empire. These symbols and icons, most of which are a legacy of Liverpool's nineteenth-century city fathers, are, as Tim Edensor observes more generally, typically encoded with masculinized, classed, and racialized meanings and ideologies (2005: 830). Landmark buildings, such as the neoclassical monument St George's Hall, the iconic "Three Graces" (the Liver, Cunard, and Port of Liverpool Buildings at Pier

Head), or the temples of consumption that dominate large swathes of the urban center today (such as Liverpool One, which, when completed in 2008 was one of the largest retail developments in Europe), convey meanings that powerfully express the dominant political and economic power structures that have defined the city's narratives and spaces of identity. Over time, although their symbolic meanings change and multiply, these and other architectural landmarks become monuments to the mercantile, industrial, or commercial interests to which they owed their conception. The representation and framing of such monuments, whether in the form of photographs, postcards, advertisements, or film, recodify the urban landscape in ways that reproduce and reentrench the dominant meanings and narratives with which they are associated.

Taking another of Wells's examples of representations of space, those of urban planning, many films of Liverpool take the form of surveys or mappings of the urban landscape in ways that incorporate moving image representations within broader discourses of planning and redevelopment. In a spatial database of Liverpool films compiled between 2006–2010 (see below), searches reveal nearly 200 films that feature scenes of construction activity, or of buildings or landscapes in the process of construction or (re)development. These include footage of road tunnels, the city's airport, housing and residential developments, docks, office buildings, factories and industrial sites, university and hospital buildings, places of worship, transport infrastructures (roads, railways, and tramways), and underground drainage systems. Often these films include maps, architectural plans, as well as models of proposed developments. Views of the city from aerial perspectives similarly "model" the urban landscape in ways that often render the distinction between the abstract space of an architectural model and that of the actual urban landscape difficult to discern. Whether through the reproduction of maps, plans or models in film, or, through framing techniques such as aerial views and overhead panoramas of the urban landscape, these forms of urban imaging fit Lefebvre's conceptual typology of "representations of space": image-spaces which are invested with power and hegemonic spatial ordering.

Issues of power and control over everyday public spaces, and the questions these pose in respect of Lefebvre's "right to the city" (Harvey 2012), are similarly raised by the "private-public spaces" (Minton 2006, 2009) of urban regeneration developments (such as the Liverpool One retail complex), which rely on the extensive use of surveillance technologies to exert disciplinary control over the consumption practices to which they play host. There is perhaps no more powerful illustration of the moving image as an abstract spatial representation as that suggested by a bank of CCTV monitors on which a panoptic mosaic of image-spaces scrutinizes the urban landscape for any sign of aberrant behavior or urban dysfunctionality. Cinema is complicit in this process of spatial abstraction insofar as it reduces the complexity of the urban social fabric to a Cartesian logic of surface phenomena where measurement, taxonomy, regulation, and normative functionality are the guiding modus operandi. Compare the image of a security worker scanning a bank of CCTV monitors with that of thousands or perhaps millions of spectators whose cognitive and experiential understandings of a city's urban spaces have been filtered through the spectacular gaze of cinema. While the latter frames a view of the city that is semiotically encoded by the textual, performative, and embodied practices that constitute the filmmaking process, the former construct an abstract space that remains impenetrable to those individuals whose urban habitus and mobility is the object of its rationalizing gaze. Where the two become convergent is in forms of urban cinematic spectacle where the spaces of the city-film are pressed into service of an overly mediatized urban discourse. In this respect, the lack of dialogic structures of spatio-visual engagement, which is a characteristic feature of many recent developments in the so-called "creative economy" of cities, positions cinema squarely in the firing line of a Lefebvrean spatial critique. The instrumental embrace of "culture" as a subservient tool of capitalist urban development has meant that moving image culture has, by extension, similarly found itself dancing to the neoliberal tune of regeneration, tourism, consumption, and "film-related" place marketing (Tzanelli 2007; Roberts 2010, 2012a). To this end, the "cinematization of space," where direct observation and lived space give way to the authority and primacy of the media image (Abbas 1997: 41), coupled with a "decorporealization of the gaze in centrifugal space" (Dimendberg 2004: 139), should alert us to the possibilities of other ways of imagining and engaging with quotidian urban spaces (past and present), and of exploring further what role the moving image and archival film practices can or should play in this process.

C. THE ARCHIVE CITY I: LIVERPOOL

The recognition that archival film practices can productively function as a form of "spatial critique" provided one of the central underpinnings to Patrick Keiller's installation and archival project *City of the Future*. As an interactive resource, *City of the Future* draws from a database of approximately 2,000 early actuality films held by the British Film Institute (BFI) National Film and Television Archive. An interactive map of topographic film footage, the installation was exhibited at the BFI Southbank in London between November 2007 and February 2008. A selection of sixty-eight items filmed between 1896 and 1909, showing street scenes and "phantom ride" views filmed from trams and trains, was viewable across a number of screens on which historical maps were also projected. Organized spatially and geographically, the footage could be accessed by clicking on points on the maps, allowing users to move back and forth between cartographic and cinemato-graphic renderings of the same landscapes. "In enabling us to see so much of this landscape," Keiller argues, "these early films are truly extraordinary, as they offer the most extensive views of the landscape of another time at or just before the moment of that landscape's transformation" (2007: 121).

Insofar as the early actuality material Keiller discusses may be described as "topographic films," they bear many comparisons with much of the foot-age of cities shot by amateur filmmakers in the post-war period. This has formed the basis of extensive ethnographic and geographical research into amateur film practice in Liverpool and the surrounding Merseyside region from the 1950s to the present day. Alongside *City of the Future*, University of Liverpool's *Mapping the City in Film* project represents one of the fore-most examples of urban cinematic cartography using archival film practices as forms of spatial critique. This interdisciplinary project, a collaboration between architects, film scholars, and anthropologists, grew out of earlier research conducted into Liverpool's urban landscape and the moving image. This had resulted in the compilation of an online database of over 1,700 films shot in and of the city of Liverpool between 1897 and the present day. The database is searchable by a number of variables, including genre, date, syn-opsis keyword, as well as, more pertinently, spatial data: building and loca-tion, spatial function (the architectural characterization of landscapes in each film) and spatial use (the ethnographic and social forms of on-screen engage-ment with the city's spaces).

The *City in Film* project is comparable with *City of the Future* inasmuch as, firstly, it was the result of extensive archival film research in which space, landscape, and place, aided by the use of database tools, were the main focus of analysis. Secondly, it shared with Keiller's project a curiosity as to both the historiographical and architectural role of nonfiction archival film materi-al in critical analyses of everyday urban spaces and the shifting socio-cultural practices that have been historically aligned with these spaces. One of the key differences, however, (alongside the fact that it comprehensively focuses on a specific city) is that, unlike *City of the Future*, the interactive resource that developed from this early phase of the Liverpool research lacked a *cartographic* space of interactive engagement. Although, as a database, the resource allowed users to search city film data by location, street or building, the limitations of the database format (and, at the time, the requisite techno-logical and infrastructural support)[4] did not readily accommodate the use of maps or for the geo-referencing of the film data. Conversely, although Keill-er's installation effectively combined historical maps alongside digitised footage of the available archival material, the disjuncture between output (installation) and the database content from which it was developed (a spreadsheet compilation of 2,000 films from the BFI archive) meant that, unlike *City in Film*, as an interactive resource *City of the Future* had limited application as an analytical tool of urban historiographical film research. Lacking the immersive and site-specific spatialities that are the raw material of a place-based archaeology of film, the cinematic geographies it sets in motion are geographically more diffuse, and more fragmented in terms of their groundedness and spatial coherence as a "totality" of archival image-spaces. As a consequence, they are far less equipped to inform processes of critical engagement with the concept of the *archive city* as a mode of urban spatial praxis.

The compilation of spatial data drawn from an extensive archival trawl of moving images of a city, and which represent a diverse range of genres, localities, and historico-spatial practices, provides the basis of an urban geo-spatial resource that is at its most effective when it is itself organized and interacted with spatially. As a *mapping* resource, the digital infrastructure of the archive city is significantly enhanced by upgrading the database model to that of a spatial database, utilizing geographical information systems (GIS) and digital mapping technologies to geo-reference a city's archival image spaces. Embracing the many possible opportunities offered by what, in 2007–2008, were relatively nascent developments in the field of urban cine-matic cartography (Caquard and Taylor 2009; Roberts 2012b; Misek 2012), the layered, contested, "navigable," and dynamic spatialities of a GIS-based model of the archive city formed the starting point for the development of the *Mapping the City in Film* research activities which grew out of the earlier project.

Of course, contradictions once again abound in the notion that a progres-sive cultural politics of film and urban space might be sought by building a virtual architecture organized around the geospatial abstractions of a world "remodelled" by GIS: the same technologies that have aided state, corporate, and imperial powers to exert ever-greater degrees of hegemonic control over everyday landscapes and mobilities. Suffice it to say, there is a far wider debate to be had here that takes us beyond the remit of the present discussion (see Roberts and Hallam 2013), but the key proviso in the uptake of these technologies is the extent to which they serve not to extend a further layer of abstraction (reinforcing rather than critiquing the illusion of transparency). It is rather to provide new critical perspectives on the visual and spatial cultures of cities by bringing into sharper relief the contradictions and heterogeneity of the urban, and by foregrounding the spatial embeddedness of moving image cultures within wider structures and dialectics of urban space. To this end, the critical potential of geospatial and digital mapping tools lies less in their Euclidean capacity to attach urban cultures to specific points, areas, or vectors in space (although this has many undoubted benefits) as in their functionality as an interface or "critical hub" from which to explore and *map across* the differential spaces of the city. Accordingly, one of the main aims of *Mapping the City in Film* was to develop a resource that could bring into dialogue different experiences, representations, and practices that have variously constituted Liverpool's historical urban landscape, whether these be archival, cinematic, cartographic, ethnographic, embodied, architectural, or psychogeographic in their inception. In other words, to explore the qualitative and humanistic imbrications of the city's built environment and lived spaces of memory, and to consider more fully the ways that "archival film practices articulate an historiography of radical memory" (Russell 1999: xv).

The qualitative dimension to *Mapping the City in Film*—the geospatial embedding of archive film imagery in a GIS map; the geo-referencing of place-specific film data drawn from extensive archival research on a wide range of film genres; the "constellation" (Benjamin 1999a: N2a, 3) of past and present geographies of film; interviews and ethnographic research conducted with amateur filmmakers and others involved in film production in Liverpool and Merseyside; site-specific fieldwork conducted in key film locations; the use of video and still photography as visual research methods—these all provide the foundations for a richer and more complex navigation of the historical geographies of Liverpool that render the archive city as much a form of spatial practice—a spatial anthropology of the city in film—as a representational space by which the city *in* film might be more extensively mapped.[5]

As the Liverpool case study shows, the elemental task of mapping the archive city can shed practice-based insights into the spatial histories and geographies surrounding the production and consumption of film texts and practices. Virtual "wayfarers" of the archive city can navigate spatial film data by decade, genre, film gauge (16mm, 9.5mm, 8mm, etc.), building and location, architectural characterization, spatial practices, or by plotting film geographies on and across layered historical maps dating back to the 1890s. They can follow routes and communications, whether journeys mapped on film around particular city locations, historic tram and ferry routes, mobility networks linked to amateur film activity in Merseyside, films shot on or around bridge crossings, or the road tunnels underneath the River Mersey (Roberts 2010). They can query attribute data relating to over 1,700 films to map correlations between, for example, film genre (e.g., amateur, newsreel, promotional, municipal, and documentary) and topographic categories of spatial function (e.g., industrial and commercial, housing, public spaces, leisure, and recreation) or spatial use (everyday life, contested and political, festivals and parades, and so on). Users can also pull up geo-referenced planners maps, such as the 1962 Liverpool Corporation map showing the proposed location of an elevated inner city motorway system. While the motorway was never built, the ability to relate film data to the map of the proposed scheme provides a further layer of spatial contextualization with which to examine films inspired by road developments in parts of Liverpool,

including those made by community groups and amateur filmmakers, as well
as activist documentaries produced as part of campaigns contesting proposed
road developments and the impacts these have had on working-class communities in Liverpool (Roberts 2012a: 122–24). In addition, the attachment of
hyperlinks to location data offers users the opportunity to view geo-referenced film clips, videos of interviews, as well as photographs of sites of all
former cinemas in Liverpool and the surrounding region, alongside related
contextual information (figure 1.1).

  Mapping the City in Film is, then, first and foremost a geospatial compen-
dium of multimedial information relating to over a century of filmmaking
and film practice in Liverpool and Merseyside. Alongside its instrumental
function as a geo-historical research tool, as an interdisciplinary "hub" of
urban historiographical engagement, the GIS resource marshals together a
range of spatial forms and practices which, deracinated from their otherwise
localized constituencies, are rendered contingent and partial. In this regard
they may be considered as interventions in a wider cultural politics of the
urban: the critical *mobilization* of space as a form of urban *bricolage*.
Viewed thus, the archive city represents an open, creative space of engage-

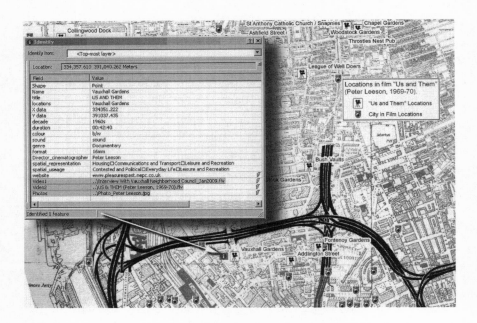

Figure 1.1.   Les Roberts. GIS map showing locations featured in the amateur
film *Us and Them* (Peter Leeson 1969-1970). The map features part of a proposed
(and subsequently abandoned) elevated motorway scheme planned for Liverpool in the 1960s.

ment in which the temporal geographies of a city's archival image-spaces reflect less the linearity of historical time than "the cautious probing of the spade in the dark loam" of urban spatial memory (Benjamin 1999b: 576). The historiographical implications are thus oriented around the navigational and dialectical possibilities of an urban cinematic geography. Understood as a relational assemblage of archival image-spaces rather than as a virtual chronology of individual filmic "narrative moments"—"like the beads of a rosary" to cite Benjamin (1999c: 255)—the archive city is, therefore, fundamentally a reservoir of spatial stories (de Certeau 1984) whose narrative pathways purposefully lead away from the abstractions of centrifugal space to the lived spaces of everyday urban practice.

D. THE ARCHIVE CITY II: BOLOGNA

Cinematic Bologna was an exhibition and series of workshops held at the Urban Centre located in the Salaborsa in Bologna city center between November 2012 and January 2013. Drawing on a wide range of amateur films shot in Bologna from 1950 to 1980, the exhibition was organized by Associazione Home Movies, the National Family Film Archive, also based in the city. The archive was founded in 2002 by Paolo Simoni and Karianne Fiorini, along with technical director Mirco Santi. Developed through collaboration with the Instituto Storico Parri Emilia-Romagna, the Regional Institute of Historical Research, named after the antifascist leader Ferruccio Parri, Associazione Home Movies has built up a collection of some 18,000 family films/home movies on a range of small-gauge formats, establishing Italy's de facto national amateur film archive and one of the largest collections anywhere dedicated to the recovery, conservation and enhancement of a nation's amateur film heritage (Edmonds 2007: 423).[6]

Marking the tenth anniversary of the founding of Associazione Home Movies, *Cinematic Bologna* provides a unique and absorbing insight into a city's cinematic geographies framed exclusively through the lens of amateur film. Spanning three decades, the films depict scenes of everyday life in and around the city. As with the case of Liverpool, the films capture an urban landscape undergoing rapid change and growth in the post-war years, although, unlike Liverpool, much of Bologna's historic urban fabric remains intact and has been spared some of the dramatic and convulsive transformations of the like visited on large parts of the port city.

As with *City of the Future* and *Mapping the City in Film*, one of the central features around which the curatorial activities of *Cinematic Bologna* revolve is a map. Dominating the main exhibition space, a large pictorial map of Bologna in black background depicts the city's prominent urban features and buildings which are hand-drawn in white chalk. Mounted at a number of locations around the wall map are small monitors on which visitors can view a selection of amateur films shot at or near the locations represented on the map (figure 1.2). With its high contrast white-on-black graphics, the aesthetic design of the map allows for a visually engaging form of cine-spatial interaction, further enhanced by the hand-drawn cartographic representation of the city that is well in keeping with the spirit and aesthetics of an amateur mode of filmic practice. Moreover, as "unofficial" or "unauthorized" forms of urban cultural heritage (Roberts and Cohen 2013), these vernacular cartographies help bolster the symbolic structures of a critical urban imaginary that offers the possibility of alternative ways of thinking about and engaging with cities than those underpinned by the logic of consumption and spectacle.

Among the other exhibits on display in *Cinematic Bologna* is a split-screen installation of a selection of home movies, which are viewable on the right hand side of the screen. On the left is video interview footage, produced by the Bologna archivists, of the filmmakers who shot and donated the films and who provide a scene-by-scene commentary on the film being simultaneously projected on the right of the screen.[7] Among the challenges routinely faced by archivists working with and cataloguing amateur films is the lack of contextual information surrounding their production, making it difficult, or in

Figure 1.2.   Les Roberts. *Cinematic Bologna* wall map (detail). The map was hand drawn by Cristina Portolano (courtesy Home Movies).

some cases impossible, to reliably determine the filmmaker's motivations, the locations filmed, or any biographical information on those involved in the production and/or consumption of the films. This lack of local knowledge is often compounded by the absence (or loss) of synchronized sound, meaning that to all intents and purposes many amateur cine productions are (or have become) silent films (Shand 2013: 197). The process of conducting video interviews and oral histories with the filmmakers and donor families can, therefore, furnish far greater insights into the social, cultural, and urban contexts that have historically shaped the production of amateur films of the city. In addition, by incorporating video ethnography and oral history methods into the standard historiographic toolkit used by film archivists, organizations such as Associazione Home Movies are pushing back and redefining the boundaries of what archival film practices can or should potentially encompass. As Paolo Simoni explains: "We are working on filmic material that is perhaps nearest to oral histories or autobiography. Memories recorded onto film mean that you need to provoke a reaction between the footage and the people to recontextualize the old images, to elaborate the gap created by the passage of time. . . . To be strictly a film archivist is not enough" (in Edmonds 2007: 424).

In the case of the *Cinematic Bologna* initiatives, the research-focused and qualitatively-enriched approach to the archival process that Simoni describes opens up the possibilities for critically engaging with amateur films (as well as other genres) as part of a wider urban historiographical project. In this respect the Bologna case study echoes many of the objectives that underpinned the Liverpool-based *Mapping the City in Film* activities discussed earlier. Both projects have sought to: (a) establish a more emphatic link between a city's archival image-spaces and its historical urban landscape; (b) explore the practical and curatorial role of maps and the geospatial embedding of a city's cinematic geographies; (c) flesh out the ethnographic layers of meaning and interpretation that underpin the *practice* and *spatial histories* of amateur filmmaking in an urban context; (d) mobilize processes of critical engagement—or, in Simoni's words, provoke a reaction—between and across the layered and heterotopic spaces of urban representation constitutive of a city's cinematic geographies; and (e) populate and "flesh out" these spaces as lived and anthropological spaces of urban habiting. In other words, to establish a more emphatic link between people, urbanity, and a city's archival image-spaces. In their different ways, then—and to bring this discussion to its conclusion—both case studies exemplify what I have described as *archive cities* on the terms elaborated throughout this chapter.

E. FROM VIRTUAL CITY TO ARCHIVE CITY

The cinematization of urban space is both a symptom and cause of wider processes of spatial abstraction that are transforming the cityscapes of late capitalist modernity. The case for a critical cartography of the city in which archival film practices are a central element is therefore problematized by the inherent spatialities of the medium. Never have cities been so extensively imaged as they are today. Yet despite or because of the "imageability" (Lynch 1960) and purported transparency of these virtual cityscapes, the concrete spaces of the city—"the [lived] space[s] of habiting: gestures and paths, bodies and memory, symbols and meanings" (Lefebvre 2003: 182)— remain opaque and intractably elusive. The more the everyday spaces of the city are reduced to spectacle the more the actual city seems to disappear. And the more it disappears the more urgent the task of imaging (and therefore archiving) the city becomes.

The capacity for archival film practices to foster critical spatial dialogue remains the measure by which cinematic cartography can serve as an analytical tool of historical urban discourse more generally. The development of a spatial anthropology of the archive city may of course encompass research into a much wider field of urban cultural practice than that specifically orientated around moving image cultures (Roberts 2012c). However, approaching film practices as forms of *spatial practice* can provide critical insights into the ways urban landscapes are—and have been—experienced, imagined, and negotiated as material and symbolic forms. Articulating what Bonnett (2010) describes as a "radically nostalgic" critique of contemporary spaces of urban spectacle, archival film practices offer a means—one among many—by which to reterritorialize the placeless spaces of the virtual city and thus to reappropriate, recultivate, and remobilize the anthropological spaces of the *archive city*.

NOTES

1. See http://www.bbc.co.uk/news/technology-19947159; http://youtube-global.blogspot.co.uk/2012/10/mission-complete-red-bull-stratos-lands.html (accessed 16 July 2013).

2. Research published in 2010 claimed that 37 percent of the Internet is made up of pornographic material, although this figure has been contradicted by other studies, see: http://www.bbc.co.uk/news/technology-23030090 (accessed 16 July 2013).

3. Google Glass is an augmented reality device in the form of a headset with spectacle frames via which users can access digital data directly as an adjunct to their embodied perceptual experiences (i.e., without interacting with separate hand-held devices such as laptops, tablets, or smart phones).

4. For a discussion of cross-disciplinary developments in GIS and film, and some of the issues and challenges these have raised, see Roberts and Hallam 2013.

5. A recent example which illustrates similar developments in digital spatial anthropology is MyStreet, an online user-generated resource that hosts geo-referenced films that can be searched via a map and by place name or postcode. Developed by anthropologists at UCL,

MyStreet is described thus: "It's where you are, who you are and how you live . . . your place on the map. MyStreet is a living archive of everyday life, encouraging you to make your mark and bring your area to life." http://www.mystreetfilms.com/ (accessed 06 August 2013).

6. See http://www.memoriadelleimmagini.it/homemovies/ (accessed 06 August 2013).

7. For an example see: http://www.youtube.com/watch?v=0NMIqid6Adc. For a selection of other films uploaded to the Associazione Home Movies YouTube channel see: http://www.youtube.com/user/archiviohomemovies (accessed 06 August 2013).

BIBLIOGRAPHY

Abbas, Ackbar (1997), *Hong Kong: Culture and the Politics of Disappearance*, Minneapolis: University of Minnesota Press.

AlSayyad, Nezar (2006), *Cinematic Urbanism: A History of the Modern From Reel to Real*, Routledge: London.

Benjamin, Walter (1999a), *The Arcades Project*, Cambridge, MA: Harvard University Press.

———. (1999b), "Excavation and Memory," in *Walter Benjamin: Selected Writings Volume 2, Part 2, 1931–1934*, Michael W. Jennings, Howard Eiland, and Gary Smith (eds.), Cambridge, MA: Belknap Press, p. 576.

———. (1999c), "Theses on the Philosophy in History," in *Illuminations*, London: Pimlico, pp. 245–55.

Bonnett, Alastair (2010), *Left in the Past: Radicalism and the Politics of Nostalgia.* London: Continuum.

Brunsdon, Charlotte (2007), *London in Cinema: the Cinematic City since 1945*, London: BFI.

Caquard, Sébastien and D.R. Fraser Taylor (eds.) (2009), "Cinematic Cartography," Special Issue of *The Cartographic Journal*, 46:1, pp. 16–23.

Coleman, Roy (2004), *Reclaiming the Streets: Surveillance, Social Control and the City*, Cullompton, Devon: Willan.

de Certeau, Michel (1984), *The Practice of Everyday Life*, Berkeley: University of California Press.

Debord, Guy (2004 [1967]), *The Society of the Spectacle*, London: Rebel Press.

Dimendberg, Edward (2004), *Film Noir and the Spaces of Modernity*, Cambridge, MA: Harvard University Press.

Edensor, Tim (2005), "The Ghosts of Industrial Ruins: Ordering and Disordering Memory in Excessive Space," *Environment and Planning D: Society and Space*, 23:6, pp. 829–49.

Edmonds, Guy (2007), "Associazione Home Movies, l'Archivio Nazionale del Film di Famiglia—An Interview with Paolo Simoni and Karianne Fiorini of Italy's Amateur-Film Archive," *Film History*, 19:4, pp. 423–28.

Harvey, David (2012), *Rebel Cities*. London: Verso.

Jameson, Fredric (1991), *Postmodernism, or, The Cultural Logic of Late Capitalism.* London: Verso.

Keiller, Patrick, (2003), "City of the Future," *City* 7:3, pp. 376–86.

———. (2007), "Film as Spatial Critique," in *Critical Architecture*, Jane Rendall, Jonathan Hill, Murray Fraser and Mark Dorrian (eds.), London: Routledge, pp. 115–23.

Lefebvre, Henri (1991), *The Production of Space*. Oxford: Blackwell.

———. (2003), *The Urban Revolution*, Minneapolis: University of Minnesota Press.

Levin, Thomas Y. (2002), "Dismantling the Spectacle: The Cinema of Guy Debord," in *Guy Debord and the Situationist International: Texts and Documents*, Tom McDonough (ed.), Cambridge, MA: MIT Press, pp. 321–453.

Lury, Karen and Doreen Massey (1999), "Making Connections," *Screen* 40:3, pp. 229–38.

Lyon, David (2002), *Surveillance Society: Monitoring Everyday Life*, Buckingham: Open University Press.

Lynch, Kevin (1960), *The Image of the City*, Cambridge, MA: The MIT Press.

Minton, Anna (2006), *The Privatisation of Public Space*, London: Royal Institution of Chartered Surveyors.

————. (2009), *Ground Control: Fear and Happiness in the Twenty-First-Century City*, London: Penguin.

Misek, Richard (2012), "Mapping Rohmer: A Research Journey through Paris," in *Mapping Cultures: Place, Practice, Performance*, Les Roberts (ed.), Basingstoke: Palgrave Macmillan, pp. 53–67.

Noys, Benjamin (2007), "Destroy Cinema!/Destroy Capital!: Guy Debord's *The Society of the Spectacle* (1973)," *Quarterly Review of Film and Video*, 24:5, pp. 395–402.

Penz, Francois (2010), "The Real in the Reel City: Towards a Methodology through the Case of *Amélie*," in *The City and the Moving Image: Urban Projections*, Richard Koeck and Les Roberts (eds.), Basingstoke: Palgrave Macmillan, pp. 233–52.

Pile, Steve (2005), *Real Cities: Modernity, Space and the Phantasmagorias of City Life*, London: Sage.

Roberts, Les (2010), "Projecting Place: Location Mapping, Consumption and Cinematographic Tourism," in *The City and the Moving Image: Urban Projections*, Richard Koeck and Les Roberts (eds.), Basingstoke: Palgrave Macmillan, pp. 183–204.

————.(2012a), *Film, Mobility and Urban Space: A Cinematic Geography of Liverpool*, Liverpool: Liverpool University Press.

————. (2012b), "Cinematic Cartography: Projecting Place through Film," in *Mapping Cultures: Place, Practice, Performance*, Les Roberts (ed.), Basingstoke: Palgrave, pp. 68–84.

————. (2012c), "Mapping Cultures: A Spatial Anthropology," in *Mapping Cultures: Place, Practice, Performance*, Les Roberts (ed.), Basingstoke: Palgrave, pp. 1–25.

Roberts, Les and Sara Cohen (2013), "Unauthorizing Popular Music Heritage: Outline of a Critical Framework," *International Journal of Heritage Studies*, 20:3, DOI: 10.1080/13527258.2012.750619.

Roberts, Les and Julia Hallam (2013), "Film and Spatiality: Outline of a New Empiricism," in *Locating the Moving Image: New Approaches to Film and Place*, Julia Hallam and Les Roberts (eds.), Bloomington: Indiana University Press, pp. 1–30.

Rogoff, Irit (2000), *Terra Infirma: Geography's Visual Culture*, London: Routledge.

Russell, Catherine (1999), *Experimental Ethnography: The Work of Film in the Age of Video*, Durham and London: Duke University Press.

Shand, Ryan (2013), "Retracing the Local: Amateur Cine Culture and Oral Histories," in *Locating the Moving Image: New Approaches to Film and Place*, Julia Hallam and Les Roberts (eds.), Bloomington: Indiana University Press, pp. 197–220.

Siegel, Allan (2003), "After the Sixties: Changing Paradigms in the Representation of Urban Space," in *Screening the City*, Mark Shiel and Tony Fitzmaurice (eds.), London: Verso, pp. 137–59.

Soja, Edward W. (1996), *Thirdspace: Journeys to Los Angeles and Other Real-and-Imagined Places*, Oxford: Blackwell Publishers.

Tzanelli, Rodanthi (2007), *The Cinematic Tourist: Explorations in Globalization, Culture and Resistance*, London: Routledge.

Wells, Karen (2007), "The Material and Visual Cultures of Cities," *Space and Culture*, 10:2, pp. 136–44.

Chapter Two

Capital, Mobility, and Spatial Exclusion in Fernando León de Aranoa's *Barrio* (1998)

Malcolm Alan Compitello

New turns in critical geography theorize the idea of mobility and how it affects human agency under the conditions of capital. This line of inquiry deploys concepts from the work of Gilles Deleuze and Félix Guattari, most especially their landmark *A Thousand Plateaus*, as its theoretical frame of reference is congruent with the post-structuralist turn that has become a significant thread in the current discourse of critical geography.[1] One might think that the entry of this strain of theoretical discourse into the mainstream of critical geography—which has, for decades been more materialist-oriented—might lead to a lessening of the impact of the latter. There is no doubt that this work is enlightening and exciting. Nevertheless, its theoretical orientation has a tendency to side step the real life issues of mobility and exclusion that the spaces of capital impose on society and how these issues are imbedded in cultural texts. For this reason, it is David Harvey's extensive body of work which continues to offer the most important frame of reference for those wishing to study the unequal apportionment of space under capital. Harvey's project of converting historical materialism into a geographical historical materialism (Harvey 1989: 7)—as he has developed it across four decades of seminal contributions to Marxist theory and urban dialectics—offers the tools necessary to examine this problem in its social and cultural contexts and as such forms the theoretical underpinnings for this chapter.[2]

A considerable part of David Harvey's contribution to the study of how capital forms space and human existence in its image issues is from two key concepts he developed in seminal work in the 1980s, the urbanization of capital and the urbanization of consciousness.[3] Capital reproduces itself in space as a second nature. This second nature is the built environment. This built environment, which results from the ways in which capital forms itself in space—the urbanization of capital—forms a second human nature out of the way we experience the urban—the urbanization of consciousness. The conjoining of capital and space allows Harvey to articulate these two basic tenets of his work. With the idea of the urbanization of capital Harvey suggests an inexorable link between capitalism and cities. Capital is an eminently urban form. Its evolution over the last two and a half centuries is inexorably bound up in the way it has been able to maintain and transform itself through the acts of creative destruction that have a decisive impact on the built environment of cities and on the people who inhabit them. This process creates the close relationships between money, space, time and the city. These relationships are what, in turn, form urbanized consciousness: individual and group responses to life in a city built in the image of capital.

Harvey identifies five primary areas of consciousness formation: individualism, class, community, the state and the family, whose dynamic interplay shapes urban consciousness. The task for a historical-geographical materialist interpretation of the urban process, according to Harvey, is to "[e]xamine how the ways of seeing, thinking and acting produced through the interrelations between individualism, class, community, state, and family affect the paths and qualities of capitalist urbanization that in turn feedback to alter our perceptions and our actions" (1989: 231). Moreover, it is in the urban context that, to again quote Harvey, "firmer connections between the rules of capital accumulation and the ferment of social, political and cultural forms can be identified. In so doing I reiterate that the urban is not a thing, but a process and the process is a particular example of capital accumulation in real space and time" (Harvey 1989: 247). Capital shapes consciousness, and consciousness is both formative of and formed by cultural and social forms. This process-based view represents an important corrective to analyses that focus simply on cultural products or texts in isolation from their context. It underscores the shortsightedness of approaches to the city and its problems that assume that a rearrangement of the built environment in and of itself solves anything. Building is thus only an intermediary step in the continuing process of answering the basic question about social justice and the city: "Whose city is this?"

As capital extends itself more and more through space as a way to confront changing economic realities, it does so unevenly. Capital, as Harvey points out, has used space to its advantage. The spatial fixes it attempts to impose account for this uneven development, since "capitalism has survived not only through the production of space, as Lefebvre insists, but also through superior command over space—and that truth prevails as much within urban regions as over the global space of capitalist endeavor" (Harvey 1989: 58). Harvey is right on the money when he asserts that instead of concerning ourselves with globalization and its effects—(capital has been transnational and globally oriented since its inception)—emphasis should be placed on the disastrous effects that this uneven development and expansion of space has had on place, and on each of the individual cities or urban regions touched by it.

Fundamental to the arguments this chapter proposes is an understanding of the idea of the cartographic imaginary. "Monument and Myth: The Building of the Basilica of the Sacred Heart" (Harvey 1989: 200–28) is the British geographer's most famous essay on the cartographic imaginary. By far his most sophisticated explanation of how the relationship between the fictional imaginary and political, economic, and spatial processes functions in narrative fiction is his essay on Balzac (Harvey 2003: 23–48). He believes that novels have "inspired the imagination, influenced conceptions and imaginaries of, for example, the city, and therefore affected material processes of urbanization" (Harvey 2003: 28).[4] They also help create what Harvey calls a "consensus of the imagination" in which "certain kinds of political-economic action suddenly seem both possible and desirable" (2003: 28). This chapter launches an analysis of how the director embeds his cartographic imaginary into *Barrio*'s visual disposition; how it makes visible the lack of congruence between urban reality and claims to an equitable distribution of wealth and access to and control of space. Examining key sequences in the film demonstrates how they highlight the protagonists" fixedness in place in a world where mobility is essential. In this way the film's visual structure lays bare the fate of those left behind or pushed aside by that expansion.

An analysis of this kind helps humanists to "think like geographers," as Harvey (2001a) puts it, and in this way ameliorate the differences between humanists and social scientists when it comes to space and culture. It enables humanists to understand that to scrutinize the production of imaginary spaces in a cultural text is to also excavate the real built environment constructed by real people in real space and time. At the same time, to think like a geographer from Harvey's perspective will enable those whose work deals with real space to understand the subtleties and constructive moves that allow an artist to imbue *form* (not only content) with the meaning of a text's cartographic imaginary. The formal analysis of film that this chapter adduces draws on the foundational analyses as proposed by David Bordwell and Kristin Thompson (2001) while recognizing that there is a substantial body of work that has emerged on the relationships between film and space.[5]

A. STRUCTURING FILMIC RESISTANCE

The urban processes emphasized in Harvey's work plays a fundamental role in the nature of the transformations Madrid underwent as it expanded and responded to different tactics for managing its urban growth. Moreover, they seep inexorably into the consciousness of cultural creators. Mobility—and the lack thereof—becomes central in a Madrid whose expansive tendencies increased geometrically from the 1980s until the financial crisis of 2007 burst the housing bubble and plunged Spain into a recession.[6] During that period, the city of Madrid continued to absorb outlying townships at a vertiginous rate and then assimilated its new condition as both city and the last of the autonomous regions approved by the articles of the Spanish Constitution of 1978—articles which restored federalism as a form of government in Spain. Madrid therefore had to deal with its new political identity at the same time it navigated the problems of being the site of not only city but also state and national governments. This complex identity brought to the fore political negotiations and tensions dependent upon which political parties controlled each of the administrations. Mobility becomes problematic during this period since the expansion of the "megapolis" made problematic fundamental tenets put forth in the official plans for the city. As it was first articulated in *Recuperar Madrid* (1982: 138–234), that is, the study volume published a few years before the final plan (*Plan general de ordenación urbana de Madrid 1985 Memoria general*)—urban planning in Spain's capital sought to "*Garantizar el derecho de la ciudad a todos*" ("Guarantee the right to the city for all").[7] Over time, however, this noble goal was lost as the idea of what planning should accomplish and how the city should be organized changed. What happened—to once again cite a principle articulated by Harvey (1990)—was that progressive urban planning ceded to the parochial interests and collusion between the public and private sectors that characterized urban design.

These developments must necessarily shape how we understand the Madrid we see in Fernando León de Aranoa's film. The director is one of a group of younger Spanish filmmakers who the critic Carlos Heredero labeled the "*cosecha de los noventa*" ("harvest of the nineties") because they all began their directorial careers in the 1990s in the wake of the artistic and economic success of Pedro Almodóvar's films. Of all of these directors, León de Aranoa has produced the most consistently socially critical body of film which focuses on space and capital—while never letting his films degenerate into mere political pamphleteering. As such his films play into the urban process, in the way Harvey discussed above, through their skillful thematization and visualization of the spatial inequity wrought by capital. *Barrio* is mediated by a cartographic imaginary that contests the uneven expansion of Spain's capital city. León, like his fellow *madrileños*, would have been acutely aware of this inequity especially as it played out as crucial elements in the battles over city planning in Madrid after the restoration of democracy in the late 1970s.[8] In this light, *Barrio*'s central characters are the victims of the periodic bouts of creative destruction that are the essence of capital precisely because they do not have the resources to keep up with the vertiginous pace of change. The film shows them caught in a web of transportation networks, which paradoxically fix the young protagonists in space because they only serve those with more resources than the teenagers and their families possess and which proves inadequate to provide access to the city for all of its residents.

León de Aranoa is cognizant of the role of the spaces of capital in this film asserting that the images of his film form a synthetic space out of the real places of the run-down neighborhoods of Madrid's southern tier.[9]

> *Esta es una película sobre la periferia de las cosas, sobre aquello que las rodea, que las sostiene. Sobre la periferia de las grandes ciudades. . . . Transcurre en un barrio cualquiera, a los que no llega ni el metro ni el dinero. Un barrio gris, cuatelero, hermético, un barrio que en la realidad no es ninguno y quiere ser todos.* [This is a film about the periphery of things, about that which surrounds them, which sustains them. About the periphery of the great cities. . . . It unfolds in what could be any neighborhood whatsoever, a neighborhood to which neither the metro nor money has arrived. A neighborhood that is gray, insular, self-contained, one that in reality is not a neighborhood, and yet wants to be all neighborhoods.] (León de Aranoa 2000: 275)

The city that León de Aranoa presents stands in stark contrast to how Madrid is portrayed in sleek thrillers like *Tesis* (Amenábar 1996), *Abre los ojos* (Amenábar 1997), and the spate of youth films that filled out the urban imaginary vision of Madrid, from *Historias del Kronen* (Armendáriz 1995) and *Mensaka* (García Ruiz 1998). In some ways, León de Aranoa's vision is much closer to Saura's groundbreaking *Deprisa Deprisa* (1980) than to films made by other directors who began their careers in the 1990s and even to the portrayal of the city in most of the films Pedro Almodóvar. Pursuing this approach leads León de Aranoa's work in directions far removed from the theater of imaginary family filmed in his first feature, *Familia* (1997), and roots *Barrio* in the drama of real social relationships, a direction he has pursued in subsequent films, especially *Los lunes al sol* (2002) and *Princesas* (2005).

Images of mobility, or the lack thereof, and of spatial exclusion center how the director chooses to visualize the problems inherent in Madrid's urban process.[10] Decades ago Eduardo Leira pointed out that Madrid expanded not rationally, but as a *mancha de aceite* (oil stain) responding to speculators" ability to marshal capital in support of its desire or organize space to its advantage sometimes with, sometimes without the collusion the public sector (Leira et al. 1981). The desire to ameliorate the physical and social distances between what Carmen Gavira has labeled "*la ciudad y la no ciudad*" ("the city and the noncity")—a constant problem as Madrid expanded through the twentieth and into the twenty-first century—has been far less than seamless. The inability of numerous planning documents to address these inequities, the shifting priorities of the political bodies who enact the plans and the role of the private sector in thwarting some of the more progressive solutions essayed has had the effect of fixing spatial exclusion in place, denying segments of the population the right to the city or even to the autonomous region. Therefore, León's assertion that his film could take place in any of the areas that circle Madrid's core is both true and not quite true, it could be any part of the outskirts of the city that is left behind, first because of lack of access to public transportation, later because of the bursting housing bubble. Those who reside in these areas are financially unable to surmount the spatial divide that makes them both "out of site" (to borrow a term from Diana Ghirardo [1991]) and out of sight in other parts of the city.

Barrio develops this critique of capital's appropriation of urban space through its depiction of the lives of three fifteen-year-old boys (Javi, Manu and Rai) who reside in an area where *chabolas* (shanty towns) give way to cheap housing supplanted in time by higher rise *ciudades dormitorios* (bedroom communities), crisscrossed by various iterations of beltways and train tracks that themselves fracture the landscape. It is August: the boys and their families are suffering through hard times and they have no place to go. All they have is their dreams of spending vacation time someplace else perhaps a beach in a resort in Spain or elsewhere, fueled by their incomplete vision of the world outside of their own barrio, lavish publicity campaigns and media reports. They inexorably get bound in circuits of frustration that eventually lead to tragedy.

· León de Aranoa plots this visually through a brilliant portrayal of the relationships of space, time, and money that mediate the protagonists'' lives. The film foregrounds the interconnectedness of space and the interpretive acts the spectator needs to deploy to decipher how the film forms its critical vision of space from *Barrio*'s opening credits [00:00:00–00:01:49].[11] The neighborhood in which they live, a series of aging older buildings, is brought into sharper focus at the beginning of the film. The use of a hand-held camera, and quick crosscutting of disconcerting shots of short duration leave the viewer struggling to form meaning from the visual introduction to space. The need to grasp a puzzling spatial maze presented in a disconcerting manner contrasts vividly with the informational function that film credits normally provide. In this way, the film problematizes the meaning-making process from the beginning and forces the viewer into the role of active participant in making-meaning. The sequence ends with a series of enabling shots. Each one draws back, unveiling another layer of urban construction, newer and taller than the previous one that supplants it, further out from the center of the city in a way reminiscent of how Alex de la Iglesia films both the Capitol building and the Torres Kío en *El día de la bestia* (1995) and Pedro Almodóvar films the last shots of *¿Qué he hecho yo para merecer esto?*

(1984). This technique heightens viewers" disconcertedness as each shot displaces the center of the action and recontextualizes it in a way that shows its scale in relationship to other moments of construction of the city.[12] A dissolve to white advances the film to the next sequence and to the three young protagonists. The end result is to open the eyes of the viewer capable of making sense of the material and the manner in which it is presented. In this way it visually underscores that in order to process what will follow, the viewer must be willing to proceed with eyes wide open through the layers of poor urban planning that fixes this inequality in space.

Mobility, the capacity to control space through the ability to move through it with impunity, helps establish one's right to participate fully in the urban experience. This concept is central to the message that *Barrio* presents, but as an absence since the film focuses on how capital constrains the movements of those who reside on the city's periphery. David Harvey points out how cultural works spatialize class relationships (1989: 178). For example, the fluidity with which characters traverse space in Dickens stands in sharp contrast to the space in novels by Gissing where capital is seen as imposing much stricter limits on freedom of movement. A significant number of sequences in León de Aranoa's film engage with this concept as a way of offering resistance to the role of capital in carving up urban space and constraining movement. Of the eighty-seven sequences that comprise *Barrio* (including the opening and closing credits) fifty-six portray spatial issues and twenty-eight of those treat issues of spatial exclusion. Of these, modes of transportation (cars, vans, subways, highways, trains, buses, and others) figure prominently in thrity-three of them.[13] Several stand out for the incongruous connections they portray between needs, desire, and what reality holds out. The most emblematic—the pizza delivery sequences (18–21 [00:23:14–00:25:10])—explore how the lack of mobility limits access to employment. Manu applies for a job as a pizza delivery boy in order to earn some money to shore up the fragile economic situation at home; his father has lost his job and is supporting Manu's older brother who is a homeless drug addict. He professes to have a *moto* [motor bike] to get the job, but since he does not have one, he has to deliver the pizzas by bus and by foot, demonstrating the tortuously slow rate of public transportation in the neighborhood for all those who do not have an automobile. The fractured nature of the urban landscape makes it even more difficult to navigate. With the band Amparanoia's song "*Hacer dinero*" ("Making Money") blaring in the background, Manu is filmed through a series of shots that depict him crisscrossing space as he attempts to surmount the lack of public transportation to do what the song and capital demands, make money. At each turn space places more obstacles in his way, steep stairs to descend, overpasses to traverse, busses to catch, fields to cross. They are filmed in such a way as to make it appear that at each turn he gets further away from his goal, rather than closer to it and in so doing the election of shots disorients the viewer leaving one in the dark as to where Manu is headed. At one point—in a shot reminiscent of the passage in Luis Martín-Santos" *Tiempo de silencio*, where Pedro thinks he has arrived at his destination of the *chabolas*, only to find out that he has not— Manu climbs a hill and the low angle shot leads one to believe he has arrived at his destination. When the camera pulls back the viewer realizes that he is still far away [00:24:49]. By the end he is reduced to a small figure against looming new apartments in the background, emphasizing his loss of agency and control of the situation. Manu and the boys wind up eating the pizza he is unable to deliver.[14]

The most vivid symbol of being stuck in space are the jet ski sequences (34–36, 48, 63). Rai wins the vehicle in a contest by sending in the tops of yogurt containers, which he has to steal from a local supermarket since his mother will not buy that brand of yogurt because it is too expensive as she tells him in Sequence 3. He wants the vacation offered as first prize, one that would allow him to escape his spatial confinement. He wins the jet ski that eventually will sit uselessly in front of his family's apartment building until it is ultimately stolen. The useless prize indicates the boys" fixedness in space in a society where the winners are those with the ability to traverse space with impunity. Even when they win, they lose. Once again the shots Léon de Aranoa uses to construct this sequence highlight the incongruity of the situation. Three short shots cut together seemingly without connective threads begin the sequence. The viewer can suture the elliptical shots by connecting the juxtaposed material in a way that is alert to what has already happened; that is to say if one is attentive, following Harvey—see above—to time and space at the same time. A sound bridge leads to a shot of Rai in his bedroom [00:37:33–00:38:05] as his mother hands him a letter which he begins to read. The second, a long shot, is of a white van arriving outside of an apartment building. [00:38:06–00:38:10]. The juxtaposition—a technique the director uses assiduously to create meaning—can lead the viewer to suppose that the letter Rai receives has something to do with the one he sent when he entered the contest but not necessarily with what the van holds, since the only time the contest was mentioned Javi and Rai discussed the contest's first prize, the trip. How one should connect these two shots is established by the two succeeding ones with which they are juxtaposed. The camera frames Rai with his mother and father looking out of a small window in their building [00:38:11–00:38:18] at the end of which Rai leaves the shot and a reverse angle shot captures the van and some men beginning to unload it [00:38:19–00:38:24]. The next shot establishes a relationship between the jet ski and Rai as he exits the apartment [00:38:24–00:38:42]. Subsequent ones situate Rai and the jet ski (medium one of him, disconcerted [00:38:42–00:38:58]; medium long shot of him and contest representative and the vehicle [00:38:58–00:39:12]; then a long shot of him and the ski

[00:39:12–00:39:52]). At the end of the latter, the representative asks Rai if he likes his new vehicle, which is met with a look on the youngster's face which belies the word "*mucho*" ("a lot") that he utters.

A jump cut transitions to the next sequence (Sequence 36 [00:39:13–00:40:54]) which takes place sometime later. The three boys and the jet ski overtake the dimensions of Rai's diminutive room where the jet ski has come to rest intensifying the message from the exterior shots about how out of place it is. Rai lets the viewer know of the ultimatum from his mother to get the vehicle out of the house—subsequent sequences will see the jet ski chained to the light pole outside the apartment building (Sequence 48 [00:51:29–00:51:40])—and will be the cause of its being stolen (Sequence 63 [01:13:41–0114:19]).[15] The boys" jokes about the ski disarm the situation of melancholy—saying it would be much more useful if it had wheels, like a car, and Manu's observation that in that way he could use it to deliver pizzas—because there is nowhere else for it to go since the gift is useless. Through this juxtaposition León de Aranoa points out how space constrains the boys" actions, the importance of private vehicles in a place where public transportation is insufficient to the needs of the population, even though the space is crisscrossed with train tracks and, as importantly, how the boys build a community to surmount their situation.[16]

The defining sequence of exclusion is one that frames the boys as they sit on an overpass of a highway watching cars go by (Sequence 14) which occurs early on in the film [00:17:00–00:18:54]. Their fixedness stands in sharp contrast to fluidity with which space is traversed in other less critical movies that thematize Madrid and in the "road pictures" that have become an interesting subgenre in recent Spanish film. Moreover coming as it does early in the film it offers a stark contrast to the frenetic movement of the opening credits. In this sequence the stasis is just as disconcerting as the fast pace of the opening. The shots in this sequence frame Javi, Manu, and Rai through a series of close angle, reverse angle shots through the bars of the rails of the overpass offering an image of entrapment as they sit locked in space on the edge of the highways that crisscross the area and play a game imagining which car will be theirs. Javi and Manu win, but the car that Rai identifies does not come, and no cars appear for a considerable period of time, emphasizing the fixedness and emptiness of their situation. The boys get up one by one and leave. The minute that Rai exits, the camera pans back to a wide enabling shot as cars again appear on the motorway and the viewer experiences the vertiginous pace of vehicular traffic as it glides to all of the places announced on the signs above the highway.

Javi, Manu, and Rai's private hideaway (sequences 5, 39) offers another visual image of their condition. It is situated in a ditch near a culvert amid piles of refuse besides one of the numerous highways which whisk people with means of private transportation around and beyond the city. The boys sit on car seats, "liberated" from discarded vehicles or that were simply abandoned at the side of the road or in a garbage container and dream of a life beyond their neighborhood. The space constitutes the safe haven for the community they have formed to shield them from the problems each faces in their own families. Their interactions here are sometimes filmed against the sight and sound of vehicles streaming by. In this way the camera captures both their solidarity as a community and the tragedy of their situation since, as with other sequences already examined, they can only observe the passing vehicles, simulate the experience, and not live it. This solidarity stands in stark contrast to the tensions that characterize the family lives of the three protagonists.

Nothing represents the incongruence of spatial relationships more than the sequence filmed in the abandoned Chamberi metro stop (Sequence 60 [1:07:27–1:10:10]).[17] The boys miss the last metro at the Iglesias metro stop and decide to walk through the metro tunnels.[18] Through a series of angle/reverse angle shots of various distances from medium close to long, the viewer sees the youngster's reactions as they see close the hidden living conditions of immigrants. The contextualization of their plight as outsiders in the city with those of immigrants whose living conditions and social and political status was exacerbated by the regressive policies of the Partido Popular is similar to the visual contextualization strategy that León de Aranoa uses at the beginning of the film when shot after shot draws the camera further back to contextualize one layer of urban growth against the previous ones. While a number of those sequences underscore this relationship of spatial exclusion, this particular one helps draw into sharper focus the scales at which this exclusion plays out in the film.[19] In essence they are out of site both in the center of the city and in the *no-ciudad* (noncity) where they should be in place.

That *Barrio*'s tragic ending—the death of Rai at the hands of a plain clothes policeman who lives in Javi's building—is vehicle-related is telling. Rai has become infatuated with Javi's sister, Susana, who flirted with him early in the film (Sequence 9 [00:12:00–00:13:02]) and whom he and the other boys observed leaving a vehicle after having sex (sequence 75 [01:09:21–01:13:05]).[20] Sequences 79–81 ([01:13:13–01:13:30]) are an interchange between Rai and Susana. He calls her on the intercom from outside her building and asks if she wants to go out, she accepts and tells him to wait ten minutes while she takes care of some things. In sequence 82 [01:13:31–01:22:06] the camera then frames a series of shots involving Rai as he waits for Susana. First it films him repeating an action he has done before, walking along a piece of discarded wire simulating a high-wire artist perched on the edge of danger as he traverses the wire.[21] The danger becomes real as the camera shoots angles and reverse angles of Rai and a car parked nearby. The youngster leaves the wire and walks toward the vehicle, one that the viewer may remember from a previous sequence, belongs to the plainclothes officer who lives in Rai's building. He starts to jimmy the lock when he is confronted by the policeman who levels his gun at him.[22] The camera fixes on Rai who looks upward as a reverse angle shot films the upper floor windows of the building in which Javi's family lives. The camera then captures Rai through the glass of the driver's side door window and the reflection of the plainclothes officer. Probably because he was already arrested for distributing drugs—a sequence in which vehicles also play prominent roles—and feels he has no future, he attempts to flee and is shot by the police officer, who, significantly and in character with the paranoia he has displayed in previous sequences in which he has appeared, never identifies himself as such before firing.[23] The camera films the policeman firing, but not Rai being shot. The next two sequences (83–84) shift in rapid succession to Susana and her grandfather in their apartment as she hears the shot and moves toward the window[24] then to Manu giving Javi the news of Rai's demise when the latter enters a subway car. Significantly we never hear the conversation and can only observe, not hear, Javi's violent reaction to the tragic news—all filmed through the windows of the subway car. We hear only the voice of famous television anchorman, Matías Prat Luque, announcing the news of Rai's death in a voiceover that the viewer must assume is a news broadcast similar to the ones presented in earlier sequences which are discussed below.

The ambiguity of these sequences reduces Rai's agency, objectifying his death and denying the viewer direct access to the reactions of his family and most importantly the close friends who form his small community, an alternative to the stressful situation of their families. The method chosen to film these sequences also intensifies the sense of ambiguity the film presents and they problematize how the viewer might come to grips with what is being presented; struggle to construct meaning. At the same time these scenes emphasize how far Rai was willing to go to have access to the kinds of transportation he hoped would be liberating but which proves to only be the ultimate exclusion. The fact that Javi receives the news while in a subway car intensifies the relationship between mobility and exclusion even more.

The social relationships *Barrio* explores—especially its family relationships—are also fundamental in how the movie underscores the effects of uneven capital development in space, time, place, how capital fixes in place spatial exclusion, and inequality.[25] The film emphasizes this early on through the way the director addresses the difficult financial times that affect Javi, Manu, and Rai. The way León de Aranoa constructs the spaces they inhabit and how he films their residences highlights how space fits into their problems and underscores their position of marginality. The spaces are a realistic representation of lower middle class apartments typical of these developments on the edge of the city, carved up into very small rooms, the result of unchecked speculation by developers bent on maximizing profits. In *Barrio* these spaces are filmed in a way that makes the space seem too cramped for the people who occupy it, highlighting a sense of spatial exclusion through the way capital apportions space based on class an element of the film's structure and meaning already evident in the jet ski sequence and how it is filmed.

This is most evident in the scenes filmed at meals in Javi, Rai, and Manu's houses. *Barrio* highlights the importance of these family gatherings by featuring them early on in the film. First, a meal at Javi's house (Sequence 2), juxtaposed to one at Rai's (Sequence 3), then, shortly after, one at Manu's (Sequence 7). All three foreground financial issues and underscore tensions that will develop throughout the film sequences. The director weaves the first of the two together through recourse to the newscast by Matías Prats Luque that is playing on the television in the dining room. The director highlights this by ending the sequence prior to the one at Javi's house with a sound bridge (Sequence 2 [00:03:37–00:03:40]) of the newscast expounding on the fact the most important national news was the beginning of summer vacations and the arrival of millions of Spaniards to beaches on the coast. This contrasts with the condition in the boys' neighborhood seen in the previous sequences and then in the one inside Javi's house which erupts into a conflict over family values. This continues into the next sequence in Rai's house, introduced with a sound bridge to the end of the same newscast [00:05:00–00:05:02]. This links the sequences visually, aurally, thematically, and structurally to the one at Rai's house which also ends in a conflict over money over missing money. Family tensions and issues of money continue in the sequence in Manu's house a few minutes later in the film. Subsequent sequences in Javi's and Manu's house as well as the tension over the jet ski in Rai's house discussed above exacerbate the situation. The conflicts become tenser over time as family and personal crises heighten. A second scene over the dinner table in the apartment of Javi's family underscores this. Once again it is filmed with the television offering visions of people on the beach enjoying their summer vacations and Matias Prat Luque offering the positive economic forecasts—congruent with the Partido Popular's message of that period. All of this clashes directly with the content of the scene which brings home again the tense economic situation that is tearing the household apart and which will eventually lead to the divorce of Javi's parents and the need for the viewer to judge reality with open eyes.[26] Opening one's eyes—and ears—after all is what affords the viewer the discursive power to understand the protagonists" plight, contextualize it, and challenge the discourse that normalizes their situation.

B. CONCLUSION

As mentioned at the beginning of this chapter, David Harvey reconfigures historical materialism as geographical-historical materialism recognizing the need to spatialize Marxist theory given the power that capital wields over the configuration of space and the social relationships of those who inhabit the spaces of capital that it tries to mold in its image. Spatial battles became fundamental as Spain moved beyond the period of the Franco dictatorship and tried, for a time, to suture the wounds predatory capital's speculative urban processes inflicted on the city. Although the Marxist-based attempts of the socialist/communist-based government elected in Madrid in 1979 to change this dynamic with a plan, whose intent was to guarantee the right to the city for all inhabitants, would fail as urban planning ceded to urban design in subsequent less enlightened urban administrations, the idea of equality, and the battles of the city became part of the urbanized conscious-ness of those living in the city. León de Aranoa's body of filmic work stands as a monument to how cultural creations form part of the urban process and particularly how they can form important spaces of resistance against specu-lative urbanism. *Barrio* is one of the clearest examples of this. It underscores how the inversion of the ciudad/no ciudad dynamic has skewed the nature of urban consciousness. The periphery is now the center for these teenagers without access to the money and means necessary to suture the relationship between the component parts of the urban in Madrid. At this point in time Aznar's famous *"España va bien"* ("Spain is fine") pronouncement is made to ring hollow against the visual evidence of a city and region that still excludes part of its population. Through the skillful use of the visual tech-niques the film articulates through its visual imagery, content, themes, and *dispositio* a coherent view of how capital skews space in a way that fixes the protagonists in place through processes of spatial exclusion based on the power of capital to rebuild space in its image. It affords a powerful antidote to less contestatory cultural creations and contributes to the debates over the rights to the city by articulating what is at stake if they are not preserved.

NOTES

1. Tim Cresswell has been at the center of mobility studies see Cresswell (2006). The volume he edited with Deborah Dixon (2002) is particularly germane to the study of the film under scrutiny in this essay.

2. Merrifield (2002) contextualized Harvey's seminal work in the field of Marxist urban-ism. Castree and Gregory (2006) is an important collection of essays that offer a variety of views of Harvey's contributions that underscore his position as the preeminent critical geogra-pher of his time and as a leading Marxist theorist.

3. The most condensed explanation of these concepts can be found in Harvey (1989: 17–58; 229–58).

4. Compitello (2013) offers a more expansive explanation of the concept of the cartographic imaginary in another analysis focusing on Madrid.

5. David Clarke (1997) is one of the classic studies on this subject. Cresswell and Dixon (2002) offer recent takes on the subject of space and film.

6. Fernández Durán (2006) predicted a crisis that, with hindsight, has generated considerable critical attention.

7. Compitello (2013) delves into the sources for the planning vision of the 1985 plan.

8. González Esteban (2001) is a succinct overview of the planning process as it plays out throughout Madrid's modern history. De Terán (1981: 37–52; 1999a; 1999b) offers the most comprehensive study of the 1985 plan. Compitello (1999: 199–219; 2003: 403–11; 2012: 75–94; 2013: 41–63) studies the effects of planning on culture and the urban process as does Larson (2003: 395–402).

9. Carlos Badessich (2010) offers interesting important comments on the material this essay develops but does not fully develop a contextual frame that includes the urban transformations that mediate the characters" predicament and its relationship to capital.

10. The fact that it is impossible to highlight all of the images of this type in a paper of this length underscores just how important they are to understanding the film's meaning.

11. I thank Professor Carlos Velázquez Torres who did the segmentation of this film when he was working as my research assistant while completing his doctoral work in Spanish at the University of Arizona. A copy of the segmentation is available by emailing compitel@email.arizona.edu.

12. The concept of scale as socially constructed as Sallie Marston points out in her seminal article on this subject is important in this film, since this León de Aranoa's film is one of the first of the period to respond to the expansion of Madrid from the point of view of those living on the periphery who, necessarily see the relationship between the city and noncity as Carmen Gavira (1999) posits the difference from a completely different perspective. This remains outside the parameters of analysis that circumscribe this essay but are part of a larger view of the author's work and the urban process in Madrid now in progress. It is worth noting here that Marston's corrective to a totally production based view of scale's social impact, one which takes into account family relationships and space is completely germane to remarks about social exclusion made in this paper.

13. These include cars (13, 55, 75, 82), busses (18, 19, 21, 45, 46, 47, 68), cars on highway (5, 14, 39, 71), and the jet ski and others (34, 35, 36, 48, 49, 63).

14. Subsequent sequences (45, 76) film Manu delivering pizzas as well, indicating that in spite of the obstacles the need to "*hacer dinero*" ("make money") as the song says keeps him making his torturous journeys of foot and with public transportation.

15. Sequence 63 is juxtaposed to two sequences in a local trophy store. Rai jimmies the lock and the boy's enter and take home some trophies to console Javi who is disconcerted over his parents" divorce and its deleterious effects on his family. As they arrive at Rai's house in sequence 63 they see that the jet ski has been stolen and all that remains is the chain that held it to a pole. Rai's comment "mierda de barrio" is an accurate assessment of the place in which they live and a liberating statement that allows the three friends, as they did earlier in Rai's room, to laugh about the incongruity of their situation. In this way it also serves to allow the viewer the critical distance to examine how capital skews social relationships, a sequence in which the boys break into a trophy store and take home some.

16. Community is one of the five elements that David Harvey identifies as constitutive of urban consciousness. The others are class, individual, family, and the state. See Harvey (1989: 229–55).

17. The station now forms part of the Andén 0 metro exhibit in Madrid. See http://www.esmadrid.com/anden0/. Araceli Masterson-Algar (2012) essay offers a wonderful contextualization of the Andén 0 project.

18. The sequence is set up in Sequence 15 when Manu tells his friends about an abandoned metro stop his father, who worked for the Metro, had told him about.

19. Among the most important are ones that demonstrate that Javi, Manu, and Rai's spatial exclusion is class based. They include one filmed in a department store where although Rai has enough cash on hand to purchase the music they are listening to, the private security guard tells

them to leave and one filmed in a club frequented by slightly older young people of another class who make no bones about the difference. This scene allows León to Aranoa to establish a stark difference between his portrayal of young people and that found in Gen X fiction, especially the work of José Angel Mañas and the films based on those written narratives such as *Historias del Kronen* and *Mensaka* mentioned above.

20. What remains unclear is whether the motivation for Susana's sexual act is monetary, based on the precarious financial situation that her parents" divorce has precipitated, as well as Rai's motives.

21. Sequence 16 filmed Rai doing the same kind of simulacrum of a high-wire act on a discarded piece of wire.

22. Rai's ability to open closed cars came out in sequence 49. As the three boys observed an armored truck and Rai informs his friends that he can open that and any vehicle. He demonstrates his ability by opening the door of the car against which he is leaning. This provokes the ire of Manu who leaves instantly. The nature of all of Rai's illegal activities in the film seems to be something that the director uses to blur the boundaries between black and white, guilt and innocence, adolescence and adulthood and hammer home how difficult the teenagers" lives are in this neighborhood that capital seems to have marginalized.

23. In sequence 17 Javi's grandfather peers through the window of their apartment seeing the police officer in his bathroom. When he realizes someone is looking, he rapidly closes the window in a belligerent way that casts his actions in a negative light. In sequence 26 he confronts Rai when the latter enters his building and Javi has to come to his friend's defense. In the following sequence Javi informs Rai he is a police officer. In sequence 55 the police officer's rampant paranoia is revealed in a way that sets up the final confrontation, as we see him peering under his car looking for a bomb with a the same kind of mirror device the Spanish military regularly used to look for explosives planted by ETA. It is important to note that while family and community figure prominently in the film the state is only seen in its inability to manage spatial and social inequities and as a force of repression. It is also interesting that Rai's brother is a private security guard at AZCA and that the scenes filmed there, especially Rai's simulating Russian roulette with his brother's revolver while the former leaves his post to have sex with his girlfriend, are indicative of Rai's state of mind and foreshadow his violent death.

24. The shot is also important because it appears that Javi's grandfather, who is supposedly deaf, has heard the shot. This is another element that the film deploys to unsettle viewer expectations at crucial moments of *Barrio*'s advancement.

25. Steven Marsh (2004) and Nuria Cruz-Cámera (2005) study these relationships in their excellent articles on *Barrio* which help immensely to contextualize and understand the family dynamics and the social contexts that inform them.

26. Significantly the preceding sequence (23 [00:27:53–00:00:28:23]) shows the three boys filming an employment announcement in such a way that demonstrates that Javi's youthful innocence and their incapacity for dealing with real world economic situations. Significantly while the other two have to come more to grips with hard economic times and their deleterious consequences, in Javi's family it appears that it is his sister Susana who confronts the situation more directly. This parallels the first set of family encounters, which were also preceded by a sequence that demonstrated how little the boys seem to understand the surroundings outside of their neighborhood (Sequence 2 [00:01:48–00:03:35]).

BIBLIOGRAPHY

Almodóvar, Pedro (dir.) (1984), *¿Qué he hecho you para merecer esto?*, Producción Cinematográfica Española.

Amenábar, Alejandro (dir.) (1996), *Tesis*, SOGEPAQ.

———. (1997), *Abre los ojos*, SOGEPAQ.

Armendáriz, Monxo (dir.) (1995), *Historias del Kronen*, Alta Films.

Badessich, Carlos (2010), "Espacio urbano e identidad: adolescencia marginada en *Barrio* de Fernando León de Aranoa," *ACTAS del XVI Congreso de la Asociación Internacional de Hispanistas: nuevos caminos del hispanismo, París, 9 al 13 de julio de 2007*, pp. 1–6.

Bordwell, David and Kristin Thompson (2001), *Film Art An Introduction*, sixth ed., New York: McGraw Hill.
Castree, Noel and Derek Gregory (eds.) (2006), *David Harvey: A Critical Reader*, London: Blackwell.
Clarke, David B. (ed.) (1997), *The Cinematic City*, London: Routledge.
Compitello, Malcolm Alan (1999), "From Planning to Design: The Culture of Flexible Accumulation in Post-Cambio Madrid," *Arizona Journal of Hispanic Cultural Studies*, 3, pp. 199–219.
———. (2003), "Designing Madrid, 1985–1997," *Cities* 20: 6, pp. 403–11.
———. (2012), "A Good Plan Gone Bad: From Operation Atocha to the Gentrification of Lavapiés," *The International Journal of the Constructed Environment*, 2: 2, pp. 75–94.
———. (2013), "City Present in City Past: Rafael Chirbes' Cartographic Imaginary," *International Journal of Iberian Studies*, 26: 1–2, pp. 41–63.
Cresswell, Tim (2006), *On the Move: Mobility In the Modern World*, New York: Routledge.
Cresswell, Tim and Deborah Dixon (eds.) (2002), *Engaging Film: Geographies of Mobility and Identity*, New York: Rowman and Littlefield.
Cruz-Cámara, Nuria (2005), "El simulacro desde el extrarradio: *Barrio* de F. León de Aranoa," *Bulletin of Spanish Studies*, 82: 1, pp. 59–73.
De la Iglesia, Alex (dir.) (1995), *El día de la bestia*, SOGEPAQ.
Deleuze, Gilles and Félix Guattari (1987), *A Thousand Plateaus. Capitalism and Schizophrenia* (trans. Brian Massumi), Minneapolis: Minnesota University Press.
De Terán, Fernando (1981), "Notas para la historia del planeamiento de Madrid (De los orígenes a la Ley Especial de 1946)," in *Madrid: Cuarenta años de desarrollo urbano 1940–1980*, Vol. 5, Temas Urbanas, Madrid: Ayuntamiento de Madrid, pp. 37–52.
———. (1999a), *Historia del urbanismo en España III Siglos XIX y XX*, Madrid: Cátedra.
———. (1999b), *Madrid: Ciudad-Region. Entre la ciudad y el territoria en la seguna mitad del siglo XX*, Madrid: Comunidad de Madrid-Consejería de Obras Públicas, Urbanismo y Transporte.
Fernández Durán, Ramón (2006), *El Tsunami Urbanizador Español Y Mundial. Sobre Las Causas Y Repercusiones Devastadoras, Y La Necesidad De Prepararse Para El Posible Estallido De La Burbuja Inmobiliaraia*, 2nd ed., Barcelona: Virus.
García Ruiz, Salvador (dir.) (1998), *Páginas de una historia. Mensaka*, Alta Films.
Gavira, Carmen (1999), "La ciudad y la no ciudad, Madrid (1567–1993)," *Madrid centro y periferia*, Madrid: Biblioteca Nueva, pp. 111–48.
Ghirardo, Diane (ed.) (1991), *Out of Site. A Social Criticism of Architecture*, Seattle: Pay Press.
González Esteban, Carlos (2001), *Madrid Sinopsis De Su Evolución Urbana*, Madrid Ediciones La Librería.
Harvey, David (1989), *The Urban Experience*, Baltimore: Johns Hopkins University Press.
———. (1990), *The Condition of Postmodernity*, Cambridge, MA: Blackwell.
———. (2001a), "Cartographic Identities: Geographical Knowledges under Globalization," *Spaces of Capital. Towards a Critical Geography*, New York: Routledge, pp. 208–36.
———. (2001b), "The Art of Rent: Globalization and the Commodification of Culture," *Spaces of Capital. Towards a Critical Geography*, New York: Routledge, pp. 394–411.
———. (2003), "City Future in City Past: Balzac's Cartographic Imagination," *After-Images of the City*, Ithaca: Cornell University Press, pp. 23–48.
Heredero, Carlos (1997), "Cosecha de los noventa," *Espejo De Miradas. Entrevistas Con Nuevos Directores De Cine Espanol De Los Años Noventa*, Alcalá: Festival de Cine de Alcalá de Henares, pp. 23–75.
Larson, Susan (2003), "Shifting Modern Identities in Madrid's Recent Urban Planning, Architecture and Narrative," *Cities* 20: 6, pp. 395–402.
Leira, Eduardo et al. (1981), "Madrid: Cuarenta Años De Crecimiento Urbano," *Madrid: Cuarenta Años De Desarrollo Urbano 1940–1980*, Vol. 5, Temas Urbanas. Madrid: Ayuntamiento de Madrid, pp. 135–63.
León de Aranoa, Fernando (dir.) (1997), *Familia*, Alta Films.
———. (1998), *Barrio*, Warner SOGEFILMS.

————. (2000) "Periferia." *Barrio. Guion de Fernando León de Aranoa*, Madrid: Academia de las artes y las ciencias cinematograficas, pp. 275–76.

————. (2002), *Los lunes al sol*, Warner SOGEFILMS.

————. (2005), *Princesas*, Warner SOGEFILMS.

Marsh, Steven (2004), "Tracks, Traces and Common Places: Fernando León de Aranoa's *Barrio* (1998) and the Layered Landscape of Everyday Life in Contemporary Madrid," *New Cinemas: Journal of Contemporary Film*, 1: 3, pp. 165–77.

Marston, Sallie A. (2000), "The Social Construction of Scale," *Progress in Human Geography*, 24: 2, pp. 219–42.

Martín-Santos Ribera, Luis (1981), *Tiempo de silencio*, definitive ed., Barcelona: Seix Barral.

Masterson-Algar, Araceli (2012), "Digging Madrid: A Descent into Madrid's Subway Museum, Andén 0 [Platform 0]," in *Trains, Culture and Mobility: Riding the Rails*, B. Fraser (ed.), Lanham, MD: Lexington Books, pp. 205–34.

Merrifield, Andy (2002), *Metromarxism*, New York: Routledge.

Plan General De Ordenación Urbana De Madrid 1985 Memoria General (1985), Madrid: Ayuntamiento de Madrid, Oficina Municipal del Plan.

Recuperar Madrid (1982), Madrid: Oficina Municipal del Plan, Ayuntamiento de Madrid.

Saura, Carlos (dir.) (1980), *Deprisa, deprisa*, Elias Querejétera.

II

THE HUMAN SENSES
IN URBAN CONTEXTS

Chapter Three

Henri Lefebvre in Strasbourg

The City as Use Value in José Luis Guerín's
Dans la ville de Sylvie *(2007)*

Benjamin Fraser

French Marxist geographer-philosopher Henri Lefebvre's relatively brief stint teaching ethics and sociology in the city of Strasbourg represents a crucial and still underappreciated shift toward the formulation of his urban theory. That is, although today Lefebvre is widely and almost immediately recognized as an "urban thinker," this was not always the case. Born in Hagetmau in the Basque Pyrenees in 1901, he attended classes at the Sorbonne in the 1920s; he published early translations of Marx and Hegel and texts on Nietzsche, alienation, and dialectical materialism in the 1930s; and he went on to take part in the resistance in southern France during the Second World War. Lefebvre's intellectual work up through this point showcased the interdisciplinarity that would become the hallmark of his later urban theory—but it did so notably without prioritizing the urban phenomenon itself. The Philosophies group he ran with during the 1920s took on "poetry, sociology and political economics, philosophy, history, novels, literary criticism and psychology" (Burkhard 2000: 28); and Lefebvre also drank "wine and coffee with leading Dadaists and surrealists (like Tristan Tzara and André Breton)" (Merrifield 2002: 72; Elden and Lebas 2003: xvi; also Merrifield 2006). While part of the French Communist Party (PCF, 1928–1958) he wrote essays "appropriating classical authors, that is, French cultural capital [books on Diderot or Rabelais, for example], for Marxist purposes" (Elden and Lebas 2003: xiii; see also Léger 2006: 145, who cites Poster 1975; Kelly 1982). Lefebvre later worked in "collaboration" with Guy Debord and the Situationists (Shields 2011: 280; also Kofman and Lebas 1996: 11–12;

43

43

Kitchens 2009; Nadal-Melsió 2008; Ross 2004; Shields 2005), employed author Georges Perec to do fieldwork in 1960 and 1961 (Kofman and Lebas 1996: 15) and continued to write on aesthetic questions throughout his entire life—most notably producing the book *La présence et l''absence* [Presence and Absence] (1980), itself an underappreciated text and at the time of this writing still untranslated into English (available in Spanish: Lefebvre 2006a). Most important is that although many in the humanities fields would pass over the fact that Henri Lefebvre was a committed Marxist, he would have contested this appropriation of this hought (e.g. Lefebvre 1947; 1948; 1964; 1982; 1988; 2008; also Elden 2007; 2006a; 2006b; 2004; 2001).

Considered marginal in Anglophone scholarship for many years even after the 1991 publication of Donald Nicholson-Smith's English translation of the French thinker's watershed text *The Production of Space* from 1974 (Lefebvre 1991a), Lefebvre's popularity is now sharply on the rise in urban humanities work. Nonetheless, what many current approaches overlook is that Lefebvre had defended his thesis on rural sociology in the early 1950s, and that it was only by the late 1950s that his interest began to shift from the agrarian question and his sustained critique of everyday life toward a critical evaluation of the concept of the city and of urban matters themselves. He spent the period spanning October 1961 to October 1965—when he became professor of sociology at the University of Paris-Nanterre—commuting from Paris to the University of Strasbourg. While in Strasbourg, Lefebvre lectured on urban questions, supervised research studies, and moved in an impressively interdisciplinary circle of "colleagues, students and artists" whose intellectual reach ranged from mathematics/catastrophe theory, to acoustic engineering, to the sociology of work and religion and more (Stanek 2011: 20–23). More important, still, is that his co-creation of the *Institut de sociologie urbaine* [Institute of Urban Sociology] (ISU; formed 1962–1963, Stanek 2011: 19) dates to this period. While his subsequent publications on the city might have attracted more attention given their relevance to the events of May 1968 (see also Mendieta 2008)—his books *The Right to the City* (1968), *The Explosion* (1969), and *The Urban Revolution* (1970), for example, are key in this regard—Strasbourg occupies a privileged place not merely in his life but also in the development of his urban research profile.

Significantly, the beginning of Lefebvre's time in Strasbourg (1961–1965) also marked the final moments of his famed friendship with Guy Debord and the Situationists. Lefebvre later reflected on this friendship and its terminus in an interview:

> The Situationists . . . it's a delicate subject, one I care deeply about. It touches
> me in some ways very intimately because I knew them very well. I was close
> friends with them. The friendship lasted from 1957 to 1961 or '62, which is to
> say about five years. And then we had a quarrel that got worse and worse in

conditions I don"t understand too well myself but which I could describe to you. In the end it was a love story that ended badly, very badly. (Ross and Lefebvre 1997: 80; quoted in Merrifield 2005: 31)

In brief, the Situationist International had formed in 1957 drawing from a number of other Eurpoean avant-garde groups (Knabb 2006: ix). Its collaborators imagined a radically disalienating and interdisciplinary urban practice that linked desire and action—art, life, and critique—as a way of dismantling the pillars of contemporary capitalist society (see also Debord 1961; 1995; Knabb 2006; Merrifield 2005; Nadal-Melsió 2008). In the aforementioned interview, Lefebvre regards the Situationists" reading of his own *Critique of Everyday Life* (vol. I, 1991b; originally published in 1947) as a fundamental inspiration for their formation (Ross and Lefebvre 1997: 70). The Situationists' early experiments with Unitary Urbanism, for example—which aimed to connect disparate parts within the city, a hallmark of the Situationist notions of psychogeography/dérive—unfolded in Strasbourg, specifically (along with Amsterdam). In fact, the group's first brochure was handed out by the thousands in Strasbourg even before Debord and others disseminated it in Paris (Ross and Lefebvre 1997: 73–74).

Though the Situationists and Lefebvre often engaged in heated arguments and eventually split because of disagreements both theoretical and material (Ross and Lefevbre 1997: 73–75), they also shared a central understanding. This was the insight that everyday urban life was a battleground, one that was increasingly important not merely for assessing how capitalist power operates in contemporary urbanized society, but also for resisting and contesting that power through both play and direct action. In the end, Strasbourg as a material urban site is an historical point of reference essential for understanding the evolution of Situationist and Lefebvrian ideas. But more important, still, in the present context, is its concrete appearance in a recent film by Barcelona-based director José Luis Guerín (b. 1960). Guerín's film *Dans la ville de Sylvie* (In the City of Sylvia, 2007) offers an opportunity to reflect upon the Marxian dimensions of Lefebvre's body of work, now applied to the city, and also to see how this film—taken as a particular type of cultural production with somewhat unique formal properties—can bring his urban insights to light.

What this chapter of *Marxism and Urban Culture* proposes is an analysis (or rather what Lefebvre called a "rhythmanalysis") of *Dans la ville de Sylvie*—which takes place entirely in Strasbourg. This reading showcases the film's representation of urban rhythms—not merely to advance a Marxist reading of cinematic urban space but also as a way of returning to several of Lefebvre's key insights on the urban phenomenon. Lefebvre's time spent in Strasbourg constitutes an implicit point of departure for this discussion of the on-screen presentation of the city, but it is his concept of *Rhythmanalysis*

([1992] 2006b), developed as part of his multi-volume *Critique of Everyday Life* (1991b, 2002, 2005, 2006b), which best allows the viewer to appreciate director José Luis Guerín's filmic vision of its urban fabric. On the whole, this chapter harnesses Lefebvre's reconfigured spatial and urban Marxism (Lefebvre 1988; 1996; 2003b) and his notions of rhythmanalysis, use versus exchange value, the right to the city, and the notion of play as resistance, in making sense of a most difficult and masterful film. While Guerín's "silent film with sound" (Kuehner 2008: 11; 2011) features almost no dialogue whatsoever, its use of sets, editing, shot composition, and seemingly naturally occurring (if diegetic) sound, foregrounds a Lefebvrian vision of the urban that is defiantly at odds with the ideological content of urbanism and planning as it has developed over the past two centuries. In this "virtually wordless, but never silent" city film (Kuehner 2008: 11), urban life is itself the protagonist; through the language of a "pure" cinema (Kuehner 2008: 11), the sights and sounds of Strasbourg take on a more universal meaning—a meaning which Lefebvre's rhythmanalytical Marxian method is uniquely equipped to explore.

A. JOSÉ LUIS GUERÍN AND THE LIVED CITY: A MARXIAN-LEFEBVRIAN APPROACH

Having already directed *Los motivos de Berta* (Berta's Motives, 1984), *Innisfree* (1990), and *Tren de sombras* (Train of Shadows, 1997) among other shorts and documentaries, with 2001's *En construcción* (Under Construction) José Luis Guerín established an international reputation for himself, winning the Premio Nacional de Cinematografía that same year. The director himself has aptly described that film's theme as "*cotidianidad quebrada por el estruendo de los derribos*" ("everydayness fractured by the thunder of demolitions") (quoted in Smith 2005: 174)—and *En construcción* takes on the recent urban changes in his native city's urban core quite directly. These urban changes must be approached simultaneously, of course, with reference to both the local and global scales (see Kipfer 2009): that is, since the nineteenth century, the Catalan capital city has continually engaged in what one scholar has termed *Barcelona's Vocation of Modernity* (Resina 2008a; see also Loxham 2006; Núñez 2012; Fraser 2012a). Some may be unaware, for example, that the extensive and more well-known urban shifts introduced by Haussmann into the built environment of nineteenth-century Paris (Harvey 2006; Choay 1969) are in many ways complemented by urban designer Ildefons Cerdà's somewhat similar plan of 1859 for the Catalan capital (Cerdà 1867; Fraser 2011a; 2011b). But Barcelona's urban changes also speak more broadly to how capitalism has evolved over the past two hundred years by turning to the urban form as a vehicle for its accumulation strategies (Harvey

1996; 2000; 2012; Lefevbre 1976; 1991a; 2003a). Understanding these global changes and their local expressions—which were at the core of Guerín's
earlier film—is important if we are to appreciate Strasbourg's appearance in
the film *In the City of Sylvia*.

In particular, the Marxian distinction between use value and exchange
value—already central in the opening pages of volume I of *Capital* (Marx
1977: 125–27 and onward; see also Harvey 2010: 17)—is one of the core
themes brought to life through Guerín's cinematic oeuvre. To see how this is
so we need to grapple with these concepts as they have been explicitly
urbanized in the theory of Henri Lefebvre. In *The Right to the City*, the
French urban philosopher points to the nineteenth century as a crucial hinge
moment when the city as an exchange value begins to trump its use value
(Lefebvre 1996: 167; see also Harvey 1989: 199; Marx 1977). That is, instead of being a lived space used by its inhabitants—to whom the city should
inarguably belong if we follow the thinking of Lefebvre, David Harvey, and
Manuel Delgado Ruiz—the city is not merely a site for exchange but also
increasingly a vehicle for capital accumulation through gentrification, a
product to be bought and sold through intercity competition and even an
object of consumption constructed through touristic discourse (Lefebvre
1996; 2003a; Harvey 1996; 2000; Delgado Ruiz 2007a; 2007b). For Lefebvre, the nineteenth century marks a key moment in which the nascent ideological bourgeois system of urban planning shifts from creating "an urban reality
for "users"" toward the production of a city ripe for exploitation by "capitalist speculators, builders and technicians" (Lefebvre 1996: 168). Lefebvre's
critique of this practice is sharpest in *The Urban Revolution* and *The Right to
the City*, but is also broadly supported by insights from *The Survival of
Capitalism* and by the central thrust of the multi-volume *Critique of Everyday Life*—that is, daily life is understood as both "an encounter and a confrontation between use (use-value) and exchange (exchange-value)" (Lefebvre 2005: 12).

In 1968's *The Right to the City*, Lefebvre makes an impassioned call for
defending use value, for asserting the value of the city as a lived space:

> For two centuries, industrialization has been promoting commodities—which
> although they pre-existed were limited by agrarian and urban structures. It has
> enabled the virtually unlimited extension of exchange value. It has shown how
> merchandise is not only a way of putting people in relation to each other, but
> also a logic, a language, and a world. . . . What is at stake is an overtaking by
> and in practice of a change in social practice. Use value, subordinated for
> centuries to exchange value, can now come first again. How? By and in urban
> society, from this reality which still resists and preserves for us use value, the
> city. (Lefebvre [1968] 1996: 167; see also Attoh 2011; Purcell 2002)

Later—in *The Explosion* (1969)—Lefebvre in effect turns to one particular aspect of the city's use value in highlighting the contestatory power of urban demonstrations. This book, which was written in the wake of the events of 1968, in part called for further reflection on contestation as a radical way of linking economic and political factors and of rejecting the pernicious logic and power of both institutions and the people who identify with them (Lefebvre 1969: 65, 67). As discussed there, a key part of contestation is spontaneity (1969: 70–71; see also Nadal-Melsió 2008: 161), a factor that has often been linked with the urban in general (Jacobs 1992; also Fraser 2009; 2012b). "It was in the streets that the demonstrations took place. It was in the streets that spontaneity expressed itself—in an area of society not occupied by institutions" (Lefebvre 1969: 71; see also Delgado Ruiz 2010). Contestation as theorized in *The Explosion* is already a specifically urban practice— and yet our understanding of this fact is deepened when it is considered in light of Lefebvre's later Marxian work on space and capitalism (e.g., in *The Urban Revolution*, *The Production of Space*, and even the less clearly spatial *Rhythmanalysis*).

As Lefebvre explores more fully in *The Urban Revolution* and *The Right to the City*, modern urban planning develops in the nineteenth century as an ideological practice rooted in the urbanization of bourgeois capitalist society (Lefebvre 1970; 1996; see also Fraser 2011a; 2011b; Harvey 2006; 2012). In somewhat simple terms, a provisional Lefebvrian distinction between the "city" and the "urban" distinguishes the built environment as it has been constructed by "capitalist speculators, builders and technicians" (in this case the "city") from lived urban spaces (in this case the "urban") (see Delgado Ruiz 2007a; Fraser 2007; 2008; 2014; Lefebvre 1996; 2003a). This distinction in effect recapitulates the Marxian contrast between use and exchange as mentioned above: the "city" has an exchange value while the "urban" has a use value. As Lefebvre writes in *The Survival of Capitalism*:

> It is worth remembering that the urban has no worse enemy than urban planning and "urbanism," which is capitalism's and the state's strategic instrument for the manipulation of fragmented urban reality and the production of controlled space. . . . The urban, defined as assemblies and encounters, is therefore the simultaneity (or centrality) of all that exists socially. (Lefebvre 1976: 15)

Here we can see that the necessarily collaborative production of modern city space by diverse power structures—the state and capital being the strongest among these political, economic, and social influences—involves an instrumentalization of lived space. For Lefebvre, defining the urban in terms of ephemeral encounters is closely related to the potential of the city streets for unmasking, critiquing, and contesting capitalist power. And following from the basic premise outlined in the introduction to this book—and although contestation nevertheless must continue in the city streets themselves—cultural products do nevertheless play a key role in legitimizing or contesting systems of power (Hopkins 1994; also Cresswell and Dixon 2002; cf. Harvey 1990).

In essence, both of Guerín's most famous films—*En construcción* and *Dans la ville de Sylvie*—spring from the same spirited directorial defense of the city as a use value, from the same intuitions regarding the spontaneous nature of urban life and its potential for contestation. That is, while the former film's unadorned critique of gentrification explicitly pits the city as it is experienced on the ground as a lived space against the city as it has been designed and built by "capitalist speculators, builders and technicians," the latter film continues this critique, albeit in somewhat modified form. Here the fleeting moments of street life are taken to the extreme as Guerín constructs a lyrical cinematic urban poem of sorts (perhaps a visual version of Spanish poet Luis García Montero's *Poesía urbana* [Urban Poetry], collected in 2002; Cabello 2005 would see it as a "cinematic essay"). The next section of this chapter explores Guerín's more recent film itself as a visual urban poem in the Lefebvrian key. We should keep in mind that, as one critic has written, "*L'approche de* Dans la ville de Sylvia *est beaucoup plus ludique, plus téorique et philosophique aussi* [*In the City of Sylvia*'s approach is much more playful, and also more theoretical and philosophical]" than that employed in *En construcción* (Darras 2008: 44). And yet, even if *Dans la ville de Sylvie* is less overtly political than *En construcción*, it is no less political in essence. That is, just as Lefebvre's own writings on rhythmanalysis themselves (not merely those included in the posthumously published *Rhythmanalysis* but also those appearing in the second and third volumes of the *Critique of Everyday Life*) cannot be understood apart from his sustained critique of capitalism's ideological production of space, Guerín's 2007 cinematic and rhythmanalytical and cinematic poem acquires its political force when viewed in light of the overt critique of urbanism in his earlier film. Although space is indeed a limitation here, the present argument should be seen as building upon previous urban studies of Guerín's cinematic work (Loxham 2006; Núñez 2012; Resina 2008b; Smith 2005; Viestenz 2009).

B. RHYTHMANALYZING STRASBOURG: THE SIGHTS AND SOUNDS OF *DANS LA VILLE DE SYLVIE*

This chapter is novel not merely for its choice of object, but also for its method. Previous discussion of *Dans la ville de Sylvie* has tended to assert its entanglement with questions of desire and memory from a largely subjective perspective instead of grappling with the imbrication of these themes in an urban reality that is at once subjective and objective, both immaterial and material (see Latham and McCormack 2004). A relatively minor but some-what illustrative example of this is a review of the film penned by Jay Kuehner and published in the journal in *Cinema Scope*, which reads: "At the stark core of the film's latent narrative is a memory, perhaps irretrievable, of a beloved's face. For the lover, a dreamer, the beauty of a face and the enigma of a stranger are reciprocally entwined—an economy of desire that takes looking, and subsequently a of a lot of walking, as its currency" (2008: 11). There is no question that—as the director himself asserts—the film takes on the "male dilemma, the paranoic process of the disenchanted lover" (Kuehner 2008: 12); but for all its possible failings, the film's urban critique persists.

The story I want to tell about *Dans la ville de Sylvie* folds urban space into filmic space and film form. At the center of these relationships there lies the city of Strasbourg itself:

> *Dans la ville de Sylvia* unfolds in an unnamed European city of cobbled lanes and chiming cathedrals—Strasbourg in reality—in which the dreamer in ques-tion (Xavier Lafitte) is a young artist cut from the same blue cloth as Goethe's Young Werther (whose love was also Strasbourg-based). (Kuehner 2008: 11)

The French city's central streets and locations are omnipresent (as in a not-able sequence unfolding on the terrace of the Théâtre National de Strasbourg [Darras 2008: 45], the appearance of the bridge over the River Ill at 0:05:50, and so on) as this protagonist-dreamer seems to wander around Strasbourg in search of a lost love. With map in hand, he strolls Strasbourg's arteries and sits at its cafes, his quest ultimately unrealized at the end of the film. While certainly not a Situationist experiment in Unitary Urbanism, there is nonethe-less a palpable (psychogeographical) tension presented between the immate-riality of desire and the materiality of city form in this wandering—one which heightens the cinematic depiction of Strasbourg's sights and sounds. This depiction of the poetry of urban movement—one can say with little hesitation—takes center stage in *Dans la ville de Sylvie*. Just as Jane Jacobs (Jacobs 1992: 50, 153) had observed what she called the "sidewalk ballet" on her own Hudson Street in New York (Fraser 2012b: 24), Guerín througout immerses us in the flows and movements—the spontaneous encounters—so central to theories of the urban (not merely Jacobs, Lefebvre, and Debord but also Benjamin 1999; Certeau 1988; Delgado Ruiz 2002; cf. Guerín 2000). As many have pointed out, there is an historical, dialectical interaction at the center of our relationship to cities: "in making the city, man has remade himself" (Harvey 2012: 4; who draws on Park 1967; 1968; see also Mumford 1970: 5). In this context, Kuehner's brief but astute review of the film appro-priately characterizes the film as, in part, an "architectural tango" (Kuehner 2008: 12)—one that takes on "the human morphology of the city" (Guerín's phrase; quoted in Kuehner 2008: 12)—but he does not subject the film to the thorough urban analysis it requires. Likewise, Txetxu Aguado's (2011) chapter discussing *Dans la ville de Sylvie* offers a robust cinematic treatment of the urban film—emphasizing that architecture is a notion that applies to both emotions and physical structures—but even his welcome analysis could be strengthened by connections with Lefebvre's work.

Strasbourg is a perfect location for the film's cinematic representation of urban theory not merely on account of its fundamental role in early Situationist practice and in Lefebvre's professional trajectory but also because of its own unique history. Seen in many ways as a "prototypical European city" (Kuehner 2008:12), Strasbourg is "a metropolis that can rightfully claim to being at once a crossroads, a crucible, and a showcase for the making of Europe" (Wacquant 2012: xv). It is a city which may be taken as emblematic of transnational Europeanness, "neither French nor German but a marchland blending of those cultural realms" (Western 2012: 3). As a long-standing point of contact, center of migration, and perhaps even a fulcrum for historical and religious transition, Strasbourg can also be seen as emblematic of changes that are urban in nature (Ford 1996; Western 2012). These historical processes notwithstanding, the film's real contribution is to be found in how it represents and thus defines the urban phenomenon. In order to appreciate how it functions to poetically/cinematically destabilize the instrumentalizing ideology of urban planning, we must turn to Lefebvre's rhythmanalytical project.

Commenting on *Dans la ville de Sylvie*, the director himself has said that "It's a film as much to be heard as seen" (Guerín, quoted in Kuehner 2008: 12), a characterization which in effect offers a concise tribute to Lefebvre's notion of rhythmanalysis. That is, opposed to the largely visual and flattened spatial, even geometrical logic of space as conceived by urban planners as an ideological project of late-capitalism (Resina 2003: 76; Sennett 1992; Fraser 2011a; 2011b; Lefebvre 1991a: 33), Lefebvre asserted the city as a lived temporal space. He saw the assertion of the use value of lived time and urban temporality as a key part of contestation in general and of specific contestatory practices as embodied historically in the festival (Lefebvre 2005: 135). In 1970, in *The Urban Revolution*, he remarked that the urban phenomenon "is made manifest as movement" (2003a: 174); and in his later writings, he turned more and more toward appreciating space as a lived and temporal experience—not visually but by focusing on rhythms and sounds. He first broached the topic of rhythmanalysis—borrowing the term from Lucio Alberto Pinheiro through Gaston Bachelard (Lefebvre 2006b: xiii)—in the second volume of the *Critique of Everyday Life*, and Lefebvre came to see his rhythmanalytical method as a "critique from the left" (Lefebvre 2006b: 7; Fraser 2008; 2011a).

As collected posthumously in the 2006 volume *Rhythmanalysis* by Stuart Elden, Lefebvre's writings on rhythms called for a return to embodied temporality via the senses:

> The rhythmanalyst calls on all his senses. He draws on his breathing, the circulation of his blood, the beatings of his heart and the delivery of his speech as landmarks. Without privileging any one of these sensations, raised by him in the perception of rhythms, to the detriment of any other. He thinks with his body, not in the abstract, but in lived temporality. (Lefebvre 2006b: 21)

In light of his earlier work in *The Urban Revolution* and *The Right to the City*, understanding the urban as a sensory experience is necessary in order to contest the static conception of cityspace, one activated through the capitalist production of the city in the interests of accumulation and accelerating turnover time for investment. The rhythmanalist "listen[s] to a house, a street, a town as an audience listens to a symphony" (Lefebvre 2006b: 22; see also Meyer 2008). So it can be said that in *Dans la ville de Sylvie*, the city of Strasbourg itself functions as this Lefebvrian symphony. The images of the film function to reorient consciousness in a way befitting the central premise of rhythmanalysis. As we work through a few of the film's key sequences and traits, we must keep in mind what Guerín has said about his work: that is, he sees

> *El cine como un fenómeno de comunicación no tanto cuantitativo, de grandes audiencias, sino cualitativo, de intensidad. Porque yo siempre he entendido el cine como algo donde es la intensidad lo que importa.* [Cinema as a communicative phenomenon that is not as much quantitative, one of large audiences, as it is qualitative, one of intensity. Because I have always understood cinema as something where it is intensity that matters.] (Quoted in Pérez et al. 2002: 30)

Though *Dans la ville de Sylvie* deserves much more attention than can be devoted here, the opening scenes in particular establish how Guerín's cinematic approach to the urban phenomenon will unfold.

The film's opening sequence marked "1st night" fades from black to a dimly lit interior where exterior nighttime light is filtered through waving curtains. Recalling the implied reader's viewpoint from Lefebvre's "Seen from the window" (2006b: ch. 3) here the film's spectator is encouraged—from the outset—to "*let oneself go*, give oneself over, abandon oneself to duration" (Lefebvre 2006b: 27, original emphasis). As it is in that written text, this visual text from the outset allows the viewer "to situate oneself simultaneously inside and outside. A balcony does the job admirably, in relation to the street. . . . In the absence of which you could content yourself with a window" (Lefebvre 2006b: 27–28). Through the initial sequence, one hears—or may be induced to imagine hearing—the soft sounds of a quiet night; one sees the wind rendered visible in the movements of the curtains. The camera dwells on a hotel room's interior—light and shadow intermittently pass over a door with a collared shirt on hanger descending from the knob next to an armchair bearing an open suitcase (0:00:30–0:00:44). These are static objects connoting the travel, or even the tourist, experience. And yet through (indexical) cinematic light and sound they are immersed in duration, as are viewers who have willingly abandoned themselves to the latter.

Cut to another set of objects resting on a wooden desk—a coaster from the bar Les Aviateurs bearing a city map hand-drawn in ink, itself resting atop a map of Strasbourg taking up more than half of the frame; to the right a labeled key to room #307 on a metal keychain atop a tan notebook with sharpened wooden pencil (0:00:44–0:01:06). We may take these objects to be static, but the director's continuing play of light and sound once again immerses them in temporality. Lefebvre reminds us thusly:

> [W]e have to distinguish between appearances—which are themselves a reality—and what is actually inside these things. For example, they seem inert (this wooden table, this pencil, etc.) and nonetheless they move. . . . The object before me is the product of labour; the whole chain of the commodity conceals itself inside this material and social object. (Lefebvre 2006b: 82)

In the simple capture of these objects within the temporal filmic image Guerín wants to draw us from the philosophical viewpoint of objects within space toward a more complex view of a shifting space-time, an urban time, folding sets of relations into one another. One must keep in mind that this scene acquires its significance in light of the meaning of the entire film. If *Dans la ville de Sylvie* is a difficult film requiring spectators to actively construct its meaning, this shot poses a series of initial questions ranging from the subtle plot of the film to more philosophical inqueries: What happened at Les Aviateurs? What is the meaning of the hand-drawn map? How is urban space conceived and represented through static forms—and how is it lived? The next shot of the objects pulls back to reveal other objects on the surface of the desk: another city map, some fruit and a clock (remember the distinction between duration as lived time vs. quantified clock-time crucial to both Lefebvre and his philosophical predecessor Henri Bergson; Bergson 1912; 1998; 2001; Lefebvre 2005; Fraser 2008; 2010). This is ultimately a cinematic epigraph, a still life portrait brought into time, one whose objects suggest the interplay between space, cartography, temporality, corporeality, and the city (0:01:06–0:01:12). These seemingly abstract notions—and their necessarily philosophical interrelation (see Fraser 2014)—are at the core of Guerín's Strasbourg film.

The function of the opening sequence is not merely to introduce the key lines along which the film's urban poetry will unfold, but also to transition from interior subjectivity toward the external objective realm of the city—importantly maintaining the former in the presentation of the latter. Following a ten-second long take of a tree branch waving in the wind outside the window—now in broad daylight (almost two full minutes from 0:01:22 until 0:03:11)—we watch the male protagonist as he sits on the bed in room #307, pencil and notebook in hand, staring intently into space. Given his silence—along with the long duration of the take—viewers must actively struggle to place themselves in his position, attempting to intuit an interior monologue whose content is suggested only by the questions implicit in previous static camera shots. This is a long take that would be equally at home in a film by Antonioni or De Sica (see Deleuze 2001)— broken up only by subtle movements of the pencil in line with a slowly advancing train of thought and the protagonist's move to begin writing something down at the three-minute mark. The shot-composition and mise-en-scene remain essentially unchanged despite a small number of gradually accelerating edits until a sharp cut thrusts us outside into the streets of Strasbourg (0:03:57). From here onward—even as the film's reconciliation of memory, desire, and city space and the protagonist's somewhat aimless search for a past love take on greater form—*Dans la ville de Sylvie* is about the city of Strasbourg as a lived urban space, about urban use value.

Frequently, Guerín's camera is characteristically static, capturing urban moments in time—urban movements—from a fixed point; his take of choice is the long take. For example, in the first cut to exterior space (mentioned above), the camera faces into a T-shaped intersection, the movements of urbanites echo against the walls of what are presumably apartment buildings and what a sign designates as the "Hotel Patricia." Already we see the lived city pitched against the tourist city—which is one aspect of the Marxian use versus exchange value contrast subsequently elaborated upon by Lefebvre and Lefebvrian thinker David Harvey (Harvey 2009)—a fact that is highlighted when a man drags an obtrusively large black suitcase loudly down the short stretch of street before us. The static camera allows Strasbourg to become a series of vectors, flows, and rhythms: a woman runs away from the camera down the short block, her footsteps resounding loudly; a pair of women who appear to be students soon cross the T-intersection left to right, followed by a bicyclist in the same direction; after which a woman walking intently crosses right to left; then the man with the suitcase enters at our left. The movements seems to be carefully choreographed to evoke the simultaneity and rhythms of the "sidewalk ballet": each urbanite enters the frame just before others have left, overlapping one another, sharing the space and working together to evoke the complex totality of the urban phenomenon. We have the use of light and shadow determined by the sun's placement out of sight at the upper left corner of the frame, here as elsewhere accentuating the reality of time and hinting at the intersection of rhythms that are alternately (in the case of the city, "both") natural and constructed by humankind. After the man with the large (and loudly rolling) suitcase disappears in the distance at stage right there is a period of relative calm (0:04:19–0:04:32) before the unnamed male protagonist steps out of the Hotel Patricia's door in the right mid-ground. Staring a moment at the large map he carries, he vacilates before walking slowly past us—after which traffic picks up: we see more pedestrians (both young children and an older man walking with a limp, a man with a cane, a couple), bicycles, and even a car. These are geometrical flows that lean toward evoking Yasujiro Ozu's geometrical use of deep space in *Good Morning*, mirroring also the static camera of that film, capturing life from a single point in space-time. Note that a full two minutes have passed—and yet from 0:03:57 to 0:05:50 the camera has not moved an inch. There is thus a Lefebvrian conceit in Guerín's cinema: like the theorist, the director also wants to immerse us in the duration of the city, he wants us to experience the urban phenomenon first of all as movement and to see Strasbourg as a lived space.

The above scenes and images should be taken as representative of *Dans la ville de Sylvie* in this sense: they are cinematic attempts not merely to represent the urban phenomenon in terms of movement (Lefebvre 2003a: 174), but moreover to thrust viewers into those very rhythms (Lefebvre 2006b). Just as in *En construcción*, but perhaps even more so, here, in *Dans la ville de Sylvie* the long take, the absence of dialogue, the use of sparing and natural sound, the persistent use of light and shadow—these are all strategies purposefully allowing for the triumph of the city as an iconic and indexical cinematic sign (see Wollen 1972; Prince 1999; cf. Kracauer 1968). Just as it is with *Rhythmanalysis*, the real success of Guerín's film is that it deals simultaneously both with everydayness and with the urban environment as two poles of what Lefebvre's work establishes as "the whole chain of the commodity" (Lefebvre 2006b: 82; 2005). That is, both what we understand to be the natural world and also the constructed built environment are equally building blocks of capital accumulation, subject to the reifying processes of the capitalist (re)production. The film is a cinematic complement to a passage of *Rhythmanalysis* which Lefebvre intends to be disalienating in the widest sense possible:

> Now look around you at this meadow, this garden, these trees and these houses . . . they offer themselves to your eyes as in a simultaneity. Now, up to a certain point, this simultaneity is mere appearance, surface, a spectacle. Go deeper. . . . You at once notice that every plant, every tree has its rhythm. . . . Henceforth you will grasp every being, every entity and every body, both living and non-living, "symphonically" or "polyrhythmically." You will grasp it in its space-time, in its place and its approximate becoming: including houses and buildings, towns and landscapes. (Lefebvre 2006b: 80)

As the film advances—and despite or even in tandem with the purported storyline of memory, nostalgia, and desire—Guerín's portrayal of Strasbourg becomes more and more layered. We begin to see that "houses and buildings, towns and landscapes" are also part of "the whole chain of the commodity"; we see long takes portraying central Strasbourg, its infrastructure of transportation—train tracks and movement which can only be considered as separate from the industrial origins of urban capitalism if one effects a most curious reification (see Schivelbusch 1986; Harvey 1989: 24; 2009: 305–07; Lefebvre 1996: 177; 2007: 47, 134, 195). At the film's end another typical long take (from 1:19:37 to 1:20:55) captures a curved section of the electric tramway line, a corner grocery, shops and residential buildings. Here Strasbourg's ubiquitous foot traffic is once again scaled-up to include not merely bicycle and car traffic but also travel by traincar. We thus begin and end *Dans la ville de Sylvie* with an intense and qualitative awareness that the urban is alive "symphonically" and "polyrhythmically."

Viewers of Guerín's film have no choice but to ask themselves, why is there all this looking and seeing, this staring, listening, spontaneous wandering, and rhythmanalyzing? The answer is that without understanding the history of urban planning in practical and/or intellectual terms, without understanding either Lefebvre's explicitly Marxian method or on the other hand the central premise of street demonstrations as realizations of urban spontaneity—without seeing *Dans la ville de Sylvie* as building upon *En construcción*—viewers will be unable to advance anything but an aestheticized interpretation of the urban or of Strasbourg's touristic or voyeuristic beauty. Yet, the goal of Guerín's 2007 film is not a self-congratulatory or ontological acceptance of the fact of city life, but instead an implicit contestation. Under the guise of melodrama, he emphasizes the city not as planned from above, but rather as lived on the ground (Harvey 1989; Certeau 1988). The tools employed in this contestation are the hallmarks of the lived experience of the city: sights and sounds, movement and meandering. The director cinematically returns the streets to the urbanites, reclaiming the city sidewalks as the space and the time of urban rhythms. This is the city as a use value and decidedly not the city—as it has been planned for centuries by a specialist class of urbanists—as an exchange value.

As an artistic inspiration for further contestation, *Dans la ville de Sylvie* joins Lefebvre in painting the urban in human terms as a site for spontaneous play and direct action. As Lefebvre would be the first to argue, cinema—art, in fact (Lefebvre 1980; 2006b)—is either obsolete, a bourgeois alienation, or else it is part of the reorientation of consciousness required to disalienate ourselves from the omnipresent capitalist rule of exchange.

BIBLIOGRAPHY

Aguado, Txetxu (2011), "Anatomía de una gestualidad urbana en José Luis Guerín: De *En construcción* y *Unas fotos en la ciudad de Silvia* a *En la ciudad de Sylvia*," in *Un hispanismo para el siglo XXI: Ensayos de crítica cultural*, Rosalía Cornejo Parriego and Alberto Villamandos (eds. and intro.), Madrid: Biblioteca Nueva, pp. 139–55.

Attoh, Kafui A. (2011), "What *Kind* of Right is the Right to the City?," *Progress in Human Geography* 35: 5, pp. 669–85.

Benjamin, Walter (1999), *The Arcades Project* (trans. Howard Eiland and Kevin McLaughlin), Cambridge; London: Belknap Press.

Bergson, Henri (1912 [1896]), *Matter and Memory* (trans. Nancy Margaret Paul and W. Scott Palmer), London, G. Allen & Co., ltd.; New York, Macmillan Co.

———. (1998 [1907]), *Creative Evolution* (trans. A. Mitchell Mineola), New York: Dover Publications Inc.

———. (2001 [1889]), *Time and Free Will. An Essay on the Immediate Data of Consciousness* (trans. F. L. Pogson, M. A. Mineola), New York: Dover.

Burkhard, Bud (2000), *French Marxism between the Wars: Henri Lefebvre and the Philosophies*, Amherst: Humanity Books.

Cabello, Gabriel (2005), "Construyendo tiempo: los ensayos cinematográficos de José Luis Guerín," *Ciberletras*, 12: no pagination. http://www.lehman.cuny.edu/ciberletras/v12/cabello.htm. Web. Accessed 29 Jan. 2013.

Cerdà, Ildefons (1867), *Teoría general de la urbanización* (2 vols.), Madrid: Imprenta Española.

Certeau, Michel de (1988), *The Practice of Everyday Life*, Berkeley: University of California Press.

Choay, Françoise (1969), *The Modern City: Planning in the 19th Century*, New York: George Braziller.

Cresswell, Tim and Deborah Dixon (eds.) (2002), *Engaging Film: Geographies of Mobility and Identity*, Lanham, MD: Rowman and Littlefield.

Darras, Matthieu (2008), "*En construcción / Dans la ville de Sylvia*," *Positif*, 571, pp. 44–45.

Debord, Guy (1961), "Perspectives for Conscious Changes in Everyday Life," *Internationale Situationiste* 6: pp. 20–27.

———. (1995), *The Society of the Spectacle* (trans. Donald Nicholson–Smith), New York: Zone.

Deleuze, Gilles (2001), *Cinema 2: The Time-Image* (trans. B. Habberjam), Minneapolis: University of Minnesota Press.

Delgado Ruiz, Manuel (2007a), *Sociedades movedizas: pasos hacia una antropología de las calles*, Barcelona: Anagrama.

———. (2007b), *La ciudad mentirosa. Fraude y miseria del "modelo Barcelona,"* Madrid, Catarata.

———. (2010), "La ciudad levantada: la barricada y otras transformaciones radicales del espacio urbano," in *Hacia un urbanismo alternativo* (*Architectonics, Mind, Land & Society* 19/20), Barcelona: UPC, pp. 137–53.

Elden, Stuart (2001), "Politics, Philosophy, Geography: Henri Lefebvre in Recent Anglo–American Scholarship," *Antipode*, 33: 5, pp. 809–25.

———. (2004), *Understanding Henri Lefebvre: Theory and the Possible*, London; New York: Continuum.

———. (2006a), "Some are Born Posthumously: The French Afterlife of Henri Lefebvre," *Historical Materialism*, 14: 4, pp. 185–202.

———. (2006b), "Rythmanalysis: An Introduction," in H. Lefebvre, *Rhythmanalysis* (trans. Stuart Elden and Gerald Moore), London; New York: Continuum, pp. vii-xv.

———. (2007), "There is a Politics of Space because Space is Political: Henri Lefebvre and the Production of Space," *Radical Philosophy Review*, 10: 2, pp. 101–16.

Elden, Stuart and Elizabeth Lebas (2003), "Introduction: Coming to Terms with Lefebvre," in *Henri Lefebvre: Key Writings*, S. Elden, E. Lebas and E. Kofman (eds.), New York; London: Continuum, pp. xi–xix.

Ford, Franklin L. (1996), *Strasbourg in Transition 1648–1789*, New York: W. W. Norton.

Fraser, Benjamin (2007), "Manuel Delgado's Urban Anthropology: From Multidimensional Space to Interdisciplinary Spatial Theory," *Arizona Journal of Hispanic Cultural Studies*, 11: pp. 57–75.

———. (2008), "Toward a Philosophy of the Urban: Henri Lefebvre's Uncomfortable Application of Bergsonism," *Environment and Planning D: Society and Space* 26: 2, pp. 338–58.

———. (2009), "'The Kind of Problem Cities Pose': Jane Jacobs at the Intersection of Philosophy, Pedagogy and Urban Theory," *Teaching in Higher Education*, 14: 3, pp. 265–76.

———. (2010), *Encounters with Bergson(ism) in Spain: Reconciling Philosophy, Literature, Film and Urban Space*, Chapel Hill: University of North Carolina Press [Studies in the Romance Languages and Literatures #295].

———. (2011a), *Henri Lefebvre and the Spanish Urban Experience: Reading the Mobile City*, Lewisburg: Bucknell University Press.

———. (2011b), "Ildefons Cerdà's Scalpel: A Lefebvrian Perspective on Nineteenth–Century Urban Planning," *Catalan Review*, 25, pp. 181–200.

(2012a), "A *Biutiful* City: Alejandro González Iñárritu's Filmic Critique of the "Barcelona Model"," *Studies in Hispanic Cinemas*, 9: 1, pp. 19–34.

———. (2012b), "The 'Sidewalk Ballet' in the Work of Henri Lefebvre and Manuel Delgado Ruiz," in *The Urban Wisdom of Jane Jacobs*, Diane Zahm and Sonia Hirt (eds.), London; New York: Routledge, pp. 24–36.

———. (2014), "Editorial: Urban cultural studies—a manifesto [part 1]," *Journal of Urban Cultural Studies*, 1: 1, pp. 3–17.

García Montero, Luis (2002), *Poesía urbana (Antología 1980–2002)*, Laura Scarano (ed.), Sevilla: Renacimiento.

Guerín, José Luis (dir.) (2007), *Dans la ville de Sylvie* (perf: Pilar López de Ayala, Xavier Lafitte), Cameo.

———. (2000), *En construcción* (perf: Juana Rodríguez Molina, Iván Guzmán Jiménez, Juan López López), S.A.V.

Harvey, David (1989), *The Urban Experience*, Baltimore, MD: Johns Hopkins University Press.

———. (1990), *The Condition of Postmodernity*, Cambridge, MA and Oxford: Blackwell.

———. (1991), "Afterword," in H. Lefebvre, *The Production of Space* (trans. Donald Nicholson–Smith), Oxford: Blackwell, pp. 425–34.

———. (1996), *Justice, Nature and the Geography of Difference*, London: Blackwell.

———. (2000), *Spaces of Hope*, Berkeley: University of California Press.

———. (2006), *Paris, Capital of Modernity*, London & New York: Routledge.

———. (2009), *Social Justice and the City*, Athens: University of Georgia Press.

———. (2010), *A Companion to Marx's Capital*, London; New York: Verso.

———. (2012), *Rebel Cities*, London; New York: Verso.

Hopkins, Jeff (1994), "Mapping of Cinematic Places: Icons, Ideology, and the Power of (Mis)representation," in *Place, Power, Situation, and Spectacle: A Geography of Film*, S. Aitken and L. Zonn (eds.), Lanham, MD: Rowman and Littlefield Publishers, pp. 47–65.

Jacobs, Jane (1992), *The Death and Life of Great American Cities*, New York: Vintage.

Kelly, Michael (1982), *Modern French Marxism*, Baltimore: Johns Hopkins University Press.

Kipfer, Stefan (2009), "Why the Urban Question Still Matters: Reflections on Rescaling and the Promise of the Urban," in *Leviathan Undone? Towards a Political Economy of Scale*, Roger Keil and Rianne Mahon (eds.), Vancouver; Toronto: UBC Press, pp. 67–83.

Kitchens, John (2009), "Situated Pedagogy and the Situationist International: Countering a Pedagogy of Placelessness," *Educational Studies*, 45, pp. 240–61.

Knabb, Ken (ed.) (2006), *Situationist International Anthology*, Berkeley: Bureau of Public Secrets.

Kofman, Eleonore and Elisabeth Lebas (1996), "Lost in Transposition—Time, Space and the City," in H. Lefebvre, *Writings on Cities,* E. Kofman and E. Lebas (eds.), Malden, MA.: Blackwell, pp. 3–60.

Kracauer, Siegfried (1968 [1960]), *Theory of Film: The Redemption of Physical Reality*, New York; Oxford: Oxford University Press.

Kuehner, Jay (2008), "José Luis Guerín's Point of View," *Cinema Scope*, 33, pp. 11–13.
——. (2011), "*Guest*: José Luis Guerín," *Cinema Scope*, 45, pp. 42–43.
Latham, Alan and Derek McCormack (2004), "Moving Cities: Rethinking the Materialities of Urban Geographies," *Progress in Human Geography*, 28: 6, pp. 701–24.
Lefebvre, Henri (1947), *Marx et la liberté*, Geneva: Editions des Trois Collines.
——. (1948), *Le marxisme*, Paris: Presses Universitaries de France.
——. (1964), *Marx*, Paris: Presses Universitaries de France.
——. (1969), *The Explosion: Marxism and the French Upheaval*, New York; London: The Monthly Review Press.
——. (1976), *The Survival of Capitalism: Reproduction of the Relations of Production* (trans. Frank Bryant), New York: St. Martin's Press.
——. (1980), *La présence et l'"absence: Contribution à la théorie des représentations*, Paris: Caterman.
——. (1982), *The Sociology of Marx* (trans. N. Guterman), New York: Columbia University Press.
——. (1988), "Toward a Leftist Cultural Politics: Remarks Occasioned by the Centenary of Marx's Death" (trans. David Reifman), in *Marxism and the Interpretation of Culture*, Lawrence Grossberg and Cary Nelson (eds.), Chicago: University of Illinois Press, pp. 75–88.
——. (1991a), *The Production of Space* (trans. Donald Nicholson–Smith), Oxford: Blackwell.
——. (1991b), *Critique of Everyday Life*, Vol. 1 (trans. John Moore), London; New York: Verso.
——. (1996), *The Right to the City*, in *Writings on Cities* (eds. and trans. E. Kofman and E. Lebas, Oxford: Blackwell, pp. 63–181.
——. (2002), *Critique of Everyday Life,* Vol. 2 (trans. John Moore), London; New York: Verso.
——. (2003a[1970]), *The Urban Revolution* (trans. Robert Bononno), Minneapolis: University Minnesota Press.
——. (2003b), *Henri Lefebvre: Key Writings*, S. Elden, E. Lebas and E. Kofman (eds.), New York; London: Continuum.
——. (2005), *Critique of Everyday Life,* Vol. 3 (trans. Gregory Elliott), London; New York: Verso.
——. (2006a), *La presencia y la ausencia: contribución a la teoría de las representaciones* (trans. Óscar Barahona and Uxoa Doyhamboure), México D.F.: Fondo de Cultura Económica.
——. (2006b), *Rhythmanalysis* (trans. S. Elden and Gerald Moore), London; New York: Continuum.
——. (2007), *Everyday Life in the Modern World* (trans. Sacha Rabinovich, introd. Philip Wander), Eleventh paperback ed., New Brunswick and London: Transaction Publishers.
——. (2008), *Dialectical Materialism* (trans. John Sturrock; pref. Stefan Kipfer), Minneapolis: University of Minnesota Press.
Léger, Marc James, (2006), "Henri Lefebvre and the Moment of the Aesthetic," in *Marxism and the History of Art: From William Morris to the New Left*, Andrew Hemingway (ed.), London: Pluto Press, pp. 143–60.
Loxham, Abigail (2006), "Barcelona Under Construction: The Democratic Potential of Touch and Vision in City Cinema as Depicted in *En construcción* (2001)," *Studies in Hispanic Cinemas*, 3: 1, pp. 35–48.
Marx, Karl (1977), *Capital*, vol. 1 (trans. Ben Fowkes; intro. Ernest Mandel), New York: Vintage.
Mendieta, Eduardo (2008), "The Production of Urban Space in the Age of Transnational Mega–urbes: Lefebvre's Rhythmanalysis or Henri Lefebvre: the Philosopher of May '68," *City*, 12: 2, pp. 148–53.
Merrifield, Andy (2002), *Metromarxism. A Marxist Tale of the City*, London; New York: Routledge.
——. (2005), *Guy Debord*, London: Reaktion Books.
——. (2006), *Henri Lefebvre: A Critical Introduction*, New York; London: Routledge.

Meyer, Kurt (2008), "Rhythms, Streets, Cities" (trans. Bandulasena Goonewardena), in *Space, Difference, Everyday Life: Reading Henri Lefebvre*, Kanishka Goonewardena, Stefan Kipfer, Richard Milgrom and Christian Schmid (eds.), New York; London: Routledge, pp. 147–60.

Mumford, Lewis (1970), *The Culture of Cities*, New York: Harcourt, Brace Jovanovich.

Nadal–Melsió, Sara (2008), "Lessons in Surrealism: relationality, event, encounter," in *Space, Difference, Everyday Life: Reading Henri Lefebvre*, Kanishka Goonewardena, Stefan Kipfer, Richard Milgrom and Christian Schmid (eds.), New York; London: Routledge, pp. 161–75.

Núñez, Natalia (2012), "Whose Vanguardist City?: The Barcelona Urban Model as Seen from the Periphery in José Luis Guerín's *En construcción* (2001)," in Helena Buffery and Carlota Caulfield (eds.), *Barcelona: Visual Culture, Space and Power*, Cardiff: University of Wales Press, pp. 89–103.

Ozu, Yasujiro (2004 [1959]), *Good Morning* [Ohayô] (perf: Keiji Sada, Yoshiko Kuga, Chishû Ryû), The Criterion Collection.

Park, Robert (1967), *On Social Control and Collective Behavior*, Chicago: Chicago University Press.

———. (1968), "The City: Suggestions for the Investigation of Human Behavior in the Urban Environment," in R. E. Park, E. W. Burgess, and R. D. McKenzie (eds.), *The City*, Chicago; London: University of Chicago Press, pp. 1–46.

Pérez, Jordi, José Luis Guerín, Manuel Quinto and Toni Comín (2002), "José Luis Guerín: "Jamás se me ocurren películas caras"," *El Ciervo*, 51: 619, pp. 30–33.

Poster, Michael (1975), *Existential Marxism in Postwar France: From Sartre to Althusser*, Princeton: Princeton University Press.

Prince, Stephen (1999), "The Discourse of Pictures: Iconicity and Film Studies," in *Film Theory and Criticism,* Fifth ed., Leo Braudy and Marshall Cohen (eds.), Oxford: Oxford University Press, pp. 99–117.

Purcell, Mark (2002), "Excavating Lefebvre: the right to the city and its urban politics of the inhabitant," *GeoJournal*, 58, pp. 99–108.

Resina, Joan Ramon (2003), "From Rose of Fire to City of Ivory," in Joan Ramon Resina and Dieter Ingenschay (eds.), *After-Images of the City*, Ithaca and London: Cornell University Press, pp. 75–122.

———. (2008a), *Barcelona's Vocation of Modernity*, Palo Alto, CA: Stanford Universtiy Press.

———. (2008b), "The Construction of the Cinematic Image: *En construcción* (José Luis Guerín, 2000)," in Joan Ramon Resina, Andrés Lema-Hincapié (eds.), *Burning Darkness: A Half Century of Spanish Cinema*, Albany, NY: SUNY Press, pp. 255–76.

Ross, Kristin (2004), "Lefebvre on the Situationists: An Interview," in *Guy Debord and the Situationist International: Texts and Documents*, Tom McDonough (ed.), Cambridge, MA: MIT Press, pp. 267–84.

Ross, Kristin and Henri Lefebvre (1997), "Lefebvre on the Situationists: an interview," *October*, 79, pp. 69–83.

Schivelbusch, Wolfgang (1986), *The Railway Journey: The Industrialization of Time and Space in the 19th Century*, Berkeley and Los Angeles: University of California Press.

Sennett, Richard (1992), *The Conscience of the Eye: The Design and Social Life of Cities*, London and New York: W. W. Norton.

Shields, Rob (2005), *Lefebvre, Love and Struggle: Spatial Dialectics*, London; New York: Routledge.

———. (2011), "Henri Lefebvre," in Phil Hubbard and Rob Kitchin (eds.), *Key Thinkers on Space and Place*, London: Sage, pp. 279–85.

Smith, Paul Julian, (2005), "La construcción del tiempo: dos documentales creativos," in *Casa encantada: Lugares de memoria en la España constitucional (1978–2004)*, Joan Ramon Resina and Ulrich Winter, Madrid/Frankfurt: Iberoamericana/Vervuert, pp. 173–80.

Stanek, Lukasz (2011), *Henri Lefebvre on Space: Architecture, Urban Research, and the Production of Theory*, Minneapolis; London: University of Minnesota Press.

Viestenz, William (2009), "Cinematic Ethics within the Picnoleptic Moment in José Luis Guerín's *En construcción*," *Bulletin of Hispanic Studies*, 86, pp. 537–53.

Wacquant, Loïc (2012), "Foreword: Prismatic Identities: Memory, Migration and the Making of Europe," in John Western, *Cosmopolitan Europe: A Strasbourg Self-Portrait*, Farnham, Surrey (UK); Burlington, VT: Ashgate, pp. xv-xviii.

Western, John (2012), *Cosmopolitan Europe: A Strasbourg Self-Portrait*, Farnham, Surrey (UK); Burlington, VT: Ashgate.

Wollen, Peter (1972), *Signs and Meaning in the Cinema*, Third ed., Bloomington: Indiana University Press.

Chapter Four

Sensing Capital

Sight, Sound and Touch in
Esteban Sapir's La antena *(2007)*

Benjamin Fraser

It seems, at first, to be a difficult task to subject Esteban Sapir's *La antena* (2007) to a unifying approach. It is at once a dystopic urban film, a critique of the media saturation that evolves with capitalist consumer society, a metaphor for brute political corruption and domination, a cautionary tale about the social dangers of technological and scientific advance, and—perhaps most of all—a deeply self-reflexive engagement with cinema itself. That is, its superbly but eclectically stylized visual language borrows from extensively silent film, noir, German Expressionism, and even the early cinematic works of Georges Méliès. Yet each of these aspects of the film are linked through the theory of everyday urban life advanced by Marxist philosopher Henri Lefebvre. Illustrating insights outlined in Lefebvre's *Critique of Everyday Life*, *Rhythmanalysis*, and *The Urban Revolution*, the importance of the senses (here: sight, sound, and touch) as developed in *La antena* simultaneously posits urban everyday life as both the site of alienation and the staging area for resistance to the many alienations of capitalist production. This filmic analysis has the effect, moreover, of recuperating the "sensuous Marx" whose thoughts have been left out of overly deterministic/purely economic models of Marxian thought but who was so important for Henri Lefebvre's urban philosophy

Although Esteban Sapir is considered by some to be a precursor of the new Argentine cinema (Chamorro 2011: 94n2, 138; see also Aguilar 2006; Falicov 2003), he has made relatively few films. In truth, his only film prior to the one under discussion was *Picado fino* (1996) and since that film's release the director had been working in publicity and advertising—professional activity which had no small effect on *La antena* (Wells 2012: 352). The film's diegesis unfolds in the year XX in a dystopian, media-saturated city controlled by a man known merely as Mr. TV (played by Alejandro Urdapilleta). Mr. TV runs the single television channel watched by the film's urbanites, who are beholden to a hypnotic symbol—a spinning wheel resembling a "6," a "9," and also a question mark ("?")—which is ubiquitous throughout the film's mise-en-scene. It appears not only on the urbanites' television screens but is also visible on billboards atop the city's skyscrapers and on the packaging of the foodstuffs branded as "Alimentos TV."[1] Not only are *La antena*'s urbanites passive consumers enthralled to the visual spectacle of urbanized capital, but they are also unable to speak audibly. Silence in this city is said to be "hereditary," and ultimately the film makes it clear that the words of the citizenry are in fact the raw materials used in creating the Alimentos TV that are then sold back to them for consumption. In this way, the people themselves are alienated from their own speech, and function both as producers and consumers in a capitalist chain of accumulation which strives for ever-greater profit. Although it may be suggested that the film's story is a foil for the dictatorial political rule that has characterized some moments in Argentina's twentieth-century history (see Paz 2011, discussed below), this point is insufficient. At a certain point in the film, even the visual mode of communication used by the characters (discussed below) is appropriated by Mr. TV's system of production, the implication being that for this capitalist mode of production, it is not just a stable profit margin that matters but a continually increasing rate of profit that is essential to the self-perpetuation of that capitalist system. The character named Dr. Y (Carlos Piñeiro) is a scientist whose work allows Mr. TV to continually rethink the technological means of production. There is also a rat-like henchman (Raúl Hochman) who does Mr. TV's bidding—chief among his duties (and evident at the end of the film) is that of protecting the machinery of production from co-optation by the proletariat. Significantly, there are two characters who are—presumably by some chance transmission of genes—able to speak audibly: a female singer named La Voz (The Voice) (Florencia Raggi) whose genius has been appropriated by Mr. TV and her son, a blind boy named Tomás, who keeps his "gift"of speech a secret so as to avoid enslavement to the capitalist Mr. TV. These characters provide further illustration of the way in which capitalist systems thrive on and co-opt the unique cultural capital produced by others (both in practice and potentially) as a source of profit.

The central protagonists of the film, however, are not La Voz and her son Tomás, but instead a family constituted by a curiously unnamed TV repairman (Rafael Ferro), his daughter Ana (Sol Moreno), his ex-wife who is a nurse (Julieta Cardinali) and Ana's grandfather (Ricardo Merkin). As a scene cut from the film but available in the extras section of the DVD makes clear, the population may "*sume puntos y vuele*"("collect points and fly") by consuming the Alimentos TV—thus becoming eligible to be the "*Hombre globo del mes*" ["The Flying Person of the Month"]. Eating this manufactured foodstuff as part of this ongoing promotional contest, these urbanites are actually, of course, consuming their own alienated speech. As estranged laborers, they are producing the raw product which is being sold back to them and from whose sale they derive no profit. The repairman, his daughter, and her grandfather together are responsible for physically launching and tethering the "Flying Person of the Month"—a job from which they are fired early in the film due to an accident on the job, also discussed below. Fired from their job, and due also to other circumstances—a botched delivery attributable to the fact that an insufficiently stabilized "6" on Ana's house suddenly becomes a "9," which is instead the last digit of the address of La Voz and Tomás—this (separated) family consisting of the repairman, daughter, and nurse eventually takes on the role of resisting Mr. TV's plans for continued economic, political, and social control of the city and of its inhabitants.

It is testament to the film's originality and depth that there have been a small number of highly compelling articles written on *La antena* in recent years. I want to turn briefly to three of these recent articles on Sapir's film to chart out the benefits and limitations of how the film has been studied so far—Melinda Blos-Jáni's book chapter "Is Silence Hereditary? Written Word and Acoustic Events in a Contemporary Silent Film: Esteban Sapir's *La antena* (2007)" (published in the 2008 volume *Words and Images on the Screen: Language, Literature, Moving Pictures*, edited by Agnes Petho), Mariano Paz's article "Vox Politica: Acousmatic Voices in Argentinean Science Fiction Cinema" (published in a 2011 issue of the *New Review of Film and Television Studies*) and Sarah Ann Wells's "*Viaje a través del tiempo:* anacronismo y distopía en *La antena* (2007), de Esteban Sapir"(published in a 2012 issue of *Revista Iberoamericana*). I believe that, while providing insight into important aspects of the film, each has—in its own way—left out something important. Given the film's content, form, and message—a critique of both the material and immaterial forms of capitalist alienation in urban contexts—in each case, the fact that something has been "left out" is absolutely crucial. That is, my position is that the film portrays the Marxian notion of totality and emphasizes the role of the human senses in resisting the many alienations of urbanized capital. Clearly, it is difficult in a chapter-length publication to explore all aspects of such a complex and visually stunning film, and these previous scholars have done important work that I would like to unashamedly build upon here. But to leave the film's Marxian critique out when analyzing *La antena*—to approach a film concerning totality from a purposely restricted viewpoint—is simultaneously to replicate the fragmenting and alienating logic of a capitalist system that thrives on visual spectacle as a way of hiding the real conditions of its own operation. This is, after all, the main point of Esteban Sapir's film: to recuperate a sense of the interconnectedness of an organically unified if complex society that seems otherwise to be constituted by so many fragmented and isolated areas. The act of resistance in the film—as follows from a Marxian understanding of capital—is made possible only by the movement of a disalienating thought which questions the image of what appears to be a fragmented social world housing seemingly autonomous areas of experience.

Melinda Blos-Jáni is the critic who best understands and most thoroughly interrogates the visual communication method used by the film's urbanites. That is, watching the film for the first time, it may seem unclear to some whether the silenced characters themselves can see and manipulate the on-screen intertitles standing in for their speech of whether these are merely incorporated for the practical benefit of the viewer. Mariano Paz, for exam-ple, in his otherwise intriguing essay writes of the film that "People under-stand each other by reading their lips, while subtitles inform the audience of what is being said" (2011: 16). This understanding of the film's intertitles as a communication merely accessible to the film's audience—as it would have been in the times of silent film—is, however, not only a grave reduction of the artistry of Sapir's film, but moreover a misunderstanding of the fact that the director wants to join *La antena*'s diegetic space with the space of the filmic spectator. Blos-Jáni, for her part, says it most directly in her splendid book chapter: "they communicate using titles":

> the characters are aware of the words floating around them, and they treat them
> as visible parts of the world, sometimes as objects: the texts hang above them
> as burdens, they can look up on them . . . the letters can be moved and held . . .
> they can be hidden when communicating a confidential information, punches
> can be given with them . . . the missing letters can be replaced with signs
> formed by cigarette smoke . . . or by hand. (Blos-Jáni 2008: 139)

In her chapter, Blos-Jáni gives an informative historical contextualization of the use of intertitles in film (2008: 135–36; also previous studies of them on pp. 133–34) and notes "the physicality and haptic nature of the words" (2008: 139), arguing convincingly that: "here the titles are not situated on the plain surface of the image, but they are within the illusory three-dimensional space, as an organic part of the profilmic world, just like the inscriptions indicating street names or the advertisements signs" (2008: 139). The critic's enviable analysis of the "graphic strangeness" (2008: 137) and "three dimen-sional presence of the plain titles" (2008: 140) is, however relatively depoli-ticized, and is certainly not carried out in the context of capitalist production and alienation.

In contrast, Mariano Paz does engage the political aspects of the film's diegesis and their link to extra-filmic Argentina in the relatively brief section on the film included in his article (pp. 16–21 only). Therein, he writes of the film's "dystopian world"/"totalitarian government" and its links to George Orwell's *1984* and also what is known as the *Proceso* (Paz 2011: 17–18; for further historical background on this period see Romero 2002: 215–54):

> In this sense, an analogy can be established between this fictional world (or novum, to put it in Suvinian terms [here Paz references science fiction scholar Darko Suvin]) and the military dictatorship that ruled Argentina between 1976 and 1983, and which is commonly known as the *Proceso*. The *Proceso* was a severely repressive authoritarian regime based on heavy censorship, the military regulation of most areas of the civil society such as the media and academia, the ban of political parties, and the persecution and murder of all sorts of political dissidents who dared to raise their voices against the government (politicians, journalists, social activists and so on). (Paz 2011: 18)

Though the analogy is relevant and certainly enlightening, there are two potential issues with Paz's characterization as it appears in that publication. First, given the temporality referenced through *La antena*'s visual style (confirmed in the DVD extra as the 1930s and 1940s; see also Page 2012), it would be better to reconcile filmic and extra-filmic reality through reference to earlier periods in the history of repressive rule in Argentina. Luis Alberto Romero, for example, describes the political turmoil of the first third of the country's twentieth century in detail. His description includes a "strike wave that culminated between 1917 and 1921" (Romero 2002: 36), as well as the fact that in the early 1930s "the flow of foreign capital, which had traditionally nourished the national economy, ceased" (2002: 65). As a response to this, "the economy as a whole gradually shut itself off from the rest of the world in which relatively closed markets were also clearly emerging" (2002: 67)— a description that squares with the relative isolation of Mr. TV's production-consumption system as imagined on screen in Sapir's film. Also relevant is the fact that the 1930s in Argentina also saw the birth and growing strength of certain trade unions and workers' movements (Romero 2002: 77–78), and this, of course, in the context of a growing counterrevolutionary movement (Deutsch 1986). The second issue with Paz's characterization, however—and the most important one given the present article's aim—is that politics in his analysis is taken to be an autonomous area of urban experience, considered in isolation from capitalist production strategies.

Sarah Ann Wells's chapter is significant because, in opposition to Paz and to Blos-Jáni, she writes of the film from a vantage point grounded specifically in the context of an international neoliberalism (Wells 2012: 349)—for example, critiquing Mr. TV in light of work by Adorno and Horkheimer (2012: 351–52). Nevertheless, pursued outside of a deeper understanding of tactility and disalienation, her discussion of "*trabajo manual*" ("manual labor") (2012: 359) in the film is incomplete and will be built upon in what follows. Moreover, her remark that Sapir's is *"un cine claramente anti-re-alista"* ("a clearly anti-realist cinema") (2012: 349) is provocative and similarly deserves attention, but as will be discussed below, reveals a problematically alienated perspective on film which reduces it to being merely a text; that is, she ultimately separates film from the extra-filmic ideologies, relations and alienations of contemporary urban capitalism with which *La antena* explicitly dialogues and which also themselves deal with the notion of reality. It is necessary to add that there is, notably, a fourth article on the film—"Retrofuturism and Reflexivity in Argentine Science Fiction Film: The Construction of Cinematic Time" by Joanna Page (2012), published in the *Arizona Journal of Hispanic Cultural Studies*—which is just as attentive to capitalist neoliberalism. This article makes some splendid insights into *La antena*, but its argument—not unrelated to my own—focuses more on capitalist temporality than it does the human senses specifically. Moreover, Page's nonetheless astute analyses of Sapir's film are forced to share the space of her article with discussion of another Argentine film (*La sonámbula* [1998] by Fernando Spiner; also addressed by Paz). It is necessary to say that the present chapteer thus repeats some arguments made by Joanna Page, but it also elaborates further on them, applying them to the film more extensively and using more space than was available to her there. Here, that is, I want to thoroughly engage the theme of the senses and capital in *La antena* in a way that has not been possible in previous criticism, either because scholars have adopted a different focus or because discussion has unfolded in a limited space. In addition, I see this effort as a complement to the scholarly studies of filmic Buenos Aires undertaken by Laura Podalsky (2004), Page (2009) and Alberto Chamorro (2011), even though it takes on a time period and a work not addressed by those book-length studies.

Appropriately, the first section of this chapter (Totality, Alienation, and the "Sensuous Marx") explores the extension of Marx's ideas on the senses—as originally presented in the *Economic and Philosophic Manuscripts of 1844* (1964)—by Marxian urban philosopher of the everyday Henri Lefebvre (1901–1991). In the end, it is Lefebvre's approach to urban everyday life that provides the most unifying understanding of *La antena*'s contestatory message and often spectacular formal aspects. The second section (Sensing Capital through Sight, Sound, and Touch) analyzes the role of the senses in *La antena* from this Lefebvrian perspective. It is divided into three subsections, each of which focuses on a single human sense and each of which leads into the next: sound into sight, sight into touch. What holds these analyses together is Lefebvre's reconfigured Marxian emphasis on the human senses—and on tactility as a privileged sense among them—as comprising a dual field subject to alienation and also potentially constitutive of resistance.

A. TOTALITY, ALIENATION, AND THE "SENSUOUS MARX"

In order to make sense of the roles played by sight, sound, and touch in Esteban Sapir's dystopic work *La antena* (2007), it is necessary to understand that Marxian vision which both underlies the director's stunning film and also motivates the analysis advanced here. Exploring the Marxist dimensions of the word "totality" can help us to understand the contemporary alienations suffered by the urbanites depicted in Sapir's work of art before moving to analyze, in succession, the importance of the senses in *La antena*. It is significant that in the *Economic and Philosophical Manuscripts of 1844*, Marx wrote that "The transcendence of private property is therefore the complete *emancipation* of all human senses and qualities, but it is this emancipation precisely because these senses and attributes have become, subjectively and objectively, *human*" (1964: 139).[2] In the end, both Sapir's film and the reconfigured Marxism elaborated by urban theorist Henri Lefebvre foreground how the human senses are directly implicated in the battle between colonization and resistance that rages on in everyday urban life. As discussed in this first section, to work with Lefebvre's theories of capital is at once to recover the "sensuous Marx" for whom transcendence of private property went hand in hand with the emancipation of the human senses.

The notion of totality is asserted by Lefebvre—building on its role in Marx's thought (see Marx 1964: 139; also Kolakowski 2005: 1000–01; also Merrifield 2002)—as a response to the various alienations of contemporary urban capitalism.[3] One way to explain this response is to point out that capitalist ideology obscures the relationships between the seemingly fragmented aspects of contemporary urban life—separating the political from the economic from the cultural from the social and prohibiting a holistic assessment of the way each of these areas are aspects of a variegated but organically interrelated and continually shifting capitalist mode of production. It is perhaps necessary to make clear from the outset that, despite the way in which Marxian thought was misinterpreted and misused in totalitarian dictatorships of the twentieth century, totality for Lefebvre (as for Marx) suggests not a static, coherent, authoritarian, and proscriptive sense of the (false) unity of humankind, but rather the processual and dynamic move toward disalienating oneself and one's society from the effects of that capitalist ideology. That is, in Lefebvre's work, human history itself is defined as the continual movement from alienations toward disalienations which in turn spawn new forms of alienation.

To understand totality as an ongoing process is to refuse to passively accept the many alienations that structure life under contemporary capitalism—alienations that are for Lefebvre not merely ideological but also economic, social, political, and philosophical (Lefebvre 1991b: 249); "In fact, there are many alienations, and they take many forms," he writes (Lefebvre

2002: 207).[4] Disalienating oneself from the mystifications contemporary urbanized life—as the characters in Sapir's film are ultimately able to do—
refusing to live through alienation, brings an awareness of how what appear
to be fragmented human relationships and isolated areas of human experience are in fact integrated into a constantly shifting and complex, if also
organic, shared social world. In humanistic circles, it is much more widely
acknowledged that Lefebvre had refashioned Marxism to better explain the
spatial character of urbanized forms of twentieth century capitalism, as in the
widely cited book *The Production of Space* (1974, translated into English by
Donald Nicholson-Smith in 1991) and the lesser-known *The Survival of Capitalism* containing the dictum that capitalism has survived throughout the
twentieth century "by producing space, by occupying a space" (Lefebvre
1976: 21). But his recalibrated concept of Marxian alienation is no less
important (Shields 2005; Elden 2004; Fraser 2011). In his book *Lefebvre,
Love and Struggle: Spatial Dialectics*, Rob Shields has concisely articulated
the value of Lefebvre's innovation on Marx's concept:

> Marx had identified three forms of alienation. People could be alienated from
> their work and activities: they might be alienated from each other through
> excessive competitiveness, for example; and they might be alienated from
> their own essence, their "species being" or human-ness, which meant that they
> misunderstood what it was that made them human. . . . Lefebvre located these
> all-pervasive forms of alienation not just in the workplace but in every aspect
> of life. Estranged from our activities, ourselves, and from each other, we still
> barely experience our lives, moving in a daze from obligation to obligation,
> programmed activity to programmed activity. (Shields 2005: 40; also Elden
> 2004: 42; Kolakowski 2005: 114–16)

As scholar Andy Merrifield draws out in his own discussion of Lefebvre,
"The antithesis of alienated man was the "total man," a character Marx
alludes to in *The Economic and Philosophical Manuscripts* (see "Private
Property and Communism")" (Merrifield 2002: 78). In Lefebvre's reconfigured Marxism, this is someone able to reintegrate the fragmented areas of
human experience that, in contemporary urban life, seemed to have an autonomous existence: that is, the individual's economic, social, political, and
philosophical circumstances and understandings.[5]

What is so important—and here is another area of Marx's thought that has
been overlooked—is the way in which this (again, necessarily ephemeral)
disalienating transformation into a "total person" could not occur without
reclaiming the world of the senses from their ideological appropriation under
urban forms of capitalism. As many have discussed, there is, co-existing
alongside the hardline materialist Marx, also a "sensuous Marx." That is,
despite the attention that he himself placed on the senses, Karl Marx's
thought continues to be subjected to myopic appropriations that reduce it to

being a mere economic determinism or a simplistic materialism.[6] The periodizing theses which abound—differentiating the "young" Marx from the "mature" Marx—are well known; as are the battles between scientific and humanistic Marxism which notably flared up in the 1970s (e.g., Louis Althusser; see Merrifield 2002: 15; Elden 2004: 17–19). Rather than rehash these unavoidably solipsistic arguments about whether to authenticate the work of Marx the political economist over Marx the philosopher (or vice-versa),[7] it is important to assert how an entire tradition of Marxism—one evident already in the 1960s and enduring to the present day—has not merely recognized the "sensuous Marx" but has also elaborated upon the relevance of the senses to contemporary capitalist alienation. Andy Merrifield explains, quoting from Marx:

> "The positive supersession of private property," Marx writes, "means the *sensuous* appropriation of the human essence and human life." Human essence doesn" t just revolve around possession, around simply having or owning: people, according to Marx, appropriate their integral essence in an integral way, as "total people." Thus, "human relations to the world—seeing hearing, smelling, tasting, feeling, thinking, contemplating, sensing, wanting, acting, loving—in short, all the organs of his individuality . . . are in their *objective* approach or in their approach to the object, the appropriation of the object." (Merrifield 2002: 78; also 17–18)

This original insight, of course, has not been totally overlooked by activists and scholars. One can see echoes of it in many radical movements of the 1960s—not least of which are the dérives of Guy Debord and the Situationists (Debord 1995; Knabb 2006; Merrifield 2005) whom Lefebvre came to know well and from whom he was ultimately estranged (see Ross 2004).[8] Yet Lefebvre's work in particular recuperated the sensuous Marx—perhaps most poetically in the essays posthumously published as *Rhythmanalysis* (1992 [2006a]) as discussed elsewhere (Fraser 2008, 2011, 2014) but also in his theorizations of everyday life as carried out in his multi-volume project titled the *Critique of Everyday Life*.

Grounded in previous analyses of capitalism's mystifications carried out, in part, along with Norbert Guterman, Lefebvre published the first volume of his *Critique of Everyday Life* in 1947, the second in 1961, and the third in 1981. (It is accepted, also, that the insights published as *Rhythmanalysis* were to form part of a fourth volume in the *Critique*; Elden 2006). In the second volume, Lefebvre invoked the phrase "the colonization of daily life" (as had Debord 1961; 1995) to refer to the fact that "capitalist leaders treat daily life as they once treated the colonized territories: massive trading posts (supermarkets and shopping centers); absolute predominance of exchange over use; dual exploitation of the dominated in their capacity as producers and consumers" (Lefebvre 2005: 26). But everyday life now was not merely colonized but also riven through with contradiction. Marc James Léger writes that,

> Although conceptions of the everyday can be found in the work of Nietzsche, Simmel, the Surrealists, Lukács and Heidegger, Lefebvre sought to align the everyday with the notion of alienation rather than the banal or the trivial. The everyday in this sense becomes dialectically bound up with the potential for disalienation, for an opening onto new possibilities" (Léger 2006: 149). [9]

Lefebvre himself explains, in his work *The Explosion: Marxism and the French Upheaval*—written in the wake of the events of 1968—how, given the concentration of the social and technological contradictions governing labor in urban environments, in the city, "The many forms of alienation are experienced obscurely and provoke muffled and profound anxiety. This is the source of the surge of spontaneity" (Lefebvre 1969: 98; also 1976: 19). This is precisely, in fact, what we see happen in Sapir's film.

B. SENSING CAPITAL THROUGH SIGHT, SOUND, AND TOUCH

The fictionalized world presented to us through Esteban Sapir's *La antena* clearly harnesses the human senses to critique the contradictions and aliena- tions of contemporary urban capitalism. In fact, as the director notes in an interview included on the DVD of the film, sensations and feelings were an important part of his creative process: "*Nunca partí de la historia, ¿no? sino que partí de, de detalles y de sensaciones y de, y de, y de cosas que sentía*" ("I didn't begin with the story, you see? Instead I began with, with the details and with sensations, and with, and with, with things I was feeling"). While Marx's original critique as posited during the accelerating capitalist industri- alization of the nineteenth century is also deeply relevant to the film, Lefebv- re's Marxian understanding of how capital operates in twentieth-century eve- ryday urban life is much better suited to elucidate Sapir's visual, auditory, and tactile critique. Having contextualized this study in previous research on the film and having already recuperated Lefebvre's Marxian insights into the power of the human senses, this section of the chapter thus engages in a close reading of *La antena*'s portrayal of sight, sound, and touch through succes- sive subsections. I find that the film showcases a nested but dialectical cri- tique of the way in which humans have become alienated, too, from their own sense-world. Precisely due to that alienation, this sense-world is simul- taneously a potential staging ground for disalienation and resistance. This reading—which also explores Sapir's own engagement with the nature of cinema itself as a visual spectacle—ultimately privileges the role of touch and tactility. In the end, both the film's director and Henri Lefebvre (and

Marx) suggest that the sense of touch constitutes the last bastion of resistance to capital's multiple alienations.

1. Sound

In the context of his radical and multi-volume *Critique of Everyday Life*, Henri Lefebvre's later creation of a rhythmanalytical project—one that remains understudied still today (see Elden 2006; Fraser 2008, 2011)—sought to value sound (and also movement) over vision in understanding the urban phenomenon.[10] Drawing implicitly on a Bergsonian inheritance from which he had distanced himself in his early years and imbuing it with explicitly political dimensions (Fraser 2008, 2010), his insight was that vision encourages a spatial understanding of the city, whereas sound (and movement) install us in a mobile temporality (Lefebvre 2006a: 20–22; see also chapter 3 of this volume). Though his descriptions may seem abstract, when they are properly understood in the context of Lefebvre's extensive oeuvre their political dimensions are clear: as Stuart Elden has written, the theme of the body within capitalism is central to Lefebvre's work (2006a: viii). We may, therefore, look at how sound in *La antena* is at once—following Lefebvre's critique of the colonization of everyday life—a battleground between both alienation and resistance.

As critics have already pointed out, the hereditary silence of *La antena*'s urbanites is a clear mark of political repression (e.g., Paz 2011; Wells 2012). Unable to speak, their voicelessness is a clear and transparent symbol of their lack of political agency in the closed, authoritarian society controlled by Mr. TV. What is important is that their words have been refashioned in this original diegetic and self-reflexively cinematic world as visual signs. These signs, as previously explored by Blos-Jáni (2008), can be manipulated by the characters in interesting ways. Yet it is significant that both the ruling technological class (e.g., Mr. TV and Dr. Y) and the proletariat working class (e.g., the repairman's family) are similarly voiceless, and also that they are similarly able to manipulate the visual signs they produce. From a Marxian perspective on the film, this is an indicator that the power structure in place in city XX is subject not merely to the law of dictatorial political rule but also to the contradictory laws of capital accumulation. As opposed to a politically repressive dictatorial system where there is one set of laws governing the dominated, and another reserved for those in power, the laws of capital structure affect both capitalist and proletariat, leading to periodic crises that—according to Lefebvrian Marxist geographer David Harvey—are inherent to the system (like the one which was occurring in 2008, one year after the release of the film). That is, by acting in their own interests to accumulate individual capital, capitalists actually work against their own class interests (those of the capitalist class; similarly, by acting in their own individual interests, the proletariat work against their own class interests). In *La antena*, the fact that Mr. TV and the urbanites are subject to the same repression indicates that we are dealing with a more complicated fusion of political and economic power structures than those implicit in the notion of a simple political system that exists as an autonomous realm of experience.

This is not to say that there are no elements of strictly political repression in the film, for of course there are—it is just that they are articulated via their relationships with more complex economic forces. These brute political elements are clearly at play in the storylines that concern La Voz and her son Tomás. Mr. TV has struck a deal with La Voz that he will provide her blind son with a set of eyes if she does what he asks. La Voz, who (only) appears to be the single voice in this silent society, sings, makes recordings for radio broadcasts, and also submits to have her voice harnessed by Dr. Y's technological contraption as part of the bargain. Dr. Y's contraption will use her voice to further extract raw materials for production from the already silent urbanites. That is, having already used their spoken words, this invention will steal their visual words as well (the film's intertitles); demonstrating, of course, the classically Marxist need of the bourgeoisie to continually revolutionize the means of production. The situation in which La Voz finds herself, however, also finds an apt historical intertext in the economic realities of radio broadcasting in the first third of the century in Argentina. Jorge Finkielman's *The Film Industry in Argentina* (2004) notes the "extremely fast development" of broadcasting in Argentina between 1920 and 1924 (2004: 107), alluding to a battle between the state regulation of radio channels and the broadcasters themselves (2004: 111) and pointing out that the activities of vocal artists were closely controlled. Such artists were, in the beginning, unable to perform on the radio live, while it was at times appropriate to play a recording over the airwaves.[11] Interestingly enough, there is, in fact, a relevant scene in *La antena* where a woman singer appears to be lip-synching to a recording by La Voz—pressed as a record with a swirling and hypnotic "6" / "9" / "?" logo in the center—while it is being played over the radio.[12] In the end, La Voz may even be, perhaps, a composite historical figure constructed from the cultural capital of popular Argentine singers like Mercedes Simone and Sofía Bozán.[13]

The radio was then and still is, of course, a medium where listeners use their imaginations to produce visual representations to accompany sonorous signals. Toward that end, it is not irrelevant that the sport of boxing—which plays a recurring role in *La antena*—was big during the 1920s and 1930s in Argentina and was a radio hit. Finkielman writes that "With the transmission of the Firpo vs. Dempsey boxing match in 1923, radio found a show with which to attract a large audience to the radio sets, anxious to follow the details of the events" (2004: 109). Boxing appears in Sapir's film as a theme (i.e., human beings warring with each other, a parallel for the market competition that is ominously absent in Mr. TV's monopolistic but still capitalist empire), a recurring motif (e.g., the way the repairman "boxes" two halves of a photo of himself and his ex-wife together, demonstrating for the viewer the antagonistic nature of their failed relationship) and also as a reality. Mr. TV in fact seems to run (i.e. own) a boxing ring and business. In fact, at the very moment in which the urbanites are lulled into sleep by the power of La Voz's voice as augmented by Dr. Y's contraption, there is a boxing match taking place—suggesting that sport is yet another way of lulling an urban population into passive conformity and consumption practices.

But given the film's self-reflexive engagement with cinema itself (discussed by Page 2012), the point is that the everyday speech of the urbanites, the auditory performance(s) of La Voz (whether live or recorded), and the appeal of boxing for radio audiences are rendered for viewers on screen by Sapir as a *visual* spectacle. In the same way, the intertitles seen by viewers are more than *either* a merely nondiegetic explanation of the silent film's action *or* a diegetic part of the film's action—they are a *visual* bridge between one and the other. Just as the citizens of city XX are beholden to visual spectacle (of their televisions), we, too, as viewers, are beholden to the film's visual spectacle (of our own screens). The genius of the film is that *La antena* alienates its fictional citizens from their own words at the same time that as spectators we are deprived also of sounds. Consistently, then, the auditory is essentially replaced by the visual, sound is replaced by sight, and we take part—willingly, passively as consumers of the visual—in what is effectively the society of the spectacle so denounced by Guy Debord (through his Situationist texts) and by Debord's one-time friend Henri Lefebvre (through his rhythmanalytical project).

And yet, just as sound is—for diegetic urbanite and *La antena*'s viewer alike—the realm of alienation, it is also a potential staging ground for resistance to capital. That is, while the sound of La Voz's voice is transmitted as a way to revolutionize the means of production and acquire ever greater quantities of raw materials for Mr. TV's factory system, it is the sound of the voice of her son Tomás that, once broadcast from the rural antena, disrupts Mr. TV and Dr. Y's ingenious accumulation strategy. Meeting the capitalist appropriation of sound with the proletariat's reappropriation of sound effects a liberation from the auditory repression governing *La antena*'s population. As viewers, we hear Tomás's calls for his mother—the phatic function of language ("*¿mamá?, ¿estás allí?* [Mama, are you there?]")—such an exaggerated number of times that it is meant to overwhelm us during the film's climactic scene. In the context of a film that has been mostly silent, the sound is even more powerful, delivering us—and also the film's characters—back into a sound-filled sense-world from which both groups have been deprived for too long (for the duration of the film, in our case, and for multiple generations, in the case of *La antena*'s characters).

2. Sight

As suggested above, Sapir's masterpiece alienates us from the auditory world
just as it substitutes for sound through sight. That is, given that we are—as
are *La antena*'s urbanites—deprived of sounds (for the most part), the film's
spectacular visual style and cinematic citation becomes even more overwhelming. The oft-repeated tropes of the film—in particular the hypnotic
image of the "6–9–?"—provide indications that the visual is not to be trusted.
In addition, we may look to the blind boy Tomás as a symbol of the need to
distrust images. In this context, he becomes a powerful figure in the film
precisely because he is not beholden to the spectacular image of the city—
what Debord would call the visual forms assumed by capital and what Lefebvre would denounce as the link between the visual/spatial on one hand
and the auditory/temporal on the other. The boy Tomás, then, exists in lived
temporality—as Lefebvre asks the rhythmanalyst to do (2006). From a Lefebvrian perspective, this suspicion of the visual which crops up in *La antena*
is doubly important.

First, that is, this distrust of the visual can be seen as a metaphor for the
way capital has, since the nineteenth century, helped to construct the city as
an exchange-value instead of a use-value, an image instead of a lived space.
As explored in Lefebvre's *The Urban Revolution* and *The Right to the City*,
the nineteenth-century city was envisioned as a geometrical abstraction, a
two-dimensional space conceived by planners and architects who embodied a
dynamic partnership with the bourgeois science of urbanism—whether they
were conscious of this fact or not. As has been explored elsewhere in much
greater detail, in this way, Lefebvre's reconfigured Marxian thought applied
an understanding of the circuits of capital which Marx had originally explored to the spatial dimensions of to contemporary urban life (Lefebvre
1996, 2003a; Fraser 2008, 2011; Marx 1977; Harvey 2009, 2010). The work
of Lefebvre's one-time collaborator, Guy Debord, is also relevant here, in
that the notion of the *Society of the Spectacle* which he articulated held that
urbanized capital had evolved to such a point that it had become mere image
(Debord 1961, 1995).[14] But—and this is the second importance of adopting a
Lefebvrian perspective on the film's engagement with sight—the insight
common to both Debord and Lefebvre's distrust of the visual concerns the
Marxian notion of alienation. Just as the film's revolutionary family of characters (repairman, daughter, and ex-wife) is eventually disalienated from the
visual and ideological spectacle of urbanized capital, so too are we as viewers visually disalienated from the impression of reality that is synonymous
with the spectacular character of cinema.

To explain: one of the chief filmic properties of *La antena* is its visual
complexity. The ingenious and ubiquitous use of intertitles, the original and
visual inspiration for the film (the extensive storyboarding described by Page

2012), and the connection with the visual style of comics are all significant here, and they acquire ever greater force in a stunning black-and-white final product (a stark contrast which itself ties into the Marxian theme of the dialectic between the capitalist class and the proletariat). But the method of cinematic citation employed by Sapir in the film is the most significant of these strategies of visual complexity. Creating a mise-en-scene that draws from German expressionism—films like *The Cabinet of Dr. Caligari* (1924), *Nosferatu* (1927), and *Metropolis* (1927), as analyzed by Blos-Jáni; and also, in the final sequences, *Voyage to the Moon* by Georges Méliès—*La antena* is further involving the film's audience in a discourse on alienation and the ideological nature and function of representations. To see how this is so, we must turn to the work of film theorist Christian Metz. In a classic article titled "On the Impression of Reality in the Cinema"—one given the privileged position of opening his anthology titled *Film Language*—Metz ruminated on the reality of artistic representations. The distinction he drew there between the theater and the cinema is quite useful in the present context. That is,

> One of the most important of the many problems in film theory is that of the *impression of reality* experienced by the spectator. Films give us the feeling that we are witnessing an almost real spectacle—to a much greater extent [. . .] than does a novel, a play, or a figurative painting. Films release a mechanism of affective and perceptual *participation* in the spectator (one is almost never totally bored by a movie). They spontaneously appeal to his sense of belief— never, of course, entirely, but more intensely than do the other arts, and occasionally films are, even in the absolute, very convincing. They speak to us with the accents of true evidence, using the argument that "It is so." (Metz 1974: 4)

Building, via Roland Barthes, from the photograph's "real unreality" (Metz 1974: 6) to the distinction between cinema and theater, he acknowledges that the presence of movement and the so-called corporeality of objects are key factors in the cinema's impression of reality; but he also suggests there is more to it than that (1974: 7). There is, of course, an illusion of tactility in the cinema which fades as soon as we stretch our hand out toward the screen (1974: 8)—one that is greatly relevant to Sapir's film as discussed in the final section below. Yet while the cinema convinces us of its reality, "the theatrical spectacle . . . cannot be a convincing duplication of life, because it is itself a part of life, and too visibly so . . . the stage setting, for example, does not have the effect of creating a *diegetic* universe; it is only a convention within the real world" (1974: 10). To paraphrase Metz's conclusion, as a convention, the theater is clearly a representation of reality, whereas the cinema's "impression of reality" induces us to forget that it is a representation.

With Metz's words in mind, what is so compelling about *La antena* is that its visual complexity drives to counteract the "impression of reality" that so often accompanies the cinema. Sapir's persistent, exaggerated, and pro-

longed visual references to the stylistic mise-en-scene of classics in German
Expressionism and the early fantastic films by Méliès are so conventional
and so rooted in our extra-diegetic experience of the history of cinema that
we cannot suspend our disbelief as we might otherwise do. These references
build, of course, on *La antena*'s curious recuperation of the silent film aesthetic, which also exposes for us the representational nature of the film. The
director wants us to see this as a creation, rather than have us passively
accept its "impression of reality" and simply enjoy it as a cinematic spectacle. That is, *La antena* is undoubtedly a cinematic spectacle, but the characters are not "objects of our identification"—as so often happens in film—so
much as they are what Metz calls "objects of our dissociation"—as more
often happens in theater (1974: 9). Of course, a more appropriately nuanced
reading would have it that we both identify with and dissociate from *La
antena*'s characters, that we give ourselves over to the diegesis while simultaneously adopting a detached and questioning viewpoint that we might otherwise not sustain. The curious use of the intertitles as a way of blending the
diegesis and our reception of the film is yet another visual way in which we
are both connected to and distanced from the characters. Yes, it is possible to
adopt this intermediary or liminal position (being "betwixt and between" as
anthropologist Victor Turner would have it) with any film (see Lotman
1976), but the point is that Sapir is persistently asking us to do so through his
use of the film's formal properties themselves. To bring Lefebvre back into
the discussion, the film's formal properties guide us to critically analyze the
mystifying effects of alienating processes, to distinguish, then, between appearance and reality.[15]

We must build on Metz to see that the distinction between appearance and
reality made in *La antena* is crafted in specifically Marxian terms. This
questioning of the film's diegesis on our part is a complement to the struggle
that *La antena*'s characters are going through to disalienate themselves from
the hypnotic ideologies of urban capital in their own fictional world. Just as
the characters learn to distrust the surface appearance of their everyday lives
we are—in parallel—made aware of the representational nature of the film. It
is important to clarify that the visual is not merely an immaterial realm
opposed to a material realm. Instead, evoking the Marxian logic that unites
the material and the immaterial in a dialectical circuit, the immaterial in the
film can actually do harm to the characters. For example, when the revolutionary family uses the flying balloon to escape to the country where they
hope to reclaim the antenna—and, in the end, to reappropriate capitalist
machinery for the destruction of that same capitalist system—they are fired
upon by Mr. TV's henchmen. The guns used by these henchmen—which are
also silenced in this world, subject to the same systematic repression as the
city's people—produce visual words which initially group together near the
ground and are then thrust up into the air at their fleeing targets. As it was

with the case of sound, the realm of sight is also a place where one encounters both the reality of alienation and also the potential for disalienation. In particular, the spectacle of the film itself, *La antena* as received by contemporary film viewers, is destabilized, made to appear more real precisely by getting us to see beyond the spectacle. But in addition, the realm of the tactile, already alluded to above, is what provides the most powerful force of disalienation for the film's characters.

3. Touch

Continuing to build on the importance of the human senses for Marx and for Lefebvre, we must recognize the privileged role assigned to touch and to tactility as a potential instrument of disalienation and perhaps revolution in Marxian thought. In a passage from the first volume of the *Critique of Everyday Life*, Lefebvre refashions a classically Marxian perspective for twentieth-century urban realities when he writes that

> The proletarian "condition" has a dual aspect—more precisely, it implies a dialectical movement. On the one hand it tends to overwhelm and crush the (individual) proletarian under the weight of the toil, the institutions and the ideas which are indeed intended to crush him. But at the same time, and in another respect, because of this incessant (everyday) contact with the real and with nature through work. the proletarian is endowed with fundamental health and a sense of reality which other social groups lose in so far as they become detached from practical creative activity. (Lefebvre 1991b: 143)

In this passage, the potential advantage retained by the proletariat in the class struggle stems directly from the physical and tactile contact with everyday reality. The physical contact sustained by the proletariat with this tactile sense-world provides a "direct" experience with reality that the capitalist loses. While tactility is at work in *La antena* primarily at the level of the film's diegesis, it must not be ignored that the intertitles as analyzed by Blos-Jáni (i.e., intertitles which can be touched and manipulated) also suggest an illusion of tactility that involves both the characters and the cinematic spectator. Nevertheless, the film reveals the Marxian link between tactility/touch and disalienation most strongly in its characterization of the repairman and his family.

The repairman's profession itself speaks to his everyday experience with the tactile just as it suggests his ability to see beyond mere surface appearance into the way systems operate. This itself is a clear representation of the Marxian notion that "only the social agent which is itself a 'whole'—that is, Marx's 'universal class', the proletariat—can perceive the 'whole' in isolated phenomena" (Kolakowski 2005: 1002). The repairman not only works restoring televisions—a clear filmic representation (at the level of sets/props)

of the visually spectacular and alienating capitalist discourse of media-saturated societies—but he is also responsible for overseeing the "Flying Person
of the Month" contest. Significantly, in one of the film's first sequences, it is
implied that this profession has been passed down from generation to generation. Both the grandfather character and the repairman's daughter Ana are
seen collaborating on this task. Moreover, each of the three generations has a
prominent scar on their hand—which comes as a work-related injury stemming from the act of having to hold the tethering rope.[16] This itself can be
understood in terms of the way in which increasing industrialization, historically speaking, introduced a new element of risk and danger—if not actual
death—into jobs ranging from the mines to the factory system. But it also
draws attention to the hands of the proletariat, which are at once the instru-
ments of labor and also hold the potential for revolution.[17]

Tactility is also important in the frame-story as established for the film's
theatrical release.[18] The film opens with the image of a pop-up book: three-
dimensional buildings rise up from its pages and provide (the illusion of) not
merely a verbal artifact but rather a tactile reading experience. Once again,
this choice has the additional effect—working along with the film's eclectic
visual style as noted above—of minimizing the cinema's "impression of
reality" and showing us clearly that we are participating in a representation—
with all the alienations and ideological fictions which that implies. The sense
of touch figures also in the theme of boxing—although, as it was with the
film's visual gun sounds (above), here we are reminded of the harmful effects and even the violence that accompanies the sense of touch. Just as was
the case with sound and with sight, the tactile world is clearly also a realm
with harmful, and not solely emancipatory, effects. We do well in remember-
ing that the sense of touch is similarly a site of alienation. It is that sense
through which the laborer engages not only in the process of production but
also in the process of alienation. As Debord writes, clearly articulating a
Marxian premise found also in the work of Lefebvre:

> Workers do not produce themselves: they produce a force independent of
> themselves. The *success* of this production, that is, the abundance it generates,
> is experienced by its producers only as an *abundance of dispossession.* All
> time, all space, becomes *foreign* to them as their own alienated products accu-
> mulate. . . . The spectacle's function in society is the concrete manufacture of
> alienation. (Debord 1995: Theses 31–32; also 1961)

The repairman and his family—even his ex-wife who, as a nurse, is also
associated with the working class, and visually so through the uniform she
wears consistently—are identified with the sensuous world in a double sense.
The ubiquitous presence of tactility is a filmic indication that these are laborers who work more closely with nature than does the capitalist and also that
there are at once alienated from their own sense world.[19] Though a battle-

ground between alienation/estrangement and also the potential for disaliena-tion, touch is a privileged sense for Marx just as it is for Esteban Sapir in this film. The sense of touch is made to appear as the last sense from which the diegetic city's inhabitants have not yet been alienated/estranged. It is tactility which connects them to the reality of the material conditions which structure their lives and which invites them to challenge the progressive dispossession of their other senses: first their spoken words, and subsequently their visual words. Tactility is, in this sense, the last "thing" owned/possessed by the working class in *La antena*.

In particular, the exaggerated physical fight between the rat-like hench-man of Mr. TV and the repairman at the end of the film portrays very well the fact that the sense-world of touch is a battleground, and resonates also with the theme of boxing commented on above. This battle is a struggle at once to recuperate the human sense-world and also to destroy the machinery (and by extension also symbolically the capitalist mode of production) through which domination of the proletariat is continuously effected. The point made by *La antena*'s pervasive and structural emphasis on the senses is that the production and consumption practices in which we engage are not about the objects we produce or consume, but rather about our own human-ness, our shared human reality. In Lefebvre's words:

> The drama of alienation is dialectical. Through the manifold forms of his labour, man has made himself real by realizing a human world. He is insepara-ble from this "other" self, his creation, his mirror, his statue—more, his body. The totality of objects and human products taken together form an integral part of human reality. On this level, objects are not simply means or implements; by producing them, men are working to create the human; they think they are molding an object, a series of objects—and it is man himself they are creating. (Lefebvre 1991b: 169)

Ultimately, *La antena* does not merely critique brute political power, but rather—following the Marxian premise I hope to have traced out—it instead critiques the capitalist alienation which estranges us not merely from the products of our labor but moreover from our sense-world. As Lefebvre made clear in his reconfigured Marxism—and as Sapir's film helps us to realize—we are alienated not merely at our jobs, but also in our everyday urban lives.

It is important to remember, however, that even Marx himself—the "sen-suous Marx" outlined in the first section of this article—imagined a nonal-ienated form of production in which humankind would be able to reconstitute the totality of modern life which had been fragmented even under nineteenth-century capitalism.[20] Although the nature of this nonalienated form of pro-duction was unclear from Marx's own work—and although *La antena* stops short of suggesting its outline to us—it is clear to Marx, to Lefebvre, and to Sapir, also, I would say, that the vehicle for this transformative shift in the totality of contemporary urban life has to be the human senses themselves. Our alienation from our own sense-world (sound, sight, and touch) potentially provides the impetus for questioning the way in which our political, social, philosophical and economic worlds appear to function as autonomous areas of experience. Uniting them all is a single (if complex) capitalist system hiding the conditions of its own existence and appearing to us in our everyday lives only indirectly.

NOTES

1. One of the first scenes cut from the film exaggerates the predominance of the symbol atop what seems to be a number of different buildings throughout the city.

2. I would like to thank the twelve students of my HONS 381 class titled "The Culture(s) of Hispanic Cities: Bridging Film and Urban Studies" at the College of Charleston, a group whose contagious enthusiasm for urban films led to continued intriguing conversations each week. In particular, I thank these students: for commenting on the role of tactility in this film during the week we spent on *La antena*, which got me thinking quite a bit (inspiring this article); for their thorough explanations of deleted/cut scenes, which provided many answers for me and also suggested that I reframe the questions I was asking; and for the well-crafted initial and final student-led presentations and discussions of the film, which provided the opportunity for those intriguing conversations to unfold.

3. "Man appropriates his total essence in a total manner, that is to say, as a whole man. Each of his *human* relations to the world—seeing, hearing, smelling, feeling, thinking, observing, experiencing, wanting, acting, loving—in short, all the organs of his individual being, like those organs which are directly social in their form, are in their *objective* orientation or in their *orientation to the object*, the appropriation of that object" (Marx 1964: 139). Kolakowski's discussion of the concept (in relation to its use by Lukács, specifically) in enlightening, as when he writes "In other words, the basic dependence in social life is not between the base and the superstructure but between social being (or 'the whole', i.e. everything) and particular elements of the whole" (2005: 1001).

4. Here, Lefebvre clearly conceives of his exploration of alienation as part of a new reading of Marx. "Marx tended to push the many forms of alienation to one side so as to give it one specific definition in terms of the extreme case he chose to study: the transformation of man's *activities* and relations into *things* by the action of economic *fetishes*, such as money, commodities and capital. Reduced to economic alienation within and by capitalism, alienation would disappear completely and in one blow, through and historical but unique act: the revolutionary action of the proletariat" (Lefebvre 2002: 207).

5. Regarding the seemingly autonomous areas of contemporary urban capitalism, in *La presencia y la ausencia* (2006b [1980]), Lefebvre examines: "This: a totality that was previously present broke into pieces, an invisible center, perhaps due to being "spiritual" ceded its place to multiple partial centers; the free play of representations and of manipulations substituted for the decisive influence of the *civil*, which in turn had replaced the religious. In order to become more explicit, a multitude of capacities and forces—some ancient and others more recent— *became autonomous*, each one going its own way, affirming itself on its own, imposing itself or attempting to impose itself on the others and totalizing itself through its own strength" (Lefebvre 2006b: 242).

6. Consider also, for example, how twentieth-century work recaptured the dialectical premise underlying Marx's original critique, such as Marxist scholar Raymond Williams, who writes that "it would be more reasonable . . . to look at our actual productive activities without assuming in advance that only some of them are material" (1977: 94).

7. For Marx is neither a political economist nor a philosopher, in the sense that he advances a *critique* of political economy (through political economy) just as a *critique* of philosophy

(through philosophy). On the Marxian legacy of the latter as it has been rearticulated in the work of twentieth-century Marxist philosopher Henri Lefebvre, see Fraser 2014.

8. "Without doubt, there is no philosopher who should be more closely associated with "68 than Lefebvre, especially if we recognize that this historical moment had to do with the explosion of the urban, and a concomitant assault on the colonization of everyday life by the technocratic forces of capitalist commercialization" (Mendieta 2008: 149).

9. "Everyday life . . . possessed a dialectical and ambiguous nature. On the one hand, it's the realm increasingly colonized by the commodity, and hence shrouded in all kinds of mystification, fetishism and alienation. . . . On the other hand, paradoxically, everyday life is likewise a primal site for meaningful social resistance. . . . Thus radical politics has to begin and end in everyday life; it can't do otherwise" (Merrifield 2002: 79).

10. Lefebvre's references to this rhythmanalytical project are evident, also, in earlier work (see Lefebvre 1991a: 117; and 2002: 130, he refers to it as "a new science"). The term itself is borrowed by Lefebvre from Gaston Bachelard, and can be traced back to author Lucio Alberto Pinheiro (Elden 2006: xiii; Lefebvre 2006a: 9). In *Rhythmanalysis*, Lefebvre suggests a musical vocabulary now applicable to urban analysis, including the terms: "melody-harmony-rhythm" (Lefebvre 2006a: 12), measures (2006a: 8), harmonics (2006a: 60), musical time (2006a: 64), arrhythmia, isorhythmia, polyrhythmia, and eurhythmia (2006a: 16, 31, 67) and more.

11. Finkielman reports that: "The most famous orchestras from the cinemas and cabarets, and the most popular artists of the times, did not perform on the radios then. Nobody could pay them the money they wanted. What is more, almost all of them were under contract with recording companies, and were forbidden to perform on the radio, which was seen as a competitor" (Finkielman 2004: 107; as per 2004: 109, this did change somewhat after 1924); and also that "In the beginning, radio consisted of the live transmission of events. The technical difficulties, both in transmission and in reception, made the use of records difficult, and the big recording companies had in the beginning forbidden the reproduction of their record by the broadcasters. The artists under contract with these companies were also forbidden to perform at the radio stations" (Finkielman 2004: 112).

12. This scene is much more complex than it seems, however, given that—as is evident upon watching the scenes deleted from the film—the woman (whose face we can see, as opposed to La Voz whose included scenes hide her identity for the duration of the film) is in reality La Voz herself.

13. Finkielman writes of both women: "Mercedes Simone (probably the best female tango singer of all time and occasionally a film actress)" (2004: 121) and also Sofía Bozán, who received praise for both her voice and her cinematic appeal (2004: 122–25).

14. Consider the following statement by Debord: "The spectacle divides the world into two parts, one of which is held up as a self-representation to the world, and is superior to the world. The spectacle is simply the common language that bridges this division. Spectators are linked only by a one-way relationship to the very center that maintains their isolation from one another. The spectacle thus unites what is separate, but it unites it only *in its separateness*" (1995: Thesis 29).

15. In the *Critique of Everyday Life*, Lefebvre writes: "In mystification appearance and reality are confused, inextricably bound up together. . . . Appearance and reality here are not separated like oil and water in a vessel, but rather amalgamated like water and wine. To separate them we must *analyse* them in the most classic sense of the word: the elements of the mixture must be isolated" (original emphasis, 1991b: 147).

16. In the deleted scenes accompanying the DVD, it becomes even more clear that this scar is incurred from holding the rope. Also interesting is that, in another deleted scene, the character of La Voz takes off her glove to expose her hand, in the process revealing that she also possesses a scar of the same dimensions as the repairman and his relatives.

17. The world of the human senses is additionally equated with the repairman and his family through the store window whose display seems to have the appearance of a human face (eyes and nose) and also the communication devices used to communicate with one another, which also boast knobs appearing to be eyes, a nose, and also a small screen where the face's mouth would be where mouth movements of the communicating characters can be clearly seen and

(somehow) visually interpreted. Sapir is reminding us that the technology, although alienated from human labor, is a product of human labor nonetheless.

18. That is to say: the deleted scenes show an alternate beginning also indicate that we might have been shown that the hands of the intro and finale (typing on the typewriter and opening/ closing the pop-up book) are those of Mr. TV's son. As released, we are not assisted in making this connection.

19. "The worker can create nothing without *nature*, without the *sensuous external world*. It is the material on which his labor is realized, in which it is active, from which and by means of which it produces" (Marx 1964: 109). Also, "*All* these physical and mental senses have there-fore—the sheer estrangement of *all* these senses—the sense of *having*" (Marx 1964: 139).

20. In his 1844 *Manuscripts*, Marx wrote of the "ideal of a future 'non-alienated artistic' form of production" (Rose 1984: 79); "Although Marx had spoken of a future form of non-alienated labour in terms of artistic activity in his *Economic and Philosophic Manuscripts* of 1844, he had not yet offered a fully developed analysis of art as a form of economic production subject to the demands—and alienations—of other forms of production" (Rose 1984: 79). In this sense, Lefebvre picks up where Marx left off.

BIBLIOGRAPHY

Aguilar, Gonzalo (2006), *Otros mundos: Un ensayo sobre el nuevo cine argentino*, Buenos Aires: Santiago Arcos.
Blos-Jáni, Melinda (2008), "Is Silence Hereditary? Written Word and Acoustic Events in a Contemporary Silent Film: Esteban Sapir's *La antena* (2007)," in *Words and Images on the Screen: Language, Literature, Moving Pictures*, Agnes Petho (ed.), Newcastle: Cambridge Scholars, pp. 132–58.
Chamorro, Alberto (2011), *Argentina, Cine y Ciudad. El espacio urbano y la narrativa fílmica de los últimos años*, Mar del Plata: Eudem.
Debord, Guy (1961), "Perspectives for Conscious Changes in Everyday Life," *Internationale Situationiste* 6: pp. 20–27.
———. (1995), *The Society of the Spectacle* (trans. Donald Nicholson–Smith), New York: Zone.
Deutsch, Sandra McGee (1986), *Counterrevolution in Argentina, 1900–1932: The Argentine Patriotic League*, Lincoln: University of Nebraska Press.
Elden, Stuart (2004), *Understanding Henri Lefebvre: Theory and the Possible*, London; New York: Continuum.
———. (2006), "Rythmanalysis: An Introduction," in Henri Lefebvre, *Rhythmanalysis* (trans. Stuart Elden and Gerald Moore), London; New York: Continuum, pp. vii–xv.
Elden, Stuart and Elizabeth Lebas (2003), "Introduction: Coming to Terms with Lefebvre," in *Henri Lefebvre: Key Writings*, S. Elden, E. Lebas and E. Kofman (eds.), New York; London: Continuum, pp. xi–xix.
Falicov, Tamara L. (2003), "Los hijos de Menem: The New Independent Argentine Cinema, 1995–1999," *Framework*, 44: 1, pp. 49–63.
Finkielman, Jorge (2004), *The Film Industry in Argentina: An Illustrated Cultural History*, Jefferson, ND and London: McFarland and Co.
Fraser, Benjamin (2008) "Reconciling Film Studies and Geography: Adolfo Bioy Casares's *La invención de Morel*," *Mosaic: A Journal for the Interdisciplinary Study of Literature*, 41: 1, pp. 153–68.
———. (2010), *Encounters with Bergson(ism) in Spain: Reconciling Philosophy, Literature, Film amd Urban Space*, Chapel Hill: University of North Carolina Press.
———. (2011), *Henri Lefebvre and the Spanish Urban Experience: Reading the Mobile City*, Lewisburg: Bucknell University Press.
———. (2014), "Inaugural editorial: Urban Culture Studies—A Manifesto," *Journal of Urban Cultural Studies*, 1: 1, pp. 3–17.
———. (n.d), unpublished article-length manuscript, "Urban railways in Buenos Aires."

Fraser, B. and C. Méndez (2012), "Espacio, tiempo y ciudad: La representación de Buenos Aires en *El Eternauta,*" *Revista Iberoamericana* 78: 238–239, pp. 57–72.

Goonewardena, Kanishka (2005), "The Urban Sensorium: Space, Ideology and the Aestheticization of Politics," *Antipode* 37, pp. 46–71.

Goonewardena, Kanishka, Stefan Kipfer, Richard Milgrom, and Christian Schmid (eds.) (2008), *Space, Difference, Everyday Life: Reading Henri Lefebvre*, New York; London: Routledge.

Harvey David, (2009), *Social Justice and the City*, Athens: University of Georgia Press.

———. (2010), *A Companion to Marx's Capital*, London; New York: Verso.

———. (2012), *Rebel Cities*, London; New York: Verso.

Knabb, Ken (ed.) (2006), *Situationist International Anthology*, Berkeley: Bureau of Public Secrets.

Kofman, Eleonore and Elisabeth Lebas (1996), "Lost in Transposition—Time, Space and the City," in Henri Lefebvre, *Writings on Cities*, E. Kofman and E. Lebas (eds.), Malden, MA: Blackwell, pp. 3–60.

Kolakowski, Leszek (2005), *Main Currents of Marxism* (trans. P. S. Falla), New York; London: W. W. Norton.

Lefebvre, Henri (1947), *Marx et la liberté*, Geneva: Editions des Trois Collines.

———. (1948), *Le marxisme*, Paris: Presses Universitaries de France.

———. (1964), *Marx*, Paris: Presses Universitaries de France.

———. (1969), *The Explosion: Marxism and the French Upheaval*, New York; London: The Monthly Review Press.

———. (1976), *The Survival of Capitalism: Reproduction of the Relations of Production* (trans. Frank Bryant), New York: St. Martin's Press.

———. (1980), *La présence et l'absence: Contribution à la théorie des représentations*, Paris: Caterman.

———. (1982), *The Sociology of Marx* (trans. N. Guterman), New York: Columbia University Press.

———. (1988), "Toward a Leftist Cultural Politics: Remarks Occasioned by the Centenary of Marx's Death" (trans. David Reifman), in *Marxism and the Interpretation of Culture*, Lawrence Grossberg, Cary Nelson (eds.), Chicago: University of Illinois Press, pp. 75– 88.

———. (1991a), *The Production of Space* (trans. Donald Nicholson–Smith), Oxford: Blackwell.

———. (1991b), *Critique of Everyday Life*, Vol. 1 (trans. John Moore), London; New York: Verso.

———. (1995), *Introduction to Modernity* (trans. John Moore), London and New York: Verso.

———. (1996), *The Right to the City*, in *Writings on Cities*, E. Kofman and E. Lebas (eds. and trans.), Oxford: Blackwell, pp. 63–181.

———. (2002), *Critique of Everyday Life,* Vol. 2 (trans. John Moore), London; New York: Verso.

———. (2003a [1970]), *The Urban Revolution* (trans. Robert Bononno), Minneapolis: University Minnesota Press.

———. (2003b), *Henri Lefebvre: Key Writings*, S. Elden, E. Lebas and E. Kofman (eds.), New York; London: Continuum.

———. (2005), *Critique of Everyday Life,* Vol. 3 (trans. Gregory Elliott), London; New York: Verso.

———. (2006a), *Rhythmanalysis* (trans. S. Elden and Gerald Moore), London; New York: Continuum.

———. (2006b), *La presencia la ausencia: Contribución a la teoria de las representaciones* (trans. Óscar Barahona and Uxoa Doyhamboure), México D.F.: Fondo de Cultura Económica.

———. (2007), *Everyday Life in the Modern World* (trans. Sacha Rabinovich, intro. Philip Wander) Eleventh paperback ed., New Brunswick and London: Transaction Publishers.

———. (2008), *Dialectical Materialism* (trans. John Sturrock, pref. Stefan Kipfer), Minneapolis: University of Minnesota Press.

Léger, Marc James (2006), "Henri Lefebvre and the Moment of the Aesthetic," in *Marxism and the History of Art: From William Morris to the New Left*, Andrew Hemingway (ed.), London: Pluto Press, pp. 143–60.
Lotman, Iuri (1976), *Semiotics of Cinema*, Ann Arbor: University of Michigan Press.
Marx, Karl (1964), *Economic and Philosophic Manuscripts of 1844* (trans. Martin Milligan), Dirk J. Struik (ed and intro.), New York: International Publishers.
———. (1977), *Capital*, vol. 1 (trans. Ben Fowkes, intro. Ernest Mandel), New York: Vintage.
Meira, María and Lisandro Grané (dirs.) (2007), "Making of *La Antena*" (included with extras on DVD of *La Antena*), LadobleA.
Mendieta, Eduardo (2008), "The Production of Urban Space in the Age of Transnational Mega-urbes: Lefebvre's Rhythmanalysis or Henri Lefebvre: The Philosopher of May '68," *City* 12: 2, pp. 148–53.
Merrifield, Andy (2002), *Metromarxism. A Marxist Tale of the City*, London; New York: Routledge.
———. (2005), *Guy Debord*, London: Reaktion Books.
———. (2006), *Henri Lefebvre: A Critical Introduction*, New York; London: Routledge.
Metz, Christian (1974), "On the Impression of Reality in the Cinema," in *Film Language* (trans. Michael Taylor), Oxford: Oxford University Press, pp. 3–15.
Nadal–Melsió, Sara (2008), "Lessons in Surrealism: Relationality, Event, Encounter," in *Space, Difference, Everyday Life: Reading Henri Lefebvre*, Kanishka Goonewardena, Stefan Kipfer, Richard Milgrom and Christian Schmid (eds.), New York, London: Routledge, pp. 161–75.
Page, Joanna (2009), *Crisis and Capitalism in Contemporary Argentine Cinema*, Durham: Duke University Press.
———. (2012), "Retrofuturism and Reflexivity in Argentine Science Fiction Film: The Construction of Cinematic Time," *Arizona Journal of Hispanic Cultural Studies*, 16, pp. 227–44.
Paz, Mariano (2011), "Vox Politica: Acousmatic Voices in Argentinean Science Fiction Cinema," *New Review of Film and Television Studies*, 9: 1, pp. 15–27.
Podalsky, Laura (2004), *Spectacular City: Transforming Culture, Consumption, and Space in Buenos Aires, 1955–1973*, Philadelphia, PA: Temple University Press.
Romero, Luis Alberto (2002), *A History of Argentina in the Twentieth Century* (trans. James P. Brennan), University Park, PA: The Pennsylvania State University Press.
Ross, Kristin (2004), "Lefebvre on the Situationists: An Interview," in *Guy Debord and the Situationist International: Texts and Documents*, Tom McDonough (ed.), Cambridge, MA: MIT Press, pp. 267–84.
Rose, Margaret A. (1984), *Marx's Lost Aesthetic: Karl Marx and the Visual Arts*, Cambridge: Cambridge University Press.
Sapir, Esteban (dir.) (1996), *Picado Fino* (perf: Belén Blanco, Marcela Guerty, Facundo Luengo), 5600 Film.
———. (2007), *La Antena* (perf: Alejandro Urdapilleta, Valeria Bertuccelli, Julieta Cardinali), LadobleA.
Shields, Rob (2005), *Lefebvre, Love and Struggle: Spatial Dialectics*, London; New York: Routledge.
———. (2011), "Henri Lefebvre," in *Key Thinkers on Space and Place*, Phil Hubbard and Rob Kitchin (eds.), London: Sage, pp. 279–85.
Wells, Sarah Ann. (2012), "*Viaje a través del tiempo:* anacronismo y distopía en *La antena* (2007), de Esteban Sapir," *Revista Iberoamericana* LXXVIII: 238–239, pp. 349–65.
Williams, Raymond (1977), *Marxism and Literature*, Oxford; New York: Oxford University Press.

III

CULTURES OF URBAN PROTEST

Chapter Five

Psychoprotest

Dérives of the Quebec Maple Spring

Marc James Léger and Cayley Sorochan

In Canada and the province of Quebec, like in so many other countries where neoliberal policies have been imposed, the level of social inequality has increased dramatically, with virtually all of the income growth during the last thirty years going to the richest 1 percent (see Yalnizyan 2010). A major part of this project of class restoration is the devolution of state provision, as noticed in the practice of consecutive federal government administrations in the 1990s to disregard budget surpluses and to insist on cutting transfer payments to the provinces—payments that were previously invested in education, among other things (Lewis 2006). The commoditization of education in Canada and elsewhere has led to an exponential growth in tuition fees, making student debt a matter of political struggle.[1] In the province of Quebec, however, due to a tradition of social democratic reforms that began in the 1970s, tuition fees for postsecondary education have been relatively low, encouraging students to frequently protest right-wing initiatives to commodify educational services. In 2012, in the context of growing inequality, and after the provincial government decided to increase tuition by 75 percent over five years, hundreds of thousands of university, college, and CÉGEP students across Quebec declared an unlimited general strike. Beginning in March and through to August, students held marches and organized actions that politically transformed the experience of city space.

Claiming a right to the city often entails challenges to the dominant order that lead to state repression. The student strike, which almost led to a general social strike, was so well coordinated that the Montreal police, in an effort to criminalize dissent, transferred its student portfolio to the department of organized crime (Frappier et al. 2012: 14). Both the provincial government and the Montreal municipality imposed new laws designed to control the improvisational dimension of the demonstrations, giving the police the power to demand protest itineraries and the authority to declare the protests illegal in the case of noncompliance. Aware of the newly defined stakes involved in the radical occupation of city streets, demonstrators and citizen supporters engaged in broad-based yet unplanned street marches.

In his recent book on "rebel cities," David Harvey argues that over the last decade Henri Lefebvre's idea of "the right to the city," the right to create alternative forms of urban life that are less alienated, more playful, and more conflictual, has undergone a certain revival (2012: xi). Harvey calls on Marxists to focus on the city rather than the factory as the major site of surplus value production and argues that the ruling elites are especially vulnerable in cities and for this reason are "gearing up for militarized urban struggles as the front line of class struggle in the years to come" (2012: 131). This perception is consistent with studies that show how neoliberal regimes have begun to shift policing strategies from that of negotiated management toward criminalization. According to Leanne Serbulo, the purpose of policing in the wake of antigloballization protests is no longer the differentiation between "good/contained" and "bad/transgressive" protesters, but the incapacitation of demonstrations through the creation of a climate of fear (Serbulo 2012: 111).

In the spirit not only of Lefebvre, but in particular, of the Situationists, we would like to propose that the student protests of the 2012 *printemps érable* (Maple Spring) can be productively interpreted in the terms of the Situationist theory of psychogeography. In our case, the Situationist *dérive* is transferred to the terrain of the student demonstrations and the built environment is reconceived to include not only the given city space, but the presence and intervention of municipal and provincial police. Given that the current prime minister of Quebec, Pauline Marois, decided to diffuse student anger by stating that opposition to government policy should not turn into a "psychodrama," we have termed our application of Situationist psychogeography to street protest *psychoprotest* (Dutrisac and Gervais 2013). We make use of the early writings of the Situationist International (SI) and the Lettrist International in order to advance a cultural analysis of protest activity. While the city of Montreal has been working for decades to brand Montreal a city of festivals and urban spectacle, the psychoprotests of student demonstrators revealed the forms of repression that are at work in a system of neoliberal privatization. In this regard we reject contemporary cultural theoretical perspectives that discount the critique of the spectacle and that work to reduce radical politics to the bogeymen of totalitization, teleology, and Stalinist crime.

A. THE 2012 QUEBEC STUDENT STRIKE

On February 13, 2012, after two years of protests, petitions, and occupations, students across Quebec voted to go on a general unlimited strike against the provincial Liberal government's plan to increase tuition fees by 75 percent over five years.[2] The months following the strike declaration were the most politically intense time in Quebec or Canada in recent memory as the students" demand for a moratorium on tuition fees was representative of a broader struggle against the failed logic of neoliberal policies. This social movement declared itself *le printemps érable* (Maple Spring) in reference to the democratic uprisings in the Arab world in 2011 and as part of a global resurgence of leftist resistance. The strike ended on September 5, one day after premier Jean Charest was voted out of office and the incoming Parti Quebecois leader Pauline Marois followed through on her election promise to cancel the tuition increase. Many considered this victory—however temporary and partial in light of the larger demand for tuition-free education—to be a direct result of the student mobilization. Along with the cessation of studies during the course of the strike, students picketed classrooms, took to the streets daily, and engaged in various forms of civil disobedience and direct action.

In light of the government's initial refusal to meet with student representatives and negotiate the terms of the increase, students voted in favor of a general unlimited strike. The strike endured for 206 days, making it the longest student strike in Quebec history. At its peak, 175,000 joined the strike, that is, over half of Quebec's 342,000 postsecondary students. The three major student associations that represented the striking students included the *Fédération des étudiantes universitaires du Québec* (FEUQ), the *Fédération des étudiantes collégiales du Québec* (FECQ) and *l'Association pour une solidarité syndicale étudiante* (ASSÉ). For the duration of the strike, the ASSÉ formed a temporary coalition, *La Coalition large de l'Association pour une solidarité syndicale étudiante* (CLASSE), which was considered the most radical of the student groups and represented half of the striking students. What distinguished CLASSE (and ASSÉ) from its more moderate counterparts was its commitment to the principle of free postsecondary education as well as its organizational structure, which was based on direct democratic decisionmaking by student assemblies during weekly meetings. Instead of representatives, CLASSE had spokespeople who relayed the decisions of its membership to the government and the public.

While the minimal demand of the striking students was a moratorium on the tuition increase, the more radical demands involved a plan to move toward a tuition-free system. CLASSE pushed for the realization of this latter demand by proposing that the government introduce a small 0.7 percent tax on banks that would cover the costs of tuition for all of Quebec. The students defended their position by arguing that higher tuition diminishes accessibility to education and results in larger amounts of student debt. Rather than treat education as an individual consumer investment, the students insist that education is a social good that should be paid for through a progressive tax system.

The decision to strike and the street tactics devised by the students were informed by CLASSE's principle of combative syndicalism. This principle consists of a commitment to the progressive escalation of tactics until an objective is met. The slow escalation of tactics over the two years preceding the strike declaration, from petitions and one-day strikes to the general unlimited strike, conforms to this principle and helps to explain the widespread and sustained engagement in the strike mobilization.

The student strike became institutionally and politically significant after the establishment of picket lines. These pickets resulted in an effective freeze of teaching activities at most French universities and CÉGEPs. While students struggled to maintain picket lines and control over their strike they also engaged in regular demonstrations of between several hundred to tens of thousands of people. The twenty-second day of each month became a massive day of action that attracted the largest demonstrations of support for the student cause. On March 22, for instance, 200,000 students from across Quebec marched in Montreal. Other than the 2003 demonstration against the impending war on Iraq, this was the largest demonstration in Quebec history. Despite the massive turnout, the government refused to negotiate the issue of tuition increase. On April 22, the monthly march coincided with Earth Day and attracted an even larger crowd, estimated at 300,000. The march of May 22 became the largest act of civil disobedience in Canadian history as approximately one hundred thousand demonstrators diverged from the official route in contravention of the special law passed by the government, which criminalized spontaneous protest. Although no arrests were made during this march, the following day the police made a mass arrest by kettling 500 people. These large demonstrations continued until August and September when the crowd numbers dwindled along with the winding down of the strike.

In response to the injunctions aimed at undermining the democratic strike mandate and in light of the government's refusal to negotiate, student tactics shifted toward economic disruption. Demonstrators participated in peaceful civil disobedience by blocking bridges and major streets. Bags of bricks were thrown onto the tracks of the subway system, disabling it for several hours. The office windows of education minister Line Beauchamp were painted red and a few bank windows were broken. A red square, the symbol of the student movement, became increasingly visible across the province and was worn by students, supporters, and even some politicians from the leftist party Québec Solidaire and the nationalist Parti Québécois. The visual landscape of Montreal was transformed by a proliferation of red flags and banners suspended from balconies and taped to the windows of the homes and businesses of supporters. Just as this happened, however, the level of police violence increased, with the regular deployment of tear gas, stun grenades, and baton charges. After some of the worst police violence occurred, students began to stage "*MaNUfestation*" (Naked Bloc) marches in their underwear and with their bodies adorned with slogans in red paint in order to draw the attention of the media and to demonstrate their vulnerability and nonviolent intentions in relation to the heavily armed riot police.

Among all of these creative actions, the most significant in terms of transforming city space were the night marches. After walking out of talks on April 25, the Liberals presented a new plan that would result in an even higher increase than that of the original proposal. From the evening of April 24 onward students began to assemble nightly at 8 p.m. at Place Émilie-Gamelin and led marches throughout downtown Montreal and surrounding areas until the early hours of the morning. After almost one month of these night marches, and after negotiations broke down, the government introduced a surprise emergency bill that effectively criminalized the strike actions. Bill 78, or Law 12 (nicknamed the "billy club" law—*loi matraque*), suspended the winter 2012 term at any institution where classes were significantly interrupted by the strike and legislated a change in the fall semester start date in order to accommodate the completion of the winter term in August and September.[3] In addition, the law banned any interruption of classes and any assembly of people within fifty meters of an educational institution. The law criminalized any demonstration of fifty or more people that did not provide its itinerary to police eight hours in advance and instituted steep penalties for any individual ($1,000–$5,000 per offence), student leader ($7,000–$35,000), or organization ($25,000–$125,000) that broke its provisions (double the amount for recidivism). Institutions were also empowered to cease the collection and payment of student fees to any student federation or association found to be in violation of the law, effectively incapacitating the students' rights to represent and defend their own interests. Most problematically, the law declared that these penalties would apply not only to those who broke the law, but to student representatives or organizations that did not adequately prevent their members from breaking it. On the same day the City of Montreal introduced a municipal law that banned the wearing of masks at demonstrations.[4] As the law was denounced by the Quebec Bar Association as well as the United Nations, and as it was unlikely to stand up to constitutional challenge, it appeared to most as an undemocratic measure, however temporary.

On May 18, the night that Bill 78 was passed into law, tens of thousands took to the streets in Montreal in a willful act of civil disobedience. Police responded by declaring the march illegal and by firing rubber bullets and tear gas into the peaceful crowd. The crowds were so large, however, that they quickly reassembled and marched for hours without further incident. People continued to march every evening with police making a number of arrests. The new law emboldened police to declare the marches illegal before they had even begun and to use unnecessarily coercive tactics. Those who were arrested in Montreal, however, were not actually charged according to the provisions of Law 12, but were instead given fines of over $600 for breaking the highway safety code. By the end of the summer, more than 3,000 arrests had been made in relation to the student strike.

The arrests and police violence temporarily abated in the face of a new phenomenon. Angered by the special law and the contemptuous way that the government had dealt with the students' concerns, citizens across Montreal began at 8 p.m. to bang pots and pans in their neighborhoods, eventually taking over city streets in spontaneous marches that numbered in the hundreds and thousands and violated the unjust law. Unable to contain or follow all of these *manif des casseroles*, the police allowed them to carry on without interference. The night of May 26 marked the high point of these events with tens of thousands of people marching in dozens of groups all over the city. The *casseroles* continued every night for two weeks and inspired solidarity demonstrations across Canada and in more than seventy cities internationally. In the end, the amount that was spent on policing—over $15 million for the Montreal municipality alone—was more than enough to cover the costs of the tuition increase. Such neoliberal state attacks on democracy confirm David Graeber's observation that today's capitalism is more concerned with convincing people that there is no alternative than making itself functional (see Graeber 2013).

Based on the various aspects of the student strike, the idea of psychoprotest as a mutation of psychogeographic dérive applies most specifically to the night marches and the *casserole* marches, though some aspects of it could also be noticed in the mass demonstrations of the twenty-seconds. Before attending to some of the particulars of these street actions, however, it is necessary to contextualize the concerns of our investigation.

B. PSYCHOGEOGRAPHY

The Situationist theory of psychogeography was developed in the mid- to late-1950s as a means to overcome of the limits and failures of previous avant-garde art movements. In this regard we caution against popular studies that seek to transform psychogeography into a genre category.[5] Against the tendency to historicize, it is necessary to appreciate the significance of Hegelian Marxism to the Lettrists' and Situationists' program. When the French *Philosophies* group, which included Henri Lefebvre, was courted by André

Breton and the Surrealists in 1925, Breton very categorically told them that they should read Hegel before resuming negotiations (Hess 1988: 45). The importance of Hegel for Breton, according to Lefebvre, was the combination of unity and struggle within the real, in other words, the significance of Hegel to avant-garde movements was the importance of the concept of alienation as a constructive and disalienating concept (Lefebvre 1975: 48–50). Alienation is the essential ingredient of what the SI would later term "unitary urbanism," which itself led to the development of the methods of *dérive* and *détournement*.

For Lefebvre, the Surrealist avant-garde had come to a dead end around 1930 since it translated all struggle into literary alienation. This criticism of Surrealism is famously expressed by Lefebvre in his 1947 *Critique of Everyday Life*, in which he decried the group for its diversion of interest away from the real, for belittling the real in favor of the marvelous, for its attack on everyday life, its extreme aesthetic individualism, and the refusal of human redemption in a world of image and poetry (Lefebvre 1991: 110–12). Against the Surrealists' "fictitious negations," Lefebvre set out on a critique of capitalist abstraction and the separation of spheres of human activity by proposing a Marxist understanding of everyday life, an approach to culture and politics based on the concept of alienation. If there was to be a revolution, for Lefebvre it would not be an armed struggle, but a revolution of and within the everyday.[6] In this regard, Lefebvre prefigured the Situationist critique insofar as he advocated the method of Hegelian Marxism in his approach to the alienation of social life. Most specifically, Lefebvre gave close attention to the domain of leisure. The critique of everyday life, he argued, is enacted by humans on a regular basis through their leisure activities, which cannot be separated from the everyday aspect of work. Leisure, which includes not only traditional culture but also the mass media, film, radio, and television, breaks with everyday routines and liberates people from the realm of necessity. As compensation for the same everyday routines, however, leisure creates artificial needs and illusory contents. Whatever the analysis of culture, Lefebvre insisted that the realm of leisure should be part of everyday social practice and be based on needs that are reversible and provisional. The need to enjoy, he argues, comes into conflict with the need to accumulate and therefore, leisure should include the critique of money and mystification (Lefebvre 1991: 92). Despite the eventual disputes between Lefebvre and Guy Debord, it is necessary to underline this connection between unity and struggle in the SI's "desacralization of culture" and in its affirmation of negation in the need for a revolutionary overthrowing of bourgeois tradition (see McDonough 2002).

From out of the postwar alternatives and counter-movements to Surrealism, the Lettrist International, which included Debord, put out a series of statements on urban theory.[7] The first and most important of these was written by Ivan Chtcheglov (a.k.a. Gilles Yvain) in October 1953. Titled "Formula for a New Urbanism," the statement declares a break with Dada and Surrealism as lost legacies (Chtcheglov 1995 [1953]: 1). The piece is far more imaginative than later formulations, and yet, because of this, the aspect of play and the critique of "boring" leisure are foregrounded as means to disrupt the way that modern architecture, modern conveniences, and the mechanization of desires has prolonged the conditions of work. The new world should be more fun and the goal of the avant-garde should be to "carry out an intensive propaganda in favor of new desires" (Chtcheglov 1995 [1953]: 3). Chtcheglov writes:

> We have already pointed out the need of constructing situations as being one of the fundamental desires on which the next civilization will be founded. This need for *absolute* creation has always been intimately associated with the need to *play* with architecture, time and space. . . . The principal activity of the inhabitants [of the new urbanism] will be the continuous dérive. The changing of landscapes from one hour to the next will result in complete disorientation. (Chtcheglov 1995 [1953]: 3–4)

In relation to previous European avant-garde movements, Chtcheglov's tract is the first proposal for a new architecture for which play, leisure, and imagination are set against boredom, control, and regulation. Chtcheglov tends, however, to emphasize poetic power and chance operations at the expense of political analysis. We thus find that the first descriptions of *psychogeography* appear in the Lettrist bulletin as "game of the week," with propositions such as "choose an area, build a house, furnish it, etc."[8]

The concepts associated with psychogeography are taken up by Debord in a series of far more programmatic statements written between 1955 and 1958. The first of these, "Introduction to a Critique of Urban Geography," was produced while Debord was still a member of the Lettrists (Debord 1995 [1955]). Debord states that the term psychogeography was proposed in 1953 as a materialist perspective on the determinations of life and thought. Its purpose is the search for new ways of life through processes of chance and predictability *in the streets* (Debord 1995 [1955]: 5). "Psychogeography," he writes, "could set for itself the study of the precise laws and specific effects of the geographical environment, consciously organized or not, on the emotions and behavior of individuals" (Debord 1995 [1955]: 5). Debord's formulation adds the serious element of research to the more playful aspects defined by his acolyte. Aware of the architecture of social control that has been effected through urban renewal, and in the postwar period, the opening up of cities to automobile circulation, Debord's purpose was to spoil the pleasures and the "pathetic illusions" of happiness and privilege that are promoted by capitalist production. He wished to provoke a crisis in advertising spectacle and cinematic happiness by "turn[ing] the whole of life into an exciting game" (Debord 1995 [1955]: 6). Against overproduction and overaccumulation, the method of psychogeography studies the various ambiances of city space, overcoming the usual, prescribed influences, for instance, between rich and poor neighborhoods, between commercial and historical zones, and against the grain of specially designated activities like tourism, sports, and shopping.

In his text on "Methods of Détournement" Debord set the stage for psychogeography as a new avant-garde method designed to overcome the limits of cultural heritage. The method of *détournement* is a kind of parody and educative propaganda (Debord 1995 [1956]: 9). Détournement is brought to bear on city space through the psychogeographic dérive. In his first tract as part of the soon to be formed Situationist International (SI), which broke off from the Lettrists in 1957, Debord defines the project of the SI as being specific to the critique of urbanism (Debord 1995 [1957]). The new art should be formed at the level of urbanism, he argues, which uses psychogeographical research to study urban development and to propose "hypotheses on the structure of a situationist city" (Debord 1995 [1957]: 23).[9] Opposed to the conditions of the modern spectacle, with its increase in leisure time and imposition of bourgeois tastes, the method of psychogeographical observation is both a moral choice, he argues, and a game that negates the element of competition. Its form is the dérive, a practice of strolling that changes the way one perceives the city. In the first issue of the *Internationale Situationniste* journal, Debord defines the dérive as a "mode of experimental behavior linked to the conditions of urban society: a technique of transient passage through varied ambiances" which "liberate[s] the tendency toward play," an "experimental form" of a "game of revolution" that is opposed to games that represent a regression to an infantile stage (Debord 1995 [1958]: 44).

As a final, programmatic statement on the theory of the dérive as part of a Situationist study of the effects of the geographic environment, Debord considered the dérive in terms of four elements: chance, scale, duration, and terrain.[10] In the process of drifting, one or more people drop their usual work and leisure activities and let themselves be drawn by the different ambiances of the urban terrain. In the process, the play of *chance* is overdetermined and diminished by the psychogeographical relief of the city, with its "currents," "fixed points," and "vortextes." One does not simply improvise one's way as one goes, but becomes aware of and attentive to the calculation of possibilities, which Debord says are both relative and absolute. To fully appreciate the method of psychogeography, the determining aspects of city space must be utilized and not simply ignored or disavowed. Dérive is therefore not a practice of transgression or even of direct action. He writes: "The objective passional terrain of the derive must be defined in accordance both with its own logic and with its relations with social morphology" (Debord 1995

[1958]: 50). Chance, he argues, tends to reduce things to habit and to limit possibilities. Progress therefore lies in breaking away from chance by creating new conditions that are favorable to *revolutionary* purposes. In this regard Debord avoided the aimless strolling and nostalgia of predecessors like Baudelaire, Breton, and Aragon.

Nowhere is the difference between psychoprotest and the psychogeographic dérive more evident that on the matter of *scale*. Debord recommends dériving alone or in small groups of two or three people, in particular, people with the same level of political awareness. Since the goal is to achieve certain objective conclusions, the increase of scale to four or five persons diminishes the specificity of the method. Any more than ten people, he contends, causes the group to break up into smaller groups. In this regard, on the other hand, the way that a demonstration of anywhere from 1,000 to 100,000 people tends to involve smaller groupings of individuals, friends, and associated parties, may very well have a potential kinship to psychoprotest. This affinity is also borne out on the matter of *duration*. The average duration of a dérive is one day, sometimes merging into the night, after which fatigue naturally sets in. While it may, Debord says, last from three to four days, it is more likely limited to a period of three to four hours. At the outer edges, dérives have been known to last two months and according to Chtcheglov, a 1953–1954 dérive lasted for three or four months, adding: "It's a miracle it didn't kill us."[11]

Lastly, in terms of *terrain*, the psychogeographer, in the action of studying, may become disoriented by the randomness of wandering. The point of departure, Debord says, does not usually lead far beyond a city or its suburbs; it may be limited to a certain neighborhood or may remain within one specific location for an entire day. The goal is the calculation of directions of penetration rather than the search for the exotic. The psychogeographer may not know who s/he will be meeting at the rendezvous point; he may converse with people not directly implicated in the game, and may make unexpected turns. In other words, there is in this avant-garde practice an openness to chance operations that undermine the logic of duty, discipline, and obedience to rules. Movement may involve hitchhiking or wandering into spaces that are "forbidden to the public" and so implies a certain level of civil disobedience or delinquency.

The goal of psychogeography is to discover "unities of ambiance," the main zones of influence of the built and symbolic environment, and to fathom its possible transformation. The only known representation of the city created by the Situationists is Debord's 1957 map of Paris, known as *The Naked City* (figure 5.1). The map cuts up city neighborhoods into a collage of fragmented parts rearranged into a new configuration with large gaps in between and connected by arrows that connote a dance chart, alluding to the importance at that time of new dances influenced by the then-popular jazz

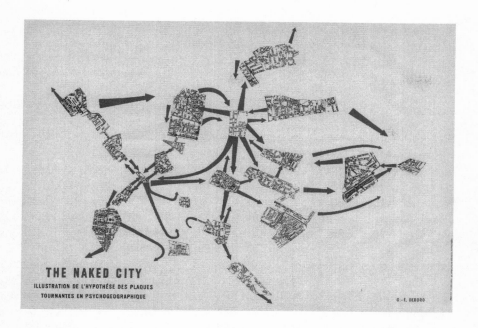

Figure 5.1. Guy Ernest Debord, *The Naked City, Illustration de l'"hypothèse des plaques tournantes en psychogeographique,* 1957. Courtesy and collection of David Tomas.

and rock and roll sounds—not to mention its reference to a 1948 American film noir as well as a book of crime photographs by Weegee. The image enlists the pleasure of popular music and dance as well as the sinister aspects of crime for the purposes of social critique and the construction of a radical perception of urban space. The function of this appropriated map is to propagandize a practice of insubordination of urban directives. While Tom McDonough argues that the dérives' spatial practices reject a totalizing view, echoing in the process the distinction made by Michel de Certeau between pedestrian speech acts and the Archimedian view from atop the World Trade Center, we would note that *The Naked City* does in fact present just such a retotalized, or "dialectical" depiction based on the remapping of human needs and emphasizing the results of militant research. [12]

C. PSYCHOPROTEST

In the following psychogeographical notes on the student protests we draw on our combined experience as participants in the Montreal marches. We have organized these observations according to the four elements that Debord used to define the dérive. Our purpose here is not to provide an exhaustive description but rather a sketch of some of the ways in which the notion of psychogeography is pertinent to our experience of the protest marches, especially those that occurred while it was still unknown to what extent the special law would be enforced.

1. Chance

Situationist psychogeography is concerned with the determining aspects of city space, with its currents, fixed points, and vortexes, leading in the dérive to a game of improvisation that is coordinated with social and not just physical morphology. Like the dérive, protest activity epitomizes the breaking of habits for leftist political purposes.[13] The conditions of illegality that were occasioned by Bill 78 made the protests far more intense. While attending to the "fixed points" of city space, we consider that in this case, such legal fixed points were directly reflected in the slogans that developed. For example, three of the chants that were often used were: *"On est plus que 50!"* ("We are more than 50!"), which was chanted in a mocking manner and referred to the fact that although the march involved more than fifty demonstrators, no one had notified the police, *"La loi special—on s'en calisse!"* ("The special law—we don't give a fuck!"), and *"SSPVM—police politique"* which criticized the Montreal police (Service de police de la Ville de Montréal) for not protecting citizens and for siding with the powerful. Also popular was *"Charest—yoooo hooooooo,"* chiding the prime minister for not meeting with students and daring him to come out of his hiding place. After Charest had told the news media that he had jobs for discontented students up North—referring to his government's plan to subsidize extensive resource extraction in the province's northern regions—the chanting included *"Charest—Dehors! On va't trouver une jobe dans le Nord"* ("Charest—Out! We'll find you a job up North"). The invention of new marching slogans allowed for a counter-construction of fixed points within the movement itself, focusing on shared meanings and allowing for the creation of new solidarities. By producing and repeating this repertoire of common slogans, the improvizational element is provided with swing and momentum, transforming fear and anxiety into collective moral indignation.

Psychoprotest, unlike psychogeography, takes place under the constant watch of police, who are trained in crowd control. Police tactics seemed at times to be highly organized, while at other times they seemed relatively unorganized and casual. Police tactics contribute dramatically to defining the terms of engagement and influence the mood and attitudes of protesters. In terms of legal superstructure, the fixed point of reference used by the Montreal police was not the provisions of Bill 78 but an excerpt from the Quebec Highway Safety Code that reads:

No person may, during a concerted action intended to obstruct in any way vehicular traffic on a public highway, occupy the roadway, shoulder or any other part of the right of way of or approaches to the highway or place a vehicle or obstacle thereon so as to obstruct vehicular traffic on the highway or access to such a highway.

An interesting archive of documents in relation to Bill 78's insistence on the provision of protest itineraries is the web site Manifencours. The site documented the trajectories of the marches and allowed people to post cell phone pictures while also displaying a live Twitter feed. The dates that are archived on this site are mostly from late April and May 2012.[14] What the itineraries show is the general range of the marches, which remained mostly in the downtown zone, Hochelaga-Maisonneuve, the Plateau, Mile End, Outremont, and Little Italy. Using the same streets created a sense of ritual and narrative, allowing new slogans and styles to develop within the march form as an open structure. These improvised itineraries reflect the decision of the students to violate an unconstitutional law designed to dispossess them of their political rights and power. The confrontational aspect of this choice is reflected in a map that began to circulate on the Internet sometime in May and which shows a march itinerary in the form of a "fuck you" finger (figure 5.2). The improvised marches also reflect the constituent aspect of the demos and the absence of any designated leaders. In contrast to anti-globalization marches, there was no stewarding of the marches, and no designated green (nonviolent) and red (direct action) zones. The marches broke the circulation habits of downtown streets for political purposes, creating an emotional intensity designed to maximize the chances of success for the student strike.

The ludic character of the psychoprotests began to worry city officials, especially during the planned disruptions of the Grand Prix auto race activities, which spread skepticism concerning what Attila Kotányi defined as the "racket" and "protected crime" of officially designated leisure activities.[15] The experimental living of those who attempted to disrupt the Grand Prix was a clear denunciation of existing conditions of alienation, materializing freedom by appropriating and disrupting the macho and crime-ridden scene that echoed the corruption charges that plagued the former mayor of Montreal, Gerald Tremblay, and which eventually led to his removal from office. Our experience of the protesting of the Grand Prix was also highly uneven. In a daytime demo we marched and *casseroled* through the race car displays on Crescent Street without any problems, whereas at night, within a larger group of protesters, we were blocked by police charges, tear gassed, and maimed with stun grenades.

While the interventions that affected the Grand Prix were heavily policed, the casseroles were far too popular and broad-based for the police to do anything more than act as chaperones. After the pots and pans began to sound

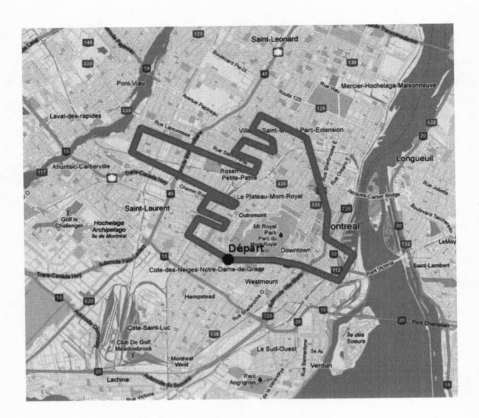

Figure 5.2. Anonymous map of protest itinerary defying the provisions of the "billy club law," Bill 78/Law 12. Source: Internet

at 8 p.m., we would look for a busy corner. It was never possible to know on any given day how many people would turn out and whether or not the gathering would develop into a march. As we experienced it, people would gather on a street corner, following the traffic lights and moving from corner to corner, cheering while passing one another. After there was enough momentum, people would take the street, blocking traffic entirely. Once a group started marching, the direction and aim of the demonstration was again very open and directed by crowd feeling. The imponderables of chance included the choice to find other groups of supporters, whether or not to stay a small group or coalesce with others, whether to follow the police car escort or escape them for fun, what *casserole* groove to get into, and how to influence the direction of the entire group. We tended to first follow a nearby march that would wind through the neighborhoods north of Mount-Royal Avenue and then go searching for others near the larger Saint Denis or Saint Laurent

Figure 5.3.   Manifencours maps of protest itinerary for April 29. Source: http://manifencours.diametrick.com.

Boulevards. We would cheer when merging with another group and then start to work our way downtown. On a few occasions the *casserole* night marches assembled into massive swarms and rivers of demonstrators numbering in the tens and possibly hundreds of thousands.

2. Scale

Debord emphasizes the fact that the group of psychogeographers should have the same level of social consciousness. In the case of psychoprotest, the name of the game is to enhance the level of political awareness as the movement grows in size. The solidarity networks that comprised the student strike were based on assemblies and involved individuals through participation and coordination. Previous strike activism had made the students well informed of the stakes and the forms of mobilization. While the duration of the protests influenced the learning process, so did its scale, which included institutional actors, in particular, Amir Khadir, the (former) leader of Québec Solidaire, and the only significant social democratic actor who struggled against government and media efforts to delegitimize the students.

Collective goals cannot be limited to one person, however, but are based on dense informal networks that allow people to enter and exit the movement at will. The strike was not about personal change, personal empowerment or

**Figure 5.4. Manifencours maps of protest itinerary for May 8. Source: http://
manifencours.diametrick.com.**

identity politics, nor was it a cultural-artistic movement or countercultural
movement, but was instead based on gaining support for a specific issue.
Many small groups marched alongside the students, including *Profs Contre
La Hausse* (Professors Against the Tuition Hikes), *Mères en Colère* (Angry
Moms), *La Coalition Opposée à la Tarification et la Privatisation des Services Publics* (Coalition Against Tarifs and Privatization of Public Services),
Occupy Montreal, and the anarchist Coalition Large Anti-Capitaliste. All of
these groups share an understanding of what is involved in fighting neoliberal austerity. We regret to note the significant absence of labor unions, especially insofar as the students attempted to transform the *printemps érable* into
a broad-based social strike. We disagree, however, with those social movement analysts who consider that the student protests are beyond the labor-
capital conflict. Although the students have different class backgrounds, as
workers they represent the lowest rungs of the educational system. In this
regard the unions of Quebec failed to recognize the student strike as an
important political event. [16]

As the *printemps érable* became significant to the international student
movement, the organizing CLASSE group attempted to define the scale of
the movement by issuing in July the manifesto *Nous sommes avenir* (Share
Our Future). That the struggle against neoliberal capitalism is understood by
the CLASSE in radical democratic terms, involving a diversity of struggles,

Figure 5.5. Manifencours maps of protest itinerary for May 23. Source: http://manifencours.diametrick.com.

including feminism and environmentalism, was confirmed at press conferences given by spokespersons Gabriel Nadeau-Dubois and Jeanne Reynolds.[17] A pragmatic description of the "associated institutions" that comprise the student movement, and certainly one that would come close to the CLASSE's general social movements outlook, is provided by David Harvey's list of nongovernmental organizations, anarchist and autonomous grassroots organizations, traditional left political parties and unions, social movements guided by the pragmatic need to resist displacement and dispossession, and lastly, minority and identitarian movements. Harvey considers communist anyone who understands and struggles against the destructive tendencies of capitalism.[18]

Protesting in large numbers allowed demonstrators to disrupt routines and also provide an avenue for political involvement beyond elections, merging politics with everyday life. The larger the demonstration, the safer one feels—and this was especially true after Bill 78 was put in place. A march could sometimes feel *too* safe and *too* large if it attracted those who were not as enthusiastic or committed to demonstrating. In some of the twenty-second day marches, for example, the focus, energy, and collective feeling was diffuse in comparison to the solidarity that was experienced on night marches. The scale also varied based on government actions. When the government angered people the demonstrations would grow. On the other hand, although the large demonstrations were less cohesive, they were broadly popular, allowing people to enter the political process with a sense of security in numbers and giving public legitimacy to the activities of the hard core as they attempted to shift the terms of the strike to popular struggle.

3. Duration

The duration of the psychoprotests pushes against the upper limits that Debord describes in the duration of dérives. While each separate march would only last for a few hours, the student strike endured for many months. The way in which the constancy of the events altered participants" experience of daily life leads us to consider the strike as a collective city-wide dérive that persisted with varying degrees of intensity. Aside from a small core, most participants did not attend every march. The constancy of the dérive was therefore sustained by people attending when they could in constantly rotating "lines" or "shift work."

The spatial extension of protest also comprised a temporal extension into the evening hours and reconfigured everyday rhythms. The evening start time meant an incursion into leisure time, allowing those who work days to participate and adding a ludic quality to the nocturnal marches that sometimes included fireworks. The night marches would begin at 8 p.m. at Émilie-Gamelin and would at times return to this "home base" at around 10 or 11 p.m., only to start again and continue until 12 or even 2 a.m. Many of these very late marches came to an end without incident when people grew tired and went home. Yet, as the crowd shrank to only a few hundred or a few dozen, the risk of arrest or forced dispersal by the police increased.

Those who became regular participants in the daily and nightly marches experienced a destabilization of their former daily rhythms. In our case, marching for hours for many evenings in a row, watching the live partisan coverage on Concordia University TV (CUTV) when we were not marching, and reading all of the news coverage on the strike eventually led to a delirious state of exhaustion. This fatigue would quickly dissipate when on a "night off" a march would pass by our street and we would find ourselves magnetically drawn toward its chanting vortex.

4. Terrain

On the level of terrain the Quebec Maple Spring was more expansive than typical Montreal protests had been. Rather than remain strictly in the downtown core, and rather than orient marches toward a symbolic site of power, the night marches extended into the surrounding neighborhoods. On particular occasions the night marches did target a site with political significance, as in the May 21 march to the home of Jean Charest in the wealthy municipality of Westmount. That night, the behavior of demonstrators changed dramatically from the respect shown toward residents in Hochelaga-Maisonneuve as compared to that exhibited in Westmount, where pranksters ran across lawns and rang doorbells, a shift that acknowledges Kotányi and Vaneigem's statement that "one doesn't live somewhere in the city; one lives somewhere in the hierarchy" (Kotányi and Vaneigem 1995: 65). The same march destroyed some of the signage in the downtown "Quartier des Spectacles," a managed zone of programmed commercial leisure. More generally, however, the marches did not target any specific site but were oriented toward maintaining a constancy of presence.

Richard Day has argued that recent tendencies in social movements exhibit a different logic from those of the past that were oriented toward a "politics of the demand" (Day 2004: 733–34). Social movements that are based on a politics of the demand are reformist and risk reinforcing the legitimacy of existing institutions by appealing to them for particular changes. Day contrasts this with a "politics of the act," which describes the rejection of hegemony by localist and anarchist activists who focus on creating alternative ways of life that do not depend on existing institutions. The temporary autonomous zones, informal networks, and affinity groups that constitute this form of social struggle are often referred to as horizontalist politics. It is possible to understand certain dimensions of the Maple Spring as exhibiting horizontalist tendencies. The extension of the marches away from physical sites of power could be seen as a rejection of a politics of the demand. The use of social media produced a set of counter discourses and representations that were unconcerned with the mainstream media news coverage and generated an alternative and autonomous media sphere.

The spatial orientation away from centers of power in a psychoprotest reflects this ideology to a degree, but we would contend that the success and power of the movement was largely due to a dialectical relation between these horizontalist tactics and those that acknowledge the actuality of hegemonic struggle through formal organizations. While whether to engage in negotiations with the government was a fraught question within CLASSE, the link to the existing power structure was never fully ignored or severed. The machinery of official negotiations and the recognition of representative power were regarded with a critical distance on the level of the political consciousness of the student organizations, and yet in practice were utilized and played with strategically. Maintaining this link gave legitimacy to the students" position while also displaying the unwillingness of the government to respond to democratic demands.

The orientation of the night marches outward from downtown into the mixed and residential neighborhoods had the effect of producing an interpellation of city residents. They addressed the public street by street, quarter by quarter, and offered people an immediate opportunity to take part, if only by cheering on the marchers or dismissing them. We can recall one young woman in a downtown pizza parlor giving us marchers two big "fuck you" fingers, as if unafraid of our collective power. What this demonstrates is the way the street marches became a diffuse medium of address through which the students cultivated an image of cheerful collectivity that contradicted the image of violent protesters that was disseminated elsewhere. We contend that the *casserole* marches would not have emerged had people not witnessed the students march through their neighborhoods and been interpellated by them through this spatialized address. A night march in early May that stands out in our memory was one that took us through the southeast of the Plateau. We marched through normally quiet residential streets and were received with supportive enthusiasm from the people who watched us from doorways and balconies. This was an exhilarating experience for those among us who are used to protesting in downtown Montreal and are accustomed to receiving blank or hostile looks from shoppers. Only a few weeks later the *casseroles* would begin in these same residential streets.

D. CONCLUSION

Having considered the affinities between the Situationists' theory of psychogeography and the dérives of psychoprotest, one cannot help but wonder about the relevance of the SI for the events of May 1968 and how this might relate to the *printemps érable*. Beyond the Situationists' politically revolutionary goal of overcoming aesthetic alienation and the hold of the spectacle on the everyday, the Situationists dedicated themselves to an avant-garde critique of the bureaucratic power of the Stalinist communist parties. However, in their reflections on the student protests that were published in the September 1969 issue of *L'Internationale Situationniste*, in particular in the essay "The Beginning of an Era," the SI acknowledged that among those groups of students who did the most to spearhead the strikes and occupations were those who had been educated in Trotskyite and Maoist political movements—in other words, those who understood what they were doing in terms of the return of the proletariat as a historical class.[19] May 1968, they argued, was not a student movement, it was a revolutionary proletarian movement. "Stalinists!" ran one of the slogans, "Your sons are with us!"

In Québec in 2012 and among contemporary social movements in general, there is far less interest in the notion of a revolutionary proletariat and so in a vanguard leadership, and yet, despite this, is this not exactly what was provided in the form of the ASSÉ and the CLASSE, with their weekly assemblies, organized structure, and philosophy of combative syndicalism. Of the 300 books that were published on the subject of the 1968 strike in France in the following year, the SI argued that only a handful of these were worth reading. In general, they argued, the books either misinformed readers or falsified the facts. In 1969 the French Larousse dictionary added an entry for the term *situationniste* which effectively reduced the SI's revolutionary politics to a youthful protest and a problem of generation gap. In today's context the generational conflict is replaced by the problems of intersectional theory, with the radical democracy that advocates the equivalence between struggles based on race, class, gender, and sexuality. According to Slavoj Žižek, the postmodern game of plurality makes it necessary that "we do *not* ask certain questions (about how to subvert capitalism as such, about the constitutive limits of political democracy and/or the democratic state as such)," and thereby avoid the question of "the political act proper."[20] Žižek argues further that the contingency of plural political struggles is not opposed to the totality of capital, but rather that the latter forms the very condition of emergence for the myriad of shifting political subjectivities. In this regard, the diversity of the social movements that participated in the psychoprotests of the *printemps érable* represents the inherent conflictual nature of neoliberal global capitalism itself. The excessive policing and systematic repression of the Quebec student strike was part of a global capitalist offensive that produces the now common features, the determining aspects, of a globally produced terrain that today's psychoprotesters have learned to subvert.

NOTES

1. Student strikes against rising tuition and cuts to education have been particularly acute in Chile, Honduras, Columbia, Brazil, Italy, Greece, and the UK. In the United States, for instance, the government now receives approximately $50 billion in annual revenue from student loan interest, an amount that is equal to the combined profits of the four largest U.S. banks. For information on the significance of student debt to the Quebec struggle, see Andrew Gavin Marshall (2012).
2. For a more detailed chronology than is provided here, see Sorochan (2012).
3. The details of Law 78 are available on the Québec government website: www2.publicationsduquebec.gouv.qc.ca.
4. The municipal mask law P-6 is still in effect today and a similar law, titled Bill C-309, was passed by the federal Harper government in June 2013.
5. This is the case with Merlin Coverley's *Psychogeography* (2006).
6. According to Ben Highmore, this approach to gradual and reformist revolution allowed Lefebvre to have a "more amenable relationship with government agencies and institutions" (2002: 142).
7. On the relation between Situationism and Surrealism, see Mikkel Bolt Rasmussen (2004).
8. See *Potlatch* #1 and #2 (1954).
9. As the first significant example of psychogeographical research, see Abdelhafid Khatib, "Essai de description psychogéographique des Halles," (1958). A three-day dérive was also proposed as part of an SI exhibition that was to have taken place at the Stedelijk Museum in Amsterdam in 1959 in "Die Welt Als Labyrinth," *Internationale Situationniste* #4 (June 1960) 5–7.
10. See Guy Debord, "Theory of the Dérive," (1958). We prefer the term "terrain" in this case to Knabb's use of the word "space."

11. Ivan Chtcheglov, "Letters from Afar," *Internationale Situationniste* #9 (1964) cited by Knabb in an editor's note (in Knabb 1995: 373).

12. See Thomas F. McDonough, "Situationist Space," (1994). See also Michel de Certeau, *The Practice of Everday Life*, (1984).

13. According to della Porta and Diani (2006: 165), protests represent "nonroutinized ways of affecting political, social, and cultural processes."

14. See http://manifencours.diametrick.com.

15. See Kotányi, "Gangland and Philosophy," (1995).

16. The failure to pursue the social strike is described in detail by Frappier et al., *Le printemps des carrés rouges*.

17. See "Nous sommes avenir: Manifeste de la CLASSE," July 2012, available at http://issuu.com/asse.solidarite/docs/manifeste_classe/3, also available in English as "The CLASSE Manifesto: Share Our Future," *rabble.ca* (July 12, 2012), available at http://rabble.ca/blogs/bloggers/campus-notes/2012/07/classe-manifesto-share-our-future.

18. See David Harvey, *The Enigma of Capital* (2010: 253–59). For an analysis of social movements in Quebec, see Francis Dupuis-Déri (ed.) *Québec en mouvements. Idées et pratiques militantes contemporaines* (2008).

19. "The Beginning of an Era" (in Knabb 1995: 225–56; originally from *Internationale Situationniste* #12 (September 1969). On the contributions of the Situationists to the events of May 1968, see René Viénet, *Enragés et situationnistes dans le movement étudiant* (1968).

20. Žižek, "Class Struggle or Postmodernism? Yes Please!" in Butler, Laclau and Žižek (2000: 98–99). See also Laclau and Mouffe, *Hegemony and Socialist Strategy: Towards a Radical Democratic Practice* (1985).

BIBLIOGRAPHY

Bolt Rasmussen, Mikkel (2004), "The Situationist International, Surrealism, and the Difficult Fusion of Art and Politics," *Oxford Art Journal*, 27: 3, pp. 365–87.

Certeau, Michel de (1984), *The Practice of Everyday Life* (trans. Steven Rendall), Berkeley: University of California Press.

Chtcheglov, Ivan (1964), "Letters from Afar," *Internationale Situationniste* #9, pp. 38–40.

———. (1995 [1953]), "Formula for a New Urbanism," in *Situationist International Anthology*, K. Knabb, (ed.), Berkeley: Bureau of Public Secrets, pp. 1–4.

Coverley, Merlin (2006), *Psychogeography*, Harpenden, Herts, UK : Pocket Essentials.

Day, Richard (2004), "From Hegemony to Affinity: The Political Logic of the Newest Social Movements," *Cultural Studies*, 18: 5, pp. 716–48.

Debord, Guy (1995 [1955]), "Introduction to a Critique of Urban Geography," in *Situationist International Anthology*, K. Knabb, (ed.), Berkeley: Bureau of Public Secrets, pp. 5–8.

———. (1995 [1956]), "Methods of Détournement," in *Situationist International Anthology*, K. Knabb, (ed.), Berkeley: Bureau of Public Secrets, pp. 8–14.

———. (1995 [1957]) "Report on the Construction of Situations and on the International Situationist Tendency's Conditions of Organization and Action," in *Situationist International Anthology*, K. Knabb, (ed.), Berkeley: Bureau of Public Secrets, pp. 17–25.

———. (1995 [1958a]), "Preliminary Problems in Constructing a Situation," in *Situationist International Anthology*, K. Knabb, (ed.), Berkeley: Bureau of Public Secrets, pp. 43–45.

———. (1995 [1958b]), "Theory of the Dérive," in *Situationist International Anthology*, K. Knabb, (ed.), Berkeley: Bureau of Public Secrets, pp. 50–54.

"Die Welt Als Labyrinth" (1960), *Internationale Situationniste* #4 (June), pp. 5–7.

Dupuis-Déri, Francis (ed.) (2008), *Québec en mouvements. Idées et pratiques militantes contemporaines,* Montréal: Lux.

Dutrisac, Robert and Lisa-Marie Gervais (2013), "Le Sommet sur l'enseignement supérieur—Désaccord persistant sur les droits de scolarité, 'Essayons de réfléchir au fait qu'il faut sortir de ce psychodrame', dit Pauline Marois," *Le Devoir* (February 26), Accessed 24 October 2013. http://www.ledevoir.com/politique/quebec/371878/desaccord-persistant-sur-les-droits-de- scolarite.

Frappier, André, Richard Poulin and Bernard Rioux (2012), *Le printemps des carrés rouges: Lutte étudiante, crise sociale, loi liberticide, démocratie de la rue*, Montréal: M éditeur.

Graeber, David (2013), *The Democracy Project: A History, A Crisis, A Movement*, New York: Spiegel and Grau.

Harvey, David (2010), *The Enigma of Capital*, Oxford: Oxford University Press.

———. (2012), *Rebel Cities: From the Right to the City to the Urban Revolution*, London: Verso.

Hess, Rémi (1988), *Henri Lefebvre et l'aventure du siècle*, Paris: A.M.Métailié.

Highmore, Ben (2002), *Everyday Life and Cultural Theory: An Introduction*, London: Routledge.

Khatib, Abdelhafid (1958), "Essai de description psychogéographique des Halles," *Internationale Situationniste* #2 (December), pp. 13–17.

K. Knabb, (ed.), (1995 [1969]), "The Beginning of an Era," in *Situationist International Anthology*, Berkeley: Bureau of Public Secrets, pp. 225–56.

Kotányi, Attila (1995 [1960]), "Gangland and Philosophy," in *Situationist International Anthology*, K. Knabb, (ed.), Berkeley: Bureau of Public Secrets, p. 59.

Kotányi, Attila and Raoul Vaneigem (1995), "Elementary Program of the Bureau of Unitary Urbanism," in *Situationist International Anthology*, K. Knabb, (ed.), Berkeley: Bureau of Public Secrets, pp. 65–67.

Laclau, Ernesto and Chantal Mouffe (1985), *Hegemony and Socialist Strategy: Towards a Radical Democratic Practice*, London: Verso.

Lefebvre, Henri (1975), *Le Temps des méprises*, Paris: Editions Stock.

———. (1991 [1947, 1958]), *Critique of Everyday Life,* Vol.1 (trans. John Moore), London: Verso.

Lewis, Avi (2006), "Students of the World Unite: Nothing to Lose but Everything," lecture presented at the University of Lethbridge, February 14.

Marshall, Andrew Gavin (2012), "Student Strikes, Debt Domination, and Class War in Canada," *Andrewgavinmarshall Blog* (April 17), Accessed 24 October 2013. http://andrewgavin-marshall.com/2012/04/17/student-strikes-debt-domination-and-class- war-in-canada-class-war-and-the-college-crisis-part-4/.

McDonough, Tom (1994), "Situationist Space," *October*, 67 (Winter), pp. 59–77.

———. (2002), "Introduction: Ideology and the Situationist Utopia," in *Guy Debord and the Situationist International*, T. McDonough (ed.), Cambridge: The MIT Press.

della Porta, Donatella and Mario Diani (eds.) (2006), *Social Movements: An Introduction*, Second ed., Oxford: Blackwell.

Serbulo, Leanne (2012), "This is Not a Riot: Minimization, Criminalization and the Policing of Protest in Seattle Prior to the 1999 WTO Shut-Down," in *Protest and Punishment: The Repression of Resistance in the Era of Neoliberal Globalization*, Jeff Shantz (ed.), Durham, NC: Carolina Academic Press.

Sorochan, Cayley (2012), "The Quebec Student Strike: A Chronology," *Theory and Event*, 15: 3, special supplement (Summer), Accessed 24 October 2013. http://muse.jhu.edu/login?auth=0&type=summary&url=/journals/theory_and_event/v015/15.3S.sorochan.html

Viénet, René (1968), *Enragés et situationnistes dans le movement étudiant*, Paris: Gallimard.

Yalnizyan, Armine (2010), "The Rise of Canada's Richest 1%," *Canadian Centre for Policy Alternatives* (December 1), Accessed 24 October 2013. http://www.policyalternatives.ca/publications/reports/rise-canadas-richest-1.

Žižek, Slavoj (2000), "Class Struggle or Postmodernism? Yes please!," in *Contingency, Hegemony, Universality: Contemporary Dialogues on the Left*, Judith Butler, Ernesto Laclau and Slavoj Žižek, London: Verso, pp. 90–135.

Chapter Six

The *Huelga de Dolores* and Guatemalan University Students' "Happy and Wicked" Reproduction of Space, 1966–1969

Heather A. Vrana

Dressed in camouflage, jungle boots, and an army-green beret, University of San Carlos (USAC) philosophy student Juan Luis Molina Loza transformed into the legendary Che Guevara.[1] In his enactment of the life, passion, and death of the recently-assassinated Che, Molina Loza carried a heavy wooden cross through Guatemala's commercial center, Sixth Avenue (*La Sexta*). Carved on the cross were the phrases "the Latin American Revolution" and "Latin America." In 1969, as Molina Loza walked as El Che, other students marched with placards that declared governmental corruption, depicting President Colonel Alfredo Enrique Peralta Azurdia in a number of compromising positions that mimicked his submission to international business, the United States, and the military.

Molina Loza's walk to Calvary was not an ordinary protest. It was part of a venerable and distinctly Guatemalan university tradition called the *Huelga de Dolores* ("Strike of Sorrows"). But neither strike nor sorrowful, this annual event most resembled carnival and included a costume parade, a theatrical revue, a newspaper called the *No Nos Tientes* (literally, "Do Not Tempt Us"), and various ludic bulletins. It was a hybrid of religious procession and political manifestation. The words of the students" hymn for the occasion, "*La Chalana*," capture this fusion well: "Laugh at the clergy, laugh at the military pigs. . . . Homeland, ancient word, so long exploited. . . . Today our homeland is an old woman, discredited, not worth fifty cents in this nation of traitors. Students—in sonorous loud laughter beat them down—Ha, ha!"[2]

The Huelga took advantage of the venerable tradition to lob political critiques at the nation's most powerful institutions, but always with a twisted smile.

The 1969 *Huelga* coincided with a brief pause in the government repression and the forced disappearances that had besieged the nation for a decade. In 1954, a counterrevolutionary coup led by Carlos Castillo Armas and aided by the U.S. State Department had overthrown democratically-elected President Jacobo Arbenz. Since the counterrevolution, the people of Guatemala endured a series of military presidents and the progressive restriction of their civic freedoms. This gradual repression was punctuated by dramatic flashpoints of violence between the so-called popular sectors—including university and high school students, labor unions, and some neighborhood organizations—and the military, paramilitary, and police forces that protected the interests of U.S. businesses and the powerful agricultural export federation Committee of Agriculture, Culture, Industrial, and Financial Institutions(CACIF). Between 1954 and the mid-1960s, the Constitution of the Republic was rewritten twice, states of exception were frequent, and disappearances and assassinations were increasingly common.

Yet the government rarely cancelled the *desfile* during these years. On the contrary, various government ministers defended the raucous event, affirming that the students (who called themselves *San Carlistas*) were simply blowing off steam. It was not a difficult argument to make, as some of the Huelga's most important activities included drinking, cross-dressing, discharging fireworks, and congregating to share delicious meals, participate in outrageous recitations, and enact satirical theater productions. Further, all elder statesmen were USAC alumni, and since the event had occurred annually since 1898, most government officials fondly remembered participating in some form or another. For instance, in 1956, San Carlos alum and former Secretary of Congress Mario Alvarado Rubio issued a passionate defense of the Huelga. He wrote, "There is no way that the students are going to stop being happy and wicked; and it would be evil for us to ask seriousness of them, when we still spend time yearning for those happy years of irresponsibility before economic and familial problems, for those years—a lot of years—during which we were the despair of professors and deans."[3] This sense of legacy was pervasive.

From the university's foundation in 1676 to the early twentieth century, USAC students constituted a privileged group. Intellectual elites such as congressmen, lawyers, doctors, editors, and engineers—a small group, and all of them San Carlistas—had tremendous power over the rest of Guatemalan civil society. As men of letters with access to editorial boards and publishing companies, these San Carlistas wrote newspaper editorials, paid political advertisements, commercial advertisements, memoirs, and scholarly monographs that circulated readily throughout Guatemala City and the countryside. In the mid-twentieth century, national economic reforms and the post-World War II economic boom enabled many Guatemalans to acquire unprecedented wealth. Suddenly, university attendance was possible for sons of small business owners, managers, and professionals. Yet even as university enrollment surged, higher education remained beyond the reach of many Guatemalans.[4]

Attendance at USAC came to define the Guatemalan middle class through encounters between students, the university, and the Guatemalan government. In these decades, the university played a determinant role in Guatemala's long process of state-making. With the 1944 Revolution against dictator Jorge Ubico, San Carlistas emerged as architects of the government. Young students like Manuel Galich would serve as congressmen in the morning, and then rush off to class in the afternoon. But the 1954 counterrevolution and subsequent civil war turned the university's vanguard social, political, and cultural role into a liability—a real risk.

Growing antagonism toward the counterrevolutionary government and the exceptional violence of the civil war came to cast San Carlistas as *contra*-state actors. USAC campus became a battleground in a national revolution, international counterrevolution, the Cold War, and a civil war that would linger for more than three decades (Vrana 2013). Year after year, regardless of the political climate, students from USAC romped through city streets, restless and defiant of the order of the day. By 1969, the order of the day was electoral fraud, military government, and restricted civil liberties.[5]

On March 6th, 1966, Julio César Méndez Montenegro won the general presidential election and put an end to the long line of military presidents dating from the 1954 counterrevolution.[6] Despite formidable opponents on the right that included the incumbent Institutional Democratic Party (PID, whose name was misleading) and the military's National Liberation Movement (MLN), Méndez Montenegro won the presidency. San Carlos students, labor organizers, and other neighborhood leaders believed they were witnessing a new dawn (Levenson 1994: 39, 41; Editorial [2] 1966). Méndez Montenegro even campaigned as the "Third Government of the [1944] Revolution." Nevertheless, before long, it became common knowledge that Méndez Montenegro had signed a deal that guaranteed military immunity to federal prosecution and retained a certain number of formal and informal advisory seats for officers. At first an emblem of democratic promise, Méndez Montenegro's administration brought the institutionalization of the civil war, expansion of military power and paramilitary death squads, and growing disappearances and assassinations. Political consensus was hard to come by, as the government and right-wing paramilitary squads circumscribed free debate and public protest.

University students and professors continued to engage with national and international political questions using a variety of strategies, including protests and strikes, discussion groups, and paid political advertisements, but these methods became increasingly risky. Consequently, seemingly apolitical or "cultural" publications, programs, and events, including the Huelga de Dolores, were high-stakes affairs. For both USAC students who were long involved in resistance to the chain of military presidents and those who were less political, the Huelga became a crucial moment in which to voice anti-government critique without too much risk of violent response. Thus, when Molina Loza-as-Che Guevara carried the cross of the Latin American Revolution, he mourned not only the death of Guevara in 1967 at the hands of U.S.-trained Bolivian soldiers, but also the loss of democratic promise. He foreshadowed students" martyrdom on sidewalks and street corners. He memorialized hopelessness and disappointment.

Just nine months earlier, French Marxist Henri Lefebvre had spoken of the revolutionary "moment"—rupture, pure possibility, and euphoria—to thousands of Parisian students from his lectern at the University of Paris X-Nanterre. The gathered students were in the midst of the legendary university movement against the government of Charles de Gaulle. As dissent grew and spread on campus, Lefebvre's "moment" seemed nigh. In fact, Lefebvre was as inspired by the student movement as the student activists who crowded into his lectures. Uniting his earlier work, his contentious engagement with the Situationists, and his observations of the May 1968 protests, Lefebvre formulated an analysis of spatial production, reproduction, and possibilities of a revolutionary spatial practice that appeared in the publication *La production de l'espace* in 1974.[7]

Building on his other works, such as *The Right to the City* (1968), *The Explosion* (1969), and *The Urban Revolution* (1970), in *Production,* Lefebvre confirmed that space was constructed to suit state power. "On the backs of the old cities" a new spatial superstructure was built that codified relations of power between social sectors (1991 [1974]: 47). The new spatial code represented the rise of the centralized state and, even more, the city's architecture and landscape disciplined its citizens. At the same time, Lefebvre argued that a spatial code served as more than a tool to read or interpret space. He argued that it could also serve as "a means of living in that space, of understanding it, and of producing it"; it is a collection of "verbal" and "non-verbal" signs. Lexicons and grammars joined music, sounds, and architecture in shaping the city (1991 [1974]: 47–48). In other words, spatial practices reframed the façades and perspectives of capitalist modernity in relation to what he called representations of space and spaces of representation, in urban settings.

Lefebvre's central subject was spatial practice sparked by the indelible mark of the crisis of modernity, which Lefebvre wrote of in terms of a "shattered" space:

The fact is that around 1910 a certain space was shattered. It was the space of
common sense, of knowledge (*savoir*), of social practice, of political power, a
space hitherto enshrined in everyday discourse. . . . This was truly a crucial
moment. (1991 [1974]: 25)

Lefebvre referred to his readers as "witnesses" of the consolidation of the
state on a global scale, including the state's regimes of rationality and alongside the rise of the nation-state. Where before Lefebvre's insistence on the
propitiousness of a "moment" referred to the student movements of 1968,
here the "moment" was modernity itself.

In Guatemala, modernity arrived in much the same moment, between the
late 1880s and 1920s (Grandin 2000; Way 2012; Woodward and Lee 1993;
Martínez Peláez 2009). Two Liberal presidents who ruled as oligarchs, José
María Reina Barrios (1892–1898) and Manuel Estrada Cabrera (1898–1920),
promoted a platform of national stability, progress, and civilization. Exports
such as cochineal, cotton, cattle, sugarcane, and coffee fueled Guatemala's
economy under the managerial aegis of European immigrants, especially
Germans, who brought foreign capital and business models. North American
capital investment soon followed.

Elite Guatemalans built their city on profits from primitive accumulation
in the image of a Paris of the Tropics. Electric and telegram lines and paved
roads crisscrossed the city. Under Estrada Cabrera, the Guatemalan modernizing project took the form of massive building campaigns, including grandi-
ose temples to Minerva the goddess of knowledge, theaters, and grand pla-
zas. Recursively, these expensive building projects, which were financed by
capital accumulated in a worldwide boom in coffee prices, cultivated an
image of prosperity and success, which in turn made the nation seem more
worthy of expanded European and North American investment. The downtown blocks near Central Park on Sixth Avenue became the locus of commerce in the city. There, Guatemalans from various classes frequently
crossed paths, as wealthy families, professionals, and small businessmen
lived and worked alongside one another and amidst a much larger class of
domestic and manual laborers. In opposition to the progressive, forward-
thinking, efficient use of space that capitalist modernity required, San Carlistas staged the Huelga de Dolores parade (*desfile*) on the same city blocks.
Yet these San Carlista contestations were not about the *right* to occupy space,
unlike other land rights and squatter settlement practices that are well-studied
in Latin American history. Students wasted time and wasted space as the
parade disrupted commerce and created an eyesore amidst the most prized
and spectacular spaces in urban Guatemala (Vrana 2012).

It is especially interesting to read the *desfile* of the Huelga de Dolores
alongside the spatial theorization of Lefebvre because he and the San Carlistas of the 1960s were also contemporaries in a global surge of protest move-

ments; but more interestingly, because San Carlista spatial practice differs from Lefebvre in ways that are suggestive of temporal possibilities of protest and popular memory. The students" Huelga parade and political funerals were not practices of the "right to the city." Instead, these events were challenges to representations of space, articulated by students through bold anti-imperialist claims and an unusual temporality. Lefebvre's project was to "detonate" common sense—"to foster confrontation between those ideas and propositions which illuminate the modern world even if they do not govern it, treating them not as isolated theses or hypotheses, as "thoughts" to be put under the microscope, but rather as prefigurations lying at the threshold of modernity" (Lefebvre 1991 [1974]: 24). But San Carlistas, so "happy and wicked" during the Huelga, staged this confrontation as a contentious reproduction of space. They began with long histories that contextualized student dissent within the injustices of Guatemalan governments and understood the people's salvation to be in the hands of the righteous, rebellious students.

A. *"¡NOSOTROS LOS ESTUDIANTES, TAMBIEN SEGUIMOS SIENDO LOS MISMOS!"* ("WE THE STUDENTS, ALSO CONTINUE TO BE THE SAME!")

In anticipation of the 1956 Huelga, a student journalist from the school newspaper *Informador Estudiantil* penned a long history of the event, emphasizing its relationship to the government and the police. The journalist wrote that the Huelga began in 1898 under the tyranny of Liberal dictator Estrada Cabrera (1898–1920), when it served as an opportunity for elite and ambitious students to challenge the personalist politics that limited their future prospects. He characterized these years in the following way:

> *Siempre fuerza se ha opuesto a ella: en 1903 la policía mata a un estudiante; en 1906 se cierra la Escuela de Medicina, y la tiene que hacer en la calle; en 1913 policías militares entran al Instituto y Escuela del Derecho, hay heridos, presos y expulsados; en 1917 la policía llega también a la Escuela de Medicina, hay expulsados también.* [The powerful have always been opposed to (the Huelga): in 1903, the police killed one student; in 1906, they closed the School of Medicine and (the Huelga) had to be held in the street; in 1914, the military police entered the Institute and the School of Law, there were injuries, imprisonment, and expulsions; in 1917, the police also entered the School of Medicine and there were expulsions (then), too.] ("Biografía sintética" 1956: 1)

From the beginning, the Huelga involved the presentation of a decree or bulletin that critiqued the government's actions over the previous year, to the sounds of marimba and firecrackers, and plenty of beer. After the first few years, businesses realized the opportunity for profit and loaned cars to the students for the construction of elaborate parade floats. Similarly, the wealthy Castillo family, manufacturers of Gallo beer, donated kegs to the students. Students donned costumes and carried painted placards that defamed the president. After the 1920 coup that overthrew Estrada Cabrera, the Huelga de Dolores expanded. These were fecund years for Guatemalan literature and art. In 1926, the *desfile* became a real public spectacle and large crowds of capital city residents gathered to view the students" costumes, floats, and placards (Barrios y Barrios 1999: 57). This creative florescence ended in 1931 with the presidency of liberal dictator Jorge Ubico, who went to such extremes as to change the university class schedule in order to prevent the Huelga's occurrence.

But even after the 1944 Revolution, in which USAC students played a leading role, the Huelga retained its anti-government attitude. For instance, in 1945 a student named Warner Ovalle stood below President Arévalo's balcony at the National Palace and drunkenly proclaimed, "Hail, oh great *Chilacayote*, from the garden of righteous pride" ("Biografía sintética" 1956: 1).[8] Then a trumpet proudly sounded. As the student journalist for *Informador* wrote in 1956, the Huelga had always been and would always be anti-government. He wrote, *"Se hizo mofa de todo y de todos; en lo social, de la aristocracia, en lo político de todos los de arriba y en lo religioso desde la Virgente* (sic) *Santísima hasta el Espíritu Santo, pasando por toda la Corte Celestial, fue un alarde de irreligiosidad"* ("It made fun of everything and everyone; socially, of the aristocracy; politically, of all of those on top; and religiously from the Virgin Mary to the Holy Spirit, including the entire Celestial Court, it was a display of impiety") ("Biografía sintética" 1956: 1). Arévalo's successor, Jacobo Arbenz, fared little better in the hands of the irreverent students.

After the 1954 counterrevolution, anti-communists and supporters of the revolutionary presidents vied for control of student politics; meanwhile, the new president Carlos Castillo Armas maneuvered to exercise influence over USAC. As a result, the Huelga continued, but the press rarely commented on the events as it had during the Ten Years' Spring. Many newspaper editors after the coup were reluctant to critique Armas, some because they feared reprisals and others because they were steadfast supporters of the coup. Armas" government provided a fertile context for the expansion of the power of Guatemala's traditional and conservative sectors: foreign business, the military, and the Catholic Church. These sectors were obvious targets of student *huelgueros*' rancor; naturally, these conservative sectors also detested the students. In 1956 and again in 1962, the Archbishop of the Catholic Church of Guatemala, Mariano Rosell y Arellano, excommunicated students who participated in the event.

President Armas was assassinated in 1957 in circumstances that have remained opaque. The following year, Miguel Ydígoras Fuentes (1958–1963) was elected with broad support from university students and professors, and capital city professionals. Students were involved in campaigning for Ydígoras and eagerly met with him (and his wife) at the beginning of his term in office. They were quickly disappointed. The new president was less inclined to hear the requests of students than to make meetings simply to maintain the peace. Fed up, students led two months of urban protests in March and April 1962. The streets of Guatemala City became a battleground. The first volleys were fired in a civil war that would last for more than three decades.

During the civil war, Huelga events were important spaces for social dissent. Direct violence against students during the Huelga was discouraged, as most citizens understood it to be a civic and cultural tradition. Opposition was certainly common, but it usually came in the form of pastoral letters to the public or letters to the editor (Vrana 2012, 2013; Kobrak 1999; Alvarez Aragón 2002). The week around the Huelga de Dolores became a temporary political and social opening, one that USAC students and the public seized. In this repetitive, ongoing, but singular time, San Carlos students remade the social topography of urban Guatemala City.[9] They marked sites where protest, play, and empathetic memory could come together to form a volatile union. The San Carlistas" language of struggle was by turns diffuse, ambivalent, and tongue-in-cheek, then earnest and even fundamentalist. Their calls to action relied less on puns, satire, and turns of phrase, and more on nonlinear temporality, dignity, and authenticity.

By the mid-1960s, San Carlista ontologies were shaped by an agonistic relationship to the government of the Republic of Guatemala and a tutorial role toward the rest of Guatemala. The inspiring earnestness of the *No Nos Tientes* editorial in 1966 marked the change in student affect during the Ydígoras presidency. The depth of this change was best captured in its opening lines:

> *Pueblo querido de Guatemala: en este Viernes de todos los Dolores, del año en Desgracia de 1966, la Voz del Estudiante Universitario—de ese estudiante de la Universidad Autónoma de San Carlos, que se debe y se muere por vos—, en esta ocasión además de un puñado de jacarandosa alegría viene a ofrecerte un RECORDATORIO, que no puedes en momento alguno relegar al Olvido: QUE LOS CHAFAROTES DE GUATEMALA, FUERON Y SIGUEN SIENDO LOS MISMOS!* [Beloved *pueblo* of Guatemala: on this Friday of Sorrows, of the tragic year of 1966, the Voice of the University Student—of that student of the Autonomous University of San Carlos, that relies upon and dies for you—, on this occasion in addition to a handful of spirited joyousness [the Voice of the University Student] comes to offer you a REMINDER that you cannot for one single minute relegate to Obscurity: THAT THE *CHAFAROTES* OF GUATEMALA WERE AND CONTINUE TO BE THE SAME!] (Editorial [1] 1966: 9)

The remainder of the editorial was a play on a classic USAC student polemic, entitled *"Somos los mismos"* ("We are still the same"), written in 1922, and circulated in 1944, 1955, and then again in 1966. As in the 1956 *Informador Estudiantil* editorial discussed above, the students wrote that they would "do a little history" and demonstrate how the status quo had been preserved throughout Guatemala's history. The popular text detailed the ongoing and historic struggle of students against tyranny. It also affirmed what students referred to as a political obligation to fight the *chafarotes* who wished to "screw over the *pueblo*" (Editorial [1] 1966: 9).

The students wrote that the *chafarotes* remained the same *"que tanto durante el Tiempo en que fuimos Colonia de España como durante el Tiempo en que venimos siendo Colonia de los Estados Unidos"* ("from the time when [they] were a Colony of Spain, to the time when [they] became a Colony of the United States"). *Chafarotes* were, in the students" words, "a caste of the insatiable "new rich"," who would *"reniegan de su origen humilde para convertirse en choleros de la Oligarquía criollo, aliados de la Clerecía reaccionaria y marionetas del Imperialismo, para todos juntos ahogar su Soberanía y asfixiarte"* ("deny their humble origins in order to become the foot soldiers of the creole Oligarchy, allied with the reactionary Clergy and marionettes of Imperialism, willing to drown and asphyxiate their Sovereignty"). Against the *chafarotes* stood the students: *"Siguen pues, siendo los mismos . . . pero también Nosotros . . . ¡NOSOTROS LOS ESTUDIANTES, TAMBIEN SEGUIMOS SIENDO LOS MISMOS!"* ("They continue being the same . . . but We . . . WE THE STUDENTS, ALSO CONTINUE TO BE THE SAME!") (Editorial [1] 1966: 9).

And so students drew the battle lines: the duplicitous *chafarotes* against the authentic, dignified students. The students were the same as those who defeated the Cabrera and Ubico dictatorships, and who opposed the traitorous counterrevolutionary, Armas. These students were the same as those who "gave a tribute of youthful blood" in street protests that erupted in June 1956 and March and April 1962. These students were the same as those who led *"la resistencia al ydigorismo corrompido, en Marzo y Abril de 1962, con otro tributo de sangre joven, que ensucia las manos de chafarotes 'absueltos '"* ("the resistance against the corrupt Ydígoras government in March and April 1962, with another tribute of young blood that dirtied the hands of the 'pardoned' *chafarotes*") (Editorial [1] 1966: 9).

B. THE HUEGLA DE DOLORES AS ANTI-COLONIAL ANGER

In fact, the streets where students paid blood tribute were the very same as those covered by the Huelga parade. Except in rare years when it was forbidden to leave the classroom buildings, the parade always departed the old

School of Medicine, continued past Central Park and in front of the National Palace, down Sixth Avenue, through the main streets of the historical center, and ended at the Law School. Students built on older histories and meanings of Sixth Avenue, at the same time as this route accrued meaning in the San Carlistas" geography of the city through the repetition of the annual parade. For instance, the parade passed the offices of the hydroelectric company (which would merged with General Electric's Electric Bond and Share Company in 1968), a commercial center owned by the very wealthy and influential Aycinena family, and the offices of various national companies, as well as popular hotels and lunch counters owned by Jewish, German, and Chinese immigrant entrepreneurs.

By staging the Huelga in and around these spaces, students confirmed Guatemala's national commercial history. They also linked this history to the contemporary problem of economic development. In 1966, the *No Nos Tientes* masthead depicted two prisoners, hooded, tortured, and assassinated; one torture manual; one military cap with the words "Dictatorship Made in the USA" printed in English across the front; two protesting students with big banners; one smoking Molotov cocktail; and Lady Liberty, chained, bound, and stabbed by a dagger, the emblem of the official MLN party. Drawn by law student and student leader Mario López Larrave, the masthead was always provocative, but this year it set the tone for the rest of the paper: the authentic students were engaged in a battle for Guatemala against tyranny directed from abroad.

Unlike previous editions of the newspaper, the 1966 *No Nos* had little room for jokes, instead preferring strong indictments of the Alliance for Progress and the Interamerican Development Bank (IDB) and other intrusions of foreign governments within the university. A terrifying cartoon of the Statue of Liberty accompanied a long history of the Alliance for Progress in Guatemala and elsewhere in Central America. Lady Liberty held aloft one missile instead of the torch of liberty, one automatic pistol instead of the book of law, and donned combat boots, a mask, and a shoulder-holstered scabbard. The editorial argued that intellectual freedom and the free exchange of ideas were necessary for the progress of scientific and cultural knowledge, but they also articulated a nationalist critique of foreign knowledge. They argued that intervention and direct interference in the educational and pedagogical plans of a nation had dire consequences for both ideological freedom and the free development of culture.

Importantly, San Carlistas" insurgent spatial practices were consciously and distinctly *Guatemalan* spatial practices. They formed in response to the particular to the context of the late 1960s, when government-sponsored kidnappings and forced disappearances increased. But they also responded to scholarly debates on development theory that circulated at Latin American universities.[10] Innovative scholarship in these years took a dependency rather than modernization theory approach. Many USAC professors taught that distinctly Guatemalan innovations and technology were crucial to national economic and social advancement. Latin American structuralists such as Raúl Prebisch and Celso Furtado, and American Marxists Paul A. Baran and Paul Sweezy, and later, Andre Günder Frank, guided classroom discussions of core/periphery, accumulation, and progress (Vrana 2013). Students were animated by the differences between these thinkers and organized frequent discussion groups and roundtables. Many students wrote theses on dependency theory. The majority of San Carlos students were critical of the role of U.S. imperialism in their nation's ongoing poverty, and they combined dependency theory with earlier ideals from the 1945 revolutionary constitution in their critiques (Letter 1966).

Along with their critiques of the U.S., San Carlistas participated in a wave of Latin American art and music that celebrated natural resources, martyrs, the glory of Guatemala, and anti-Americanism ("Canto y llanto" 1966). The figure of indigenous leader Tecun Uman was especially celebrated. Uman was the last indigenous king of the K'iche' Maya and symbol of resistance to colonialism and imperialism. In 1960, the Guatemalan government declared Uman to be a national hero. That year, the Huelga's entrance ticket (*tarjeta*) featured cartoon and short poem, a nearly nonsensical mash-up of origin myths starring Uman alongside Roman emperor Nero, Plato, and the god Mercury, as well as Uncle Sam.[11] In the image, Plato's belly bulges, while his legs are thin and weak; he holds a lyre and wears a crown of laurels; by contrast, Tecun Uman wears only a loincloth over his trim and toned muscled body. On his head is a traditional Mayan ceremonial headdress. He holds a spiked club in his right hand, suggestive of his legendary battle with conquistador Don Pedro de Alvarado. Plato and Uman share a tray of bananas while Uncle Sam looks on.

The short poem makes explicit the homoeroticism and sexual economy suggested in the image above, through references to Plato's same-sex desires and the circulation of ideal indigenous bodies in the form of the muscled body of Uman. The poem begins with a corpulent Nero arranging the sale of Uman to Uncle Sam: "*Desde este gran almohadón en que asentara su pan*" ("From this huge cushion on which sits his *pan*"). But then Uman revolts: "*y al ver tal proposición, 'huevos!' le dijo Tecún*" ("And upon seeing such a proposition, / Tecún told him, 'To hell with that!'") (Tarjeta 1966). *Pan*, Spanish for bread, can signify money; but *pan* is also the first syllable of the word *panza*, meaning belly or paunch, and youth slang often involved excising a syllable from common words. Thus, selling bodies like bread, the sexual economy critiqued in the sonnet was specifically about the selling of the meat of the nation to the United States.[12] Yet, Uman's cry of resistance, "*huevos*," was another common word in student slang. With the student's cry, Uman refuses his sale.

San Carlistas also created a cartoon figure named Juan Tecú as a foil for the heroic Tecun Uman. Tecú, unlike Uman, was childish, illiterate, and scrappy. At the same time, he represented a bold threat to the government as a regular feature of the weekly student newspaper *El Estudiante*. From the late 1950s into the 1980s, Tecú ridiculed the nation's most powerful in a column called "Juan Tecú's Slingshots." The 1966 *No Nos Tientes* included a half-page image of Tecú, chasing conservative presidential candidates Juan de Dios Aguilar de Leon (PID) and Miguel Angel Ponciano (MLN), and President Miguel Ydígoras Fuentes, shouting, "*A la mierda chafarotes!*" ("Go to hell, chafarotes!") The caption reads, "*¡Este es el pequeño, el mediano, y el gran deseo de toda Guatemala!*" ("This is the small, medium, and large desire of all of Guatemala!"). The politicians perspire and grimace as they run. Money falls from President Ydígoras Fuentes' pockets. Tecú holds a broken chain in one hand and with the other, he discards a ballot marked March 6, 1966.

As the year progressed and the national political climate declined, student artists used Tecú to manage more serious ambivalences (*El Estudiante* [1] 1966: 1; CEH 1999). In October 1966, from his usual spot in the bottom right corner of the front page of *El Estudiante*, an angry Tecú defiantly confirmed, "*Al que me caiga mal, lo molesto al que me moleste, lo insulto; al que me insulte, le pego; al que me pegue, lo mato; y al que me mate, lo espanto*" ("Those who would rub me the wrong way, I will mess with; Those who would mess with me, I will insult; Those who would insult me, I will strike; Those who would strike me, I will kill; and Those who would kill me, I will frighten") (*El Estudiante* [2] 1966: 8).

Tecú was powerful as he assaulted the politicians, but his image captured some of the ambivalences of university students during the mid-1960s. In most instances, Tecú smiled grotesquely through a wiry moustache and enormous teeth. His clothes were ripped and patched, his hair was untamed, his feet were always bare, and he was drawn with a caricatured and stereotypical Mayan nose. San Carlistas were intellectual elites in a peripheral nation. They attended university in a nation where only 22 percent of Guatemalans had attended *any school whatsoever*, including primary grades by 1950 (Dirección General de Estadística 1957). National illiteracy was about 72.2 percent in 1950 and primary and secondary schools remained uncommon until the 1970s (*Sexto Censo General* 1957).[13] As educated, urban, and non-indigenous men, San Carlistas were quite unlike the majority of Guatemalans. Despite their anti-imperial celebrations of Tecún Uman and the natural beauty of Guatemala, and their rejection of North American intervention, San Carlistas reiterated the prejudices and stereotypes that cast indigenous citizens as dupes, illiterates, and uncivilized. In their use of Tecú, this was an asset as his unpolished candor attained value because it was "authentic." Tecú could "get away with" uttering bitter insults.

Yet their physical presence on Sixth Avenue prevented business as usual and unraveled regimes of common sense. And they did so with a spatial practice that was distinctly Guatemalan—a significant project of reproduction of space coming from Latin America, and even more, from a periphery within Latin America—that was contemporary to that of Lefebvre and Parisian students.[14] While it was true that many San Carlistas were training to become architects of the very facades, public buildings, and palaces, and regimes of power and prestige that they (and Lefebvre) criticized, as spatial theorists, they offered a counter-reading of the logics of the commercial space of Guatemala City, its usage, and its social construction.[15] Of course Lefebvre allowed for as much in his understanding of the "moment." But the temporary nature of San Carlista insurgent spatial practices, in tension with San Carlistas" narratives of historical legacy ("San Carlistas de siempre"), exceeds Lefebvre's spatial theorization.[16]

If a San Carlista's spatial rebellion, even wastefulness, was only fleeting, it relied upon rhetoric of timelessness—the eternal student, or *San Carlista de siempre*—for significance. The narratives of generation and the timelessness of the resistance describe and initiate "genealogies of affect" (Vrana 2013). An individual voice resonated with the voices of the other thousands of *San Carlistas de siempre*. The eternal student repetitively, cyclically, undermined the spatial logic of capitalism. Remember, for instance, the oft-reprinted 1922 *No Nos Tientes* editorial that proclaimed, "*Somos los mismos de entonces . . . . y ¿qué? . . . Nosotros no hemos variado. Nosotros somos siempre iguales. Ayer contra aquellos porque eran estúpidos ahora contra éstos porque son torpes. Y si como ayer, vamos a los calabozos de la secciones, estaremos muy contentos de poder gritar ¡Que distinto Más Pior!*" ("We are the same as before . . . and so what? We have not changed. We are always the same. Yesterday we opposed those [rulers] because they were stupid; now, we oppose these because they are senseless. And if, as then, we go to the dungeons, we will be very happy to scream: 'What a dreadful honor!'") (Editorial [3] 1955). The article established students' eternal duty to resist tyrannical leaders. If the students had not changed, then what, indeed, had?

Put simply, the revolution that Guatemalan university students struggled for in the 1960s would not merely change ideological superstructure—it would change the practices of space and of life itself. To mark this moment of watershed change, San Carlistas held a funeral for democracy in 1962 ("La Asociación de Estudiantes Universitarios al Pueblo de Guatemala . . . ," 12 April 1962; "Presidente de la AEU Tal Declara," 10 April 1962). Confronted with the violence of more and more kidnappings, disappearances, and assassinations at the hands of both the state and clandestine paramilitary groups, students argued that a real revolution required first a change in the notion of life: agentive death. Funerals as political tools disrupted the notion that the end of life meant the end of agency. In students" political funerals, death marked a transformational moment that required an adjustment in protest strategy. The Huelga parade formed a ludic counterpart to students" political funerals—a living space that increasingly referred to the spaces of the dead as the routes of political funerals and the Huelga parade coincided on Sixth Avenue.[17]

In the dual expression of funeral and Huelga, students demonstrated that changing the substance of life was a viable tool in their repertoire of contention. On the other hand, during the Huelga, students used the cover of historical legacy and the university's elite status to smooth over sharp political critiques and personal attacks with levity. The political funeral generated political agency in death and the ludic Huelga hid the student's anti-government offensive behind humor. This willing ruse characterized San Carlista spatial practice, moving San Carlista spatial practice beyond Lefebvre's "momentary" temporality and his insistence upon "lived" experience.

C. PUBLIC PERCEPTION OF THE
HUELGA PARADE AND SAN CARLISTAS

Lefebvre's project in *The Production of Space* was to demonstrate "how space serves, and how hegemony makes use of [a 'system' . . .] on the basis of an underlying logic and with the help of knowledge and technical expertise." From a Lefebvrian perspective, then, government repression of the *desfile* and the public's response demonstrated how effectively San Carlistas threatened hegemonic space (Lefebvre 1991 [1974]: 11).[18] In 1966, the government used several means to pressure students to cancel the parade. Instances of police harassment of students increased in the days approaching the event. Students who attempted to read the year's first bulletin over a loudspeaker were chased through the Elma apartment building near Central Park. Just off the main square, a group of *huelgueros* gathered on the balcony of the third floor of the Elma building and began to read the bulletin over a loudspeaker. The act was interrupted mere minutes later when a number of police patrol cars encircled the gathered crowd and issued citations for listening to the bulletin. The committee of *huelgueros* had announced and demonstrated by the reading that the Huelga would take to the streets, "like it or not." In this short battle between students and authorities, the students won. The police were unable to capture students and their loudspeakers because they simply hid on another floor of the Elma building ("Policía dispersa reunion estudiantil" 1966). Another newspaper reported that dozens of students were arrested. Regardless, the government's strong-armed position on the year's huelga and the students' refusal to comply were made clear.

All civic groups who wished to hold an event were required to file a Petition to Assemble before the event could be planned. This was usually a formality, but the week following the failed effort to read the first bulletin, the city government denied the student's permit application. In his summary of the decision to deny the petition, Colonel Ariel Rivera Siliezar said that the government had "well-founded reason to think that certain individuals want to take advantage of the good faith of university students in order to provoke disorder that would distort the light-hearted, incisive and ironic spirit of the tradition." These people would also endanger the lives of university students and the rest of the community. Students were encouraged to organize events indoors ("Huelga de Dolores . . . se sugiere a los estudiantes, 26 March 1966). Five days later, AEU president Gonzalo Yurrita complied. He announced that the traditional celebration would be held in public when times were better and when a regime that "permitted the lively expression of humor and critique of public functionaries again ruled" ("Huelga de Dolores se desarrollará este año en el ámbito universitario," 31 March 1966).

But Colonel Siliezar's denial of the protest petition also included the restriction of the publication of the *No Nos Tientes*. Unlike Yurrita, the *No Nos* editors did not comply. On April 1, police entered the AEU offices and arrested a number of AEU members, including the vice president, secretary, and treasurer. They were taken to the Second Squad, a police unit increasingly focused on counterinsurgency techniques. Police seized about two hundred copies of the *No Nos Tientes* ("Cateo en Casa de la AEU y Aprehendidos" 1 April 1966; AHPN 2011). The national press responded by carrying news of the search and arrests, but journalists were disinclined to level a more direct critique, lest their papers be confiscated.

As for on the left, the leadership of the Revolutionary Armed Forces (FAR) distrusted the university, even as most of its leadership were former San Carlistas. They wrote,

> *Todos sabemos (a no ser que lo hubiesen olvidado los estudiosos académicos), que estas instituciones pertenecen a la superestructura de una sociedad y que para poderlas cambiar hay que cortar de raíz los cimientos en donde se erigen tales instituciones. Para cambiar la mentalidad pequeño-burguesa de una capa o clase social, vamos a librar la lucha ideológica.* [Everyone knows (unless you have forgotten your academic studies), that these institutions are part of a social super-structure and that to be able to change them, one would have to cut them off at the root. To change the petty-bourgeois mentality of a caste or social class, we will wage an ideological war.] (FAR 1973: 4–5)

They argued that in this historical conjuncture, the university, like electoral politics, the judiciary, the military, and the cultural elite, promoted a heterogeneous ideological complex that could only enable each group's own selfish material aspirations. The FAR was skeptical of the democratic revolution of

the Ten Years' Spring, which had been many San Carlistas' finest achieve-
ment. They argued that ultimately, the revolution "guaranteed capitalist
rights, known as 'human rights'" and installed "the dictatorship of the bourgeoisie." The FAR elided Arévalo, Arbenz, Armas, and all of the other
presidents as part of a bourgeoisie who fought for capitalism, under the guise
that it could be made "just" and "modern" through "democracy, progress,
and popular welfare." For the FAR, bourgeois law, nationalism, oligarchy,
and international imperialism were entwined (FAR 1973: 17–19; FAR "Causa Proletaria"). Like San Carlistas who read development theory, the FAR
located the causes of Guatemala's "underdevelopment" in economic dependency and lack of self-determination. But the difference was that the FAR
understood the university to be irrevocably bourgeois and foreign. As national intellectual elites at the public university, San Carlistas occupied an uncertain position—possibly implicated in these repressive systems (Rolz Bennett
1978: 30).[19]

USAC students, especially those on the political left, understood this
tension. They were hesitant agents of developmental interpellation, involved
in a modernizing project, albeit through the creation of national knowledge
and attempted revision of relationships between the university and the *pueblo*. At times these fantasies and ideals seemed to confirm guerrillas" suspi-
cions that the university was inexorably bourgeois (Cuevas del Cid,
Hernández Sifontes, Beatriz de Cazali 1978). But they also reflected new
possibilities for the university and its students in national guerrilla and
worldwide intellectual networks. This was a difficult negotiation for San
Carlistas who were hard at work trying to think through a new relationship to
the periphery and questions of the university and representation (Asociación
de Estudiantes Universitarios: 5). San Carlistas" playful representations of
Guatemala vis-à-vis the United States, in parade floats, costumes, signs,
cartoons, and editorials, were part of their vexed reckoning with the guerrilla,
the university, the government, and even capitalism.

D. CONCLUSION

In the guise of an annual and historic event, San Carlistas took city planning
away from adults and placed it into the hands of student agronomists, economists, dentists, doctors, and engineers. These were students whose lives were
at risk in other moments, but who lived with abandon during the Huelga
parade. They understood that the superficially carefree parade was at once
traditional and insurgent, Guatemalan and global; it was both good fun and
deeply significant. Dressed as Che, student philosopher Molina Loza presented all of these seemingly contradictory characteristics. Not only was he the
reigning winner of the Huelga's Ugly King pageant, he was also the presi-

dent of the Philosophy Student Association, a student member of the Humanities governing body, and the president of USAC's first Humanities Congress. Molina Loza was also a member of the radical left student group CRATER and he joined with the New Revolutionary Combat Organization (NORC, which later became the Guerrilla Army of the Poor [EGP]) around 1970.

On January 13, 1971, Molina Loza and a handful of other students went missing. When they failed to appear for a few days, USAC students responded by going on strike. By the January 19, six *facultades* at USAC had joined the strike (Architecture, Pharmacy, Medicine, Humanities, Law, and Economics). Days later, policemen and soldiers encircled the Medicine *facultad* in an effort to squash student dissent. The striking students did not back down, but actually expanded their strike and sought support from the professional *colegios* and the national teacher's union ("Desaparece estudiante guatemalteco" February 1971). Meanwhile, Molina Loza's mother kept a vigil in Central Park, near where her son had paraded as "our Redeemer, El Che" less than two years earlier (Kobrak 1999: x; "Paros Docentes" 19 March 1971).

Molina Loza never reappeared. He remained a "happy and wicked" San Carlista "de siempre," who would go on fighting against tyranny as it beset the people of Guatemala. He was remembered as an Ugly King and a student martyr, in both life and death, reproducing the spatial and temporal practices of modern Guatemala City.

During the annual *desfile* of the Huelga de Dolores, students reproduced urban geography of Guatemala City at the same time as they launched broader contentions of the place of Guatemala City in the global distribution of labor. The spatial practices of the Huelga de Dolores—including the parade, but also the theatrical revue, newspaper, and bulletins—enacted new spatial imaginations of the urban space of Guatemala City in the world. The Huelga challenged the underlying logic of dependency theory and its transformation of the worldwide division of knowledge and labor. First, the proclaimed continuity between the past and present— "We are the same ones . . . " (*"somos los mismos"*)—challenged the forward march of modern capitalism. Second, the Huelga staged a distinctly Guatemalan spatial practice. It was similar to, but distinct from, carnival traditions found in Europe and Latin America. Importantly, the event's financial practices reflected dependency theory's call for national investment in knowledge-production and technology. Huelga funds came from the pockets of the Guatemalan government, small donations from a few individuals, and, mostly, from Guatemalan businesses. Even more, students took the opportunity of the cover of the annual farcical *desfile* to level increasingly aggressive critiques against the Guatemalan and U.S. governments. Their critiques often centered on presidents

and ministers who were willing to sell the nation, its people, and its resources, to the highest bidder.

Finally, and importantly, the parade was a wasteful spatial practice. It
aggravated commerce by interrupting the flow of traffic in the nation's most
important commercial area. Students" behavior—drinking, skipping class,
cross-dressing, and urinating in the streets—undermined narratives of national order and progress. Students" parade floats weakened fictions of political
cohesion and stability. As Molina Loza demonstrated, San Carlistas" insurgent spatial practices were alternately strategic and senseless, from membership in clandestine guerrilla organizations to simply parading as a martyred
Guevara.

For these characteristic spatial practices, the Huelga parade offers a
unique vantage point from which to expand Lefebvrian spatiality, as students
utilized space to agitate—and make fun of—the underlying logic of a system
from the urban periphery of Guatemala City. The spatial logics of the Huelga
and students" engagement with dependency theory did not permanently reshape the city's social space. Instead, students paired the ludic parade with
political funerals to disrupt—cyclically—the business of living through anti-
colonial anger toward the United States, and national elites, including the
military.

As unique temporal invocations of history and myth narratives of the
rural and urban, all of which intersected with protest strategies including
street manifestations and student-authored insurgent texts, student contestations of dependency theory offered an emergent theoretical frame with which
to understand spatial practices of global youth in the late 1960s. Taken together, these characteristics of spatial practices engaged the cultural and
political logics of dependency theory and its iteration in Cold War contexts
of circulation of knowledge and labor.

Ultimately, this chapter answers Lefebvre's call for scholarship that accounts for the "coming into being" and "disappearance," of spatial codes
(1991 [1974]: 17–18). But where Lefebvre looked for a singular moment,
San Carlistas agreed: *"somos los mismos."* We are the same . . . and with the
Huelga de Dolores, students created an insurgent spatial practice that joined
Guatemala's past, present, and future in a project *for* the people and *against*
imperialism.

NOTES

1. Thank you to Paolo Vignolo, Abel Sierra Madero, David Sartorius, David Kazanjian,
Pam Voekel, Bethany Moreton, Alex Dawson, and Lynn Morgan for very helpful comments on
an early version of this chapter at the Tepoztlán Institute for the Transnational History of the
Americas. Thank you to Benjamin Fraser for helpful comments in this chapter's later stages.
2. Translation by Greg Grandin. All other translations herein are by the author. A note on
the translation of *"seguir siendo los mismos"*: for the sake of readability in English, this has

been translated as "continue to be the same." Yet the meaning of the phrase is much closer to "continue being the same," which suggests that both the students and the *chafarotes* continue to be the same individuals, the same type of individuals, and—importantly—continue being (existing, living) in the same manner as their predecessors.

3. Years of accusations of graft and corruption created the necessity for strict regulations, and the selected members had to be: an active member in their respective student association and the AEU in the present and previous year; enrolled in their second year or third academic cycle, at least; could not have belonged to the Huelga committee the previous year; must be "secular," here signifying that the individual could not be a prominent or powerful member in a political party, workers' syndicate, or religious body, and neither could they be a member of the active military, nor a public figure; finally, the individuals had to have experience managing funds of a student organization in the previous two years and have evidence of the appropriate management of those funds. Beginning in 1957, the committee of the Huelga de Dolores would be comprised of as many as five representatives from each student association (by Facultad). The Huelga was one of the few university events that united students from all faculties who were otherwise fairly separated in terms of course of study, class schedule, and even classroom location. For more on the administration of the Huelga de Dolores, see Articles 3, 4, and 9 of Decree 10 of the Constitution of the Consejo Superior Estudiantil, February 20, 1957; and Letter, Juan Francisco Manrique, Secretary of Organization of the AEU, February 17, 1959, Archivo General de la Universidad de San Carlos (AGUSAC).

4. In 1930, 569 students attended USAC; by 1947 that number more than tripled to 1,804; in 1954, 3,368 students attended; this numbered jumped to 5,584 in 1962; enrollment continued to grow, albeit more slowly in the 1960s, counting 6,138 students at the Guatemala City and Quetzaltenango campuses, and 8,171 in 1966 and 9,388 in 1967. In 1969, enrollment reached 11,319 students. The 1976 Catalogue of Studies accounts for this dramatic increase in enrollment by noting that more private and public secondary schools were built nationwide, thus permitting more students to reach the university level; but the university also created a number of shorter programs of study for new careers (34). Nevertheless, prerequisite secondary school, not to mention the cost of university education and time away from work to attend class, limited enrollment to urban ladino men. For instance, in 1964, 14,060 men and women had attended some duration of university classes; of these, some 40 students were indigenous. For more information on enrollment statistics, see the Departamento de Censos y Encuestas, Dirección General de Estadística, *Censo de Población de Guatemala de 1964* (Guatemala: Ministerio de Economía, 1964); *Boletín Estadístico Universitario*, 1973. AGUSAC. In the 1964 census, only one-quarter of the school age population (seven to twenty-four) currently or previously attended classes. While this percentage was on the rise since 1950 when school attendance was about 14 percent, this left very few young people with the option of attending school. Again, the 1964 census data revealed that 0.4 percent of the Guatemalan population had attended any university education, while 67.8 percent had not passed any school grade whatsoever.

5. In the decade since the 1954 counterrevolution, San Carlistas created new traditions of struggle and made dramatic changes in protest strategy and structures of feeling. Some of these included building broad alliances with groups outside the university, making appeals to international student and government bodies, entertaining little communication with the president, and openly critiquing the government. From the swelled street protests of March 1962 initiated by university and secondary school students to the huge youth presence in the MR-13 and the FAR guerrilla groups, greater numbers of *universitarios* made it clear that they were willing to risk a lot in the name of democracy, justice, and freedom. Students had on various occasions successfully seized control of major highways and radio stations. They had gained experience organizing multi-class alliances within neighborhoods, not just along partisan or professional affiliations. Although these promising early moments gave way to early disappointments, students subtly changed the meaning of autonomy to include a guarantee of campus sovereignty, which was put into practice as a secular "sanctuary." In general terms, San Carlistas had become antigovernment.

6. In "The 1966 and 1970 Elections in Guatemala: A Comparative Analysis," Kenneth F. Johnson noted that interest in the election was minimal; of a population of five million, only

944,170 individuals were eligible to vote, about 20 percent of the population. Half of these eligible voters abstained. The total vote counted 531,200 ballots and 101,082 of these ballots were nullified. Even within this very limited electorate, no candidate won a majority of votes (1971: 34–50).

7. Lefebvre's *El derecho a la ciudad* was translated in 1969 in Barcelona; in 1970, *La revolución de hoy: de Nanterre para arriba* was translated by Editorial Extemporaneos in Mexico; *La revolución urbana* was translated in Madrid in 1972 and *Espacio y política: el derecho a la ciudad II* was translated in Barcelona in 1976.

8. The San Carlistas' cheeky nickname for Arévalo was *"chilacayote,"* a variety of edible gourd common to Central America and Mexico.

9. It may interest readers to note that Lefebvre accounted for cyclical time in the later texts *Critique de la vie quotidienne, III. De la modernité au modernisme (Pour une métaphilosophie du quotidien)* (1981) and *Éléments de rythmanalyse: Introduction à la connaissance des rythmes* (1992).

10. Interestingly, Lefebvre writes about the space of primitive accumulation prior to and after 1910.

11. The brief poem here references the fifth Roman emperor Nero's rumored barbaric sexual practices, including Sporus and Doryphorus (see Tacitus and Suetonius). How Plato who had lived and died by about 348 BC could be Nero's (37–68 AD) boy toy is irrelevant. But both Nero and Plato were known for their same-sex interests, Nero's recorded by Suetonius and Tacitus as part of his sadistic tendencies and Plato's extended dialogue in *The Symposium*. Also of note: in mid-March 1960, Tecun Uman was officially declared Guatemala's national hero.

12. Appropriately, the event's financial practices reflected dependency theory's call for national investment in knowledge-production and technology.

13. Literacy has gradually increased in Guatemalan national censuses; in the 1994 national census, national literacy was 64.62 percent; in 2002, literacy increased to 71.18 percent. Instituto Nacional de Estadística, *Censo 1994* and *Censo 2002* (Guatemala: INE).

14. To be clear, I am not concerned with whether San Carlistas acted as disciples of Lefebvre or even how they understood May 1968. In fact, USAC students were part of wide reaching international student congresses (the International Student Union and the Coordinating Secretariat of National Unions of Students) that welcomed student protest and post-colonial struggles from the early 1950s.

15. This is distinct from urban spatial practices such as land occupation and squatter communities, about which there are many good monographs and articles from any number of ideological perspectives, see David Harvey, *Rebel Cities*, (2012); Loic Wacquant, *Urban Outcasts*, (2008); in Latin America, William Mangin, "Latin American Squatter Settlements: A Problem and a Solution," *Latin American Research Revew* 2:3 (Summer, 1967), pp. 65–98 and Joao Costa Vargas, "When a Favela Dares to Become a Gated Condominium," *Latin American Perspectives* 33:4 (Jul., 2006), pp. 49–81 and Anthony Stocks, "Too Much for Too Few: Problems of Indigenous Land Rights in Latin America," *Annual Review of Anthropology* 34 (2005), pp. 85–104; in Guatemala, see Deborah Levenson, *Adiós Niño*, (2013) and Kevin Lewis O"Neill and Kedron Thomas, eds. *Securing the City*, (2011).

16. While some Lefebvre readers might draw a comparison between the San Carlistas" protests and the "right to the city," one critical intervention of San Carlistas was a spatial politics in excess of "right." This was crucial in the context of Guatemala during the civil war, where crisis and impunity obscured juridical legitimacy. In fact, San Carlistas took to the streets in levity and death in a spatial practice that refused to be productive, orderly, or "right." What I call their "wasteful" spatial practice refers to students" insistence on disrupting commerce and traffic and the status quo during the Huelga parade and political funerals.

17. In "The Political Economy of Death: Communication and Change in Malagasy Colonial History," Gillian Feeley-Harnik (1984) discusses political funerals in terms of political economy; related, Allen Feldman writes in "Political Terror and the Technologies of Memory: Excuse, Sacrifice, Commodification and Actuarial Moralities," of the commerce in memory and political terror. Both articles encouraged me to think of death and death commemoration as a secular form. *Radical History Review* 85 (Winter 2003): 11.

18. It is all too easy to interpret the Huelga de Dolores as a Bakhtinian carnival, that is, as a socially conservative steam-valve for dissent or unrest. But the Huelga permitted direct political critique. Texts produced for and about these crucial protests *cum* annual popular events in the USAC calendar demonstrate how narratives of generation conscribed individuals to various state, religious, popular, revolutionary, or reformist politics.

19. Until 1961, USAC was the only university in Guatemala. In this year Universidad Rafael Landívar was founded as an alternative to the increasingly politicized San Carlos. Five years later, Universidad Mariano Galvez and Universidad del Valle were founded; Universidad Francisco Marroquín was founded in 1971. Each of the private universities was oriented toward a particular political, economic, or religious interest: Rafael Landívar was known for its focus on business and full use of natural resources; Mariano Galvez was oriented toward scientific and technological development but within an evangelical Christian schema; Universidad del Valle emphasized research and educational technology; and Marroquín enjoyed the support of North American businesses and focused on advanced studies. Notably, the offices of the national student union were labeled *"territorio libre"* around 1965. Autonomy was articulated in spatial sovereignty terms.

BIBLIOGRAPHY

Alvarez Aragón, Virgilio (2002), *Conventos, Aulas y Trincheras*, Vols. I and II, Guatemala City: Facultad Latinoamericana de Ciencias Sociales.
Archivo Histórico de la Policia Nacional (AHPN) (2011), *Del Silencio a la Memoria.* Guatemala City.
Asociación de Estudiantes Universitarios y la Facultad de Ciencias Económicas de la USAC (s.f.), "Jornadas de Agosto de 1977."
Barrios y Barrios, Catalina (1999), *La huelga de Dolores: 100 años y 1 más* . . . Guatemala City: s.n.
Biografía Sintética de la Huelga del Viernes de Dolores (1956), *El Informador Estudiantil.*
"Canto y llanto" (April 1966), *No Nos Tientes.*
Catálogo de Estudios (1976), Guatemala City: IIME.
"Cateo en Casa de la AEU y Aprehendidos" (1 April 1966), *Prensa Libre.*
Comision para Esclarecimiento Historico (1999), "Caso Ilustrativo No. 68," *Memoria del Silencio*, Guatemala City: Oficina de Servicios para Proyectos de las Naciones Unidas.
Costa Vargas, Joao (2006), "When a Favela Dares to Become a Gated Condominium," *Latin American Perspectives,* 33: 4, pp. 49–81.
Cuevas del Cid, Rafael, Julio Hernández Sifontes, and Lilian Beatriz de Cazali (1978), *Pensamiento Universitario: Enfoque Crítico.* Guatemala: Editorial Universitaria.
Departamento de Censos y Encuestas de la Dirección General de Estadística (1966), *Censo de Población 1964: Resultados de Tabulación por muestreo,* Guatemala City: Ministerio de Económica.
"Desaparece estudiante guatemalteco" (1971), *Jornada: Publicacion mensual de la Secretaría Permanente del Consejor Superior Universitaria de Centroamérica (CSUCA)*, II, 7.
Dirección General de Estadística (1957), *Sexto Censo General de Población, 1950.* Guatemala: s.n.
Editorial [1] (April 1966), *No Nos Tientes.*
Editorial [2] (August 1966), *El Estudiante*, época IV, no. 2.
Editorial [3] (April 1955), *No Nos Tientes.*
El Estudiante [1] (August 1966), 4: 2.
El Estudiante [2] (October 1966), 4: 4.
Feeley-Harnik, Gillian (1984), "The Political Economy of Death: Communication and Change in Malagasy Colonial History," *American Ethnologist*, 11: 1, pp. 1–19.
Feldman, Allen (2003), "Political Terror and the Technologies of Memory: Excuse, Sacrifice, Commodification and Actuarial Moralities," *Radical History Review*, 85, pp. 58–73.
Fuerzas Armadas Rebeldes (FAR) (1973), "Hacía una interpretacion nacional concreta y dialéctica del Marxismo Leninismo."

————. (2000), *The Blood of Guatemala*, Durham, NC: Duke University Press.
Grandin, Greg (2011), *The Guatemala Reader: History, Culture, Politics*, Durham, NC: Duke University Press.
————. (n.d.), "Causa Proletaria, Expresión de los Obreros Revolucionarios."
Harvey, David (2012), *Rebel Cities: From the Right to the City to the Urban Revolution*, London: Verso.
"Huelga de Dolores se desarrollará este año en el ámbito universitario" (31 March 1966), *Prensa Libre.*
"Huelga de Dolores . . . se sugiere a los estudiantes hacer sus celebraciones dentro de sus propias facultades" (26 March 1966), *Prensa Libre.*
Johnson, Kenneth F., (1971), "The 1966 and 1970 Elections in Guatemala: A Comparative Analysis," *World Affairs*, 134: 1, pp. 34–50.
Kobrak, Paul (1999), *Organizing and Repression in the University of San Carlos, Guatemala, 1944–1996*, Washington, DC: American Association for the Advancement of Science.
"La Asociación de Estudiantes Universitarios al Pueblo de Guatemala . . . " (12 April 1962), *Prensa Libre.*
Lefebvre, Henri (1991 [1974]), *The Production of Space* (trans. Donald Nicholson-Smith), Malden, MA: Blackwell.
Letter, Escuela Nacional de Economia Sociedad de Alumnos to AEU (22 July 1966).
Levenson, Deborah (1994), *Trade Unionists Against Terror*, Chapel Hill: University of North Carolina Press.
————. (2013), *Adiós Niño: The Gangs of Guatemala City and the Politics of Death*, Durham, NC: Duke University Press.
Mangin, William (1967), "Latin American Squatter Settlements: A Problem and a Solution," *Latin American Research Revew*, 2: 3, pp. 65–98.
Martínez Peláez, Severo (2009), *La Patria del Criollo*, Durham, NC: Duke University Press.
O'Neill, Kevin Lewis and Kedron Thomas (eds.) (2011), *Securing the City: Neoliberalism, Space, and Insecurity in Postwar Guatemala*, Durham, NC: Duke University Press.
"Paros Docentes en Seis Facultades" (19 March 1971), *El Imparcial.*
"Policía Dispersa Reunion Estudiantil" (19 March 1966) *La Hora.*
"Presidente de la AEU Tal Declara " (10 April 1962) *Prensa Libre.*
Rolz Bennett, José (1978), "Ensayo de definición de la Universidad," *Pensamiento Universitario: Enfoque Crítico*, Guatemala: Editorial Universitaria.
Sexto Censo General de Población, 1950 (1957), Guatemala: s.n.
Stocks, Anthony (2005), "Too Much for Too Few: Problems of Indigenous Land Rights in Latin America," *Annual Review of Anthropology*, 34, pp. 85–104.
Tarjeta [entrance ticket] for the Huelga de Dolores (1966).
Vrana, Heather (2012), "Revolutionary Transubstantiation in 'The Republic of Students': Death Commemoration in Urban Guatemala from 1977 to the Present," *Radical History Review*, 114, pp. 66–90.
————. (2013) "'Do Not Tempt Us!': The Guatemalan University in Protest, Memory, and Political Change, 1944–present," PhD diss., Indiana University.
Wacquant, Loic (2008), *Urban Outcasts: A Comparative Sociology of Advanced Marginality*, Cambridge, MA: Polity Press.
Way, J.T. (2012), *The Mayan in the Mall*, Durham: Duke University Press.
Woodward, Jr., Ralph Lee (1993), *Rafael Carrera and the Emergence of the Republic of Guatemala*, Athens, GA: University of Georgia Press.

IV

THE HOUSING QUESTION

Chapter Seven

Residential Differentiation in the Vertical Cities of J. G. Ballard and Robert Silverberg

Jeff Hicks

In the late nineteenth century, socialist utopian novels such as Edward Bellamy's *Looking Backward 2000–1887* (1888) and William Morris's *News from Nowhere* (1890) imagined the form of a world freed from the constraints of capitalism. While both novels left the transition to a post-capitalist world somewhat vague, each work seemed confident that such a future was not only preferable to the deplorable conditions found in its time but that a bright, socialist future was somewhat inevitable. At the same time, however, Ignatius Donnelly's *Caesar's Column: A Story of the Twentieth Century* (1890) and Jack London's *The Iron Heel* (1908) suggested that an escape from capitalism would be a difficult, if not impossible, process. These competing utopian and dystopian views of the future served to provide both hope for revolutionary change and a warning for those who believed such change would happen without a struggle. Despite the seeming incongruities between these works, one thing was for certain: each author believed that change was possible.

By the early 1970s, however, any hope for a post-capitalist future seemed to be lost. Authors working as part of science fiction's (SF) New Wave had no illusions of ever evading the confines of late capitalism and instead set their sights on identifying the mechanisms of control that kept a capitalist system in place not only structurally but mentally as well. This chapter examines two urban dystopias of SF's New Wave that focus on the living spaces of those most able to manipulate that system. An examination of the densely populated vertical cities of J. G. Ballard's *High Rise* (1975) and Robert Silverberg's *The World Inside* (1971) reveals that regardless of an urban area's size or density, the living spaces of the wealthy are marked by isolation, fear, and strict segregation based on class and social status. As Jeremiah B. C. Axelrod states of New York's vertical center:

> Although every New Yorker could read the basic marks of the metropolis and veteran urbanites could soon locate themselves within it, many city dwellers— and especially those relegated to the city's geographical, racial, and social peripheries—could really be sure only that the city did indeed have a clearly identifiable center and they were most certainly not in it. (2009: 155)

Urban dystopias focusing on the living spaces of the prosperous show that at the heart of any enclave built on exclusion lies a complex relationship between segregation by social and economic status and an isolation from even those within their own communities.

Urban dystopias rarely focus on the lives of the wealthy, preferring instead to use their proletarian protagonists to illuminate the lives of the victims of the inequities created by those in power. Most of the urban dystopias written during science fiction's New Wave relied on partial or incomplete characterizations of those in the upper classes as either part of a monolithic structure of control or as shadowy, insular figures perfectly willing to build their empires on the littered corpses of the working poor. There are, however, a handful of stories and novels that chose to question the lives of the bourgeoisie most able to manipulate urban spaces to their benefit and the vacuity that lies at the heart of the conspicuous consumption and narcissistic excess that such manipulation makes possible. In Frederik Pohl's "The Midas Plague" (1954), technology has enabled such an excess of production that the term "poor" is now used to designate citizens forced to adhere to overwhelming consumption quotas that make opulence synonymous with obligation. Charles Platt's *The City Dwellers* (1970)[1] shows what happens to the "pleasure palaces" and the gigantic automated shopping centers of the future after the city has died. Mark Adlard's T-City Trilogy—consisting of *Interface* (1971), *Volteface* (1972), and *Multiface* (1975)—describes a future where a select few technologically modified executives living in luxury control all aspects of life for those living within a giant, overcrowded, domed city.[2] In all three novels, Adlard suggests that the end of capitalism is far more likely to result in the executive class struggling to maintain their positions of authority and superiority than in any utopian dream of an equal access to enlightenment and prosperity. Each of the works listed here highlight the emptiness of a life dedicated to consumption and power, but—with the exception of Adlard's novels—they do not explicitly critique the complicity of the privileged in perpetuating restrictive land use policies.

This chapter turns away from the urban dystopias that valorized the lives of the urban poor to examine, instead, two works interested in the ways in which the very rich sought to create, control, and manage urban space in the hopes of divorcing themselves from the mass of city dwellers who also called these places home. The novels of J. G. Ballard and Robert Silverberg explored here interrogate the pervasive replication of social differentiation within the residential differentiation found in capitalist society.

Although J. G. Ballard (1930–2009) is perhaps better known for his more popular novels such as *Crash* and *Empire of the Sun*, Ballard began his career writing a revolutionary form of science fiction as part of SF's New Wave movement. Ballard's "Which Way to Inner Space?" published in the British SF magazine *New Worlds*, served as a kind of manifesto for the New Wave, urging authors to abandon the more traditional space opera and instead embrace a higher quality of fiction that would explore the psychological dynamics of its characters.[3] There are several biographies of Ballard, but thoughtful scholarship on the author is curiously lacking. Among those works worth reading, Roger Luckhurst's *"The Angle Between Two Walls": Fiction of J.G. Ballard* (1997) presents an excellent examination of the SF elements present in Ballard's work, and David Pringle's early analysis of Ballard's work, *Earth Is the Alien Planet: J. G. Ballard's Four-Dimensional Nightmare* (1979) is slim, but informative. Studies focusing on *High Rise* are even harder to find. Jeanette Baxter has edited two recent collections on Ballard's extensive canon of works, and in both, Sebastian Groes examines Ballard's critique of urban space in his early work. In "The Texture of Modernity in *Crash*, *Concrete Island*, and *High Rise*" Groes uses Dante's *The Divine Comedy* (Groes 2012: 1314–21) to suggest that those three novels encourage specific sensory reactions in the reader in order to humanize postmodern urban structures. But while Groes begins to examine the forces of late capitalism at play in Ballard's fiction, none of the works mentioned above are able to connect *High Rise* to the larger discussion of urban space being formulated by Marxist theorists of the 1970s and 1980s.

Robert Silverberg (1935–) is easily one of the most prolific SF authors there is. With hundreds of novels, short stories, and nonfiction works in print, Silverberg has covered a number of different themes and subjects in his fiction from alien encounter stories to the boundaries of human sexuality. Despite his contributions to the genre, Silverberg scholarship is severely lacking. Charles Elkins and Martin Greenberg's *Robert Silverberg's Many Trapdoors: Critical Essays on His Science Fiction*, provides a good overview of Silverberg's work, but is too short to serve as a critical study. Studies of *The World Inside* include Meritt Abrash's "Robert Silverberg's *The World Inside*" and Thomas P. Dunn and Richard D. Erlich's "The Mechanical Hive: Urbmon 116 as the Villain-Hero of Silverberg's *The World Inside*." But despite Dunn and Erlich's interrogation of the living spaces of Silverberg's novel, the scholars choose not to examine the larger political implications of the author's work.

    The sections that follow provide a background in the theories of residen-
tial differentiation and social structure before applying those ideas to a critical examination of *High Rise* and *The World Inside*. In the first section,
Residential Differentiation and Social Structure, I contrast Friedrich Engels's
views on urban segregation with those of E. W. Burgess and the Chicago
School of sociology in order to provide context for David Harvey's more
contemporary, Marxist views of residential differentiation and its ties to social structure. In the next section, Madness and Residential Differentiation in
the Vertical City, I show the influence architect and urban planner Le Corbusier had on the development of many of the major metropolitan areas of
the twentieth century and the strong reaction science fiction's New Wave had
against the utopian visions suggested in Le Corbusier's writings. Finally, I
show that Ballard's *High Rise* and Silverberg's *The World Inside* provide a
critique of both the living spaces of the bourgeoisie and the possibility of
escaping the social and residential structure that helps to support late capitalism.

A. RESIDENTIAL DIFFERENTIATION AND SOCIAL STRUCTURE

As industrialization began to permanently alter and expand existing urban
centers in Britain and abroad in the nineteenth century, social theorists began
to examine the forces behind the changing patterns of urban land use and
housing preferences in the city. Friedrich Engels's *The Condition of the
English Working Class in 1844* neatly delineates the economic contours of
the pattern of residential housing in a newly industrialized Manchester. Engels found that "[The] unmixed working people's quarters, stretching like a
girdle, [averages] a mile and a half in breadth, around the commercial district. Outside, beyond this girdle, lives the upper and middle bourgeoisie, the
middle bourgeoisie in regularly laid out streets in the vicinity of working
quarters . . . the upper bourgeoisie in remoter villas with gardens" (1935: 46).
Within this urban organization, one that clearly separated Manchester's residents by class, Engels also found a profound desire for an almost total isolation of the wealthiest citizens from the working classes: "And the finest part
of the arrangement is this, that the members of the money aristocracy can
take the shortest road through the middle of all the laboring districts without
ever seeing that they are in the midst of the grimy misery that lurks to the
right and the left"; a misery that Engels suggested was "the complement of
their wealth" (1935: 46–47). Although working mainly within Britain, Engels suggested, "[T]his hypocritical plan is more or less common to all great
cities" (1935: 47).
    Engels would later expand upon his analysis of the city in a series of
essays entitled "The Housing Question" that were published in the *Volkstaat*

between 1872 and 1873. Written in the wake of a shortage of affordable housing for workers in major metropolitan centers, "The Housing Question," anatomized the mechanisms of the housing market in order to show that it is always in the best interests of capital to manipulate housing opportunities for the proletariat so that even while living conditions deteriorate, rents will continue to increase, eventually forcing workers from their homes. In what could easily be mistaken for an outline of modern day gentrification efforts Engels explains:

> The growth of the big modern cities gives the land in certain areas, particularly in those which are centrally situated, an artificial and often colossally increasing value; the buildings erected on these areas depress this value, instead of increasing it, because they no longer correspond to the changed circumstances. They are pulled down and replaced by others. . . . The result is that the workers are forced out of the centre of the towns towards the outskirts; that workers' dwellings, and small dwellings in general, become rare and expensive and often altogether unobtainable, for under these circumstances the building industry . . . builds workers' dwellings only by way of exception. (1935: 23)

And for Engels it was very clear what needed to be done: "In order to make an end of *this* housing shortage there is only *one* means: to abolish altogether the exploitation and oppression of the working class by the ruling class" (1935: 21, emphasis in original). While Engels's work within and contributions to the Manchester School of urban studies can be seen now as a clear precursor for the work of urban Marxists working at the end of the twentieth century, his socialist deconstruction of the city would soon fall by the wayside in the wake of a new school for urban theory that would attempt to naturalize the plight of the working class while leaving the capitalist system that created it relatively blame free.

In its work in the 1920s and beyond, the Chicago School's study of urban sociology suggested that—by examining empirical data taken from those working in and observing urban areas[4]—it could be determined that environmental factors such as location, education opportunities, and population density played the strongest roles in the formation of residential segregation in the urban center. E. W. Burgess, in his concentric zone model of residential differentiation, suggested that the modern metropolis could be described as existing in a series of discrete zones that were determined by land use and land value.[5] In the center of this concentric set of rings lay the industrial center of the city or "The Loop" (1925: 50). Surrounding this zone of intense industrial concentration lay the "Zone in Transition," an area comprised of both businesses and housing for the working poor (1925: 50). Beyond the "Zone in Transition" Burgess found a "Zone of Workingmen's Homes" where second generation immigrants and "workers in industries who have escaped from the area of deterioration" might be found (1925: 50). Farther

still, Burgess identified a "Residential Zone" of "high-class apartment buildings or of "restricted" districts of single family dwellings" and a "Commut-
ers" Zone" of suburban living spaces for those wealthy enough to escape the
realities of the city (1925: 50). While the organizational model Burgess identified very closely described the realities of residential patterns in Chicago,
the causes he found for this segregation were far more problematic.

Burgess suggested that any major urban area developed naturally and that
urban growth could be seen "as a resultant of organization and disorganiza-
tion analogous to the anabolic and katabolic processes of metabolism in the
body" (1925: 53). What this meant for Burgess was that each new wave of
immigration to the city would naturally find a home within the Zone of
Transition and that eventually—after a generation lost to the acclimation to
city life—those immigrants would pass on to ever better living areas. Within
this system, the squalid living conditions of the working poor could be
blamed on the poor themselves and to their failure to adjust to life in the big
city. Even while praising the regenerative qualities of the slum, Burgess was
careful to highlight the racial or ethnic qualities of these areas of the city
describing "the Latin Quarter, where creative and rebellious spirits resort,"
and "the Black Belt, with its free and disorderly life" (1925: 56). He also
suggested that employment for immigrants to the city was determined more
by "racial temperament or circumstance than by old-world economic background" suggesting that "Irish policemen, Greek ice-cream parlors, Chinese
laundries, Negro porters, [and] Belgian janitors" were only natural (1925:
57). While Burgess admitted that "[i]n the expansion of the city a process of
distribution takes place which sifts and sorts and relocates individuals and
groups by residence and occupation," he failed to identify who or what
controlled that process, preferring instead to see mobility patterns within the
city as natural (1925: 54).

What was missing from the Chicago School models of urban development, however, was a connection between housing opportunities and economic class divisions. In the 1960s and 1970s, Marxist geographers and
urban theorists such as Manuel Castells and David Harvey began to suggest
that environmental factors alone were not sufficient to describe and define
the formation and use of urban space. David Harvey's work, *Social Justice
and the City* (2009 [1973]), outlined what Harvey saw as a revolutionary
restructuring of geographic thought. Using Engels's study of Manchester as
his starting point, Harvey explained that access to transportation and to employment required the poorest members of society to live in the center of the
city, but because of a market that used competitive bidding to determine the
use of urban land, land rents were always higher in the city's core (2009:
134–35). Because land rents are higher, the working poor are forced to live in
smaller spaces, surrounded by larger groups of people. As Harvey suggests:
"The logic of the model indicates that poor groups will be concentrated in

high rent areas close to the city centre in over-crowded conditions" (2009: 135).[6] In Harvey's *The Urban Experience* (1989)[7] he further outlines the ways in which the production of capital determines residential segmentation, mobility chances, and the conscious replication of housing and land use by capital in the hopes of furthering surplus value and undermining the possibility of proletarian revolt. Harvey shows that rather than having some semblance of choice when determining housing location, the production of capital—in particular the control of mortgage rates, land values, and borrowing possibilities by bankers and landowners—presents a very limited choice in where to live (1989: 121–22). This limited choice in turn creates a self-perpetuating cycle of residential differentiation. Those with limited housing choices pass these limitations down generation by generation. As Harvey suggests: "a white-collar labor force is reproduced in a white-collar neighborhood, a blue-collar labor force is reproduced in a blue-collar neighborhood, and so on" (1989: 118).

An essential part of Harvey's examination of the city is constituted through the links he explores between social differentiation, as determined by class, and residential differentiation, as determined by the conscious manipulation of housing markets by the forces of capitalism. Specifically, Harvey suggests that capitalism not only encourages segregated living spaces but segregated social and work spaces as well. For Harvey, capitalism supports social differentiation through a division of labor that creates a sharp divide between the managerial class and the working class and a manipulation of "ideological and political consciousness" that inspires workers to rally against their own best interests (1989: 117). The sharp social divide that Harvey identifies helps to explain what he sees as a pattern of neighborhoods organized not by race or ethnicity but by class and social status where "[r]esidential differentiation is to be interpreted in terms of the reproduction of the social relations within capitalist society" and where "[r]esidential areas (neighborhoods, communities) provide distinctive milieus for social interaction from which individuals to a considerable degree derive their values, expectations, consumption habits, market capacities, and states of consciousness" (1989: 118). These seemingly inseparable ties between social status and residential location—along with the barriers to mobility put in place by the ruling class—make it difficult for Harvey to suggest a viable path to proletarian revolt or the reorganization of urban space. However, the strength of class divisions within the city and the seeming impossibility of creating an urban space without them would fuel two of the greatest works of urban SF within the New Wave.

B. MADNESS AND RESIDENTIAL
DIFFERENTIATION IN THE VERTICAL CITY

At the beginning of the twentieth century, the vertical development of metropolitan areas such as New York and Chicago became commonplace, and soon the skyscrapers and high-rise buildings characteristic of Chicago's downtown Loop and Manhattan's impressive skyline would dominate modernist cultural representations of the city. As Axelrod suggests, the scale and size of the skyscraper "evoked strong feelings of awe in the (in comparison tiny) observer" and the buildings came to represent a utopian synthesis of "progress and modernity" (2009: 133–34). Illustrations by New York booster Moses King, pulp artist Frank R. Paul, and architect Harvey Wiley Corbett suggested towering, austere skyscrapers, linked by elevated walkways and roads, as emblematic of the city of the future. But no one would do more to promote the vertical city than the architect and urban visionary known as Le Corbusier.

Born Charles-Édouard Jeanneret, Le Corbusier would create an austere, monolithic vision of urban architecture that would influence architects and city planners for over half a century. Le Corbusier's "La Ville Contemporaine" (1987 [1929]: 163–80),[8] emphasized the need to decongest city centers by increasing their density and called for a central area dominated by towering office buildings. Believing that little could be done within existing city centers, Le Corbusier argued vehemently for razing downtown blocks entirely so that the urban planner could begin with a clean slate. Within the Contemporary City, residential areas would be strictly segregated by occupation: six-story luxury apartments for industrial scientists and artists; and mass-produced, hive-like apartments for the working classes (Le Corbusier 1987 [1929]: 163–80). After losing faith in capitalism and embracing the more egalitarian ethos of revolutionary syndicalism, Le Corbusier would expand and reimagine his views on the city in his 1933 work, *La Ville Radieuse* (Fishman 1982: 230–31). The Radiant City attempted to eliminate class division in its housing by creating Unités, giant collective apartment buildings featuring individual living units allocated by family size instead of income and limited to "the minimum space necessary for efficient existence" (Hall 2002 [1988]: 210). The Unité would be much larger than the proposed residential buildings of the Contemporary City, and these high-rise structures would come complete with gymnasiums, pools, primary school, and stores. Although Le Corbusier would never see his plans fully implemented, he was a constant booster for the vertical city, and though his call for centrally controlled egalitarian living spaces would never be taken up, his ideas would influence later planners and architects in two important ways; Le Corbusier's strategy of razing existing city centers would be used in urban renewal efforts to make room for luxury high-rise apartments, and his call for mass-produced, cramped, uniform apartment complexes would be replicated in dozens of public housing projects.

By the end of the 1960s, the utopian promise of Le Corbusier's "Ville Radieuse" had begun to come under heavy criticism in the work of science fiction's New Wave authors.[9] The idea that centralized living and work spaces could create a classless, tightly-knit community seemed out of touch with the urban realities of the 1960s and 1970s. Specifically, the image of the tall, free-standing apartment complex had become less associated with a community of equals than with the separation of a specific class of residents from the outside world. The remainder of this chapter examines the connection between the isolated, self-contained living spaces depicted in J. G. Ballard's *High-Rise* and Robert Silverberg's *The World Inside* and the residential differentiation and class segregation analyzed by Marxist urban theorists such as Manuel Castells and David Harvey as characteristic of contemporary cities. Deploying Harvey's conceptions of a just distribution of income and apportionment of urban space, as outlined in *Social Justice and the City*, I also examine Ballard's and Silverberg's depiction of how, even under seemingly ideal conditions, a utopian alternative to inequitable living standards as imagined by urban planners such as Le Corbusier simply isn't possible under capitalist social relations.

Ballard's novel anatomizes the callous existence of those at the top by exposing the class division and spatial segregation that persist even in an isolated, affluent, high-rise apartment building. This class segregation is also found in Silverberg's futuristic "Urbmons," vast tower blocks where those with the most socioeconomic power naturally reside on the uppermost floors. Although Silverberg's characters are freed by automation and other advanced technologies from the need to participate in a system of monetary exchange, the Urbmons are, nevertheless, unable to escape from a residential and social segregation based on capitalist social relations. But neither novel relies on a simple binary of haves and have-nots. Instead, both authors focus on the complicity of urban planners and building management in ensuring that such class divisions are strictly defined and enforced.

1. High-Rise

Ballard's novels *Crash* (1973) and *Concrete Island* (1973) began a critique of contemporary urban living that would continue throughout his career. These novels and Ballard's later explorations of upper class luxury resorts and isolated corporate living[10] also suggested that the decadent, technologically bound urbanity of the upper classes belied an almost universal dissatisfaction with life that would ultimately manifest itself in savage acts of violence. One of the best examples of Ballard's dystopian cities of decay, *High-Rise*, focuses on a group of wealthy, successful professionals living in the first building of a five unit complex two miles east of London. The apartment building, a forty story monument of glass and steel, although still on the borders of the larger city, is part of a recent redevelopment project that includes a medical school, television studios, and a newly completed concert hall. As many of the residents work in one of these locations, they find little reason to leave the immediate area, content to contain their existence within the radius of a single square mile. Further isolating the residents from the rest of the city is the high-rise itself, containing on the tenth floor, "a supermarket, bank and hairdressing salon, a swimming-pool and gymnasium, a well-stocked liquor store and a junior school for the few young children in the block" (2006 [1975]: 9). On the thirty-fifth floor, a second swimming pool, a sauna, and a restaurant complete any additional needs the tenants might have. The apartment building in the novel seems to cocoon the residents, insulating them from the outside world and giving them some semblance of providing for their every need. As one tenant puts it:

> The high-rise was a huge machine designed to serve, not the collective body of tenants, but the individual resident in isolation. Its staff of air-conditioning conduits, elevators, garbage-disposal chutes and electrical switching systems provided a never-failing supply of care and attention that a century earlier would have needed an army of tireless servants. (Ballard 2006 [1975]: 10)

Ballard himself said in a 1975 interview that his fiction "is really about one person coming to terms with various forms of isolation" (Pringle 1975: 15). Early on in the novel, *High-Rise* identifies the paradox of high-density building construction; tenants are ensured the ability to live individually yet surrounded by hundreds of people intent on maintaining the same level of seclusion. However, while insular living is both encouraged and catered to in the building, *High-Rise* has much more to say about the social and cultural groupings formed in the vertical city.

In Ballard's apartment of the future, there still exists a need to re-create the social and residential differentiation painfully present in the distribution of land use in greater London. Echoing Harvey's description of the social cohesion of any urban neighborhood, Dr. Robert Liang, a teaching physician living on the twenty-fifth floor initially believes that the residents of the building are "probably closer to each other than the members of any conceivable social mix, with the same tastes and attitudes, fads and styles" (Ballard 2006 [1975]: 10). But within the novel this society of equals begins to break down almost immediately. As Wilder, a tenant from the second floor observes, "an apparently homogenous collection of high-income professional people had split into three distinct and hostile camps. The old social subdivisions, based on power, capital and self-interest, had re-asserted themselves here as anywhere else" (2006 [1975]: 53). Despite their ability to afford to live in the high-rise, the residents of the lowest nine floors of the building serve as the lower class, a "proletariat" of "film technicians and air hostesses"; the middle section, or middle class of the building is comprised of "self-centered but basically docile members of the professions—the doctors and lawyers, accountants and tax specialists"; and the top five floors serve as the upper class, the "discreet oligarchy of minor tycoons and entrepreneurs, television actresses and careerist academics" (2006 [1975]: 53). Soon the three groups begin to become obsessed with a series of subtle aggravations, minor events to fixate upon until they begin to fester and blister forth into eruptions of violence. The children of the lower floors are soon blamed for noise and disruptive behavior, and their "disorderly" conduct at the pool soon angers the middle and upper floor residents. The residents on the upper floors are blamed for the noise and music of a series of never-ending parties and for their roaming packs of well-manicured dogs. The building itself then seems to egg on these neighborly squabbles as electrical and waste systems begin to fail. But rather than find ways of creating a cooperative living space, the tenants of the high-rise only amplify their offensive behavior. Children are encouraged to make noise, dogs are encouraged to bark, and bottles of champagne are carelessly dropped from upper floors. The novel makes it very clear that although each of the tenants possesses the same basic background, there still exists a need to create a set of artificial and imagined boundaries based on social status and residence location—the same set of boundaries that are wedded to the very real class and status barriers found in the residential differentiation of the late capitalist city.

Harvey challenges earlier theories of residential differentiation that suggested simply that "similar people like to, or simply do, live close to each other" (1989: 109) by identifying the role that class relations play in residential decision making. As mentioned above, Harvey asserts that social differentiation is caused primarily by "[p]ower relations between capital and labor" but also through:

> A variety of secondary forces arising out of the contradictory and evolutionary character of capitalism which encourage social differentiation along lines defined by (a) the division of labor and specialization of function, (b) consumption patterns and life-style, (c) authority relations, (d) manipulated projections of ideological and political consciousness, and (e) barriers to mobility chances. (1989: 117)

These conditions responsible for residential differentiation—especially the active creation of barriers to mobility chances—were often used by those in power to encourage residential segregation patterns that effectively forced the urban poor to concentrate within densely populated pockets of poverty. But the perpetuation of capitalist society requires that the conditions of social differentiation apply to every economic strata of society, and even within the upper class there exists the need to perpetuate antagonism and division.

As Edward Soja suggests of the "yuppies" who came to dominate urban environments in the late twentieth century:

> Never before perhaps have the top percentiles of the income ladder been so heterogeneous, so internally divided, so *déclassé*. . . . Such Upper Profession-als . . . may not constitute a cohesive class and probably do not control the highest peaks of economic and political power in the postmetropolis, but they increasingly influence daily life in the city. (2000: 276)

Ballard places these "Upper Professionals" together—in a space designed to be perfect—and their internal divisions become eerily similar to those re-sponsible for residential differentiation. While those living in the upper floors seem far more accepting of their positions within the building, Wilder becomes filled "with a growing sense of impatience and resentment," con-vinced that those on the lower floors had "an inclination to tolerate an undue amount of interference before simply packing up and moving on. In short, their territorial instinct, in its psychological and social senses, had atrophied to the point where they were ripe for exploitation" (2006 [1975]: 54). At the top of the tower, occupying the building's penthouse and attempting to or-chestrate the exploitation of the residents, is Anthony Royal, the building's architect and principal investor. Before the complete collapse of order and structure in the building, "Royal was certain that a rigid hierarchy of some kind was the key to the elusive success of these huge buildings. As he often pointed out to Anne [his wife], office blocks containing as many as thirty thousand workers functioned smoothly for decades thanks to a social hierar-chy as rigid and as formalized as an anthill's" (2006 [1975]: 70). Even after the high-rise's descent into chaos, Royal is convinced that "he had given these people a means of escaping into a new life, and a pattern of social organization that would become the paradigm of all future high-rise blocks" (2006 [1975]: 70).

Royal's attempt to nurture the same hierarchical structure of social diffe-rentiation in his building is similar to what Harvey sees as "the processes whereby residential differentiation is produced by the organization of forces external to the individual or even to the collective will of the particular social grouping" (Harvey 1989: 121). Harvey further suggests that financial and government institutions "regulate the dynamic of the urbanization process (usually in the interest of accumulation and economic crisis management) and also wield their influence in such a way that certain broad patterns in residential differentiation are produced" (1989: 121). It is no surprise that Ballard assigns the symbolic role of housing coordinator to Royal, as his position in the novel as both architect of the building and topmost resident afford him the best possible vantage point for social manipulation. Royal's ego and confidence in an architect's ability to best determine community organization is also similar to those of Le Corbusier, who strongly believed that harmonious living was only possible through the concerted efforts of a master planner.

The isolated apartment structure in *High-Rise* is also an example of what Mike Davis calls the "corporate citadel" that lies in the heart of "Fortress LA" (1992: 223). Davis argues: "we live in "fortress cities" brutally divided between "fortified cells" of affluent society and "places of terror" where the police battle the criminalized poor" (1992: 224). Davis shows that in Los Angeles, as in other major metropolitan cities, middle and upper class demand for "increased spatial and social insulation" has driven municipal policy to concentrate on "corporate-defined redevelopment priorities" that often include a conscious attempt to privatize or otherwise destroy public space (1992: 227). In *High-Rise*, as soon as open hostilities break out among the residents, it is the public spaces of the building that are the first to become battlegrounds. Children are discouraged from using the pool and the junior school, and frightened parents soon keep their children at home or in improvised classrooms in the lower levels of the building. Top floor residents are accused of letting their dogs run free, and it is suggested that the affluent are encouraging their animals to defecate in the hallways and lobbies of the lower floors. Eventually, the elevators themselves become contested spaces as residents forcefully hold them open at certain floors, restricting resident movement and protecting against any violation of their sovereign space. Soon even the stairwells become inaccessible, sealed off by makeshift blockades and protected by club-wielding guards. Food and egress through the building are fought for by raiding parties, and the fatalities slowly begin to mount.

The residents" behavior also replicates—on a much smaller scale—the distribution and defense of urban space in any major city. The conditions of the apartment building are eerily similar to Davis's descriptions of the affluent neighborhoods of Los Angeles:

> [N]ew luxury developments outside the city limits have often become fortress cities, complete with encompassing walls, restricted entry points with guard posts, overlapping private and public police services, and even privatized roadways. . . . Meanwhile, traditional luxury enclaves such as Beverly Hills and San Marino are increasingly restricting public access to their public facilities . . . even imposing a variant of neighborhood "passport control" on outsiders. (1992: 244–46)

The separation of floors and the surplus value given to the apartments closer to the top of the building, the segregation of tenants not just by location but by occupation and class, and the concerted effort by the residents to control public space perfectly mirror Davis's description of the Carceral city and Harvey's analysis of the dynamics of urban land use. Ballard might have had the desire to explore the alienation present in the urban dwellers of the 1970s, but he also created a microcosm of the injustice faced by those unable to live within the walls of any *High-Rise*.

Harvey's *Social Justice and the City* outlines the conditions necessary to eliminate the residential differentiation developed by capital and protected by the state. He argues that before any notion of equitable land use can evolve, there would need to be a "just distribution" of resources (2009: 96–119). Harvey suggests that by meeting three criteria—need, contribution to the common good, and merit—a more equitable distribution of resources could be used, and this would allow "the principles of social justice" to be applied to urban space. Under these principles: "The distribution of income should be such that (a) the needs of the population within each territory are met, (b) resources are so allocated to maximize interterritorial multiplier effects,[11] and (c) extra resources are allocated to help overcome special difficulties stemming from the physical and social environment" (2009: 116). Additionally, "The mechanisms (institutional, organizational, political and economic) should be such that the prospects of the least advantaged territory are as great as they possibly can be" (2009: 116–17). What this would mean, of course, would be a complete and total elimination of the mechanism guiding the urban land market. Harvey states:

> The mechanism in this case is very simple—competitive bidding for the use of land. If we eliminate this mechanism, we will presumably eliminate the result. This is immediately suggestive of a policy for eliminating ghettos, which would presumably supplant competitive bidding with a socially controlled urban land market and socialized control of the housing sector. (2009: 137)

After understanding the tenacity with which capitalist systems seek to maintain the replication of social differentiation, it's difficult to imagine the circumstances that might possibly bring about such a radical change in urban land use, but that doesn't mean that Harvey believed a community founded on the principles of social justice was impossible.

In *The Condition of Postmodernity*, Harvey mentions the type of community needed to escape what he saw as the constricting grip of modernist urban planning:

> The problems of minorities and the underprivileged, or of the diverse counter-cultural elements that so intrigued Jane Jacobs, get swept under the rug unless some very democratic and egalitarian system of community-based planning can be devised that meets the needs of the rich and poor alike. This presupposes, however, a series of well-knit and cohesive urban communities as its

starting point in an urban world that is always in flux and transition. (1990: 76–77)

Although Harvey might not be so optimistic about the possibilities of these communities existing in our time, we can see how a "democratic and egalitarian system of community-based planning" is the antithesis of the design and the operation of the eponymous building in Ballard's *High-Rise*. We can also see that although the small communities of isolated tenants found toward the end of the novel seem to be slightly more egalitarian, they ultimately fail, and their attempts to find even a sort of stasis within the building are thwarted by a violent devolution. In order to see what Harvey's democratic community might look like, we must turn to a more utopian vision of the future. However—as in Huxley's *Brave New World*—even a community initially designed to meet the needs of the many will eventually devolve into a classist hierarchy of those in control and those being controlled. Harvey's conception of social justice, when applied to conceptions of a future city, begins to sound like the socialist utopias of the late nineteenth and early twentieth centuries, but in Silverberg's *The World Inside*, the future is a lot less like Edward Bellamy's *Looking Backward* (1887), and a lot more like Ballard's *High-Rise*.

2. The World Inside

In *The World Inside*, the population of the Earth has been relocated to a system of hundreds of urban monads—or Urbmons—each housing over 800,000 people. In Silverberg's conception of the year 2381, the population, resource, and housing crises have been solved by concentrating the majority of Earth's inhabitants vertically, leaving the remainder of the planet to be used for agricultural production. By concentrating the housing, production, and living spaces of the Earth's population into as economical a space as possible, the global population has been allowed to reach 75 billion people. Silverberg's novel concentrates on Urbmon 116, a typical building in the Chipitts constellation of fifty buildings existing within the area that used to consist of Chicago and Pittsburgh. Urbmon 116 consists of 999 inhabited floors, with every forty floors considered a separate city, and with the exception of relying on the agricultural production found outside of the Urbmon, the building is entirely self-contained.

While many of the cities in the New Wave novels of the 1960s and 1970s were centers of poverty, crime, and intense privation, Urbmon 116 comes as close to meeting Harvey's conditions for social justice as any utopian construct. There is no monetary system within the Urbmon; food, water, and entertainment are distributed equally. Housing and location within the Urbmon is determined by employment, with industrial classes living closest to

their workplace—on the lower levels—and administrators living toward the
top. In addition, social conventions such as privacy and monogamy have
been dropped altogether to discourage conflict. In the Urbmon, residents—
usually male—are encouraged to practice "nightwalking," where the resident
is free to enter any apartment and have sexual relations with any resident
therein.

It becomes fairly obvious to the reader, however, that despite any pretense of equality or tranquility, the Urbmons are strictly segregated by a
loose construction of superstitions, taboos, and unspoken laws centering on
residence level and employment status. While "nightwalking" is encouraged—no one in the Urbmon is permitted to deny anyone sex—"nightwalking" between cities is "a violation of accepted custom" (Silverberg 2004
[1971]: 81). And although every resident in the urban monad is supposedly
assigned the position that is best suited to her, engineers, laborers, and artists
remain stigmatized while administrators and those living near the top of the
building are valorized. Dillon Chrimes, a musician in group that travels free-
ly throughout the building performing, captures the feeling of this subtle
prejudice perfectly:

> Lately he and the group have been doing the grime stint: Rekjavik, Prague,
> Warsaw, down among the grubbos. Well, they"re entitled to some entertain-
> ment too. Dillon lives in San Francisco, not so lofty himself. The 370th floor;
> the heart of the cultural ghetto. . . . The liftshaft shoots him 160 levels heaven-
> ward. When he gets off, he is in Rome. Crowded halls, tight faces. The people
> here are mostly minor bureaucrats, a middle echelon of failed functionaries,
> those who would never get to Louisville except to deliver a report. They are
> not smart enough to hope for Chicago or Shanghai or Edinburgh. Crippled
> souls; walking zeroes; better off down the chute. (2004 [1971]: 56)

And it is the threat of the chute—the threat of being sent down to the fur-
naces to be harvested as energy—that keeps this prejudice from boiling over
into outright aggression. While a sort of city consciousness allows the dwellers of the urban monad to feel a sense of pride and identity on the one hand,
on the other hand the fear of being sent down the chute discourages any
outright hostility or protest.

Throughout the novel, Silverberg introduces characters who seem to
question the organization of Urbmon life or who find it difficult to conform
to the rigidly enforced norms of the tower. Urbmon historian Jason Quevado
believes the acceptance of communal living to be genetic, and his work, *The
Urban Monad as Social Evolution: Parameters of the Spirit Defined by Community Structure*, suggests that:

> [T]he transition to an urbmon society has brought about a fundamental trans-
> formation of the human soul. . . . A more pliant, more acquiescent mode of

> response to events, a turning away from the old expansionist-individualist
> philosophy as marked by territorial ambition . . . toward a kind of communal
> expansion centered in the orderly and unlimited growth of the human race.
> Definitely a psychic evolution of some sort, a shift toward graceful acceptance
> of hive-life. (2004 [1971]: 86–87)

Despite the ability of the majority of residents to make the transition to communal living, Silverberg's choice to focus his novel on those who might be headed to the chute seems to suggest a belief in the improbability of a socialist utopia.[12] Ironically, Quevado himself finds it difficult to conform to the spatial restrictions necessary for maintaining stasis within the Urbmon. Quevado frequently breaks the social custom of nightwalking only within one's own city, and instead finds a deviant pleasure in journeying to the lowest levels of the Urbmon to find women to "top." More importantly, Quevado seems to find a specific pleasure in dominating women who appear to be socially beneath him. In one passage, as Quevado ventures to the fifty-ninth floor of Warsaw to nightwalk with a random woman, Silverberg describes his ability to convince her to accept him with a decidedly classist tone: "His educated inflections destroy her resistance" (2004 [1971]: 99). And it is not simply Quevado who chooses to violate Urbmon custom. His wife Micaela is consumed by the desire to move upward within the Urbmon, and she uses sex with one of the upper-most professionals in the building to try and make her husband jealous, an emotion thought to be long removed from humanity. At the end of their section of the novel, after a screaming match that threatens to disrupt their position within the building, Quevado and his wife assume that they"re both "[t]hrowbacks to an uglier age" and they agree that they will "have to wear better camouflage" in order to escape the chute (2004 [1971]: 119). But the irony of their situation is that almost all of the characters Silverberg introduces to the reader feel much the same way—that they can't survive within the Urbmon.

In the section following the one focusing on Quevado and his wife, Siegmund Kluver—a rising star in the Urbmon's hierarchy of administrators—introduces the reader to life at the very top of the Urbmon. Discarding even the pretense of spatial equality, the top one hundred or so floors of the Urbmon offer those in power an unheard of level of luxury that serves to motivate eager junior administrators and satiate the need of those at the top to dominate those below. As Kluver suggests, "[t]here's space to waste in Louisville" (2004 [1971]: 126). Kluver gives no indication of accepting anything other than a position at the top of the Urbmon, foregoing the seemingly classless aspirations of the Urbmon's creators for a class envy familiar to any young capitalist reading Silverberg's novel. But Kluver is torn between his overwhelming desire to rise to the top and an unshakable feeling that he doesn't belong with the elite. As one of the many women he nightwalks with remarks: "It might just happen that your passionate involvement with administrative affairs, Siegmund, represents more of a desire for mere rung-grabbing than it does a strong humanitarian concern, and you feel so guilty about your intense ambitions that you believe others are thinking about you in the same terms that yourself—" (2004 [1971]: 131). Kluver, like a number of other characters in the novel, opts for death rather than the social and spatial constraints of the Urbmon, making the novel read more like a cautionary dystopia than a socialist utopia.

The World Inside certainly points to an inability to escape the social differentiation so clearly outlined by Harvey. Within the novel, the lowest levels of the Urbmon are represented by cities often equated with working-class living conditions. Prague and Warsaw, with their Eastern European connotations serve as the lowest levels of the building and are populated mostly by maintenance workers and laborers. San Francisco, as mentioned above, serves as the home for the novel's musician, and the topmost levels—Toledo, Paris, and Louisville[13]—serve as mimetic avatars of Western power and accumulation. More importantly, location within the Urbmon—and its indication of professional status—has become shorthand for social distinction among the Urbmon's many residents. Those living at the lower levels are frequently labeled "grubbos" by the building's inhabitants, and the "cultural ghetto" of San Francisco is seen by the upper residents as a subcultural novelty—just risqué enough to visit, but never good enough to inhabit for longer than the time it takes to purchase a new work of art. Although Silverberg's choice to create his seeming utopia within the confines of a vertical city might seem a little obvious, he uses the all-too-believable reactions of his protagonists to ensure the reader has no doubt of the staying power of the very real social stratification that girds the residential differentiation within the Western world. Harvey might have been able to envision a city where every resident was given equal access to land, but, as Silverberg suggests, there will always be some urban spaces that are better than others.

Neither the tower of capitalist accumulation in Ballard's *High-Rise* nor the future utopia of procreation in Silverberg's *The World Inside* is able to escape the need to establish boundaries based on social or employment status. And as Harvey, Soja, and Davis suggest, these buildings—these worlds—are recreations of the urban spaces we live and work in. It is no wonder then that *High-Rise* ends as it begins, with a resident tucking in to a nice dinner of barbequed dog, and no surprise that *The World Inside* ends with Urbmon 116's most promising resident leaping to his death from the 1,000th floor. As Silverberg states in the final lines of his novel: "Life goes on. God Bless! Here begins another happy day" (2004 [1971]: 233).

NOTES

1. Also released as *The Twilight of the City* by Macmillan in 1977.
2. For more on these novels see Hurst, "The Prescience of Mark Adlard," (1997) and Latham, "Mark Adlard," (2002).
3. For an informative summary of Ballard's position in the New Wave, see Rob Latham's "The New Wave" (2005).
4. Burgess's almost religious belief in the superiority of quantitative research can be seen in his use of telephone records to map social mobility (1925: 60–61).
5. See Burgess, "The Growth of the City: An Introduction to a Research Project," (1925). Useful summaries of Burgess's work and the formation of the Chicago School of urban sociology can be found in Soja's *Postmetropolis* and Harvey's *Social Justice and the City*.
6. For more on Harvey's analysis of rent see *Rebel Cities: From the Right to the City to the Urban Revolution* (2012) and *Spaces of Capital: Towards a Critical Geography* (2001).
7. Harvey's *The Urban Experience* is an abridged and modified version of *The Urbanization of Capital* (1985) and *Consciousness and the Urban Experience* (1985). The chapter I make use of here "Class Structure and the Theory of Residential Differentiation" is taken in part from *Process in Physical and Human Geography: Bristol Essays* (1975) eds. Robert Peel, Michael Chisholm, and Peter Haggett.
8. "La Ville contemporaine" or "The Contemporary City" first appeared in Le Corbusier's *Urbanisme* (1924) and was later translated by Frederick Etchells as part of *The City of Tomorrow and Its Planning* (Le Corbusier 1987).
9. See Latham, "The Urban Question in New Wave SF," (2009).
10. See See *Super-Cannes* (2000) and *Cocaine Nights* (1998).
11. Harvey describes "interregional multiplier effects" as the effect of an allocation of resources in one territory on another (2009: 105–06).
12. Silverberg's true motivations for writing *The World Inside* are ambiguous at best. At times the novel seems to be both criticizing and valorizing the concentration of contemporary urban life. While he certainly stresses the psychological toll that cramped living space might have on an individual, he also makes it a point to show the dangers of close-minded rural life. The emphasis on "nightwalking" and psychotropic drug use in the novel also points to the possibility that he was merely trying to cater to readers familiar with the countercultural SF novels of Samuel Delany and Brian Aldiss.
13. While Louisville might seem like somewhat of a stretch here, I would suggest that Silverberg was attempting to connect the city to the almost antebellum descriptions of the Urbmon's de-facto leader, Nissim Shawke. There's something of a "good old boy" network operating within the administrative center of the Urbmon, and Shawke's attempts to groom Kluver might not seem out of place in a satirization of Southern gentility.

BIBLIOGRAPHY

Abrash, Meritt (1983), "Robert Silverberg's *The World Inside*," in *No Place Else: Explorations in Utopian and Dystopian Fiction*, Eric S. Rabkin, Martin H. Greenberg, and Joseph D. Olander (eds.), Illinois: Southern Illinois University Press, pp. 225–43.
Adlard, Mark (1977 [1971]), *Interface*, New York: Ace.
———. (1978 [1972]), *Volteface*, New York: Ace.
———. (1978 [1975]), *Multiface*, New York: Ace.
Axelrod, Jeremiah B. C. (2009), *Inventing Autopia: Dreams and Visions of the Modern Metropolis in Jazz Age Los Angeles*, Los Angeles: University of California Press.
Ballard, J. G. (1962), "Which Way to Inner Space?" *New Worlds*, 118, pp. 2–3, 116–18.
———. (1998 [1996]), *Cocaine Nights*, Washington, D.C.: Counterpoint.
———. (2002 [2000]), *Super-Cannes*, New York: Picador.
———. (2006 [1975]), *High-Rise*, London: Harper Perennial.

Bellamy, Edward (2007 [1888]), *Looking Backward 2000–1887*, New York: Oxford University Press.

Burgess, E. W. (1925), "The Growth of the City: An Introduction to a Research Project," in *The City: Suggestions for Investigation of Human Behavior in the Human Environment*, E. W. Burgess and Robert E. Park (eds.), Chicago: University of Chicago Press, pp. 47–62.

Davis, Mike (1992), *City of Quartz*. New York: Vintage.

Donnelly, Ignatius L. (1890), *Caesar's Column: A Story of the Twentieth Century*, Chicago: F. J. Shulte and Co.

Dunn, Thomas P. and Richard D. Erlich (1980), "The Mechanical Hive: Urbmon 116 as the Villain-Hero of Robert Silverberg's *The World Inside*," *Journal of Science Fiction and Fantasy*, 21: 4, Winter, pp. 338–347.

Elkins, Charles and Martin Greenberg (eds.) (1992), *Robert Silverberg's Many Trapdoors: Critical Essays on His Science Fiction*, Westport, CT: Greenwood.

Engels, Freidrich (1935 [1872–73]), *The Housing Question*, C. P. Dutt (ed.), New York: International Publishers.

Fishman, Robert (1982), *Urban Utopias in the Twentieth Century: Ebenezer Howard, Frank Lloyd Wright, and Le Corbusier*, Cambridge, MA: MIT Press.

Gasiorek, Andrzej (2005), *JG Ballard*, Manchester: Manchester University Press, pp. 101–40.

Groes, Sebastian (2009), "From Shanghai to Shepperton: Crises of Representation in J. G. Ballard's Londons," in *J. G. Ballard: Contemporary Critical Perspectives*, Jeanette Baxter (ed.), New York: Continuum, pp. 78–93.

———. (2012), "The Texture of Modernity in *Crash, Concrete Island*, and *High Rise*," *J. G. Ballard Visions and Revisions*, Jeanette Baxter and Rowland Wymer (eds.), New York: Palgrave Macmillan, pp. 123–41.

Hall, Peter (2002 [1988]), *Cities of Tomorrow*, Malden, MA: Blackwell.

Harvey, David (1985a), *The Urbanization of Capital: Studies in the History and Theory of Capitalist Urbanization*, Baltimore, MD: Johns Hopkins University Press.

———. (1985b), *Consciousness and the Urban Experience*, Baltimore, MD: John Hopkins University Press.

———. (1989), *The Urban Experience*, Baltimore, MD: Johns Hopkins University Press.

———. (1990), *The Condition of Postmodernity*, Malden, MA: Blackwell.

——— (2001), *The Spaces of Capital: Towards a Critical Geography*, New York: Routledge.

———. (2009 [1973]), *Social Justice and the City*, Athens, GA: University of Georgia Press.

———. (2012), *Rebel Cities: From the Right to the City to the Urban Revolution*, London: Verso.

Hurst, L. J. (1997), "The Prescience of Mark Adlard," *Vector*, 185, September-October, pp. 8–10.

Latham, Rob (2005), "The New Wave," in *A Companion to Science Fiction*, ed. David Seed, Malden, MA: Blackwell, pp. 202–16.

———. (2002), "Mark Adlard," *British Fantasy and Science-Fiction Writers Since 1960*, ed. Darren Harris-Fain, Detroit: Gale, pp. 19–24. http://dspace.dial.pipex.com/l.j.hurst/adlard.html.

———. (2009), "The Urban Question in New Wave SF," in *Red Planets: Marxism and Science Fiction*, Mark Bould and China Mieville (eds.), Middletown, CT: Wesleyan University Press, pp. 178–95.

Le Corbusier (1924), *Urbanisme*, Paris: G Crès and cie.

———. (1967 [1933]), *The Radiant City*, New York: Faber and Faber.

———. (1987 [1929]), *The City of To-morrow and Its Planning* (trans. Frederick Etchells), New York: Dover.

London, Jack (2009 [1908]), *The Iron Heel*, New York: Dover.

Luckhurst, Roger (1997), *"The Angle Between Two Walls": The Fiction of J.G. Ballard*, Liverpool: Liverpool University Press.

Morris, William (2004 [1890]), *News from Nowhere and Other Writings*, New York: Penguin.

Platt, Charles (1971 [1970]), *The City Dwellers*, London: Sphere Books.

Pohl, Frederik (1970 [1954]), "The Midas Plague," in *Nightmare Age*, New York: Ballantine, pp. 195–258.

Pringle, David (1975), "J. G. Ballard's SF for Today," *Science Fiction Monthly*, 2: 10, October, pp. 8–11.
Silverberg, Robert (2004 [1971]), *The World Inside*, New York: ibooks.
Soja, Edward W. (2000), *Postmetropolis*, Malden, MA: Blackwell.

Chapter Eight

Red Vienna, Class, and the Common

Kimberly DeFazio

As the crisis of capitalism expands globally, cities around the world are among the most intense sites of conflict. Whether reflected in the massive cuts in jobs and social spending that have hit cities hardest, or in the urban protests against austerity measures, globalization, and anti-democratic governments, the class conflict between labor and capital has made cities one of the most important contexts today for addressing the question of radical praxis. In the face of such conflicts, one of the concerns of left theorists in the global North is increasingly with the interests of the "common" and the struggle for "community." Even more significant, central to many of the new books within cultural theory which often directly respond to movements like Occupy Wall Street and the Arab Spring—e.g., Costas Douzinas and Slavoj Žižek's *The Idea of Communism*, Jodi Dean's *The Communist Horizon*, and David Harvey's *Rebel Cities*—is the effort to theorize communism and socialism in terms of new theorizations of the common. Largely informed by the writings of Antonio Negri and Michael Hardt, for whom the common represents both "the common wealth of the material world—the air, the water, the fruits of the soil, and all nature's bounty . . . [and] also and more significantly those results of social production that are necessary for social interaction and further production, such as knowledges, languages, codes, information, [and] affects" (Negri and Hardt 2009: viii), left (urban) cultural theorists have come to see many of the cultural struggles over the commons as the basis of a radical, even communist, struggle that will usher in a new era in history. "[T]he only way we are communist," Žižek argued to protestors in Zuccotti Park in October 2011, "is that we care about the commons" (Gell 2011).

But at the core of the turn to the common and communism is the historical question for the left of whether change is primarily a cultural or an economic phenomenon. That is to say, is radical praxis a matter of cultural resistance, or does transformative change require above all changing the social relations of production?

This question is at the center of debates over what has come to be called "Red Vienna": this being the period between World War I and World War II when Vienna operated under the "municipal socialism" of the Austro-Marxists. In this chapter, I examine the extensive housing projects (the *Gemeindebauten*) that have become the hallmark of Red Vienna and its social programs and policies. Red Vienna, in other words, represents a historical moment during which the principle of cultural transformation was implemented in an urban setting. An analysis of its urban programs therefore offers a particularly important opportunity to assess both the consequences of municipal socialist policies as well as the theoretical and political assumptions underlying them.

Eve Blau, for instance, suggests in *The Architecture of Red Vienna* (1999) that since the 1970s there has been a renewed interest in Red Vienna in the field of art history as well as in the broader political context of the turn toward a "third way" between communism and capitalism. Red Vienna's housing structures, she observes, are widely regarded as a radical development, both at the level of a more "heterodox" form of architecture in the interwar period as well as a more "flexible" theory of Marxism. More recently, in *Rebel Cities*, David Harvey points to the "long and distinguished history of "municipal socialism" and even whole phases of radical urban reform, such as that which occurred in 'Red Vienna,'" that need to be "recuperated" as key to revitalizing "anti-capitalist struggle" today (2012: 138). That Red Vienna is reemerging as an important site of public discussion over the future of cities is indicated in the recent exhibit held at the Austrian Cultural Forum in New York City, "The Vienna Model: Housing for the 21st Century City" (April 17–September 2, 2013). The curators of this exhibit acknowledge the roots of contemporary progressive Viennese urban design in "Red Vienna," and emphasize that they hope "to communicate to American architects, housing activists, and planners how they might apply the Viennese lessons to the development of better housing in the United States" (Förster and Menking 2013).

What, then, are the lessons of Red Vienna? What conclusions can we draw about the way it emphasized matters of public housing, common culture, and community? Does it reflect a more effective theory of transformative change, since it foregrounds cultural over economic change and as a result is more attentive to the immediate needs of the working class, as many suggest? Or does the turn to culture represent what Austro-Marxist Otto Bauer praised as "the self-restriction of the proletariat" (quoted in Loew 1979: 26) that focused on political and cultural struggles as opposed to economic ones, but whose real effect was to distract the working class from deeper-lying economic relations? I shall argue that Red Vienna is important for Marxist urban theory to reexamine because it reveals the very significant limits of the culturalist approach to social change that informed the "municipal socialism" of Red Vienna in the 1920s. Austro-Marxist culturalism cut off culture from the economic relations that both shaped inequality in Austria and connected the Viennese workers to the struggles taking part throughout Russia and Europe, consequently weakening the class basis from which to fight capital and the later rise of fascism. It is therefore particularly troubling that this approach has almost completely overtaken the left in the global North in the twenty-first century, especially in the turn to the "common" and the contemporary rewriting of communism as common-ism.

My argument develops in four stages. In the first part of the chapter I address the historical context of Red Vienna and discuss a few of its most important and widely recognized programs and their limits. I then go on to analyze the theoretical and political grounds upon which these programs were argued for by examining the writings of Otto Bauer and others. After a rereading of Friedrich Engels ("The Housing Question"), in the final section of the chapter I address the ways in which popular trends in contemporary cultural theory—following the Austro-Marxists in Red Vienna—focus on what Engels calls the "secondary" contradictions of capitalism and consequently turn class struggle into a cultural struggle over the common. In the early twenty-first century, as in the early twentieth century, the appeal to the "common" aspects of culture in the face of deepening global contradictions, I argue, obscures the class relations in culture, substitutes local reforms for the transformation of the global roots of urban inequality, and restricts class politics to updated forms of bourgeois democracy that, far from challenging capital, serve to give it a more humane veneer.

A. "UNDOING" THE EXPERIENCE OF CLASS: THE RISE OF RED VIENNA AND THE *GEMEINDEBAUTEN*

Red Vienna, as I mentioned, refers to the municipal structure of governing inaugurated in Vienna in the post-World War I moment (1919–1934). During this time, Vienna became a socialist municipality controlled by the Austrian Social Democratic Party (SDP), largely under the leadership of Austro-Marxists such as Otto Bauer, Max Adler, and Karl Renner, many of whom had been active in the labor movement and the SDP since the 1890s. The roots of the Viennese working class movement stretch back to (and beyond) the European revolutions in 1848. But its more immediate context was, on the one hand, the Russian Revolution, which had mobilized millions of workers in Russia and throughout Europe. On the other, the end of World War I had brought utter economic devastation to regions in Europe (like

Austria) that had only recently begun to industrialize and urbanize. Austria was particularly affected by both of these related developments: a growing militancy and organization of the working class and deepening economic crises.

Following World War I and the dismantling of the Hapsburg dynasty, Vienna became the capital of the First Republic of German Austria. But Vienna emerged from the war both bankrupt as well as sharply cut off from its former sources of raw materials and resources (now located in the separate nation of Germany and in the hinterlands of Austria). It lagged behind industrially relative to other parts of Europe; faced significant food, fuel, and housing shortages; lacked a strong bourgeois power structure after the fall of the monarchy; and struggled under the imposition of political and financial constraints by the Entente powers on the nation following the war. The SDP (which had formed in 1889) came immediately to power in this post-war period of economic and political crisis and won a majority in the first national election in 1919, the same year that the Viennese elected the city's first socialist mayor, Jacob Reumann. While the SDP had control of the municipal and provincial government, however, the "numerical, electoral, and governmental strength in Vienna was deceptive, for the national government remained firmly in the hands of their political opponents, the Christian Socialist party and its allies. From the beginning the country was divided into two camps—Vienna and scattered industrial enclaves against the largely agrarian and Catholic provinces" (Gruber 1991: 10), which violently opposed the socialist forms of culture initiated by the SDP.

The rise of the Austro-Marxist-led SDP and its electoral success was situated on the one hand, in opposition to a powerful conservative party, the Christian Socialists representing agrarian interests and landed property and supported by the peasants, and on the other, the Communist movement, which was rapidly growing throughout Europe and in the Republic of Austria in the wake of the October Revolution in Russia. Eve Blau describes the success of the SDP in this way: they "emerged as the only political group that was capable of controlling the masses of unemployed workers and ex-soldiers and averting a Bolshevik revolution in Austria" (1999: 4–5). In other words, they represented a reformist *opposition* to the revolutionary parties— a particularly important concern for the ruling powers, as Austrian workers and peasants were some of the most exploited and impoverished in Europe and therefore had the most to gain from a communist revolution in Austria. At the same time, the SDP represented itself as the greatest advocate of the "proletarian revolution" (Bauer 1970).

I will return to some of the central theoretical arguments that comprised the Austro-Marxist view of the socialists when I turn shortly to the writings of Bauer and others. But here it is important to emphasize that the Austro-Marxists clearly differentiated themselves from the arguments for revolution represented by the Bolsheviks, and from the arguments for slow reform represented by revisionist position of the Mensheviks and the Second International. A testament to this is not only the Austro-Marxist proposal for a "Two-and a Half International," but also what Bauer called "slow revolution" (quoted in Bottomore and Goode 1978: 26). The Austro-Marxists argued that advancing a revolutionary movement following the Russian Revolution (based on dictatorship of the proletariat to take control of the means of production) would be a disaster for the proletarian revolution, and they advocated instead for a kind of gradualism along the lines of the later Kautsky who supported parliamentary democracy over revolution. As Bottomore and Goode suggest, Bauer's notion of slow revolution appealed to "the gradual construction of a socialist society after the conquest of political power by a working-class party, through radical reforms in all spheres of social life, involving in many cases the consolidation and gradual extension of reforms already undertaken by the bourgeois state" (1978: 26). Consequently, the efforts of the theoretical leaders of the SDP were focused primarily on extending democracy and creating forms of culture that enhanced the community and welfare of the Viennese working class.

One particularly important manifestation of the programs of Red Vienna's leaders was the massive housing project, the *Gemeindebauten*, widely heralded as monuments to the working class struggle. Between 1923 and 1934 when the German fascists invaded Vienna, the city constructed over 65,000 housing units. Between 1923 and 1927 alone over 25,000 new units had been created (Lewis 1983: 336). These housing projects—many of whose architects, as Eve Blau suggests, were students of the Wagnerian school and members of private architectural firms—were designed as large housing blocks, which combined single-family unit apartments with communal facilities such as kitchens, laundry, daycare, libraries, and schools for children. The Karl-Marx-Hof (completed between 1926 and 1930) is "often regarded as the symbol of "Red Vienna"," in the words of the exhibit at the Austrian Cultural Forum in New York City ("The Vienna Model" 2013). Curators Wolfgang Förster and William Menking go on to describe the structure, designed by architect Karl Ehn, as having been planned to include "more than 1,000 apartments around several large landscaped courtyards and a central square with its impressive archee . . . and flagposts. The common infrastructure included two kindergartens, laundries, [and] meeting rooms" ("The Vienna Model"). The actual number of units completed in 1930 was 1,325.

Based on the principle of "communal" living, the *Gemeindebauten* in general sought to intervene into the alienation and individualism of capitalist social relations by providing workers with collective spaces to live, eat, and learn.[1] "Claiming decent housing to be a fundamental right of all citizens, Bauer demanded the building of municipal housing projects which would include (in every building block) "central kitchens and laundries, central heating, play and classrooms for children, common dining rooms, reading and game rooms for adults, and the cooks, laundresses, and child-care specialists required for the function of these communal facilities"" (Gruber 1991: 50), and the tenants would play a central role in the operation and supervision of the facilities. This was part of what Bauer referred to as "creating a revolution of souls" (quoted in Gruber 1991: 6), and included other cultural programs involving

> prescriptions for an orderly family life and a new definition of a woman's role in society; lectures, a vast array of publications, and libraries to stimulate and elevate the mind; associations for the enrichment of artists taste; encouragement of abstinence from tobacco and alcohol, and admonitions about sociality; organizations to instill socialist ethics and community spirit in children and young adults; a virtual sports empire to create healthy proletarian bodies . . . and mass festivals to demonstrate solidarity, discipline, and collective strength. (Gruber 1991: 6–7)

These programs functioned as a broader cultural pedagogy aimed at fostering socialist subjectivities outside of work, *external* to the space of production.

The concern with socialist ethics was also reflected in the choices of architectural style. Instead of basing the architecture of the housing programs on the popular suburban "*Sieldlungen*," in which single family apartments (with separate facilities) were built in complexes, the leaders chose the urban *Gemeindebauten*, which became known as "workers" fortresses," "people's palaces," and "superblocks." The principle behind these was that renters would have access to common eating facilities, kindergartens, laundries, etc., and that these would be provided within the blocks themselves, specifically in the center courtyards, many of which were not accessible except from the inside of the block. The complexes would thus be "self-sufficient." And, as Helmut Gruber's text hints, one of the main arguments used in developing the superblocks as opposed to the *Sieldlungen* was that the latter were premised on the traditional role of woman as domestic laborer, whereas the *Gemeindebauten* represented a "liberation" of women from the traditional role, which would be replaced, through the construction of communal kitchens and dining rooms, by a more collective approach to meeting basic needs.

Given the power of the municipality,[2] the leaders financed the new social welfare reforms and cultural initiatives through the enforcement of a progressive tax system which heavily taxed the (rich) landlords rather than the workers, whose rents were significantly lowered (from over 25 percent to under 5 percent of wages).[3] The goal was to provide the workers with affordable housing which was not only at a higher standard of living, but fostered "community" and "proletarian culture" as part of the project of creating what Jill Lewis (1983) calls "socialism in one city" in her article's title. This was central to the effort, Blau explains, to "reshape traditional *Volkskulture* (pop-ular/folk culture) into new *Arbeiterkulture* (socialized working class culture) through social and cultural institutions" (1999: 6). The *Gemeindebauten* were to be the principle sites for the development of this "new socialized urban culture" (1999: 6), drawing attention from the wider international com-munity. "Both their direct beneficiaries and the international housing com-munity—architects, planners, housing theorist, political leaders, and sociolo-gists—saw these housing programs as one of the most promising social phe-nomena of the times, indeed as evidence that Red Vienna might be a harbing-er of a better world. Building for a new humanity was seen as the essence of what was happening" (Marcuse 1985: 208). Toward this end, the leaders of the SDP focused on cultural developments, which were perceived as impor-tant in intervening into the conservative, religious climate of Austria that inculcated workers into a mythology of "individualism" that prevented col-lectivity and solidarity. For example, Otto Felix Kanitz, an educational theo-rist of the party and pupil of Adler, argued that a new form of education should "teach proletarian children to overcome their "social inferiority com-plex" and would prevent the subsequent formation of a *macht lust* in a reaction to the *ohnmacht* of life experience" (quoted in Rabinbach 1985b: 189–90). As Rabinbach clarifies, Adler "did not champion the "proletarian education" advocated by the Communists but "socialist education" in a uni-versal sense which would *undo* the effects of proletarian experience" (1985b: 190).

However—and this is one of my main arguments in this chapter—"undo-ing" the "experience" of the working class without working to "undo" the economic structures of exploitation is ultimately a means of *managing* the contradictions of capitalism without challenging its fundamental structure in any significant way. Building socialist consciousness through "communal living"—while perhaps offering a less alienating living and learning environ-ment—replaces changing the objective conditions of oppression with subjec-tive changes for a communal lifestyle *within* capitalism. It fosters the revi-sionist illusion of "capitalism with a human face"—an illusion desperately needed by the ruling class in times of crisis—under the guise of a radical resistance to capitalism.

Red Vienna, to put this differently, was the product of a cultural theory of class and class change. Despite the Austro-Marxists" critique of capitalist oppression and exploitation, they proposed that the solution was to be found not in the international struggle to end exploitation but to "undo" the effects of exploitation *within* capitalism. Socialism, Austro-Marxist Max Adler in-sisted, is "above all a cultural movement" (quoted in Rabinbach 1985b: 190). By advocating new spaces for community participation and "creativity," fos-tering a "universal" sense of identity, and treating "living" conditions as a central site of resistance to the alienating, rationalized working conditions of the working class, the Austro-Marxists taught that it was possible to establish urban socialism within wage-labor. Thus, for them, women's "liberation" (not to mention men's) had more to do with changing the relations of domestic space than it did changing women's position in production. Central to the cultural theory of socialism, then, is a double-move involving, first, the rejection of the transformation of the relations of production and, second, the rewriting of cultural change as revolutionary.

But, significantly, the cultivation of common forms of culture in housing served as a means of focusing on reproduction in such a way that it kept down the costs of production and kept up the rate of exploitation. Take, for instance, Gruber's argument that "As sole customer [of housing construction materials], the municipality succeeded in influencing the pricing policy of some firms supplying building materials. But it made no attempt to replace the host of small construction companies by encouraging the formation of production cooperatives, or to consolidate and control them. . . . The [municipal leadership] appears not to have considered the possibility of a long-range strategy to partially alter the economy of the city" (1991: 56). The concern was with reproduction, rather than production. Or more specifically in the case of housing, with the forms of proletarian consumption, which was addressed not by intervening into the relations of exploitation but by making certain items workers needed to survive more affordable through taxing capitalists and landowners. What was at stake was redistribution at the point of consumption of the surplus value privately appropriated at the point of production.[4] In fact, as Charles Gulick has shown in *Austria*,

> The real wages of Austrian workers were extremely low. . . . This enabled Austrian industry to maintain a certain position as exporter on the world market. . . . Austrian industry could successfully compete on the world market . . . only because of the export premium industry received in the form of tenants' protection. Abolition of tenants' protection would have made increases in wages unavoidable. (quoted in Marcuse 1985: 211)

Keeping rents low in communal housing, far from challenging the relations of private property, had the effect of maintaining them, because the struggle for housing was cut off from the class struggle over the appropriation of surplus value. For, at the same time they were championing cultural reforms to the workers, in their dealings with bourgeoisie, the Social Democrats"

> economic demands always had the character of advice to the government as to how best to increase the competitiveness of the Austrian economy. In this connection, the framework provided by the given social relations was always seen as unalterable, and in no way were any demands of an anti-capitalist kind raised, such as could have made possible a counter-offensive by the working

class on the basis of an alternative economic programme to the plans of the bourgeoisie. (Loew 1979: 41)

And though they openly criticized the refusal of the industrial bourgeoisie to increase wages, "time and again the Social-Democrat leaders made themselves advocates of the "objective barriers" to increased wages that flowed from the poor competitive position of the industrialists" (Loew 1979: 41). Claims about the "undoing" of the effects of class in the culture of community served to justify maintaining the rate at which capital was exploiting workers in the imperialist rivalries.

Yet championing culture could only be accomplished by actively (and at times violently) marginalizing the Communist workers and organizations. In this regard, Bauer, speaking of the situation of Austria immediately following the end of World War I, celebrates the fact that "the great temptation of Bolshevism was repulsed" (1970: 167), following the "great process of the intellectual self-mastery of the working class" (1970: 168), which had been guided by the Austro-Marxists" emphasis on electoral politics and democratic governance, rather than the need for working class control of the state to wrest ownership of the means of production from the bourgeoisie. "In the first months after the October Revolution," Bauer eagerly admits,

> the energy of the masses found employment in the *economic activities of the workers" councils, which, however, in the course of time lost their significance*. At the same time the political importance of the workers" councils became all the more marked, especially during the time of resistance to Hungarian Bolshevism. *These councils were gradually changed from organs of revolutionary encroachment upon economic administration into organs of the political class struggle.* (1970: 173, my emphasis)

The substitution of reproduction and redistribution for production (theoretically and practically) speaks to the way that Red Vienna pioneered the crisis-managing (updating) of capitalism at a time when capital was forced to create more progressive welfare programs to stall off workers" more revolutionary demands. The turn to common culture, or the common-ing of socialism, in other words, was not a sign of the strength of the working class movement toward socialism, but rather an index of the municipal leaders' economic *and* political retreat from the socialist struggles taking place around them in Europe. This became devastatingly clear in the late 1920s and early 1930s, as the bourgeoisie and the far right gained more and more political ground outside of the socialist "oasis" of Vienna, finally gaining enough power within the national government and the military to dissolve Parliament and ban the Social Democrats, who—as Loew shows in his extensive critique—reluctantly called for the working class to fight back only once there was no chance of challenging the fascists. "The February struggles of

1934," he writes, "bore witness to the still existing revolutionary determination, despite all disillusionment and defeat, of significant sections of the
proletariat, and showed up the complete abdication of the Party leadership"
(Loew 1979: 44). The Karl-Marx-Hof would become a deadly battleground
in the Austrian Uprising. During this three-day war in February 1934 many
members of the working class barricaded themselves in the Karl-Marx-Hof
and fought to defend themselves from the artillery fire of the Austrian army
and paramilitary, which killed over 100 men, women and children and in-
jured over 400, on this front alone.

In his important *Red Vienna: Experiment in Working-Class Culture
1919–1934*, Gruber (1991) is, like many other theorists today, hardly uncriti-
cal of the practices inaugurated by the SDP leaders. Nonetheless, he reads
Red Vienna as an "attempt to develop a comprehensive proletarian counter-
culture," and heralds their "attempt to explore the unknown—the blending of
culture and politics" based on their assumption that "culture could play a
significant role in the class struggle" (1991: 5). Gruber claims, therefore, that
the SDP's cultural program only "shifted" after the storming of the Palace of
Justice on July 15, 1927 by tens of thousands of workers—workers who were
frustrated by the SDP leadership's failure to take a more radical position
following the killing by fascists of a worker and a child attending a Social
Democrat meeting earlier in the year. Significantly, this protest was met with
the deadly force of police who killed eighty-five workers. Gruber writes,
"earlier it had been an instrument in the class struggle; now it increasingly
became a surrogate for politics, the arena of which shifted from electoral
contests to force and violence in the streets" (1991: 10)—but this argument
obscures the way the Austro-Marxists" theory of culture as the primary site
of class struggle provided a framework for their political and economic struggle. In fact, it shaped their reading of class struggle and the state *from the
start*. The historian implies that, had they been more consistent (and for
Gruber more democratic), they would have been more effective in bringing
about change. Rabinbach, in his own critical analysis, says something similar
when he writes that the Austro-Marxists became leaders in proletarian pedagogy once they had decided that political power was no longer an option: "it
became increasingly clear that an ever greater emphasis was being placed on
the book as an essential tool of socialist politics. Political fatalism and a
dwindling sense of efficacy in the larger social sphere were offset by the
institutionalized optimism of the pedagogical movement" (1985b: 189).
Again, the assumption here is that the (later) political practices of the Austro-
Marxists were the problem, rather than their theory of culture and class
which had led them, in the first instance, to oppose the revolutionary movements shaking the foundations of Europe. For this reason—and the fact that
so much left cultural theory is shaped by many of the same cultural assumptions that informed Red Vienna—it is necessary to turn to a closer analysis of

the Austro-Marxists" theory of culture and its legacy in the contemporary moment.

B. UNITY, COMMUNITY, AND "SOCIALIZED CONSCIOUSNESS"

As I have begun to suggest, Austro-Marxism is a response to the crisis of capitalism that emerges in Europe in the period leading up to World War I. This is a crisis in which a falling rate of profit and increasing competition between capitalists led, as Otto Bauer writes, to

> the world image of a period in which the great traditional questions of the rights of personality and humanity, of the nature of the world and God, no longer have any significance; in which politics is carried on only by economic interest groups; in which science seeks only to classify in the most economical way what we experience, and art seeks only to reproduce what we observe. (1970: 214)

However, whereas Lenin argued in response to this crisis that true and lasting changes in cultural forms and social organizations—that is, changes that "make the blessings of democracy *really* accessible to the workers and poor peasants" (1977a: 370)—required first the fundamental transformation of the mode of production, the Austro-Marxists inverted the relationship between the economic base and the cultural superstructure. They instead sought to create the conditions for socialism primarily within the culture of capitalism itself through the mechanism of municipal socialism. What I want to propose is that what is described as the Austro-Marxists" retreat "step by step, search-ing for compromises with the authoritarian right" (Fischer 2000: ix) was not a mark of poor strategy, but a consequence of their cultural theory of class. This theory represented the fundamental contradiction in capitalist society not as that between capitalist and worker, but rather—in a Kantian twist—as a transhistorical antimony between "man" and "society" that can only be overcome through the recognition of the fundamental "socialization" that serves as the basis of humanity. While they appeal to Marx's theory of historical materialism, what emerges from Austro-Marxism is actually a de-historicized theory of "alienation" which focuses on the organization of "community" as the means of social change rather than revolutionary trans-formation. This shift from Marxism to what might be called Kantian social-ism remains a critical issue today because in the contemporary moment one finds, I claim, the same post-class logic of the Austro-Marxist "strategy of a "third way" social democracy and Marxism-Leninism" (Nimni 2000: xxxiii) among left theorists of the global North, including writers such as Antonio Negri, Michael Hardt, Andy Merrifield, and Slavoj Žižek.

It is in the context of resolving the conflict between man and society that Bauer claims the Austro-Marxists'' ability to generate "living unity" among the citizens of Red Vienna as one of their central "triumphs" (1978b: 47). However, at the core of this desire for "unity" was not simply, as Bauer claims, a practical response to the local contradictions of capitalism in the Austrian context, but a long-standing theory of class which, developed throughout the work of Bauer, Renner, and Adler, argues for the necessity of incorporating Kantian practical philosophy and ethics into the workers'' movements because of what they claimed was the need to reestablish "the working class as a united, harmonious community" (Adler 1978b: 248).

The key to understanding the Austro-Marxist theory of unity and its political implications lies in their theorization of "socialized consciousness" as "a transcendental condition of experience" (Adler 1978a: 75), which is expressed through the mechanisms and development of cultural forms. For example, in articulating the connection between the transcendental philosophy of Kant and the historical materialism of Marx, Adler writes that "society is not something which emerges from interactions between men, nor is it above men, nor has it come into existence through any sympathetic impulses or as a result of selection in the struggle for existence" (1978c: 65). Instead, he writes "it is simply there" and that "as soon as man appears society is there, because man is empirically possible only among men" (1978c: 65). For Adler, the basis of communism is a romantic notion of prepolitical, preclass social ontology, the real significance of which is its spiritualizing of class contradictions.

What distinguishes this articulation from Marx is that while Marx foregrounded labor as the condition of existence of humanity in his theorization of "social being," in Adler's articulation of the foundation of society is a variation of Kant's generalized theory of community as "general reciprocal interaction" between individuals that then serves as the basis for the development of labor (Bauer 2000: 101). "Society," in this respect, becomes the transcendental condition for labor, rather than the effect of labor. This situates nonalienated society as a transhistorical state of being that must be revealed.

In Adler's notion of the social, the conflict within "society" is no longer between classes as the expression of the mode of production as Marx theorized, but rather between those who are able to live in "society" and those who are excluded and therefore "alienated" from society. As Adler argues, history is the drive of socialized man through "formal-teleological causality to realize what he considers to be morally justified" (1978c: 64). In this sense, history is the coming into being of "society" as a transcendental-ethical ideal. The economic contradictions of capitalism are merely one expression of the unfolding of this transcendental-ethical ideal or, to put it more reductively, economics becomes a reflection of the ideal, rather than its basis. Thus, whereas Marx argues that "society" is an abstraction of the relations of production and the "ideological forms" through which people become conscious of the contradictions of the economic mode of production and "fight it out" (1970: 21), within Austro-Marxism and contemporary left theories of "communism," it is the restoration of this fundamental and transcendental notion of "society" that has become "fractured" which becomes the goal of social transformation. And this is achieved primarily through culture, at the level of consciousness.

What was particularly troubling to the Austro-Marxists was the appearance of a society that, through the events of World War I and the subsequent upheaval and revolutions in Europe and Russia, was becoming *more*, rather than *less*, fractured. In turn, it is precisely because of the transcendental-ethical ideal of society that they set out to "restore" order as the basis for enabling social transformation rather than, as Lenin and others argued, seeing in the heightening contradictions the expression of the underlying laws of capitalist exploitation (1977b). It is on this basis of restoring "unity" between members of the same "society," rather than on the basis of class struggle, that the Austro-Marxists separated the work of understanding the economic situation which produces the alienation of the working class, namely the exploitation of labor, from the transformative mechanisms which bring about the end of alienation. To this point, the Austro-Marxists argued that Marxism was unable to fully address the social complexities of imperialism without appealing to a moral and ethical framework that went beyond class consciousness. For example, Bauer argues that Marx's science of society

> demonstrated that, in capitalist society, the proletariat was bound to *want* socialism as the only possibility of escaping exploitation; that it *can* obtain its goal because the concentration of property has made possible the appropriation of the instruments of labour as social property; that the working class *will* attain its goal, because it becomes the overwhelming majority of the population. (1978a: 81)

Yet he nonetheless concludes that science can give us no answer about how to bring this possibility into being because "the recognition that socialism will come into existence does not yet lead me to fight for it" (1978a: 81). In this respect he writes, "socialism is no longer a question of science, but of life" (1978a: 83). To make socialism a question of "life" here is a reference to the transcendental-ethical society which, the Austro-Marxists argue, serves as the unifying basis of all of humanity. According to Bauer, in other words, although Marxism as a science can explain the *necessity* of socialism, it is not the mechanism for uniting society because it cannot address the divisions within society that exist at the level of ideas. In turn, the more fractured identity becomes, the more one has to turn to a moral code that exceeds or operates outside of class struggle if one is to restore the order that has been fractured. Even as they privileged the unity of consciousness, what takes precedence is not the ideology critique that exposes the way cultural differences (whether national differences, gender differences, or differences between "urban" and "rural" workers) are used to fragment class consciousness, but the creation of forums for the experience of unity. The creation, in culture, of what Bauer calls an "intellectually and morally higher type of man" (1970: 177) was posited as central to the "undoing" of experience under capital.

It is on this basis that one finds in the writings of the Austro-Marxists that the fracturing of "social identity," which includes but is not reducible to class, is generally attributed to two elements: changes in the class structure of capitalism and the impact of these changes on the national question, both of which are said to require moving beyond Marxism's focus on class exploitation.

On the one hand, according to Adler, "the development of the past decade has produced changes in the proletariat itself, eliminating its unitary character" (1978b: 219) and that "at this historical moment, when the expropriators could be expropriated the working class itself has been burst asunder" (1978b: 221). The fundamental problem, according to Adler, was that in the development of capitalism, the increasing complexity of the division of labor—whether it was the extension of the service and advertising industries, managers and labor "aristocrats" within national economies, or the interactions of workers across national boundaries—had resulted in a working class that was so "riddled with such economic conflicts . . . that it is doubtful whether we can speak of a single class" (1978b: 225). In this context, he argues, the "apparently unified class of the proletariat" was actually "five different strata which, in their social-psychological development, have eventually given rise to three basic orientations that led, and still lead to great and dangerous conflicts" (1978b: 225). In other words, the very idea of revolution becomes a dangerous illusion, Adler argues, in the context of a working class that lacks "class solidarity and a community of fate" (1978b: 244).

On the other hand, in his foundational *The Question of Nationalities and Social Democracy*, Bauer extends the need for "unity" beyond just working class and argues that it is actually the nation, rather than class, which forms the basis of "a community of fate" (2000:117). Drawing, too, upon Kant's definition of community as "general reciprocal interaction" (2000: 101), Bauer goes even further than Adler and argues that class is not the basis of a "community" but rather represents a "similarity of fate" and a "community of character" that exists alongside of and as a supplement to national identity. This is indicated, he claims, by the fact that if "language is the tool of interaction" which marks that a "general reciprocal interaction" exists, then English and German workers share traits such as "the same combativeness, the same revolutionary attitude, the same class morals, the same political aspirations" (2000: 101). However, the very lack of a common language between the workers of these two countries means that "although there may be relationships based upon interaction between German and English Workers, these are much more tenuous than the relationships that link the English worker with the English bourgeois" (2000: 101). In other words, while workers from different countries might share the same fate, they lack the history and social organizations which would enable the development of a "common culture" (2000: 35). Instead, he writes,

> The individuals who belong to a nation are united by the fact that they are all the product of the same effective forces, of the same society, that the same effects of the struggle for existence of humans living together have been transmitted to these individuals in the form of their individual inherited characteristics, that the same culture, developed in the context of the struggle for existence of the same human community, has formed their individual characters. (2000: 110)

It is in this context that the class politics of the Austro-Marxists" commitment to "unity" begin to emerge. First, the emphasis on culture was shaped by a nationalist theory of community which placed national culture as more significant than class position. This, in fact, explains one of the reasons that the Austro-Marxists tried to divert the working class movement away from revolution after World War I. While they often claimed that the Austrian working class was not prepared, they perceived this "lack of preparation" in terms of the extent of national unity.

> The German-Austrians had been the dominant people of the Hapsburg Monarchy. When the national revolution of the Czechs, the Jugo Slavs, and the Poles forcibly dissolved the Hapsburg Monarchy, German-Austria was left in a terrible state of privation and impotence. Our impotence and privation imposed insurmountable barriers to our revolution. It was unable to achieve its national aim, political union with Germany. It could accomplish social transformation only within very narrow limits. (Bauer 1970: 178)

Here it becomes even more evident that the theory of culture and nation shaping Red Vienna was a petty-bourgeois notion of nationhood that ultimately saw socialism as a tool of nation-building (which could never therefore offer any significant opposition to the rising forces of fascism). In proposing that "only socialism can integrate the broad mass of working people into the national community of culture" and that the goal of socialism is not ending national divisions and rivalries, but rather "giving the nation autonomy, by giving it self-determination in regard to the development of its culture" (2000: 94) such that far from coming together socialism would result in "a growing differentiation between the intellectual cultures of the nations" (2000: 98), Bauer and the other Austro-Marxists end up privileging cross-class alliances as the means by which "fracturing" of social identities could be overcome. This of course remystified what had been violently clarified by World War I, not to mention by the Paris Commune almost half a century before it: that "Class-rule is no longer able to disguise itself in a national uniform; the national governments are *one* as against the proletariat" (Marx 1971: 96, original emphasis). Inclusiveness, to put this another way, was ultimately a code for getting rid of the communist elements within the workers councils that threatened the "common" culture of bourgeois Austria. In this way, they could carry on the illusion that the state (civil society) could be used to represent the interests of all, as a basis for opposing "dictatorship of the proletariat," "the political form at last discovered to work out the economical emancipation of labour" (Marx 1971: 75).

C. HOUSING AND CLASS

Loew observes that the Austro-Marxists have often been critiqued for their focus on the "objective" factor of historical development (its mechanical development) at the expense of the "subjective" factor (1979: 47). But in fact, it is their privileging of (socialized) subjectivity that shapes the Austro-Marxists approach to both economics and culture. Changing one's experience of class by fostering community, they purported, would bring about change in economic relations. But class is fundamentally a question, not of experience, but of one's position in the relations of production—whether one owns the means of production and thereby compels others to work for him, or whether one sells her labor in order to survive. The alienation suffered by the working class and their inability to meet but the most basic of needs is the result of the capitalist system of production, in which wages represent only a fraction of the value produced by the worker, whose surplus labor is extracted by the capitalist and forms the basis of profit. The experience of isolation and "inferiority" are themselves effects of the class relations that determine whether one is exploited or exploiter. Therefore, to limit questions of change to culture (i.e., the creation of common, nonalienating experience) is to occlude the more fundamental relation between worker and owner which gives rise to the wide-spread shortages of housing, food, medicine, education, electricity, etc.

Fifty years before the emergence of Red Vienna, Engels had theorized the housing crisis, not as a question of "culture" or "lifestyle" but in relation to the question of production. In *The Housing Question*, Engels argues that in the analysis of the current housing shortages, it is necessary to make a distinction between primary and "secondary" contradictions within capitalism.

> The so-called housing shortage, which plays such a great role in the press nowadays, does not consist in the fact that the working class generally lives in

bad, overcrowded and unhealthy dwelling. *This* shortage is not something peculiar to the present; it is not even one of the sufferings peculiar to the modern proletariat in contradictions to all earlier oppressed classes. On the contrary, all oppressed classes in all periods suffered rather uniformly from it. In order to put an end to *this* housing shortage there is only *one* means: to abolish altogether the exploitation and oppression of the working class by the ruling class. What is meant today by housing shortage is the peculiar intensification of the bad housing conditions of the workers as a result of the sudden rush of population to the big cities; a colossal increase in rents, still greater congestion in the separate houses, and, for some, the impossibility of finding a place to live in at all. And *this* housing shortage gets talked of so much only because it is not confined to the working class but has affected the petty bourgeoisie as well. (1969: 305)

In short, Engels argues, "The housing shortage from which the workers and part of the petty bourgeois suffer in our modern big cities is one of the innumerable *smaller*, secondary evils which result from the present-day capitalist mode of production" (1969: 305–06). On the basis of his analysis, Engels concludes that by virtue of the exploitative system of capitalism, it is not possible to eradicate the housing crisis without eradicating capitalism itself. At best, such programs can only result in a more "humane" capitalism that, in effect, prolongs housing shortages.

Engels' theorization has often been read by the left as rejecting reforms. On these terms, it is said Engels rejects any and all efforts to make the lives of the working class more tolerable; he is only interested in "waiting" for the distant revolution and denying the necessity of the struggle for daily reforms. This is the position that Peter Marcuse seems to align himself with when he suggests that Marxist movements never really (adequately) addressed the housing question subsequent to Engels" critique (1969: 204). More recently, Andy Merrifield argues in *Metromarxism* that insofar as Engels sees changes in housing as a "secondary" in relation to the revolution of relations of production, "Engelsian Marxism says little about cities *in the meanwhile* . . . it denies, if you will, any *here, now*. The problems of the city are displaced by the problems of revolution. The former will have to wait until after the latter are solved" (2002: 47, original emphasis). As a result, Merrifield claims, "Engelsian urban Marxism downplays the dialectics of the city, dilutes its atmosphere, fails to spot certain cultural characteristics, latent political possibilities, and human potentialities located *within* everyday city life" (2002: 48, original emphasis). He was not "interested in culture or in the everyday ambiguity of the modern metropolis . . . [he] never quite understood the city's thicker texture and richer density" (2002: 48).

But Engels is not arguing that reforms in the housing available to workers should not be demanded. The question is *connecting* housing to the other forms of oppression faced by workers so that the struggle against housing shortages and class oppression does not become isolated and thus easily appropriated, but advances revolutionary transformation. Merrifield suggests that the privileging of "everyday ambiguity" can become the foundation for a world in which all people have adequate housing. This, however, obscures the connection between the inadequate housing of the working class and their position in the division of labor. The fight for a just society requires not ambiguity—a popular left concern that makes capital's "instrumental" and alienating effects the main problem, not the structure of relations that produce instrumentalism and isolation—but reliable and totalizing knowledge of the social relations that produce class inequality. Materialism, as Jameson explains, is "the ultimate determination by the mode of production" (1988 :45). Giving up theorizing the determining role that class plays in culture (by, for instance, emphasizing the city's "ambiguous" "thick textures") means affirming the very reified forms of cultural consciousness that capital produces so as to occlude the appropriation of surplus value. It is precisely this translation of the stark binaries of class into the benign poetics of city life (a spiritualizing of material conditions) that constitutes one of the central ideological strategies of left culturalism, as I discuss at further length below.

The importance of Engels' argument is that it shows why housing demands and reforms must be situated in terms of the broader struggle against capital. He offers an explanation of why the treatment of housing as either separate from or as a substitute for the struggle to abolish the relations of exploitation cannot—whether in the context of Red Vienna or in the contemporary moment—provide a basis for meaningful social change. To set one's political horizon at provision of adequate housing for all—not to mention the creation of communal life and learning (as the leaders of Red Vienna did)— is, from the position Engels theorizes, not only a reformist strategy, but an impossible (utopian) one, since capitalism in its competitive drive to increase profits necessarily prevents, among other things, adequate housing for all.

It is not coincidental that, by the end of the socialist municipality of Red Vienna, which had successfully built 65,000 housing units, homelessness had actually increased in Vienna since 1923! What this points to is not that the Austro-Marxists and the architects who carried out their principles lacked "commitment" or "consistency" but rather that to posit housing as a "fundamental right of all citizens," as Bauer did, and build a movement based on this principle—without connecting the housing crisis to the contradictions of capitalism—is to ensure that that right, like many others, will in fact never be achieved but will remain a "formal" right only.

Merrifield's concern with the "thickness" of urban culture and his emphasis on cultural reforms are, in this regard, a symptom of the way left theory today has become overwhelmed with the details of urban surfaces, and consequently more interested in celebrating the "ambiguities" of everyday life and affirming spontaneous activism than building an expansive working class movement to bring about a world in which homelessness no longer exists. Treating Engels" analysis of the causal relation between "primary" and "secondary" determinants of social conditions in moral terms (rather than in terms of a structural analysis of the social totality), Merrifield in effect appeals to the ethico-analytical (liberal) principle that no one realm of the social is more determining than any other while simultaneously privileging the cultural. Theorizing the determinacy of class is not a moral issue. It is an analytical necessity if one is to understand the underlying relations shaping the city in a way that does not repeat, in a more sophisticated manner, the severing of culture from wage labor that now informs many urban cultural "rejuvenation" projects whose main goal is to make cities more profitable at the expense of working people. Marxist urban theory can be a guide in the struggle for a society in which the needs of all are met, only insofar as it unearths the root causes of working class experience and explains why, by its very nature, capitalism "is incompetent to assure an existence to its slave within his slavery, because it cannot help letting him sink into such a state, that it has to feed him, instead of being fed by him" (Marx and Engels 1969: 119).

D. COMMON STRUGGLE AND CLASS STRUGGLE

The lessons of Red Vienna matter in particular today. From across the political spectrum, calls can be heard for the development of independent urban enclaves as a reaction to the severe cuts in state and federal funding. Whether this takes the form of the left turn to the metropolis as the "autonomous" space of the "common" (Negri and Hardt: 2009), the New Urbanists" appeal to more integrated communities, or Benjamin Barber's claim in his new book *If Mayors Ruled the World*, that mayors can solve the problem of "dysfunctional nations"—a sentiment New York City's Michael Bloomberg, along with other representatives of capital, have strongly endorsed in a recent City Lab conference in New York[5]—the city as a cultural space cut off from the mode of production is being heralded as the basis of progressive change. What is especially troubling is that left theorizations of urban struggle do not represent a challenge to capitalism but a (familiar) accommodation to it. Among other things, they end up repeating the anti-state dictates of capital and naturalizing the economic forces that put cities (and workers) in competition with each other nationally and internationally in the era of capitalist austerity. Moreover, this accommodation also updates the Austro-Marxist appeal to common culture at a moment when the textual and cultural notions of difference and indeterminacy that dominated theory since the 1960s have become exhausted.

Under the heavy weight of deepening economic and political crises of capitalism worldwide, contemporary left theory has returned to discussions of the failing system of capitalism and to questions of "communism" and "socialism." Thus, in the Introduction to *The Idea of Communism*, editors Costas Douzinas and Slavoj Žižek proclaim that the "long night of the left is coming to a close"; "history" has "returned," now that the "new world order" promised in 1989 has collapsed and people are everywhere becoming "distanced from capitalist ideology," making it possible to turn to communism "again" (2010: vii–viii). Many theorists are even beginning to re-think the substitution of culture for class issues that has largely defined the left since the rise of "post-" discourses in the West in the 1960s. Diana Coole and Samantha Frost write in *New Materialisms* that "the radicalism of the dominant discourses which have flourished under the cultural turn is now more or less exhausted" (2010: 6). They advocate a return to "materialism" in order to challenge "the allergy to "the real"" that dominated discursive theory (2010: 6), and embrace the "renewed attention to structures of political economy" (2010: 29). Yet it is especially telling that in the new left turn to communism, what has not returned, and should not return, as *The Idea of Communism* and *New Materialisms* make clear, is neither any reference to the binary relations of class (which are causing the recent crisis), nor anything resembling socialization of production, let alone dictatorship of the proletariat. According to Douzinas and Žižek, "As the precondition of radical action, communism must be thought today by taking its distance from statism and economism and becoming informed by the political experiences of the twenty-first century" (2010: ix). Similarly, Coole and Frost insist that within the framework of the "new" materialism, "the capitalist system is not understood in any narrowly economistic way but rather is treated as a detotalized totality that includes a multitude of interconnected phenomena and processes that sustain its unpredictable proliferation and unexpected crises" (2010: 29).

Contrary to what Coole and Frost imply, however, the "allergy to the real" (like the rejection of history and communism), was not simply a theory that has now gone out of fashion. It was a theoretical proxy of capital's war on workers in the postwar period of Western capital's expansion. And it was a broad trend in which left theorists have played an active part. Attacks on history, like the attacks on binary thinking, were the theoretical relays of capital's effort to simultaneously pursue global free trade to increase the rate of exploitation while persuading Western workers that communism signaled the death of human freedom. In this regard, the turn to language and culture (a turn largely associated with the New Left and post-1968 theory but one that also came to define Western Marxism) served not only to avoid class reality. More specifically, it translated capital's fluid ability to transgress all borders in pursuit of new markets into a spectral world of "free play," ambiguity and indeterminacy from which there was no "outside." As capital increased productivity with post-Fordist techniques and commodified more and more spheres of life, the concepts of class, history, causality, ideology, ideology critique, etc. all became the crude signs of "essentialism" and were systematically rejected by the New Left and Western Marxism as acts of metaphysical closure. The problem of capitalism, the left claimed, is not that it exploits but that it homogenizes (a claim which in fact naturalized the newer, more flexible means by which capital began to appropriate surplus value, particularly after the financial crisis of 1973, and the onset of "deregulation").

By bracketing off economic relations and focusing on culture and language, the left was able to represent itself has having adapted its radical praxis to new, post-exploitative times (a "new world order") rather than as having given up revolutionary struggle for cultural struggles within capitalism. But as we have seen, this is not the first left turn to culture in place of class, for this was central to the project of Austro-Marxism. In fact, like Austro-Marxism, Western Marxism and the New Left are part of a long revisionist tradition in Marxism that has sought alternatives to the class struggle. When confronted by heightened contradictions, it has called for communities beyond class. Thus, for instance, while the representatives of capital fought to eliminate more and more of workers" basic rights to organize, collectively bargain, and strike, left theory softened the hard edges of class and translated the orchestrated defeat of labor's historical gains from the first four decades of the twentieth century into meditations on the "difference within" the binary (Derrida 1976) and "the strength of the weak" (Lyotard 1978). In short, the blurring of boundaries in left theory functioned as the philosophical artillery by which the binaries of class were conceptually destroyed. In the place of "working class," such concepts as "proletarian culture," "structures of feeling," and (more recently) the "multitude" and the "precariat" emerged, the general effect of which is to construct a familiar vision of the world in which, as Adler put it, capitalism is so "riddled with such economic conflicts . . . that it is doubtful whether we can speak of a single class" (1978b: 225). In the guise of "compensating" for the "rigid" "structuralism" and "economism" of classical Marxism, Western Marxism and the New Left undertook the role of making Marxism and class analysis more flexible (Deleuze and Guattari 1983), aleatory (Althusser 2006), cultural (Williams 1977), experiential (Thompson 1964), libidinal (Marcuse 1955; Žižek 1989), radically democratic (Laclau and Mouffe 1985), and even, in the later Derrida (1994), spectral. Another way of saying this is that what Douzinas and Žižek call the "long night of the left" was a self-induced sleep on the part of the left in the prosperous North. The charge of economism (then and now) is not so much a reflection of the rigidity of classical Marxist theory, as dominant narratives insist. Rather, it is an index of the way the left, in the aftermath of the Russian Revolution, increasingly justified its turn to a more culturalist approach in the midst of capital's growing power over labor. "Economism" is itself one of the left's favorite metanarratives.[6]

But the deepening class contradictions stemming from the falling rate of profit now require even more spiritualizing strategies to ideologically mend the gap between labor and capital. At a time when austerity has sanctioned the systematic mugging of the working class on behalf of capital, the most effective ideological strategies are those that, in a radical rhetoric, concretely address the daily realities of class and the violence of the state, while focusing primarily on their affective and corporeal significance. This logic is perhaps best captured in Coole and Frost's call for an "open Marxism" (2010: 29), which is premised on the argument that "no workable version of Marxism can advance a historical metanarrative, aspire to the identification of determining economic laws, valorize an originary, pristine nature, or envisage communism as history's idealized material destiny" (2010: 30). Such claims not only repeat the main talking points of the post-structuralist era of post-Marxism. They articulate a broader post-humanist appeal to "unity" and "socialized consciousness" in the updated post-class language of the "common" and the "subjectivities" of the "multitude."

Antonio Negri and Michael Hardt, especially in their *Empire* (2000), *Multitude*(2004), and *Commonwealth*(2009) trilogy, are among the most influential theorists in developing today's "open Marxism." Negri and Hardt's rearticulation of capital as a regime based not in the manufacture of material commodities but in immaterial production in which "productivity, wealth, and the creation of social surpluses take the form of cooperative interactivity through linguistic, communicative, and affective networks" (2000: 294) has played a key role in shifting the focus of class from exploitation to culture, and in particular to immaterial labor. For Negri and Hardt, this change in the nature of capital—from a system of exploitation to the restrictions of bio-political instrumentality—requires a new way of addressing the social, one which eschews totalities and determination and, instead, celebrates "spontaneity" and looks at "the discontinuities (be they ruptures or innovations) [rather] than on the continuities" as the only way of resisting the imposition of a system of rigid political control over the elastic boundaries of "life" (Negri 1996: 158). Whereas in the industrial era capitalism's system of exploitation produced clear boundaries between owners and workers, they claim that in the immaterial era capital has ceased to exploit labor directly but instead accumulates surplus through rents gained from the control of "life itself" (2004: 152). In this sense, who is in control of life and who is subject to this control becomes harder to discern, since all members of the community are impacted by bio-politics. It is on this basis that Negri and Hardt suggest that "The ultimate core of biopolitical production . . . is not the production of objects for subjects, as commodity production is often understood, but the production of subjectivity itself. This is the terrain from which our ethical and political project must set out" (2009: x). They thus reject what they argue are "determining" concepts, such as "class," in favor of more "open" and "fluid" concepts such as the "multitude," or "constellations of singularities and events" (2000: 60). In fact, reflecting quite similar assumptions about the class changes in capitalism, there is a growing interest among left theorists in such concepts as "the part of no-part" in Jacques Rancière (2001) and the "uncounted" in Alain Badiou (2006), since what such concepts highlight is, in the words of Jean-Luc Nancy, "the common condition of all the singularities of subjects, that is, of all the exceptions, all the uncommon points whose network makes a world" (2010: 149). Class, here, is not a relation to the means of production but an exclusion (a reading which starts from the *effects* of the alienation of working people from production).

Replacing the collectivity of labor with the common-ism of culture, the "multitude," more specifically, is a theory of affective "community" in place of class. The multitude, in other words, is an updated form of Kantianism that informed Austro-Marxism. But, unlike the humanist Kantian community, the multitude is a posthumanist species of community: a community of affective and corporeal intensities rather than reason; a community based less on identity than on "an irreducible multiplicity," since "the singular social differences that constitute the multitude must always be expressed and can never be flattened into sameness, unity, identity or indifference" (Negri and Hardt 2004: 105). In substituting multitude for working class and singularity for collectivity, Negri and Hardt oppose a politics rooted in class struggle in favor of a focus on the way myriad movements "struggle for the common" (2012: 6), because in the age of immaterial labor, "exploitation takes the form of *expropriation of the common*" (2009: 137, original emphasis). The urban context becomes particularly important on these terms. For the "metropolis is to the multitude what the factory was to the industrial working class," because it is the space where new cultural forms are created and subsequently appropriated by capital (2009: 250). As such, contemporary struggles—from the Occupy and Arab Spring movements to fights over clean water and healthcare—are read as significant because they appear not to fall into the sharp binaries of labor/capital, workers/owners, or first world/third world, or to be organized through "parties," but instead share "internal organization as a multitude" (2012). "Communism," therefore, "begins to take shape when the proletarian takes it as her objective to reappropriate the *Gemeinwesen*, the community, to turn it into the order of a new society" (Negri 2010: 156). Hardt and Negri suggest the appropriation of "community"—be this "common" spaces, knowledges, affects, natural resources— serves to resist urban exploitation along the same lines that Bauer suggested common living and learning would usher in a new communist era. Yet whereas the Austro-Marxists" were willing to use the state to force the rich to pay higher taxes and to establish an eight hour workday, Hardt and Negri

oppose any use of the state as a tool for prioritizing the public—thus taking
the Austro-Marxist's resistance to socializing the economy even further. It is
precisely in this metropolitan context that Hardt's privileging of the common
over both capitalism and socialism must be read:

> Too often it appears as though our only choices are capitalism or socialism, the
> rule of private property or that of public property, such that the only cure for
> the ills of state control is to privatize and for the ills of capital to publicize, that
> is, exert state regulation. We need to explore another possibility: neither the
> private property of capitalism nor the public property of socialism but the
> common in communism. (Hardt 2010: 131)

This, however, merely repeats the neoliberal rejection of state regulation,
naturalizing the fact that in an era of declining profit rates, capital is no
longer willing to use the state as a mechanism for redistributing public money in order to provide social programs that benefit the working class, especially as globalization of production has enabled the alternative option of
reducing labor costs through expanding wage competition rather than
through state subsidies. Representing the metropolis as the "common" outside of capitalism and socialism romanticizes the increasingly desperate conditions urban workers face as their wages decrease and the resources on
which they have relied become privatized, forcing many to find alternative
cooperative strategies of survival. The "common" translates the coping strategies needed to survive on less into a new affective ontology.

It is precisely this that has made Negri and Hardt so influential: they
appeal to Marxist concepts like labor, class, value, and communism—while
at the same time claiming that their revision of these concepts serves to
"advance" Marxism to better grasp a "new" era of capitalism.[7] But, as was
the case with the Austro-Marxists, who claimed to enhance Marxism by
hybridizing it with Kantianism, the effect of Negri and Hardt's rewriting of
labor in terms of immaterial labor, and the shift of emphasis from production
of commodities to the production of subjectivities and affect, serves in fact to
empty Marx's concepts of their explanatory value and to dematerialize the
social at a time when class antagonisms are leading to more and more open
fights between capital and labor. In their rewriting of class conflict as one of
empire and multitude, we see the same logic by which Bauer substituted
autonomous forms of common culture for struggles aimed at transforming
wage labor. This is particularly evident in Negri and Hardt's contention that
today "class struggle in the biopolitical context takes the form of exodus. By
exodus here we mean, at least initially, a process of subtraction from the
relationship with capital by means of actualizing the potential autonomy of
labor-power. Exodus is thus not a refusal of the productivity of biopolitical
labor-power but rather a refusal of the increasingly restrictive fetters placed
on its productive capacities by capital" (2009: 152, original emphasis).

Emphasizing "exodus" and "subtraction" reinscribes even more explicitly the ideology of the "autonomy" of the cultural sphere from the relations of wage labor, as if "common" cultural spaces are not shaped by the relations of production. Moreover, the concern with removing "restrictive fetters" on production not only does not challenge capital but it has been increasingly implemented by capital in the global North to enhance entrepreneurialism. For instance, developing more "creative," "comfortable" and "non-hierarchical" work environments in order to create "friction-free" conditions of labor that minimize workers" antagonism while increasing the rate of exploitation, capital has demonstrated that "autonomous" cultural zones can just as easily be put to the use of expanding productivity. Similarly, the emergence of small cultural communities that seek "autonomy" from the market has long been one of the means by which capitalism has dealt with crises of overproduction. Whether it is the "hippies" in the 1960s or "crowdsourcing" in the contemporary moment, counter-cultural resistance has been easily co-opted by capital because counter-culturalism does not challenge the underlying structure of exploitation but merely seeks more ethical terms for the sale of labor power. In this sense, "exodus" through cultural resistance is not possible because it does not matter what "form" the commodity takes but the fact that labor is exploited in the process of its production. To put this another way, the very conditions Hardt and Negri claim have "ruptured" capitalism from within—the fact that, for instance, many workers work all the time and everywhere (due to technology) not just at "work"—reflect the higher rates at which workers are being exploited (not by "capturing" the "common" nature of their "affects" as Hardt and Negri claim but by appropriating surplus value at the point of production). The celebration of cultural resistance—like the new turn to "love" and "affect" on the left—is a left-cultural expression of an economic need to inculcate in working people the idea that "People like us can't afford to get angry," in the words of one working class character to another on the new sitcom about single mothers, *Mom* ("Loathing and tube-socks" 2013). "Hospitality," "forgiveness," and "love," far from being autonomous from production, teach "people like us" how to adapt to the staggering theft that takes place during the working day.

Having given up the struggle for collective ownership of the means of production, the Austro-Marxists" and Hardt and Negri's appeal to "self-management" and "common" acts of creation are utopian at best, and at worst a symptom of collusion in the bourgeois ideological fabrication of "common" bonds between workers and owners in the face of rising working class anger. While Douzinas and Žižek may ostensibly condemn today's "supine social democrats" (2010: vii), their "alternative" (like that of Hardt and Negri) is ultimately the cultural theory of the Social Democrats of Red Vienna who substituted municipal socialism for international socialism. It is a more "flexible" updating of the culturalism that informed the Social Democratic movements in the immediate aftermath of the Russian Revolution in order to "self-restrict" the working class from engaging more radical struggles to build a new world. This was the case in Red Vienna, and it is increasingly the case with such contemporary urban movements like Occupy Wall Street (OWS), which distanced itself from communism from the start and has over the last two years moved from occupying space in defense of the 99 percent, to becoming a stop-gap charity service catering to victims of Hurricane Sandy who have been abandoned by the city and the state, to offering a new Occupy Wall Street Debit Card in a joint venture with Visa.[8] This might be comical if it were not a deeply problematic and symptomatic consequence of the way that culturalism has led the left to reject ideology critique (as "closed," "narrow," and rooted in "economism"), and to affirm the post-class "autonomy" and "spontaneity" of "self-organization"—which is to say, to capitulate to the commodified common sense that is everywhere produced by capital to normalize the appropriation of surplus value at the point of production.

To make culture the centerpiece of radical strategy, as the Austro-Marxists did, is a step backward for Marxist urban cultural theory. Struggles over "homelessness" and "housing"—which a growing number of people now lack in the United States and Europe as a result of capital's efforts to lower the cost of production—need to be seen, not as radical ends in themselves, but as part of the broader struggle of the working class to end the conditions which produce it: the revolutionary transformation from capitalism to socialism.

NOTES

1. Marcuse notes, "So central did housing issues become to the party that is was a joke of the times that it should change its name from Social Democratic Party to Tenants" Party" (1985: 206).

2. It is important to note the significant amount of power and influence that the Austro-Marxists actually did have in the municipality (e.g. their ability to enforce federal landlord-tenant legislation, among other things), in relation to their claim, that (working class) political power was not a possibility; that is, that the focus of the working class should be on pedagogy and consciousness, not changing the conditions of the working day (exploitation). In fact, Loew emphasizes that "There can be no doubt that in 1919 the Austro-Marxist leadership had been in a position to exert a decisive influence on the development of the European class struggle . . . there was the possibility of linking up with the Hungarian revolution, of strengthening the international position of Soviet Russia, of spreading the revolution to Germany and fertilizing the workers" struggles in Italy" (1979: 36), but at every turn the leaders resisted linking up with these movements.

3. Marcuse (1985: 202).

4. Of course, after World War I this became the basis of welfare capitalism throughout much of the global North. Wolfgang Maderthaner suggests in this regard that "the municipality had created all the prerequisites for a welfare-state model on the architectonic level, on the level of social infrastructure and in the area of services" (Maderthaner 2006: 33).

5. Henry Grabar, "Blue-State Nation: Maybe its Time for Cities to Secede," *Salon.com*, 12 Oct. 2013. Web. 16 Oct. 2013.

6. This is why Razmig Keucheyan's claim that the shift in Western Marxism from the economic concept of exploitation to the cultural concept of alienation was a result of the discovery of Marx's *Economic Manuscripts* is itself a cultural reading of Western Marxism (2013: 34–38). Alienation is an effect of the relations of production under capitalism (exploitation). The fact that the left read the *Manuscripts* in order to privilege (cultural) alienation over exploitation reflects the extent to which the left accepted capital's increasing deployment of culture and cultural difference to isolate members of the working class from each other at a time when capital needed to include women and workers of color more extensively into the workforce.

7. For an extensive materialist analysis of Negri and Hardt's revision of Marxist concepts, see Chapter 2 of *The Digital Condition*, by Rob Wilkie.

8. Moynihan (2013).

BIBLIOGRAPHY

Adler, Max (1978a), "A Critique of Othmar Spann's Sociology," in *Austro-Marxism*, Tom Bottomore and Patrick Goode (eds.), Cambridge and London: MIT Press, pp. 69–76.

———. (1978b), "Metamorphosis of the Working Class?," in *Austro-Marxism*, Tom Bottomore and Patrick Goode (eds.), Cambridge and London: MIT Press, pp. 217–48.

———. (1978c), "The Relation of Marxism to Classical German Philosophy," in *Austro-Marxism*, Tom Bottomore and Patrick Goode (eds.), Cambridge and London: MIT Press, pp. 62–68.

———. (1978d), "The Sociological Meaning of Marx's Thought," in *Austro-Marxism*, Tom Bottomore and Patrick Goode (eds.), Cambridge and London: MIT Press, pp. 57–62.

Althusser, Louis (2006), *Philosophy of the Encounter, Later Writings, 1978–1987*, London: Verso.

Badiou, Alain (2006 [1988]), *Being and Event*, (trans. Oliver Feltham), New York: Continuum.

Barber, Benjamin (2013), *If Mayors Ruled the World: Dysfunctional Nations, Rising Cities*, New Haven, Yale University Press.

Bauer, Otto (1970 [1925]), *The Austrian Revolution* (trans. H. J. Stenning), New York: Burt Franklin.

———. (1978a), "Marxism and Ethics," in *Austro-Marxism*, Tom Bottomore and Patrick Goode (eds.), Cambridge and London: MIT Press, pp. 78–84.

———. (1978b), "What is Austro-Marxism?," in *Austro-Marxism*, Tom Bottomore and Patrick Goode (eds.), Cambridge and London: MIT Press, pp. 45–48.

———. (2000 [1924]), *The Question of Nationalities and Social Democracy* (trans. Joseph O"Donnell), Minneapolis and London: University of Minnesota Press.

Blau, Eve (1999), *The Architecture of Vienna, 1919–1934*, Cambridge and London: MIT Press.

Bottomore, Tom and Patrick Goode (1978), *Austro-Marxism*, Oxford: Clarendon Press.

Coole, Diana and Samantha Frost (2010), "Introducing New Materialisms," in *New Materialisms: Ontology, Agency, and Politics*, Durham and London: Duke University Press, pp. 1–43.

Dean, Jodi (2012), *The Communist Horizon*, New York: Verso.

Derrida, Jacques (1976), *Of Grammatology*, Baltimore: Johns Hopkins University Press.

———. (1994), *Specters of Marx: The State of Debt, the Work of Mourning, and the New International*, New York: Routledge.

Deleuze, Gilles and Felix Guattari (1983), *Anti-Oedipus: Capitalism and Schizophrenia*, Minneapolis: University of Minnesota Press.

Douzinas, Costas and Slavoj Žižek (eds.) (2010), *The Idea of Communism*, New York: Verso.

Engels, Frederick (1969), *The Housing Question*, reprinted in *Karl Marx and Frederick Engels: Selected Works*, Vol. 2, Moscow: Progress Publishers, pp. 295–375.

Fischer, Heinz (2000[1998]), Foreword to *The Question of Nationalities and Social Democracy*, Bauer (trans. Joseph O'Donnell) [1924], Minneapolis and London: University of Minnesota Press, pp. ix–xii.

Förster, Wolfgang and William Menking (2013), "The Vienna Model: Housing for the 21st Century City" [exhibit pamphlet], Austrian Cultural Forum, 17 April—2 September, New York, New York.

Gell, Aaron (2011), "Slavoj Žižek Speaks to Occupy Wall Street," *The New York Observer*, 9 October, accessed 29 October 2013.

Grabar, Henry (2013), "Blue-State Nation: Maybe it's Time for Cities to Secede," *Salon.com*, 12 October, accessed 16 October 2013.

Gruber, Helmut (1991), *Red Vienna: Experiment in Working-Class Culture 1919–1934*, New York and Oxford: Oxford University Press.

Gulick, Charles A. (1980), *Austria: From Hapsburg to Hitler*, Berkeley: University of California Press.

Hardt, Michael (2010) "The Common in Communism" in *The Idea of Communism*, Costas Douzinas and Slavoj Žižek (eds.), New York: Verso, pp. 131–144.

Harvey, David (2012), *Rebel Cities: From the Right to the City to Urban Revolution*, New York: Verso.

Jameson, Frederic (1988), *The Political Unconscious: Narrative as a Socially Symbolic Act*, Ithaca: Cornell University Press.

Keucheyan, Razmig (2013), *The Left Hemisphere: Mapping Critical Theory* (trans. Gegory Elliott), New York: Verso.

Laclau, Ernesto, and Chantal Mouffe (1985), *Hegemony and Socialist Strategy*, London: Verso.

Lenin, V. I. (1977a), "'Democracy' and Dictatorship," in *Lenin Collected Works*, Vol. 28, Moscow: Progress Publishers, pp. 368–72.

———. (1977b [1964]), "Imperialism, The Highest Stage of Capitalism," in *Lenin Collected Works*, Vol. 22, Moscow: Progress Publishers.

Lewis, Jill (1983), "Socialism in One City, 1918–27," *European Studies Review*, 13, 3, pp. 335–55.

"Loathing and Tubesocks" (2013), *Mom*, episode 4, season 1, CBS.

Loew, Raimund (1979), "The Politics of Austro-Marxism," *New Left Review*, I, 118, pp. 16–51.

Lyotard, François (1978), "On the Strength of the Weak," (trans. Roger McKeon), *Semiotext(e)* 3: 2, pp. 204–14.

Maderthaner, Wolfgang (2006), "Austro-Marxism: Mass Culture and Anticipatory Socialism," *Austrian Studies*, 14: 1, pp. 21–36.

Marcuse, Herbert (1955) *Eros and Civilization*, New York: Random House.

Marcuse, Peter (1985), "The Housing Policy of Social Democracy," in *The Austrian Socialist Experiment: Social Democracy and Austromarxism, 1918–1934*, Anson Rabinbach (ed.), Boulder and London: Westview Press, pp. 201–21.

Marx, Karl (1966), *Critique of the Gotha Program*, New York: International Publishers.

———. (1970), *Contribution to the Critique of Political Economy*, New York: International Publishers.

———. (1971), *Civil War in France*, reprinted in *On the Paris Commune*, Karl Marx and Frederick Engels, Moscow: Progress Publishers, 1971, pp. 48–97.

Marx, Karl and Frederick Engels (1969), *Manifesto of the Communist Party*, reprinted in *Selected Works*, Vol. 1, Moscow: Progress Publishers, pp. 98–137.

Merrifield, Andy (2002), *Metromarxism: A Marxist Tale of the City*, New York and London: Routledge.

Moynihan, Colin (2013), "Coming Soon? An Occupy Wall Street Debit Card," *New York Times*, 30 September, accessed 1 October 2013.

Nancy, Jean-Luc (2010), "Communism, the Word," *The Idea of Communism*, Costas Douzinas and Slavoj Žižek (eds.), New York: Verso, pp. 145–53.

Negri, Antonio (1996), "Twenty Theses on Marx," in *Marxism beyond Marxism*, Saree Makdisi, Cesare Casarino and Rebecca Karl (eds.), New York: Routledge, pp. 149–80.

———. (2010), "Communism: Some Thoughts on the Concept and Practice," *The Idea of Communism*. New York: Verso, pp. 155–65.

Negri, Antonio and Michael Hardt (2000), *Empire*, Cambridge, MA: Harvard University Press.

———. (2004), *Multitude: War and Empire in the Age of Democracy*, New York: Penguin.

———. (2009), *Commonwealth*, Cambridge, MA: Harvard University Press.

———. (2012), *Declaration* [ebook] New York: Melanie Jackson Agency, LLC.

Nimni, Ephraim J. (2000 [1998]), Introduction for the English-Reading Audience to *The Question of Nationalities and Social Democracy*, Bauer (trans. Joseph O"Donnell) [1924], Minneapolis and London: University of Minnesota Press, pp. xv-xlv.

Rabinbach, Anson (ed.) (1985a), *The Austrian Socialist Experiment: Social Democracy and Austromarxism, 1918–1934*, Boulder and London: Westview Press.

———. (1985b), "Red Vienna: Symbol and Strategy," in *The Austrian Socialist Experiment: Social Democracy and Austromarxism, 1918–1934*, Anson Rabinbach (ed.), Boulder and London: Westview Press, pp. 187–94.

Rancière, Jacques (2001), "Ten Thesis on Politics," *Theory and Event* 5, 3, accessed 31 October 2013.

Thompson, E. P. (1964), *The Making of the English Working Class*, New York: Pantheon.

Williams, Raymond (1977), *Marxism and Literature*, Oxford: Oxford University Press.

"The Vienna Model: Housing for the 21st-Century City" (17 April-2 September 2013).

Wilkie, Rob (2011), *The Digital Condition: Class and Culture in the Information Network*, New York: University of Fordham Press.

Žižek, Slavoj (1989), *The Sublime Object of Ideology*, New York: Verso.

V

(INTER)NATIONALIZING
THE URBAN

Chapter Nine

Urban Culture as Passive Revolution

*A Gramscian Sketch of the Uneven and
Combined Transitional Development of Rural
and Urban Modern Culture in Europe and Egypt*

Jelle Versieren and Brecht De Smet

Some scholars and observers were quick to herald the Egyptian mass uprising of 2011 as the beginning of a "fourth wave of democratization" (e.g.,
Gershman 2011). This followed Samuel Huntington's culturalist-ethnical
temporalization of modernity's democratic process into three consequent
waves. Since the advent of Western colonialism, the countries in the region
appeared to have been continuously on the road to modernity, without ever
really getting there. The fourth wave would finally liberate the Middle East
and North Africa (MENA) region from the burden of "persistent authoritar-
ianism" and Islamic cultural "backwardness."

Models of linear modernization only deal with the Other as an isolated
and diachronic entity. There is no actually shared space-time: as an observer
of "traditional" societies one can only look back and urge them to "catch up"
with the predetermined course of history (i.e., capitalist democracy). Against
the backdrop of the Other's particularism and exceptionalism, one's own
historical trajectory becomes differentiated, homogenized, and normalized.
In this chapter we criticize the linear and noncontradictory conception of
modernization and modern culture through a dialogue with the Italian Marxist Antonio Gramsci. We distinguish between the logic of capitalism and its
real, fractured history. In order to understand the dialectic of the universalization of commodity production and the concreteness of capitalist transition we
compare the historical trajectory of Western Europe with that of Egypt. The
totality of modernity is characterized by unevenness and combination, not

only of economic, but also of political and cultural forces. Gramsci's Italy functions hereby as a microcosm of the uneven and combined nature of modernity. The formation of modern European urban culture is discovered as an exceptional and immanent process, rather than the teleological outcome of capital accumulation. The Jacobin moment—that is, the bourgeoisie's "pure" ethico-political project, historically expressed in the French Revolution—is quickly subsumed under the realities of combined class interests and alliances. Instead of classical bourgeois hegemony, a series of passive revolutions become the primary determinants of modernity. Precapitalist relations of power and practices of discipline are not replaced by European bourgeois leadership, but chiefly integrated into capitalist social formations by Bonapartist coercion and the social-technological prestige of American monopoly capitalism.

We show how the case of the Egyptian Mahalla al-Kubra textile manufacturers exemplifies the notable differences and similarities between European and Egyptian transitional temporalities. The modernist form of the first indigenous industries obscured their precapitalist substance: an extension of absolutist, commercial, landed, and colonial interests and social structures. Conversely, the Nasserite intervention reinforced and developed concepts and practices of modern urban culture and nationhood, uniting the logical "Jacobin" and "Bonapartist" moments, and mobilizing them against (and in accordance with) the historical forces of colonialism and imperialism of its time.

A. THE UNEVEN AND COMBINED DEVELOPMENT OF ECONOMIC AND CULTURAL FORCES: SPATIAL AND TEMPORAL CONFIGURATIONS

A Marxist analysis of different capitalist cultures starts from the empirical and conceptual supposition that "transition" does not mean the linear "purification" of a social formation of all noncapitalist structures. The uneven and combined development of capitalism intensified a contradictory hierarchy of territorial-economic scales. The asynchronous spatial emergence of the capitalist mode of production and the world market posed the problem of how precapitalist societies and modes of production related to their capitalist counterparts and to the world economy as a whole.

One of Gramsci's main themes in the Prison Notebooks was the uneven and combined development of the Italian territory and of capital accumulation (Kipfer 2013: 86). Gramsci noticed a distinct difference between precapitalist central institutions and the modern state. Communal ties and a moral economy were the main characteristics of precapitalist societies. In contrast, the modern state attempted to homogenize its social and cultural territory. It abolished the particularist nature of overlapping and fragmented institutional powers based upon common law, personal networks and entitlements, despotic powers resting upon tradition, and the corporatist organization of economic interests. In European capitalism, cities were no longer structured by extra-economic stratified relations, but by the demands of production (Morton 2013: 58). The breakthrough of the capitalist mode of production, however, is not a simple narrative of immediate successes. In Hegelian terms, the dialectic of capital and the universalization of commodity production express a logical becoming, but only a historicist analysis can give an overview of the contradictory concreteness of this becoming.

Contrary to culturalist and post-Marxist interpretations (i.e., subalternity as a purely cultural concept or politics-qua-politics), Gramsci emphasized the importance of economic processes in the formation of the cultural and invested much time and energy to understand Marxist and bourgeois economics (e.g., Krätke and Thomas 2011). Gramsci's immanent critique of the present pushed forward an often misunderstood historicist research agenda that aimed to integrate cultural, political and economic phenomena. For example, Henri Lefebvre described his notebooks as a political statist critique of the bourgeois state (Kipfer 2008: 196). Postmodern superstructuralism not only renders every practice autonomous, but also refuses to properly deal with Gramsci's strategic questions regarding the global social processes of emancipation by political means. After Mouffe's plea for a radicalization of bourgeois democracy, a new generation of post-Marxists and autonomists avoided the state debate altogether.

Regarding the capitalist state, the ideal of a complete Jacobine transformation of a national territory contradicts with the concrete different cultural and political temporalities of the historical incomplete bourgeois hegemony—a never-ending attempt to create a spatial hegemony in order to homogenize time. These uneven and combined spatio-temporal aspects of hegemony produce unique articulations of economic structures (capital accumulation) and cultural practices (the formation of the identities of capital and labor) (Jessop 2005: 424). European modernity is not a homogenous cultural complex in which capitalism came to existence.

B. GRAMSCI, MODERNITY, AND THE FALSE DICHOTOMY BETWEEN URBANITY AND RURALITY IN EUROPE

One of the principal characteristics of Gramsci's Prison Notebooks is the connection between modern culture and state formation. The fascist rise to power exposed the weaknesses of the liberal agenda of political hegemony. Throughout the nineteenth century the liberal elite of the northern cities and the incumbent politicians in the central government relied heavily on the willingness of the bourgeois landowners. They decided whether the state bureaucracy could rely on local cooperation in order to exercise the official rule of law. The preservation of the mutual interests of the northern industrialists and the southern landowners was based upon the social and spatial separation between the two regions (Gramsci 1982: 228). The North did not only underdevelop the South by restricting infrastructural investments. The rural bourgeoisie wished to maintain the status quo between the two regions and of the rural social relations within their region. For Gramsci, the Risorgimento created a deficient modern Italian state. He articulated the uneven situation of the social formation with the Italian temporal and spatial position in the world market, because

> the late entrance of peripheral European societies into capitalist relations meant that state forms were "less efficient" in creating ideological mechanisms to defer the immediate consequences of economic crisis, so that the form of state transformations in such cases was circumscribed by prevailing conditions with the international capitalist system. (Morton 2013: 58)

The social configuration of society could not be mobilized into a national-popular force to encompass the complete national space, which reflected in the narrow scope of the political discourse of the Italian Moderates. The instable political and economic features of the unification were both the inheritance and the further reproduction of a relative backwardness of the South with respect to the North (Davis 1979). It did not come as a surprise that fascism—notwithstanding their Southern petit bourgeois patriarchal attitude—was able to advance itself as the necessary force for an all-encompassing modernization of society. Its techno-scientific productivism expressed a desire to overcome the standstill of liberal political society.

Gramsci's emphasis on the inheritance and reproduction of backwardness, in order to understand modern statehood and political phenomena such as fascism, was related to his peculiar perspective of modernity. For Gramsci, modernity entailed the universalization of the capitalist mode of production and at the same time the unevenness of this universalization. Capitalist modernity expresses, as Massimiliano Tomba has aptly put, a "historical-epochal break" with the past, because the new social relations are shaped by a "historical condition that comprises a universal history" (Tomba 2013: 115–20). Nonetheless, this historical-epochal break is not a once and for all clear cut between precapitalist social relations, practices and institutions, and modernity. Capitalist culture in the core countries based upon wage labor, contractual obligations, the factory system and the division of labor, and the formal political equality of citizenship could not thrive without the integration and co-existence of numerous practices of the past. The present forms a historical repetition of the same as a necessary basis for new phenomena.

Gramsci's stance toward modernity entails a critique of the present state of things from a historical perspective. There is always a "non-identity with itself" of the present, the "non-contemporaneity of the present" (Thomas 2009: 282). The homogenous smooth representation of capitalist modernity tends to forget the dialectical process, the process of becoming and sublation, between the apparent dead past and the living present. This is the theoretical and practical site of critical research and political struggle. Gramsci's historicism consists of a reciprocal relation between his historical materialist analysis of the capitalist social formation and his philosophy of praxis, in which he finds himself as "an element of the contradiction and elevates this element to a principle of knowledge and therefore of action" (Gramsci 1971: 405).

Hegemony became a key concept in the historical understanding of the rise and degeneration of the bourgeois state, modernity, and the political practice of elites and subaltern classes (Frosini 2003: 153). Gramsci deployed the concept of hegemony in order to rupture, in a historical and logical sense, the self-referentiality and linearity of modernity as the bourgeois epoch: "Together with the transformation of the state, the labor process, household structures, and workers" subjectivities, urbanization was key to what Gramsci saw as a positive if contradictory rationalization of social life" (Kipfer 2013: 90). Therefore, Gramsci can be used to overcome the restrictions of classical Durkheimian sociology and its evolutionary point of view regarding the contradictions of the processes of political centralization and civil mentality in the economic sphere (Badie and Birnbaum 1983: 12–14). The conceptual deployment of hegemony consists of a immanent critique of the present and the representation of modernity linked to a laboratory of political practice outside the demarcations of liberal modernity itself.

In order to understand capitalist culture, the Gramscian perspective does not propose a Habermasian ethical opposition between liberal modernity and fascism, nor does it simply underscore the post-war Adornian idea of the inherent potentiality of self-destructivity of modern society and its mythical roots. Furthermore, it is not sufficient to merely note the difference between representation and the critique of its evolutionary narrative. This limited form of critique can be noted as deconstructive, constituting modernity as a system "which inscribes its otherness within its interiority." The ideological and theoretical problematic will be reduced to a "strategic skirmish [. . . more] at the level of the mind than at the level of political forces" (Eagleton 1996: 7). Nor can a postmodern and post-colonial alterity as absolute distinction from modernity or the intransparent subjectivity be of any clarification for the historical development of capitalism (Hartley 2003: 239). Hegemony is thus a necessary tool to analyse the political and cultural forces of modernity.

Within the Gramscian notion of hegemony and its noncontemporaneity it is possible to overcome the false modern dichotomy between city and countryside in classical sociological and political thought (Kipfer 2013: 92). Looking closer, the representation of two mutually exclusive lifeworlds had its roots in medieval times. First, medieval and early modern politico-economic and moral tractates—as in Aristotle's antiquity these subjects were not differentiated into separated discursive formations of knowledge—were written on behest of dominant elites. The image of the perceived peasant subjectivity was created to serve an ideological instrumentalization of the elites "as a means toward inverse self-definition" (Lis and Soly 2012: 159). Second, the discursive content and processes of signification of instrumentalization depended on the concrete relations of force and subject dispositions. Structural relations and political events together forged the image of the farmer as either a virtuous toiler, or an inferior being. The gentry relied on the patriarchal, but at the same time uneven, reciprocal commitments and entitlements—that is, the moral economy. These landowners emphasised the passivity of the peasant, glorifying the hardship of rural labor, combined with his own imagined benevolence. But peasant revolts were a constant feature in feudal times. Landlords accused peasants of being short-sighted in their illiteracy and being a force of disruption in the natural order of things. With the introduction of capitalist money-rent with a purely monetary and contractual character, peasants were perceived as an obstacle to the production of surplus and growth. A new school of agronomists argued against the underlying moral ties in the countryside and "formulated a new set of values to substantiate the rise [of] agriculture . . . [they] labelled customary methods of self-sufficient smallholders as impediments to progress" (Lis and Soly 2012: 203). Capitalist landowners, thriving upon the spread of leasehold contracts, no longer defined their interests according to the values of the moral economy. Third, a distinction has to be made between the ideological image of the peasant and the discursive evaluation of the countryside as a source of wealth. In all precapitalist societies the predominance of agricultural output and employment, combined with the umbra of famine caused by a failed harvest, determined philosophical and utopian thought. At the same time, the agricultural feudal characteristics created the specific corporatist legal and cultural framework of cities.

These cities were not bourgeois islands in direct opposition of landlord interests. The old bourgeoisie aligned themselves with aristocratic power because their commercial networks relied on political and military support. In times of medieval revolt of the subaltern strata, the bourgeoisie failed to overcome their corporatist interests and in some cases even supported repression. These corporatist interests were expressed in the self-enclosed burgesses" culture in associations and literary guilds (Morris 1983; Heller 2011: 31–2). The success of the commercialization model of early modern Europe was the economic result of the particular class configuration and the reciprocal restrictions of political action between landed property and urban bourgeoisie which lasted several centuries (Dobb 1976: 73–67). A revolution could change the articulation of the modes of production only when a historic bloc of the bourgeoisie and subaltern classes politically disturbed the balance of forces, in combination with a secular rural crisis (Gramsci 1996: 97).

Early modern tractates lacked a profound interrelatedness between cities and countryside from the point of production (e.g., the mercantilist William Petty Roncaglia 1985: 51). It was the body politic that resembled the conceptual focal point of the integration of socio-spatial differences. In the eighteenth century, the Physiocrats, the direct forerunners of modern economic thought and a main source of inspiration for Adam Smith's *Wealth of Nations*, expressed the transition toward capitalism as a multi-layered process. Albeit firmly rooted in the Enlightenment tradition, they defended, especially François Quesnay, a despotic regime of aristocrats with very limited representation (Fox-Genovese 1976). For them, agricultural output, as written before, was the only source of limited growth. Cities and its inhabitants were considered as the sterile nonproductive part of the national state. Nonetheless, they defended the modern bourgeois idea of free trade and the further centralization of state institutions and the spatio-judicial homogenization of the nation. In other words, they proposed some incipient ideas about modern bourgeois rule, albeit directly defending their own interests and thus lacking insights about ideological consent and the importance of national-popular cultural leadership. But these bourgeois elements were nothing more than a remedy for absolutist politics, therefore they culturally represented the height of absolutism and its continuous hegemonic crisis. This was because, on the one hand, "the expansion of production and exchange relations meant that feudal serfdom could no longer be politically supported by parceled manorial authority . . . which required a centralized authority" and, on the other hand, "absolutism arose in a transitional period when the monarch could play off emerging bourgeoisie and traditional nobility against each other" (Mann 1986: 476–77).

The French Revolution signified the definite break with feudalism. The creation of the bourgeois state eliminated the moral economy and its particularist cultural and political practices and identities. The sphere of civil society was torn from political society, and man as a private individual with particular interests was separated from man as a citizen of the universal community. Modern society "divorced economic practices from their diffuse symbolic valences" (Goux 1990: 122). Yet again, this epochal-historical break consisted of many temporalities. It was Marx who wrote the history of the French post-revolutionary bourgeois epoch—especially in his "The Eighteenth Brumaire of Louis Bonaparte." Marx sketched as much the making of the French working class as the becoming of a political equilibrium between the different factions of capital. In the initial post-Napoleonic years of depression the conservative side of the bourgeoisie, the rural bourgeoisie enriched by rent-seeking opportunities, only supported the central government in its ability to establish a political Restoration. The most striking feature was the relative absence of industrial capital. The early Jacobine state removed institutional and judicial barriers for the bourgeoisie in order to accommodate accumulation, for example the abolition of guilds and common law entitlements, but soon it became clear that the republican loyalists in the ranks of the middle and lower bourgeoisie opted for traditional economic activities such as money lending, and the buying and selling of land property (Kriedte 1983: 154–55; Versieren 2013). Between 1830 and 1848 concentrated money-capital used the July Monarchy as a "a joint stock company for the exploitation of France's national wealth" (Marx 1978 [1850]: 52). As long as credit was available for the rural bourgeoisie mutual agreements were possible. But underinvestment, lack of industrial productive growth, and political instability forced these elites to take recourse to a Bonapartist regime, which led to the gradual economic integration of commercial, industrial, and money-capital. But this Bonapartist regime meant the gradual dissolution and sublation of the Jacobine bourgeois hegemonic project and the moral-intellectual content of the integral class-state "vis-à-vis civil society—the organic unity of the class-as-nation" (Mann 1986: 472).

The passivity of the subaltern classes and its cultural-political alienation from the dominant class led the Bonapartist regime to its inevitable downfall. The bourgeois project encountered its organic crisis, politically and ideologically, as "the working classes" revolt . . . demanding instead political forms adequate to their own emergent class project . . . then began an epoch of passive revolution" (Thomas 2009: 145–46). The passive revolution consisted of a series of small-scale economic reforms that initiated molecular transformations, and which were based on the partial hegemony of one or more class fractions over the other ruling and subaltern social layers. "Passive revolution" is Gramsci's interpretation of "the persistent capacity of initiative of the bourgeoisie which succeeds, even in the historical phase in which it has ceased to be a properly revolutionary class, to produce sociopolitical transformations, sometimes of significance, conserving securely in its own hands power, initiative and hegemony, and leaving the working classes in their condition of subalternity" (Losurdo, in Thomas 2009: 197). The intensified class struggle and ideological oppositions need to be contained and articulated by the integral state, thus a passive revolution aims to restructure the coherence of a social formation and its state power within a further process of uneven and combined socio-geographical development (Morton 2013: 59).

C. GRAMSCI AND THE PASSIVE REVOLUTION
OF SOCIAL AND CULTURAL SCIENCES:
RURALITY, URBANITY, AND AMERICANISM

The period of passive revolution until World War I ignited a proliferation of social, cultural, and economic theories about the modern condition and its hegemonic aspirations. Bourgeois theorists struggled with the attempt to reconcile the Jacobine discursive formation about individualism and autonomy with the collective character of mass politics. In economics, a moral-intellectual conservatism took place. The "marginalist revolution" in economics aimed to discipline the labor market by both erasing the concept of class and claiming that the struggle for a higher value of labor power equated to the complete disruption of the economy. In social theory individualist rationality was linked to intentional functionalism and value-free descriptive realism. But the lack of legitimacy of bourgeois values could not be remedied by a simple acceptance and formal endorsement of the state of facts. Durkheim invented a moderate communitarian model of individual freedom of civil subjects together with a range of social responsibilities stemming from tradition and informal social control. In his analysis of the social collective consciousness Durkheim affirmed his a-social individualist and realist concept of ideology, failing to answer the question "by means of what concepts are . . . institutions and practices demonstrated to be the object of the science of sociology?" (Hirst 1975: 100). Durkheim's methodological inability to render ideology in its proper conceptual terms can be tracked in his point of view regarding urban and rural life. In a country with almost half of the population in the rural sectors—the impoverished farmers trying to meet ends with putting-out textile production—and a significant niche craft-production by small-scale industry, the ideal image of modernity conflicted with everyday economic life (Kemp 1971; Liu 1994).

Throughout Durkheim's writings on modern phenomena a classical tension can be detected between a rather nostalgic evaluation of precapitalist communal ties in rural villages and the experienced anomie of modern city life. But his call for a vague form of solidarity to combat the disintegrative tendencies of urban mentality and the social division of labor lacked any dialectical analysis of the relations of force and ideological processes that tied urban life and countryside together. For example, he practically dismissed any qualitative difference between communal identities and the modern proletarian political struggle. For him, "the traditional community has enshrined class-conscious working-class values and some conception of shared collective responsibility and, as well, shares a collective memory with venerated historical events and personages" (Chorney 1990: 76). Compared to the Gramscian or Thompsonian historicist examples of the qualitative jump from a corporatist to a class-based struggle of the proletariat, Durkheim eliminated the ideological shifts of counter-hegemonic movements. The same can be noted about Max Weber in Germany, but in a different form. Weber mediated his seemingly a-ideological individualism with the aspirations of the conservative nationalist réveil in a young nation, calling forth the cultural ideals of democratic bourgeois elitism (Mommsen 1974: 22–46; Scott 2000: 40–42). Yet again, his unblinking support for bourgeois modernization of the economic sphere and his condemnation of the rural and urban moral economy did not resolve the pressing agrarian question and the ensuing fact of unevenness between the industrial West and the Junker-dominated rural East.

Gramsci succeeded to surpass and exceed the ideological and conceptual limitation of classical bourgeois social and cultural thinkers. In order to understand the new dialectical unity between city and countryside and the related question of hegemony, he underscored the importance of changing spatial scales (Morton 2013). While in precapitalist times the cities relied on the hinterland in order to thrive and to gain regional or international dominance of some niche production or long-distance trade, most output was being consumed locally or regionally. The emergence of the economies of scale within the capitalist world market developed in interaction with the constellation of modern nation-states. The city became the most important nexus of production, a new social and cultural-symbolic territory, fuelled by a stream of landless farmers. Early on, the novelty of urban culture as a set of "new principles" of living—the social costs of the new labor process—was already recorded by scientists and governmental institutions (e.g., Fielden 1834; Cooke Taylor 1844). Gramsci and Marx, discussing the French and Italian transition toward capitalist modernity, attempted to redefine the class content of the relation between city and countryside. The most important question is how urban culture, expressing new forms of class solidarity, became ideologically self-conscious about its socio-spatial impact on the social formation as a whole:

> Gramsci saw modern(ist) urbanization as key to the demographic reordering of the "terrain" of hegemony . . . and interpreted urban space . . . as key "ideological material" for bourgeois rule. . . . He was unambiguous about the positive role urban transformations could play in multiscalar, spatially and temporally differentiated wars of position. . . . Gramsci hoped that industrial action and political self-organization in Turin would join up with the land occupations hat swept through northern and southern agricultural zones . . . and thus lay the basis for a final war of movement—the takeover of the heights of bourgeois power in Milan and Rome. (Kipfer 2013: 90–91).

Thus, neither the deficient bourgeois rule nor its proletarian contender had the decisive hegemonic upper hand when they exerted the urban war of position. The spatial differentiations need to be tied together in order to fully understand the noncontemporaneity of hegemonic practices. At the right, combined with the wartime experiences of the total mobilisation of national resources, the technicist and technocratic fetish of Americanism attracted both liberals, conservatives as nationalists. The United States, not "burdened" by the past of feudalism and communal forms of living, exported a renewed bourgeois scientific culture of Taylorism. It brought the promise of the eradication of backwardness in the exponential intensity of the social division of labor in the production process. The pure form of bourgeois modernity in the ideological images of Americanism mirrored the "imperfections" of the European origins and development of the capitalist mode of production (Gramsci 1982: 167, 188–89, 220–23).

The spread of Americanism under monopoly capitalism happened at different economic scales. Monopoly capitalism increased labor and capital productivity, the final real subsumption of labor, which increased the spatial integration of the social units of the world market and the importance thereof (Massey 1984: 46–53). Within factory walls, it became clear that the early European capitalist process still relied on a combination of premodern and capitalist disciplinary practices, which shaped modern property relations and relations of force: the daily selection of the unskilled labor force at the factory gate, monopolizing knowledge of skills of former independent artisans by contractual obligations, the promulgation of rules and monetary penalties, spatial compartmentalization, the system of overseers, and the enhancement of vertical hierarchy by bringing in domestic relations. This strategy of microphysical power was highly problematic in terms of pure economic efficiency—surplus extraction. For example, "at a time when manufacturing still depended on craft knowledge or on the secret know-how of the overlookers and foremen, graded monetary sanctions gave owners the only feasible check on, and evaluation of, the overlookers" loyalty and efficiency" (Biernacki 1995: 195). In addition, loyalty could be procured by playing the communal card of kinship and ethnicity: the hiring of families of workers and overseers outside the locality (e.g., Lis and Soly 1987: 75–76).

The factory owners legitimized their disciplinary practices through a heterodox discursive strategy. First there was a patriarchal call for obedience and the conceptualization of the factory floor as a natural chain of command. Second, the individual prudence and sense of duty of both capitalist and worker was mobilized. The laborer had the contractual duty to deliver a certain amount of commodities to the capitalist, whose profits relied on a standardized method of sale. Third, it was argued that both wage and profit depended on the competiveness of all "participants" of production in a free trade economic society. Fourth, there was an appeal to virtuous Christian work regarding diligence and piety (Versieren 2013). Taylorism used the principle of the division of labor to atomize and disarm the potential resistance of proletarian and communal subjectivity of the worker. In other words, its spatial division is not a matter of just measuring the expanding size of the company, because Taylorism established the economic and cultural form of the social nature of property relations within the political framework of a passive revolution (e.g., Massey 1984: 27). The transformed microphysics of power on the factory floor reflected the changing ideological determination of the labor market. In the centuries before early capitalism state coercion and local authorities had been the most important source of regulation of labor practices and its role in commercial and productive activities (Mann 1986: 461; Biernacki 1995: 214–45). No culture existed which promoted the creation of an exchange market for labor power. Monopoly capitalism, unleashing the productive powers through the dissemination of Americanism as the pure ideological representation and cultural practice, showed a remarkable resemblance with the political logic of the integral state (Gramsci 2007: 11). The top-down hierarchy of overseers and the culture of master and servant gradually mutated into a layered system of molecular co-optation of workers into the daily management of the production process. A "passive revolution" in the factory was necessary because its formerly direct forms of discipline contradicted the exponential growth of the division of labor. This situation thus "aggravates control problems and potentially puts the power of the ruler into further jeopardy. . . . Those in power become dependent on experts who are much harder to control than those whose work is open to common-sense evaluation" (Rueschemeyer 1986: 54). The exercise of power became more and more anonymous, in which the concrete diffusion of individual ownership, absentee ownership, blended with collusive management of administration and engineers (Veblen 1997 [1923]: 210–14). Nonetheless, in both early liberal capitalism and monopoly capitalism, status according to the position in the production process could not be divorced from cultural and political transformations. The social evaluation of skills cannot be reduced to a technical point of view. On a macro-scale, political struggle brought an urban proletarian culture into existence. The organization of the national economy, especially the socio-spatial relationships between the different class factions of capitalists vis-à-vis the subaltern forces, is itself the object of the very same struggle (Massey 1984: 41–43). Fordism expressed the cultural and political reconfiguration of labor under the expanding role of the integral state. It integrated class struggle, which became a structural element of cyclical capitalist crisis.

D. GRAMSCI IN EGYPT: THE MAKING OF MODERN CULTURE AND THE SPECTRES OF COLONIALISM AND FEUDALISM

The case of the Mahalla al-Kubra textile manufacturers exemplifies the notable differences and similarities between European and Egyptian transitional temporalities. It cannot be considered as the inevitable making of capitalist culture on micro-scale, but rather the "further innovation and perfection of artisanal weaving process" (Hammad 2009: 36). From Muhammed Ali until Nasser, the early manufacturers and urban corporatist structures resembled some of the key characteristics of the commercialization model of early modern Europe. Thus, the thesis that merchant capitalism in Ottoman times or the emergence of manufacturing under Muhammed Ali directly led to modern capitalism lacks evidence and coherence (Abdel-Malek 1983: 122; Khafaji 2004: 43). As in Europe, this commercialization of society reached its apex in a precapitalist cultural context. A few manufacturers, additional rural "proto-industrial" production, conflicts between merchants and crafts-men, subcontracting between and within guilds, all these phenomena were intricately linked to a predominant tributary mode of production with its own history of succeeding phases of centralization and decentralization of surplus extraction by the Ottoman sultanate, the Mamluk dynasty and local land-lords—a rhythm, that only ended with the decolonization of Egypt.

Under Mamluk and Ottoman, the surplus product of rural households was extracted through taxation—the multazim gentry bought the right to collect taxes and brought the tax in kind to the urban market—and extra labor was expropriated through sharecropping, corvée, and informal wage labor (Bei-nin 2001: 25; Tucker 2005 [1979]: 230). Surpluses were not reinvested in agricultural production, but flowed directly to the cities which became rich centers of trade, guild handicrafts, and state administration within the frame-work of a decentralized command economy (Hanna 2011: 37). In the cities, Mamluk military rulers or the Ottoman administration supported a policy of provisionalism—the control of the food markets in order to prevent urban riots—but neglected the necessary protectionist measures to support handi-craft production (Parthasarathi 2011). Egyptian merchants invested in politi-cal networks, architectural imagery of opulence, and above all in the secured return of tax farms. In the middle of the seventeenth century the upward economic cycle presented new opportunities for the urban populace (Ray-mond 2002). Until that time, the guilds had an egalitarian institutional cul-ture, and possessed real political influence. Later, Ottoman rule demoted the political strength and autonomy of guilds as an important source of taxation. In comparison with their European counterparts Egyptian cities could not draw "upon any concept of juridic or corporate personality to counteract the Islamic doctrine of oneness" and remained "vulnerable to government inter-ference" (Ayubi 1995: 165). Nonetheless, guilds continued to play the pivot-al role in the urban moral economy. When urban production expanded, the internal egalitarian organization slowly slipped into an oligopoly of a few master craftsmen, whose income and status rose because of their intense involvement with rich merchants and having different systems of subcontracting (Hanna 2011: 100–2). The moral economy of urban culture did not break down, but rather became verticalized (Khafaji 1984: 111).

Muhammad Ali's "modern" centralized mercantilist policies were primarily oriented toward the needs of a military bureaucracy, relying on the new feudal landlords and traditional elites in provincial towns, and curtailing the power of urban guilds and merchant capital. He attempted to control handicraft production, commercial exchange, and the input of raw agricultural material. This closely resembled the political economy of European absolutism and created internal obstructions toward the development of an indigenous industrial capitalism (Khafaji 2004: 42; Abbas and El-Dessouky 2011: 60–63). Muhammed Ali resorted to violence to force peasants into the system of cash- and sharecropping, which was met with local revolts, but eventually led to the crisis of the old family-patriarchal household economy (Sayyid-Marsot 1984: 152–57; Khafaji 2004: 31; Abbas and El-Dessouky 2011: 12). Feudal private property rights undermined the rural household economy. In response to feudalization, the village elite strengthened the stratification of everyday life (Habib 1985: 47).

At the third quarter of the nineteenth century British colonialism fully integrated Egypt into the world market. Nonetheless, at the scale of the social formation a profound articulated unevenness and combination existed between feudal rural communal life and its output in the form of sharecropping for export purposes, handicraft production in cities and rural villages alongside the proletarianization of labor in transport and intermediary commercial activities, and capitalist rentier activities of banks and credit companies of both Egyptian and foreign ownership. As time passed, the lack of political and ideological hegemony of and the unity between the royal elite, feudal landowners, and colonial forces surfaced in times of intense political crisis. Power relations were still based upon local and ethnical clientilism.

Within this framework, Mahalla al-Kubra manufacturers appeared to be completely peripheral, with regards both to output and relative importance. Foreign capitalists politically and economically defended this articulation of precapitalist and capitalist modes of production, which effectively blocked economic development. Culturally, foreign companies imported new bookkeeping, engineering, and state administration techniques. This incentive promoted the technical education of provincial state employees, who were an intermediate class, but the mismatch between the amount of hiring and the available group of new intellectuals created a growing frustration about the limitation of social mobility (Podeh and Winckler 2004: 8). Communal ties remained strong between these intellectuals, "effendiyya," and the provincial background, because for high-ranking positions the state opted for employing foreigners. At the same time, notwithstanding the import of the aforementioned techniques, the British colonial administration in concert with the rural and merchant elites tried to contain the dissemination of a modern intellectual culture. These intellectuals, mainly gathered in the liberal nation-alist Wafd Party, were under the patronage of Egyptian big landowners and merchants and shared some common images about the "ignorant peasantry," which, when having government responsibilities, limited their capabilities to articulate an hegemonic national-popular program (Ayubi 1995: 107; Abbas and El-Dessouky 2011: 192).

The disillusions about the decisions of Wafd in interwar years created an autonomous political subaltern force with nationalist sentiments, albeit ideo-logically divided. Even though everyday cultural communal ties between the new stratum of intellectuals and the subaltern classes existed, both sides attracted and repulsed each other according to growing cultural differences and political events. The middle-class intellectuals adopted the Enlighten-ment ideas of sovereignty, liberal civic values, and economic modernization. But until Nasser the articulation of modernization, equality, and the commu-nal discourse of the common good had not been made successfully. New marriage strategies brought the elites of foreign descent and Egyptians clos-er, but at the same time they further alienated themselves from their farmer-tenants because of an exuberant urban lifestyle, and, because of an increased socio-spatial separation, as they moved to the metropole. The repertoire of oppositional groups addressed the elite's failure to promote the common good, but also demanded that they invest in the modernization of the econo-my and in the education of the Egyptian people (Hammad 2009: 31; Abbas and El-Dessouky 2011: 82; 187). This elitist culture expressed the uneven relation between the resident metropole and the hinterland, an important feudal phenomenon similar to European feudalization when the immediate ties of personalistic loyalty loosened (Mann 1973). In the eyes of provincial towns and villages the metropole was parasitic and thrived upon residential expansion, consumption of luxury goods, and commercial market networks. In major cities the blossoming world trade realized large profits for the rural elites, stimulating a new urban financial sphere of credit, loans, and banking around landed property (Richards and Waterbury 2008: 38–40). This new commercial domain gave rise to a renewed merchant class in the cities, and intensified the economic ties between feudal rurality and the rentier metro-pole. Smaller cities functioned as satellite intermediaries between rural vil-lages, and Cairo and Alexandria. As in Europe, they were imbedded in the rural countryside with local production and small-scale specialization. A few could benefit from their strategic position along transportation routes or func-tioning as agricultural hubs (Hammad 2009: 38–9). The urban culture of smaller cities was based upon spatial separation: a profound social differenti-ation linked to a provincial mentality of local elites.

The establishment of new textile manufacturers in the interwar years did not produce a definite historical-epochal break with the precapitalist past. It was as much the final success of the feudal-absolutist commercialisation model as a first step to industrial capitalism. Similar to early modern Europe "rural and domestic handicrafts did not simply disappear in the face of the development of manufacture. . . . they coexisted with and were reorganized by manufacture . . . always rested on the handicrafts of towns and the domestic subsidiary industries of rural districts, over time destroying these in one form and resurrecting them in another" (Heller 2011: 182). Contrary to the European countries, the profits derived from the new rural-urban "proto-industrial" networks did not flow to the richest layer of master craftsmen or merchants—the old and new bourgeoisie (Mann 1986: 465). Instead, feudal landlords integrated these commercial networks into their rural rentier interests fuelled by easy credit and higher money rents (Abbas and El-Dessouky 2011: 53). Guild members, stripped of their former institutional corporate rights, refused to work in the manufactures and slowly joined the ranks of the proletarianised urban workforce. In addition, before World War I, fierce local labor strikes took place at colonial companies and the public sector collaborated with the guilds in protest (Toledano 1990). Only after the war did a proletarian culture began to develop organically with the communal-corporate ethics of the dwindling guilds and neighborhood solidarities, resulting in a co-existence of both vertical class and horizontal communal relations.

After the Europeans built the first ginning factories, the Egyptian landlord owners of Mahalla al-Kubra manufacturers channelled the surplus labor of their estates through the factory gates with the help of well-educated effendiyya–management and illiterate community-based violent foremen (Abu-Lughod 1984: 102; Hammad 2009: 46). These landowners wanted to diversify their investments, but at the same time they extended their already existing influence in the agricultural sector (Khafaji 2004: 53–54; Abbas and El-Dessouky 2011: 92). Malhalla al-Kubra cannot be understood as an industrial novelty, but rather as the integration of agricultural monocropping output and derivative textile activities (Hammad 2009: 40). Land laborers and peasants were preferable as a cheap labor source because of their communal rural ties—the importation of rural cultural and social relations of production. The basic "labor unit" was not the individual worker, but the extended family. Kinship and the proximity of ethnical ties primarily defined their cultural life-world, and its hierarchical component was exploited by administration and overseers in order to keep discipline and to negate the divided authority in a preliminary process of the division of labor (Rueschemeyer 1986: 56–61).

Both foreign and Egyptian industrial textile activities changed as much the outlook of the city as they reaffirmed the divided communal lines of cultural demarcation and segregation. With the help of state finances, landlords and foreigners built new residential quarters with parks and modern public buildings. Slumps, housing seasonal factory workers and recreating the original rural village environment, were added to the narrow streets of the old medieval silk center. As the manufacturers expanded, so did the demand for services in the rich quarters. In this transitional city life cultural and spatial divisions were being crossed, which created a vague sense of class distinctions (Hammad 2009: 26–52). Slowly and after years of fierce conflict, the initial hostility of urban dwellers toward the workers began to change into a sense of shared interests. Factory management, understanding that coercion did not suffice, tried to contain the disgruntled workers with the rent of their own factory houses as a renewed effort to procure obedience and docility. This measure was part of a disciplinary repertoire that enabled management to supervise and control the everyday life—and thus resistance—of the workers, which resembled closely the practices of the first generations of European patriarchal factory owners. Factory housing also limited the mobility of seasonal workers: losing a job implied the loss of housing. These means of control made the workers adapt to "the industrial life and choose when to imitate and when to differ from the model of a modern worker-subject as it was imposed upon them by the Company and the state" (Hammad 2009: 62). In the end, the burden of patriarchal culture with no regard to efficient productivity or skill acquirement—the introduction of the factory clock or apprenticeship had only a coercive function—drove down the rate of profit, provoked Luddite destruction of machinery, and ultimately expressed the inability to mediate new social relations of production. This culture prevented a smooth exchange of technology and knowledge and the accumulation of additional increments of established useful knowledge (Scott 2006: 113–14; Storper 2013: 55).

Until World War II, the different generations of manufacturers expressed the fixed and stalled transitional temporalities of the Egyptian social formation: outdated technology, inefficient discipline culture, mix of traditional and modern trade networks, communal particularism, crowding out of handicraft products by import of Western commodities, and precapitalist solidarities combined with an incipient proletarian class consciousness. Political and social groups lacked a self-defined sense of identity vis-à-vis a conceptualized form of social totality. World War II as an economic and political event broke down the instable configuration of dominant forces. Less than a decade later, the Nasserite regime, Bonapartist and Caesarist in essence (see De Smet 2014), gradually replaced the old feudal landowner class by rich semi-capitalist farmers and initiated a state capitalist industrial project.

In political and cultural terms, Nasser radically differed from his long line of predecessors. He adopted the anti-feudal modernization discourse of liberal and socialist movements and the nationalist sentiments of the subaltern classes in order to break with the feudal-absolutist-colonial deadlock. Nasser reconfigured the relationship between urbanity and rurality. He improved the living conditions of the urban workers and initiated a planned reorganization of the cityscape. In an effort to turn itself into a top-down hegemonic force, the regime superseded the political strategy of communists, socialists, and liberals in forging a link between factory floor and local and national party headquarters. Other political contenders never succeeded in connecting the metropole with the struggle in provincial towns. Land reforms and rural cooperatives served a twofold purpose: winning over the goodwill of mainly the middle farmer and a surplus siphoning for industrial investment goals.

With the spread of mass propaganda and the instalment of educational and cultural initiatives, the Nasserite state created a novel, explicitly national and modern civil culture. The old corporatism was overcome through the forceful establishment of a new, state-driven corporatism. Although the "popular classes" became the protagonists of the national play, it was the regime that wrote the script of their mobilization. The bureaucratic nature of the political hegemony was inherently fragile because it could not supersede the people/power bloc contradiction. On the one hand, the Nasserite intervention strongly interpellated a political and cultural people-nation, forging a new hegemonic bloc that temporary displaced existing social contradictions. On the other hand, the regime tended to reduce the problem of modernity and hegemony to the technical question of industrialization, raising productivity, and the technicality of a division of labor (see Laclau 1977). Thus the new regime faced the insurmountable problem of creating a modern class project that could articulate the still fluid and transitory social relations. The authoritarian nature of the Nasserite state and its "overdevelopment" was an inadequate response to manage social conflicts, in which "the intermediate strata come to achieve an inordinate importance as a social base of state . . . [these strata] are often in a state of flux and transition, and as the entire class map is quite fluid and uncertain . . . [these strata] switch and reverse their ideological and political allegiance practically overnight" (Ayubi 1995: 182). The downfall of Nasserism signalled the end of the Egyptian Jacobin moment, leading to an instable cycle of passive revolutions, embedded within neoliberal and rentier logics, from Sadat over Mubarak to the current regime (De Smet 2014). The Egyptian case of different cultural and social temporalities could not be articulated successfully, which thus lead to a rather permanent state of organic crisis. There remained few routes to a socio-spatial escape from the past which would have led to new urban localizations of industry. This situation prevented the emergence of a modern urban culture primarily determined by production (Storper 1991: 68; Storper and Walker 1989: 71–72).

E. WAVES OF PASSIVE REVOLUTION

Returning to Huntington's "waves of democratization," we conclude that we cannot simply look back and urge the Other, who is presumed to follow in our footsteps, to "catch up." The universalization of commodity production went hand in hand with a generalization of a shared space-time. However, particular social structures were not simply assimilated into the universalist capitalist project; sometimes they resisted transformations, allied with capitalist forms, or even subjugated those forms to their interests. We have shown that the early European capitalist process still relied on a combination of premodern and capitalist disciplinary practices, which shaped modern property relations and relations of force. Similarly, the colonial and independent industries of Egypt until World War II were incorporated into absolutist, landed, and commercial capitalist structures. They did not produce a definite historical-epochal rupture with the precapitalist past. It was as much the final success of the feudal-absolutist commercialization model as a first step to industrial capitalism. Because of the shared space-time, however, Egypt did not simply replicate the European process in isolation, but its diachronic development as a part of capitalism was intersected by its synchronic existence within the whole of the capitalist world market and the modern nation-state system.

In Europe, industry created the bourgeoisie as a ruling class, just as it created the worker as a proletarian, whereas in Egypt, industry was created by an already existing hybrid of landed, commercial, and colonial capital as an expansion of their rentier income. Despite its modernist features, the Egyptian factory reproduced precapitalist kinship, religious and ethnical social relations, and cultural hierarchies. The profit motive was burdened with patriarchal principles of discipline and violence to keep the workforce in check. Despite the social space of the workplace, a modern working class culture began to emerge organically, arising from struggles in the workplace and the shared and contested spaces of the city. In the political field, immanent working class subjectivities were primarily articulated along nationalist and anti-imperialist lines, and after World War II the workers" movement played a fundamental role in the resistance against British influence. Urban proletarian culture became one of the pillars of a modern, Egyptian, national culture in the years leading up to the Free Officers" coup in 1952.

This immanent urban culture was subsumed under the Nasserite project of "Arab socialism," which united both the "Jacobin" and "Bonapartist" moments of Egypt's modernity, in the sense that the mass protests and the coup of 1952 rendered revolution and restoration logically and historically contemporaneous. Just as in the Italian case, the rupture with the precapitalist era was not realized by classical bourgeois democracy, but by an authoritarian state. Passive revolution, rather than bourgeois democracy, appears as the more correct criterion through which to interpret the cultural trajectory of urban modernity, both in the West and in Egypt.

BIBLIOGRAPHY

Abbas, Raouf and Assem El-Dessouky (2011), *The Large Landowning Class and the Peasantry in Egypt 1837–1952*, Syracuse: Syracuse University Press.

Abdel-Malek, Anouar (1983), *Contemporary Arab Political Thought*, London: Zed Press.

Abu-Lughod, Janet (1984), "Culture, 'Modes of Production,' and the Changing Nature of Cities in the Arab World," in *The City in Cultural Context*, J. A. Agnew, J. Mercer, D. E. Sopher (eds.), Syracuse: Syracuse University Press.

Ayubi, Nazih N. (1995), *Over-Stating the Arab State: Politics and Society in the Middle East*, London: I.B. Taurus.

Badie, Bertrand and Pierre Birnbaum (1983), *The Sociology of the State*, Chicago: Chicago University Press.

Beinin, Joel (2001), *Workers and Peasants in the Middle East*, Cambridge: Cambridge University Press,

Biernacki, R. (1995), *The Fabrication of Labor: Germany and Britain, 1640–1914*, Berkeley: University of California Press

Chorney, Harold (1990), *City of Dreams: Social Theory and the Urban Experience*, Scarborough: Nelson Canada.

Cooke Taylor, William (1844), *Factories and the Factory System*, London: Jeremiah How.

Davis, John A. (1979), "The South, The Risorgimento and the Origins of the 'Southern Problem,'" in *Gramsci and Italy's Passive Revolution*, John A. Davis (ed.), London: Croom Helm, pp. 67–103.

De Smet, Brecht (2014), "Revolution and Counter-Revolution in Egypt," *Science and Society*, 78: 1, pp. 11–40.

Dobb, Maurice (1976), *Studies in the Development of Capitalism*, New York: International Publishers.

Eagleton, Terry (1996), *The Illusions of Postmodernism*, Oxford: Blackwell Publishers.

Fielden, John (1834), *The Curse of the Factory System*, London: Cobbett.

Fox-Genovese, E. (1976), *The Origins of Physiocracy: Economic Revolution and Social Order in Eighteenth-Century France*, Ithaca, NY: Cornell University Press.

Frosini, Fabio (2003), *Gramsci e la Filosofia. Saggio sui Quaderni del carcere*, Roma: Carocci editore.

Gershman, Carl (2011), "The Fourth Wave," *New Republic*, 14 March, Accessed 27 October 2013, http://www.newrepublic.com/article/world/85143/middle-east-revolt-democratization.

Goux, Jean-Joseph (1990), *Symbolic Economies after Marx and Freud*, Ithaca: Cornell University Press.

Gramsci, A. (1971), *Selections from the Prison Notebooks*, New York: International Publishers.

———. (1982), *Prison Notebooks Volume I*. New York: Columbia University Press.

———. (1996), *Prison Notebooks Volume II*. New York: Columbia University Press.

———. (2007), *Prison Notebooks Volume III*, New York: Columbia University Press.

Habib, Irfan (1985), "Classifying Pre-Colonial India," in *Feudalism and Non-European Societies*, T. J. Byres, Harbans Mukhia (eds.), London: Frank Cass, pp. 44–53.

Hammad, Hanan H. (2009), "Mechanizing People, Localizing Modernity. Industrialization and Social Transformation in Modern Egypt: al-Mahalla al-Kubra 1910–1958," PhD dissertation, Austin: Faculty of the Graduate School of the University of Texas.

Hanna, Nelly (2011), *Artisan Entrepreneurs in Cairo and Early-Modern Capitalism*, Syracuse: Syracuse University Press.

Hartley, George (2003), *The Abyss of Representation: Marxism and the Postmodern Sublime*, Durham: Duke University Press.

Heller, Henry (2011), *The Birth of Capitalism: A 21st-Century Perspective*. London: Pluto Press.

Hirst, P. Q. (1975), *Durkheim, Bernard and Epistemology*, London: Routledge and Kegan Paul.

Jessop, Bob (2005), "Gramsci as a Spatial Theorist," *Critical Review of International Social and Political Philosophy*, 8: 4, pp. 421–37.

Kemp, Tom (1971), *Economic Forces in French History: Essay on the Development of the French Economy*, Durham: Dobson.

Khafaji, Isam al (2004), *Tormented Births: Passages to Modernity in Europe and the Middle East*, New York: IB Tauris.

Kipfer, Stefan (2008), "How Lefebvre Urbanized Gramsci," in *Space, Difference, Everyday Life. Reading Henri Lefebvre*, K. Goonewardena, S. Kipfer (eds.), London: Routledge, pp. 193–211.

———. (2013), *City, Country, Hegemony*, in *Gramsci: Space, Nature, Politics*, Michael Ekers, Stefan Kipfer, Alex Loftus (eds.), Chichester: Wiley-Blackwell, pp. 84–103.

Krätke, Michael and Peter Thomas (2011), "Antonio Gramsci's Contribution to a Critical Economics," *Historical Materialism*, 19: 3, pp. 63–105.

Kriedte, Peter (1983), *Peasants, Landlords and Merchant Capitalists. Europe and the World Economy, 1500–1800*, Cambridge: Cambridge University Press.

Laclau, Ernesto (1977), *Politics and Ideology in Marxist Theory: Capitalism, Fascism, Populism*, London: New Left Books.

Lis, Catharina and Hugo Soly (1987), *Een groot bedrijf in een kleine stad. De firma de Heyder en Co. Te Lier 1757– 1834*, Lier: Liers Genootschap voor Geschiedenis.

———. (2012), *Worthy Efforts: Attitudes to Work in Pre-Industrial Europe*. Leiden: Brill

Liu, Tessie P. (1994), *The Weaver's Knot: The Contradictions of Class Struggle and Family Solidarity in Western France, 1750–1914*, Ithaca: Cornell University Press.

Mann, Michael (1973), *Consciousness and Action among the Western Working Class*, London: Macmillan.

———. (1986), *The Sources of Social Power*, Vol. I, Cambridge: Cambridge University Press.

Marx, Karl (1978 [1850]), *Marx and Engels Collected Works*, Vol. 10, New York: International Publishers.

Massey, Doreen (1984), *Spatial Divisions of Labour: Social Structures and the Geography of Production*, Houndsmill: Macmillan Press.

Mommsen, Wolfgang J. (1974), *The Age of Bureaucracy: Perspectives on the Political Sociology of Max Weber*, Oxford: Basil Blackwell.

Morris, Robert J. (1983), "Voluntary Societies and British Urban Elites, 1750–1850: An analysis," *Historical Journal*, 26, pp. 95–118.

Morton, Adam David (2013), "Traveling with Gramsci," in *Gramsci: Space, Nature, Politics*, Michael Ekers, Stefan Kipfer, Alex Loftus (eds.), Chichester: Wiley-Blackwell, pp. 47–65.

Podeh, Elie and Onn Winckler, (2004), "Nasserism as a Form of Populism," in *Rethinking Nasserism. Revolution and Historical Memory in Modern Egypt*, Elie Podeh and Onn Winckler (eds.), Gainesville: University Press of Florida.

Parthasarathi, Prasannan (2011), *Why Europe Grew Rich and Asia Did Not*, Cambridge: Cambridge University Press.

Raymond, André (2002), *Arab Cities in the Ottoman Period*, Aldershot: Ashgate.

Richards, Alan and John Waterbury (2008), *A Political Economy of the Middle East*, Boulder: Westview Press.

Roncaglia, Alessandro (1985), *Petty: The Origins of Political Economy*, Cardiff: University College Cardiff Press.

Rueschemeyer, Dietrich (1986), *Power and the Division of Labour*, Stanford: Stanford University Press.

Sayyid-Marsot, Afaf Lutfi (1984), *Egypt in the Reign of Muhammad Ali*, Cambridge: Cambridge University Press.

Scott, Alan (2000), "Capitalism, Weber and Democracy," *Max Weber Studies*, 1: 1, pp. 33–55.

Scott, Allen J. (2006), *Geography and Economy*, Oxford: Oxford University Press.

Storper, Michael (1991), *Industrialization, Economic Development, and the Regional Question in the Third World*, London: Pion Limited.

————. (2013), *Keys to the City. How Economics, Institutions, Social Interaction, and Politics Shape Development*, Princeton: Princeton University Press.

Storper, Michael and Richard Walker (1989), *The Capitalist Imperative: Territory, Technology, and Industrial Growth*, Cambridge: Blackwell.

Thomas, Peter D. (2009), *The Gramscian Moment: Philosophy, Hegemony and Marxism*, Leiden: Brill.

Toledano, Ehud (1990), *State and Society in Mid-Nineteenth-Century Egypt*, Cambridge: Cambridge University Press.

Tomba, Massimiliano (2013), *Marx's Temporalities*, Leiden: Brill.

Tucker, Judith (2005 [1979]), "The Decline of the Family Economy in Mid-Nineteenth-Century Egypt," in *The Modern Middle East*, Albert Hourani, Philip Khoury, Mary C. Wilson (eds.), New York: I.B. Tauris.

Veblen, Thorstein (1997 [1923]), *Absentee Ownership: Business Enterprise in Recent Times: The Case of America*, New Brunswick: Transaction Publishers.

Versieren, Jelle (2013), "The Perception of Labour and the Discursive Temporalities of Guild Organisations, Free Trade Ideologues and Early Industrial Capitalists in Western Europe 1750–1850," Conference Paper, Cultures et idéologies urbaines dans les anciens Pays- Bas. Temps et temporalités en milieu urbain, University Lille-3/MESHS.

Chapter Ten

The Urban Working-Class Culture of Riot in Osaka and Los Angeles

Toward a Comparative History

Manuel Yang, Takeshi Haraguchi, and Kazuya Sakurada

"Culture" is easily one of the most reified terms in English. Raymond Williams called it "one of the two or three most complicated words in the English language" and attributed its complexity to the varying usage of the word that "often confuses but even more often conceals the central question of the relations between 'material' and 'symbolic' production, which in some recent argument . . . have always to be related rather than contrasted" (Williams 1983: 87–93). Thirty years later, with the academic institutionalization of post-linguistic-turn theory and Cultural Studies, "culture" in the sense of "symbolic production" seems to have considerably diminished its necessary tension with material relations and social processes. Hence, the reification of the term has inevitably followed suit, despite the fact that, etymologically, it "first denoted a thoroughly material process" and "[i]n Marxist parlance, it brings together both base and superstructure in a single notion" (Eagleton 2000: 1–2).

Those of us working within a particular kind of Marxist tradition in urban studies should remind our colleagues once again that "urban culture" has always been an inseparably material and symbolic production, rooted in the historical context of class struggle. This was Williams's meaning when he stressed their relationship, not their apparent contrast, and carefully circumscribed the dogmatic pitfalls present in Marx's famous base-superstructure metaphor (as he did in his 1973 essay "Base and Superstructure in Marxist Cultural Theory"). It was also the original impulse of British Cultural Studies, which in its early permutation was both a variation of and a predecessor to what the Italian autonomists would later call *conricera* (co-research), mapping various forms of British youth subculture as dissenting pre-political expressions of embryonic urban working-class culture (most famously published in the 1975 collection *Resistance Through Rituals: Youth Subcultures in Post-War Britain*).

In 1963, the British-German sociologist Ruth Glass coined the term "gentrification" in *London: Aspects of Change*, a pioneering collection of urban studies:

> One by one, many of the working class quarters of London have been invaded by the middle classes—upper and lower. Shabby, modest mews and cottages—two rooms up and two down—have been taken over, when their leases have expired, and have become elegant, expensive residences. Larger Victorian houses, downgraded in an earlier or recent period—which were used as lodging houses or were otherwise in multiple occupation—have been upgraded once again. Nowadays, many of these houses are being sub-divided into costly flats or "houselets" (in terms of the new real estate snob jargon). The current social status and value of such dwellings are frequently in inverse relation to their size, and in any neighbourhoods. Once this process of "gentrification" starts in a district, it goes on rapidly until all or most of the original working class occupiers are displaced, and the whole social character of the district is changed. . . . And this is an inevitable development, in view of the demographic, economic and political pressures to which London, and especially Central London, has been subjected. (Glass 1964: xvii–xix)

The meaning that Glass imbued in her neologism had persevered in its subsequent, widely circulating usage. Although she describes it as a middle-class invasion, the displacement of working-class district is viewed as a predominantly impersonal economic process: large Victorian houses are "sub-divided into costly flats" and "current social status and value of such dwellings" are transformed "frequently in inverse relation to their size." We do not see who or what does the actual upgrading or downgrading. For this inversion of "social status and value" is mediated by the price mechanism of rent, apparently a part of "inevitable development" taking on a larger, virtually suprahuman urban scale. At the same time the "subject position" of this impersonal process is credited to the "middle class," rendered literally as the contemporary variant of the "gentry," while the working class appears to vanish of their own accord, as passive pebbles blown by the irresistible gale of rent hikes.

But when we shift our view from the macroeconomic wide angle to the narrower focus of working-class social experience, the said "development" appears hardly "inevitable." As we have seen in the recent U.S. housing crisis, when workers refuse to move after the expiration of the lease or cease to pay their mortgage due to financial difficulties, they are forcibly removed and arrested by the police; and those who yield to the displacement and find themselves on the streets are invariably criminalized. Glass intimated this subaltern perspective when she traced the origin of "troubles" among the newly emergent multiethnic workers of London: "the West Indians, the Irish, the Indians and Pakistanis . . . tell similar tales of troubles" and "ultimately such troubles originate not in Jamaica, or Barbados, not in the Punjab or County Cork" but "in our own history—past and present" (Glass 1964: xxxv).

In the same year that Glass was minting "gentrification" as a lived experi- ence of the postwar British working class, E. P. Thompson was documenting precisely the roots of this working-class history, as he saw a direct link between the "deterioration of the urban environment . . . one of the most disastrous consequences of the Industrial Revolution, whether viewed in aes- thetic terms, in terms of community amenities, or in terms of sanitation and density of population" and contemporary urban reality ("Some of the evi- dence, after all, remains with us in the industrial landscape of the north and of the Midlands today") (Thompson 1966: 319). Although Thompson did not focus his analytical lens on the multiracial composition of urban workers—at the outset of *The Making of the English Working Class* he insisted that he was writing a history of the *English* working class and apologized for his exclusion of Scottish and Irish workers—he was more forthright than Glass in delineating the conscious design hidden behind the rhetorical cloak of inevitability in urban development:

> Certainly, the unprecedented rate of population growth, and of concentration in industrial areas, would have created major problems in any known society, and most of all in a society whose *rationale* was to be found in profit-seeking and hostility to planning. We should see these as the problems of industrial- ism, aggravated by the predatory drives of *laissez faire* capitalism. (Thompson 1966: 322)

Thompson argued that it was not such predatory economic power that deter- mined working-class formation but the often contradictory set of traditional cultural practices and values workers themselves brought in conflict with this power. He thus elaborated graphically the creative, culturally expressed pow- er of variable capital against the seemingly inevitable economic logic of invariable capital.

Such emphasis on working-class culture—which was actually an empha- sis on agency—would come to earn Thompson, rather unjustifiably, the epi- thet of "culturalist." But he was well aware of the pitfall in so narrowly using the term as to expunge its disparate class content: "I criticised earlier the term 'culture,' because of its tendency to nudge us towards over-consensual and holistic notions"; "we should not forget that 'culture' is a clumpish term, which by gathering up so many activities and attributes into one common bundle may actually confuse or disguise discriminations that should be made between them" (Thompson 1991: 13). Indeed, the point was not so much to homogenize class struggle into the theater of symbolic production but the opposite, to valorize "culture" as a material reality of class struggle, that "a *rebellious* traditional culture" emerges in the face of "economic rationalizations (such as enclosure, work-discipline, unregulated 'free' markets in grain) which rulers, dealers, or employers seek to impose" (Thompson 1991: 9).

No mode of urban popular action expresses this "*rebellious* traditional culture" more eloquently than urban riots. Thompson's "The Moral Economy of the Crowd" rescued "riots" from the condescension of economically reductionist history and treated it as "a highly complex form of direct action, disciplined and with clear objectives" (Thompson 1991: 188). Although the essay was published in 1971, the year of the great municipal prison riot at Attica Correctional Facility, its original conception dates back to 1963, as Thompson was examining the galley proof of *The Making*. We can thus place a few of the most significant breakthroughs in Anglophone radical urban scholarship in the same period, sandwiched between the 1961 Kamagasaki Riot and the 1965 Watts Riot, two epochal urban insurrections that would come to embody in global contemporary history what Thompson and Glass were unearthing in their respective research.

A. THE TRANS-PACIFIC INDUSTRIAL WORKER

Kamagasaki is located on the southern edge of Osaka's inner city. Its neighborhood, which is located near the central business area of Minami, Shinsekai, Tennoji bristles with over two hundred *doya* (day laborer's cheap lodging) and is thus an area known as "*doya* city." This neighborhood is also known as *yoseba*. *Yoseba* refers to the day-laborer markets in Tokyo's Sanya, Yokohama's Kotobukicho, and, among them, Kamagasaki is the largest *yoseba* in Japan. The primary residents of this area are day laborers. They are involved in day labor through the *yoseba* and, making a daily payment to the *doya*, have continued to subsist and work. They are said to number from 20,000 to 40,000, but their exact number is unknown. This is because they are mobile proletarians who wander from workplace to workplace in waterfront transportation and construction across the country.

In contrast to Kamagasaki's *yoseba* system of labor recruitment, the downtown Los Angeles area of Skid Row's dominant institutional structures revolve around the business of drug addiction and rehabilitation, along with the quasi-military surveillance of its homeless population, which are estimated to range from 8,000 to 11,000. In the late 1990s the Business Improvement Districts introduced private security guards to "harass and intimidate homeless individuals and residents through illegal searches, detentions, and 'move-alongs,'" and the Los Angeles Police Department's 2006 Safer City Initiative "criminalized the largely poor, African American community, forcing many residents to flee downtown from other parts of L.A. County" (Heatherton 2011: 26, 9). These were, in effect, the application of "broken windows policing"—"first prevent small signs of 'disorder' from proliferating, such as graffiti, litter, panhandling, public urination, etc."—that "has been deployed to suppress housing and homeless struggles in the city" and exemplified "the state's attempt to produce a geographical solution to mass racialized and gendered poverty" (Camp and Heatherton 2012: 1). Skid Row thus functions as a vast urban extension of the prison-industrial complex, an area that is a socialized Panopticon for the continually growing reserved—and increasingly semi-permanent—army of labor. This was not the case until the 1980s, when Skid Row still served as a significant source of casual labor in factories, warehouses, restaurants, and high-rise buildings in downtown Los Angeles.

The modern origins of Skid Row and Kamagasaki coincide roughly in the late nineteenth century, as both Gilded Age United States and Meiji Japan set out to restructure their respective, largely agrarian populations into industrially disciplined, urban-based proletariat under the inextricably bound pressures of capitalist modernization and imperialist expansion. This forcible expropriation is usually given the name of "primary (or primitive) accumulation" in Marxist vocabulary. While orthodox Marxists, who also came of age in the late nineteenth century, interpreted this to mean a singular nonrecurring event, the next hundred-plus years have revealed it as an ongoing, necessary characteristic of capitalism, whose booms and busts require new forms of proletarianization to reconstitute the basis of accumulation. It is no coincidence that large-scale urbanization, within which Kamagasaki and Skid Row were formed, occurred in a period of late nineteenth-century intra-imperialist competition, intermittent depressions, and global wars, which all functioned effectively as mechanisms of primary accumulation. In modern history, urbanization is by definition a form of capital accumulation. Or, as two historical sociologists put it, "It is specious to say that industrialization caused urbanization or vice versa. Both were manifestations of a modal change in the social organization of production—a change from "simple" or "primitive" accumulation to the expanded reproduction of industrial capitalism" (Abu-Lughod and Hay 1979: 83–84).

In response to the ups and downs of laissez-faire capitalism, its unregulated tendency toward chaos, capitalism restructured itself. One essential factor of instability, what caused the general tendency toward rampant crisis was working-class struggle. Especially urban workers, that is, the classical industrial working class, made enormous contribution in generating this crisis and thus forced capital to establish state intervention and enter into a collective deal with workers in order to manage its crisis (variously termed Keynesian capitalism or welfare capitalism or social democracy). No less important, waterfront workers, sailors, shipyard workers, transporters, and other seafaring workers who connect major ports and cities of the world to each other formed a crucial part of this industrial working class. The very term "factory" stems from the ship and, as C. L. R. James pointed out famously in *Mariners, Renegades, and Castaways*, the nineteenth-century Atlantic sailors were precursors of the modern-day industrial workers, with their division of labor, class solidarity, and invention of the strike as a weapon of class struggle. A microcosm of this expansive conception of the industrial working class can be observed in the trans-Pacific activist relationships between Osaka and the West Coast.

At the 1903 Fifth Domestic Industrial Exposition, about 6,000 workers in Osaka had taken to the streets and rioted. Although ostensibly treated as a protest of rickshaw workers against the Expo's cruise ship that took away their customers, recent research by Sakai Takashi has shown that it drew from a far larger urban class composition involving *kyokaku* (professional gamblers), *tobinakashi* (stevedores), and other segments of ""underclass society" that, with varying degree of intensity, resonated with this rebellion," expressing a concerted response to the urban "clearance" or enclosure that the Expo had established (Sakai 2011: 80). In the same year, riots of a very different nature mottled the U.S. landscape, from Boston to Evansville, Ohio to Tonopah, Nevada, race riots against incoming black and Chinese workers who were perceived as a threat to the white supremacist public order. It was also around this period that a renegade Catholic priest Thomas J. Hagerty aided Mexican railroad workers in the U.S. Southwest, translating socialist propaganda into Spanish and defending them, with a gun, from white goons. Two years later, in 1905, Hagerty would cofound the IWW or Wobblies, design its organizational schema in "Father Hagerty's wheel," and draft its defining Preamble that proclaimed, "[t]he working class and the employing class have nothing in common. . . . By organizing industrially we are forming the structure of the new society within the shell of the old" (Industrial Workers of the World 1905).

Henmi Naozo, an Osaka native who organized the militant League of Tenants that fueled the urban insurrection of 1921 (often called "a year of the strike"), including the first May Day march, had gone across the Pacific to the Bay Area in 1899 and went through various jobs, including baker, gardener, and apple farm laborer. Henmi had first-hand experience with racist violence. Just as the Wobblies were forming in 1905, Henmi opened a ten-cent restaurant for underclass workers with two Chinese friends in Seattle, but "outlaw cowboys" hired by white restauranteurs" association "destroyed the store completely" doing irreparable damage (Sakai 2011: 379). Along with his regional compatriot and comrade Hasegawa Ichimatsu, who had also been staying on the West Coast and encountered the Knights of Labor and the Wobblies, Henmi returned to Osaka and proceeded to weave together a "temperamentally positive" pragmatic activism that they had learned much from their trans-Pacific sojourn.

> This temperament was fused with a certain kind of regional temperament in Osaka, producing a style that can be called trans-America/Osaka, radical pragmatism. From the outset it had nothing to do with the cheap morality commonly found in our society, which issues attacks from an ethically consistent position and nitpicks contradictions between "being and consciousness." It kept them at a distance from an element of "negativity" that sharply picks up on "contradictions" and "defects" in people close to them, discourages their potential production and creation, and energizes even more condemnations and denunciations, rather than think and worry about making organizational innovations, developing relationships, producing and creating theory. (Sakai 2011: 415)

This distinctive activist style that stressed direct action and created relationships that short-circuited organizational and occupational categories owes much to the Wobbly ethos of defining the industrial working class as broadly as possible, from unskilled minority workers to hobos and bums (such Wobbly songs as "Hallelujah, I"m a Bum"—which may have been penned by Kansas City hobo "One Finger Ellis"—and also Joe Hill's "Tramp" are eloquent testament to this lumpen-proletarian breadth). Indeed, if the Wobbly vision of "one big union" was so capacious in defining industrial workers, the corollary implication for defining the "city" was no less profound: the waterfront could as well be the center of revolutionary direct action as the lumberyard or the railway. In contrast to the later period of the Fordist mass worker, who was canonically placed in a fixed factory in a fixed urban environment, the industrial worker still could proudly define him or herself as a bum riding the rails and living in the "jungle," hobo camp, from the exploitative restriction of wage-labor.

Some of the most spectacular strikes that forced capital to restructure itself and brought about the regime of mass worker, in fact, took place on the waterfront. For example, of the three major general strikes in 1934 (Minneapolis Teamsters, Toledo Auto-Lite, and San Francisco general strikes), the West Coast Waterfront Strike was led by Harry Bridges, an ex-Wobbly.

The strike established the seafaring workers as a central component of the industrial mass worker and forced the Roosevelt administration to reform the classical laissez-faire form of industrial capitalism to overcome its "hostility to planning" and mute its "predatory drive" in exchange for workers" acceptance of fragmented, rationalized labor process on a mass scale, supervised by conservative business unions. Twenty-four years later, Bridges would play a crucial role in forging trans-Pacific solidarity between West Coast and

Osaka waterfront workers, who were drawn directly—especially in loading and unloading coal—from the pool of day laborers at Kamgasaki's *yoseba*. A year after the first Kamagasaki Riot, on March 27, 1962, the Japanese Dockworkers Union (JDU)—which was formed in 1946 after the Osaka dockworkers organized and called for a national union—and the ILWU, co-founded and led by Harry Bridges, carried the energy of the riot into a "trans-Pacific strike" that made possible the passage of 1965 waterfront labor law in Japan.

> This action began with a letter delivered to the JDU across the Pacific from the American continent. In the first letter dispatched from the International Longshore and Warehouse Union (ILWU) on 9 August 1958, it stated that "many of our problems are similar to each other" and proposed holding an international meeting of all waterfront-related labor unions on the Pacific coast. A letter delivered in the same year on December 2 and signed by ILWU President Harry Bridges proposed the international meeting to take place between April and May of 1959 in Tokyo. According to the first volume of *The Movement History of JDU*, "When the United States kept testing hydrogen bombs in the Pacific, the JDU and the ILWU exchanged opinions on the serious threat that radiation from exposed ships would pose to the dockworkers's health, a discussion that expanded and developed the conception of the international meeting." The fate of radioactive exposure, which dockworkers shouldered in common, undeniably intensified the trans-Pacific character of the dockworkers and became the stepping ladder for their global solidarity. (Haraguchi 2012: 196–97)

The solidarity also may have had personal resonance for Bridges himself. In 1958 he had tried to marry a Japanese-American activist Noriko Sawada in Reno, Nevada, but, unable to do so due to anti-miscegenation law on the books since 1846, the couple demanded a marriage license to be issued by the District Court, which led to the repeal of the law a year later. Sawada was the daughter of immigrant Japanese fieldworkers in Gardena, L.A. County, survivor of the wartime Japanese-American internment camp near Poston, Arizona, and, after the war, became involved in the Berkeley Interracial Committee, AFL-CIO, and worked as a legal secretary to civil rights lawyer Charles Garry, who would later defend the Oakland Black Panther Party leaders Huey P. Newton and Bobby Seale.

From the perspective of class composition, the emergence of the Black Panther Party can be historically understood as a lumpen-proletarian struggle against the mass worker's deal with capital, which preserved the discriminatory structure against racial minorities, temporary workers, and women. Although their immediate ideological compass was Maoism and Third World Revolution, the Black Panthers was demanding a return to the broader Wobbly working-class redefinition of an earlier period, albeit narrowly focused according to the necessary imperative of the ghettoized city, and would exert similar trans-Pacific reverberations.

B. *YOSEBA* AND THE HOOD: MAKING OF *ROMUSHA* AND LUMPEN-PROLETARIAN CULTURES

Like the Wobblies and black working class of South Central Los Angeles, the origins of Kamagasaki day laborers, ranging from Kyushu and Okinawa to Hokkaido, are also multitudinous. The majority of them are children of farmers who had to leave home due to mechanization of agriculture or are ex-coal miners who lost their jobs due to the closing of mines during the mid-1950s to early 1970s "high economic growth," the Japanese variant of Keynesianism. Funamoto Shuji, a core member of *Boryoku-tehaishi tsuiho Kamagasaki kyoto kaigi* ("Kamagasaki Solidarity Congress for Expelling Violent Recruiters," abbreviated as Kama-kyoto), said:

> The anko's[1] circuits toward Kamagasaki are the farming and fishing villages, unliberated communities, Korean communities, and Okinawa, the closed coal mines and mountains. They are the voiceless people who, as a result of working hard, had their farming and fishing villages dismantled by the will of the state, got fired because of mechanization, were "forcibly transported" from Okinawa, and were expelled from the buraku due to discrimination or impoverished life, and the Kamagasaki area is the stopping point for these voiceless people. (Funamoto 1985: 56)

Yoseba was a system to absorb the thus produced "voiceless people" as an urban surplus labor-power and utilize them efficiently. During "high economic growth," the mainstream Japanese working class became integrated into the middle-class (or a suburban) lifestyle characterized by ownership of their own homes and cars. The Kamagasaki day laborers, on the other hand, were incorporated into the lowest layer of the multilayered subcontract system. And they were placed under the rule of *tehaishi* (recruiters), the middlemen of labor-power, under the rule of labor bosses (at times affiliated with organized crime) had their wages skimmed, exposed to discrimination and violence. The government either acquiesced to or officially approved this as an exception, utilizing them as irreplaceable labor-power. For example, the construction of the main hall for the 1970 "Japan World Exposition," the first world exposition in Asia, and its accompanying urban reconstruction could not have been achieved without the day laborers" labor-power.

The parallel with the position of black, Native American, lumpen-proletarian, and other marginalized workers who fell outside or at the bottom of the mass-worker hierarchy in postwar U.S. history is striking. The U.S. analogue of the Japanese "high economic growth" period is the 1950s when the mass worker's Keynesian social compact was acquired in exchange for ideological and social conformity, expressed most explicitly in anti-communist demonology and middle-class suburbanization of industrial and white-collar workers. Despite the racial and wage discrimination against African-American workers, they responded to the rapid growth of postwar industries that built numerous plants and factories in Southern California by making a second wave of the Great Migration and forming a vibrant working-class neighborhood in South Central Los Angeles. White youth gangs harassed these newcomers on the streets and black youths organized gangs of their own in self-defense—the origin of the urban black youth gangs whom the Panthers reorganized into their ranks and who, after the dissolution of constructive political organizing, become some of the fiercest urban guerrilla capitalist adherents of free market principles.

Working-class racial division on the streets mirrored institutionalized hierarchy on the job. Harry Bridges, who had transmitted the Wobblies" international culture of direct action from the first decade of the twentieth century to the organized militance of the collective worker on the waterfront in the 1930s, had functioned exactly as a labor bureaucrat under the new postwar rule of Keynesian labor regimentation. In 1959, when the International Longshoremen's and Warehousemen's Union created a new hiring category of low-ranking, irregular B men in San Francisco and seven hundred B men—who were excluded from union meetings, given the worst jobs, and readily fired—protested, Bridges and other ILWU leaders eliminated representation for the B men and fired eighty-two "B" men whom they considered dissidents. Stan Weir, one of the fired B men reps, summarized the ideological significance of the struggle as follows:

> Still unnoticed anywhere, for example, is the fact that by simple self-interest and self-preservation B men became critical of Harry Bridges because of the conservatism of his leadership and his eager acceptance of the employers" new technology program. Quite logically, those who cast their lot with the B men or came to their defense both from inside the industry and from the public, were persons who were viewed as having a more radical worldview than Bridges; probably a very threatening experience for a labor official whose entire method of operation historically had been based upon presenting himself as a leftist. (Weir 2004: 67)

When we place the radicalism of the ILWU's B men *vis-à-vis* the growing conservatism of industrial union labor leadership in the context of postwar urban history, we see how the African-American struggle for civil rights and black nationalism can be reinterpreted convincingly as a working-class history of the racialized B men and women against the conservative black leadership that maintained equipoise with the white supremacist bourgeois order. Rank-and-file urban workers played a critical, even defining role in this respect. The December 1955 Montgomery Bus Boycott, for example, is un-thinkable without the black workers" mass boycott of segregated public tran-sit, an act of strike that usually occurs at the point of production now recon-figured into the urban sphere of circulation. Nor was this an isolated incident; it was an organic outcome of many other interconnected small struggles of what Robert Korstadt dubbed "civil rights unionism" among Southern black workers. The lynching of fourteen-year-old Emmett Till, from Chicago's Southside, eight months prior to the bus boycott had exposed the fatal conse-quence of a young black man speaking equally, with intimate overtones, to a white woman in the Mississippi Delta—in other words, acting as if the back-woods of the Deep South was an extension of the black Northern cityscape. The Montgomery Bus Boycott was an urban black working-class expression of self-organized militance, which could no longer be contained within the industrial factories and unions but treated the entire city as a site of socialized production and reproduction.

If the collective, carefully organized black urban response to the murder of Emmett Till in Mississippi took about half a year to reemerge in Alabama, the urban working-class call and response of the first Kamagasaki Riot six years later were immediate (significantly, this area of Osaka is also popularly known as "Deep South," a demotic recognition of common geographically subaltern concerns). On August 1, 1961, a taxi cab ran over a day laborer and killed him on the street. The police officer who arrived on the scene, howev-er, merely draped a straw mat over the deceased worker and otherwise ne-glected the dead body. This discriminatory treatment by the police triggered an explosion of collective rage among Kamagasaki residents and a riot broke out, continuing for the following five days. Terashima Tamao spoke thus on the riots.

> That Kamagasaki workers" energies are cheaply sucked dry by Japanese in-dustry is a clear fact that does not require much evidence. In short, even if their energy is not potential but manifest, it is skillfully and mercilessly consumed by others. Riots are an angry wailing that says, I hate that, really hate that! Because it's a wail, it's spasmodic and its meaning is unclear but who can put a stop to a wail? (Terashima ca. 1973)

As is evident from the naming of the 1961 riot as the "first Kamagasaki Riot," riots broke out from the 1960s through the mid-1970s. But there was rarely anybody within the movement who resonated with the series of riots until the 1960s (the first labor union in Kamagasaki was finally formed in 1969). Hence the riots of the 1960s remained continuously as "wails," but in the early 1970s, especially as the currents within the student movement con-verged into Kamagasaki, a political culture, engendered by the social energy of riots, flourished suddenly. In the process, a "wail" transformed into a "scream."

The 1965 Watts Rebellion also originated in traffic with police involvement. Twenty-one-year-old Marquette Frye, behind the wheel of his mother's 1955 Buick with his brother Ronald in the passenger seat, was pulled over by California Highway Patrol officer Lee Minikus as a suspected drunken driver. Frye was unemployed and had ties to the local youth gang, and, during the sobriety test, stumbled, prompting Minikus to call for police back-up to impound the Buick. Meanwhile, as Ronald brought their scolding mother Rena Price who lived two blocks away, a few hundred onlookers had gathered. Altercation followed, with the police pulling a shotgun and arresting all three Price family members. The crowd threw rocks and concrete at the police who tried to disperse them, and this typical everyday incident of police harassment turned into a full-blown series of riots that continued for six days and turned a 73–square-mile area of L.A. into a war zone, damaging $40 million worth of property, leading to the arrest of nearly 3,500, injuring over a thousand, and killing thirty-four people.

Both the riots in Kamagasaki and Watts created a new working-class culture and identity. Those who had been excluded from and discriminated by the capital-labor "social compact" that defined the legitimate mass-worker according to a labor hierarchy that placed them at the bottom due to their precarious or unskilled working conditions, race, criminality, and geography, expressed their grievances through direct action on the streets. Riots cut through the bureaucratic red tape in which workers" grievances had been endlessly bound and generalized the identity of workers from a narrow, industrially defined, company-based one to an identity in which anybody who took to the streets and participated in the rioting became at once agents of class struggle. What Martin Glaberman, long-time auto worker and labor sociologist, observed about the wildcat strike in an industrial factory can be extended to the power of riots in the city, which had become a socialized factory without walls:

> The workers, organizing in the CIO, wanted to establish their control over production and to remove from the corporations the right to discipline. Their method was direct action—the carrying out of their own plans for the organization of production to the extent possible. . . . Their answer to company discipline was the wildcat strike. It was a common practice in the auto shops for negotiations on the shop level to consist of the steward, surrounded by all the men in a department, arguing with the foreman. No one worked until the grievance was settled—and most of them were settled in the workers" favor without the red tape of a bargaining procedure, appeals, and umpires. (Glaberman 1973: 11)

Indeed death by traffic as a point of origination for both riots is indicative of how the capitalist socialization of labor and urbanization had become virtually indistinguishable (the comprehensive plan for the construction of the Southern California freeways was developed in 1947 and formed a critical linchpin in the region's postwar Keynesian economic growth for the next two decades). When we contrast these riots to the riots of an earlier epoch, such as the 1860s-1920s racist white riots against minorities—comparable to Church and King mobs of the 1790s—or the eighteenth-century bread riots, which defended popular customary rights and moral economy against the new imperative of market economy and privatization, we see that they are neither popular enactment of the repressive state apparatus as in the former case nor the artisan and peasant refusal to be dispossessed of their traditional subsistence economy as in the latter. They are the acts of those already dispossessed and experience this dispossession on a daily basis, even from the stable regime of industrial labor with a modicum of institutional protection, and do not so much make demands that can be absorbed and instituted into law or collective bargaining as negate the fundamentally exploitative contradiction of the city as a whole by widespread destruction. The Luddite machine-breakers only targeted the textile mechanical apparatus that was supplanting their artisan labor. By the 1960s the most exploited and neglected segment of urban workers recognized the city itself as a capitalist machine that had to be uprooted root and branch.

Moreover, the riots reclaimed an affirmative social agency of class. Between these two riots, in 1963 E. P. Thompson questioned the economic reductive definition of the working class and wrote, "class happens when some men, as a result of common experiences (inherited or shared), feel and articulate the identity of their interests as between themselves, and as against other men whose interest are different from (and usually opposed) to theirs" (1966: 9). These riots were nothing less than a genesis of a class that was happening, as day laborers and ghetto residents put their bodies on the line against police power to prove indeed that they did not patiently endure discrimination and violence. As exemplified in the Kama-kyoto slogan "*yararetara yarikaese*" ("if they fuck with us, we"ll fuck with them"), *yoseba* was also a place where the day laborers developed their own culture and manifested their oppositional energy, which rioting most dramatically expressed. In fact, the very language of *yoseba* (which literally means in the passive voice "a place of being gathered together") changed, as workers came to rename it in the active voice, as a *yoriba*, "place to gather together": ""*Yoseba*" is a term that stresses the meaning of bringing workers together and implies the establishment's concentration, management, and surveillance of day laborers. On the other hand, "*yoriba*" is a term that emphasizes the subjectivity of workers gathering together and connotes the possibility of workers joining together and transforming themselves into a collective subject" (Haraguchi 2011: 185).

"In Osaka, the period of high-economic growth peaks with the 1970 Expo, which also coincides with the capital's process of proletarianizing the majority of the population" (Sakurada 2012: 214). And it is during this decade, as proletarian political practice in Kamagasaki flourished, that *romusha* culture came into being. *"Rōmusha"* was a discriminatory term generally used by the mainstream media during most of the twentieth century, denoting casual laborers living on a daily wage and distinguishing them from usual or regular "workers" in general. The subversive usage of the word *"romusha"* circulated from Osaka during this time, when some working-class activists published a series of newsletters entitled *Romusha Tosei: Kamagasaki Tsushin (Drifting Life of Romusha: Kamagasaki Correspondence)*. Terashima Tamao, a poet who had worked as a day laborer in Kamagasaki as early as the 1960s and lived as a resident of *doya* city, denounced the discriminatory use of *romusha* in the late 1960s and made the Osaka municipal government acknowledge this fact. But in the early 1970s the term shifted into a subversive sense, one of its decisive factors being the U.S. Black Power movement. Kama-kyoto members were directly stimulated by the Black Power movement and reread the black consciousness slogan "black is beautiful" into *"romusha* is the true worker." They argued that in Japanese society of the period, when organized regular workers were entirely subsumed into the system of high economic growth, the day laborers had become the defining revolutionary subject. Funamoto Shuji recalled the historical genealogy of the term and elaborated its internationalist, universal implications.

> In the prewar era, because there was a decisive lack of *romusha* domestically, violent *tehaishi*/emperor's military forcibly transported Chinese and Koreans from the continent and the peninsula. After the war . . . a structure reproducing "forcible transportation" of *romusha* from the farming and fishing villages, closed coal mines and mountains was set in place and, since that was still not enough to fill in the labor shortage, Okinawa was finally reverted to mainland Japan. And the specific misery, specific repression, specific impoverishment of *romusha* were concentrated in the history of Japanese capitalism and *romusha*, and the will of the state against the *romusha* . . . was carried out essentially not against the buraku *romusha*, the agrarian *romusha*, or the fishing *romusha* but against the specific Korean and Chinese *romusha*. We observe the historical, universal destiny of the *romusha* in the Korean and Chinese *romusha*. (Funamoto 1985: 199–200)

Terashima, who was seeking to abolish the term *romusha* in the latter half of the 1960s, concurred. In his zine "for Kamagasaki workers by Kamagasaki workers," *Romusha Tosei*, he declared:

> Originally, workers were us. But now . . . the fools all over the world discriminate us as *romusha*. Therefore, we argued, "we are the real workers, we are the ones whom you should call workers!" It's true that . . . I was also among the first to make that argument. Then, as to why we call ourselves *Romusha Life* now, it's because we don"t have any desire in asking to join the company of

those whom the general public . . . consider workers. The word "worker" is already dirtied with spit and vomit, smeared in lies and pretensions. . . . So we changed our mind and shifted our argument to "*romusha* is fine, we are *romusha!*" . . . If we are made to join the company of workers, only half-heartedly by way of a word, our freedom is weakened and narrowed, and so *romusha* is fine. No, actually, we"d rather actively seek to be *romusha*. (Terashima 1975b: 25; 1975a)

Tracing the course of the phrase "black is beautiful" can give us an insight into the dialectical workings of subaltern linguistic micro-history. The phrase is attributed originally to a March 1858 speech made by the black abolitionist lawyer and doctor John Stewart Rock, on the occasion of Crispus Attucks Day in Boston's Fanueil Hall. The phrase as such does not appear in Rock's speech, which was largely a defense of the black man's courage, with the Haitian Revolution as a historical reference point, in the wake of the Dred Scott decision that denied African-American citizenship and attacked the abolitionist cause. One line does refer to racial physical features, favorably comparing African to Caucasian characteristics:

> When I contrast the fine tough muscular system, the beautiful, rich color, the full broad features, and the gracefully frizzled hair of the negro, with the delicate physical organization, wan color, sharp features and lank hair of the Caucasian, I am inclined to believe that when the white man was created, nature was pretty well exhausted—but determined to keep up appearances, she pinched up his features, and did the best she could under the circumstances. (Marable and Mullings 1999: 110)

In the following hundred years, the aesthetic sentiment of black racial pride became condensed into a singularly memorable phrase, whose demotic authorship—like blues and folk music—was anonymous and collective.

The South African anti-apartheid activist Steve Biko popularized it and explained its meaning during his May 1976 trial under cross-examination:

> When you say "black is beautiful" what in fact you are saying to him is: man, you are okay as you are, begin to look upon yourself as a human being; now in African life especially it also has certain connotations; it is the connotations on the way women prepare themselves for viewing by society, in other words the way they dream, the way they make up and so on, which tends to be the negation of their true state in a sense a running away from their colour; they use lightening creams, they use straightening devices for their hair and so on. (Biko 1987: 104)

Malcolm X had criticized conking for the same reason in his *Autobiography*, published a decade earlier in the year of the Watts Rebellion, and, a year later on October 29, 1966, Stokely Carmichael characterized the emerging political symbol of revolutionary black nationalism as "a black panther, a beautiful black animal" in his "Black Power" speech: "In Lowndes County, we developed something called the Lowndes County Freedom Organization. It is a political party. . . . We chose for the emblem a black panther, a beautiful black animal which symbolizes the strength and dignity of black people, an animal that never strikes back until he's backed so far into the wall, he's got nothing to do but spring out" (Asante and Robb 1971: 280). What was at once a phrase that aimed to dismantle racial self-hatred, manifesting predominantly in existential and aesthetic awareness, became a politically articulated vision of a rebellious class-for-itself. After all, Rock's original class notion reflected his professional background in what would later be deemed the "black bourgeoisie," as he stated in the same speech, "When the avenues to wealth are opened to us, we will then become educated and wealthy, and then the roughest looking colored man that you ever saw, or ever will see, will be pleasanter than the harmonies of Orpheus, and black will be a very pretty color" (Marable and Mullings 1999: 110).

But the Afro-American Orpheus of the mid-1960s and thereafter was not to be one of "educated and wealthy" bourgeoisie. As filmed in Marcel Camus's *Black Orpheus* (1959), which was shot in the Leme favela of Rio de Janeiro and retold the Greek myth as an allegory of the black slums, a succession of African-American class struggles dialectically transformed John Rock's monetary aspiration of racial beauty into a militant desire for proletarian revolution in the black ghetto, which other ethnic minorities and even day laborers in Osaka across the Pacific could translate into their own terms of struggle. As Mike Davis noted, "It is not really surprising, therefore, that in the late 1960s the doo-ragged, hard-core street brothers and sisters, who for an extraordinary week in 1965 had actually driven the police out of the ghetto, were visualized by Black Power theorists as the strategic reserve of Black Liberation, if not its vanguard. . . . There was a potent moment in this period, around 1968–69, when the Panthers—their following soaring in the streets and high schools—looked as if they might become the ultimate revolutionary gang" (Davis 2006a: 297).

While the Black Panther Party, in their most constructive endeavors, organized children's breakfast programs, healthcare, armed self-defense from police brutality, and generally empowered the agency of the black lumpenproletariat, the Suzuki-gumi struggle constituted the maturation of *romusha*'s political culture in Kamagasaki. In May 1972, when a day laborer went "*tonko*" (fleeing) from the workplace of the Suzuki-gumi Construction Company, ran by an organized crime syndicate, Suzuki-gumi punished the worker by beating him up. Young activists and day laborers responded immediately with denunciation and succeeded in making the yakuza boss get down on his knees to apologize in front of the workers. The day laborers, who had meekly accepted the violence of organized crime and *tehaishi* in the workplace, were overjoyed that the boss was made to express his apology in the customarily most servile posture. This created the momentum to organize Kama-kyoto, and, in a short period, Kama-kyoto successively formed bases throughout Kamagasaki. First, their victory in the Suzuki-gumi struggle overturned the *tehaishi*'s domination in the day laborer market. Next, they seized Sankaku-koen ("Triangle Park") that heretofore had been their turf and hosted the Kamagasaki Summer Festival that proclaimed "festival organized by workers for workers." Finally, they started transforming the parks inside Kamagasaki as a base for their winter struggle (*etto toso*).

At the beginning and the end of the year, death on the street is common in Kamagasaki because unemployed workers are forced to live out in the open. Hence "to survive until spring" is itself a life-or-death struggle and, in order to preserve their lives, tent camps and soup kitchens are set up. This is the winter struggle. From the outset, the tent village of the winter struggle continued to be threatened by the riot police's attack and forcible expulsion, but, after repeated battles in which they occupied other parks after being removed from the originally occupied parks in Kamagasaki, the workers finally succeeded in making the so-called *shikaku-koen* (Square Park) into a base. Alongside the summer festival, the winter struggle has taken root as Kamagasaki's distinct political culture that continues to this day.

The new urban working-class cultures that Kama-kyoto and Black Panthers forged were thus materialist through and through, seeking to preserve life and facilitate subsistence as autonomous self-activity, while proudly affirming the existential reality of their "bare life" as revolutionary agency. They were about nothing less than the biopolitics of the revolutionary commons.

C. A RETURNING SEASON OF RIOTS IN THE NEOLIBERAL AGE OF HOMELESS AND PRECARIOUS LABOR

When an urban riot occurs, more often than not it signals a recomposition of the working class who participate in it, as it functions as a new centripetal social force that rips open, to use Marx's famous metaphor for the peasantry, the sack of isolated potatoes and forms—now shifting to a Deleuze-Guattarian image—newly interconnecting rhizomes between them. The riots of the early 1990s Kamagasaki and Los Angeles, no less than those in the 1960s and 1970s, signified such recomposition. However, there was considerable change in historical context. For one, in order to combat the powerful moment of recomposition and its accompanying black lumpen-proletarian, Osaka *romusha* cultures of the militant slums that the previous cycle of riots had established most visibly in the organizational form of the Black Panthers and Kama-kyoto, capital had unleashed a strategy to decompose this power. From the 1970s through the 1980s, this strategy of decomposition had variously assumed the concrete forms of COINTELPRO, Trilateral Commission, supply-side economics, Thatcherism/Reaganism, which sought to contain and roll back the "excess democracy" (that the elites, in their typical Orwellian inversion, interpreted it as a "crisis of democracy") that these urban figures of dissent, among others, so obviously represented. In short, the neoliberal dispensation was at hand, with its unbridled state repression, capital flight and deindustrialization that left in their wake industrial wastelands in the Unitd States and "shutter city" in Japan. Even the mass worker was being cut down from its Keynesian roots and forced to join the ever expanding reserve army of labor. The late 1970s closure of industrial plants and factories that produced the consequent mass unemployment and poverty of the once flourishing working-class community of South Central L.A., exposing depoliticized youth gang members to the principle of the free market that accelerated drug dealing and turf violence into a microcosmic mirror-image of deregulated finance capital and hostile corporate takeovers, is symptomatic of this neoliberal turn. Thus, when the 1990s riots erupted, they were not a bid to join or form an urban working class in the traditional sense, for this very class was in dissolution.

In 1978, E. P. Thompson wrote on the nature of eighteenth-century English plebs" bread riots and customary defense of the commons against the emergent laissez-faire capitalist enclosures and wondered if it were not a "class struggle without class." For in their struggle to defend their traditional popular culture against privatization, posing their customary consciousness of moral economy against the merciless calculus of political economy, the English peasants, artisans, and plebs, in Thompson's view, did not yet constitute a singular class identity. The urban cultural efflorescence of slum workers had similar ramifications for class recomposition of the 1970s, albeit in the post-industrial context of late capitalism. Progressive commentators, whose homogeneous notion of the working class owes much to the brief historical phase of the Fordist mass industrial worker's dominance in Keynesian and state capitalist regimes, responded with their confused "farewell to the working class" (Andre Gorz) or awkward formulation of the "new social movement." But it is more accurate to describe the general impact of these urban insurrections as a class struggle that destroyed "class" in the hierarchic, industrially homogenous sense, leading, in the U.S. case, to the radicalization of automobile workers (as exemplified in the Dodge Revolutionary Union Movement in Detroit) and concomitant "crisis in the auto sector," prison riots (1971 Attica Rebellion and 1980 New Mexico State Penitentiary Riot), indigenous rights" movement (American Indian Movement's 1969–1971 occupation of Alcatraz, 1973 Wounded Knee Incident), and widespread municipal fiscal crisis throughout the decade.

While the U.S. Keynesian system in response radically remodeled itself according to formative policies of neoliberalism, the Japanese equivalent was moving in the opposite direction, with the economic and cultural standardization of middle-class life and corporate monopolization of society. While the Vietnam War was another crucial factor that pushed the United States toward its long structural economic decline, it was instrumental in stimulating Japanese economic growth, unburdened by the weight of maintaining economically inefficient military bases throughout the world and of generating a vast array of domestic and international social antagonisms. At the same time, the Kamagasaki Riots that recurred from the 1960s to the early 1970s ended when the mid-1970s structural recession pushed Kamagasaki day laborers into a state of permanent unemployment. The economic bubble boom of the 1980s resulted in rapid decrease of job offers but still no riot occurred. But in the 1990s, a season of riots returned to Kamagasaki in October 1990 and October 1992.

The 1990 riot broke out when the Nishinari police sergeant in charge of organized crime was discovered to be receiving considerable sums of cash from a high-ranking member of an organized crime family in the Yamaguchi-gumi lineage, in exchange for leaking investigative information. Workers gathered in front of the Nishinari Police Department and threw stones, dragged cars into a heap and set fire to them, and built a barricade in protest, demanding, "Bring out the police chief!" This was a first full-scale riot in almost twenty years. The workers" insurrection forced the Nishinari police chief to apologize at a press conference.

The 1992 riot erupted despite the severe unemployment in Kamagasaki and, therefore, was named the "anti-unemployment riot." Heretofore, the general theory held that riots only took place during periods of prosperity, but this riot was a unique event that overturned that theory. But it may not be precise to call the riots of 1990–1992 "Kamagasaki Riots." As days went by, youths instead of day laborers became the agents throwing stones in these riots, which took on the characteristics of a "youth revolt" (this was how the mass media presented the event, regarding "the youths who participated in riots" as a social problem; there was also divided opinion even within Kamagasaki, over whether or not to consider the youths as comrades). Because these youths came from Osaka generally, particularly the busy district of Minami, it may be more appropriate to employ the term "Osaka Riot" (or at least "Southern Osaka Riot"), rather than "Kamagasaki Riot." This geographic and generational expansion in the class composition of the 1992 Osaka Riot signaled, on the one hand, the incipient end of "high economic growth," its widely touted "bubble economy," of Japanese capitalism and, on the other, the ever-expanding scope of class struggle without a singularly reducible class identity.

The dissolution of the bubble economy directly affected Kamagasaki day laborers earlier than anybody else and took away their jobs. As jobless workers could not pay the rent for the *doya* and were abandoned by the social security system, many of them were forced to live a permanent tent life. The emergence of homeless issues as a relatively major "social problem" in the mid-1990s thus corresponds closely with the collapse of the so-called "bubble economy" and the onset of Japanese neoliberalism. The day laborers lost their jobs rapidly because their labor market is much more sensitive to economic depression than that of regular full-time workers. Everyday unemployment means lack of the daily wage for all basic living necessities, such as food, clothing, and shelter, in short, the minimum ability to reproduce their labor-power. Many unemployed day laborers left Kamagasaki, where they lived for many years and started to live a tent life in various parks throughout Osaka City. The loss of their lodging thus made them visible on the metropolitan streets. Visibility made homelessness a major social issue, but the mainstream media mostly represented the homeless as a negative figure who threatened the "citizen's safe and clean urban life" due to their supposed dirtiness, laziness, or danger, although it was in fact the homeless who were actually assaulted by some citizens, including boys on a wilding spree. Osaka was thus joining New York and Los Angeles in becoming, to use Neil Smith's designation, a "revanchist city," where "archetypal neoliberal revanchism *vis-à-vis* homeless people: a residue of sympathy activated by thinly disguised hatred and abhorrence" was frequently expressed in "active viciousness that attempts to criminalize a whole range of "behavior," individually defined, and to blame the failure of post-1968 urban policy on the populations it was supposed to assist" (Smith 1996: 221–22).

Nonetheless, the reality of unemployment and poverty, which had been heretofore enclosed and concealed, had become a permanent fixture in public space and refused to dim its visibility to civil society. While the existence of *"nojukusha"*("one who sleeps in the open air") came to be treated as a social problem, as "the homeless problem," the actual source of the problem, namely the structural contradictions of neoliberal polices, was consistently left uncommented. The impoverishment of unemployed workers forced to live outside was not limited to the absence of clothes, food, and shelter. Robbing them of their work also meant robbing their agency of being a *romusha*. In order to reorganize their lives and produce a kind of alternative society, some of the homeless occupied riverbanks and parks, and lived communally, building their own camps with blue tarps because squatting on private facilities is strictly criminalized in Japan. Building their tent shacks with their own hands in public spaces, forming tent villages by coming together, and unfolding their own subsistence economy in this manner, they expressed their residual stubbornness as *romusha*, a desperate scream in refusing to be robbed of their last remaining dignity.

A decade after the 1992 Osaka Riot, the emergence of youthful precarious labor would also become even more pronounced. *The Big Issue*, a street newspaper written by journalists and sold by homeless individuals to provide the latter with a daily income and thereby help them to reintegrate into society, was founded in the United Kingdom in 1991, in the interregnum between the two Osaka riots. The newspaper started its Japanese publication in 2003 as evictions and various forms of criminalization were on the rise. Some of the young "*freeters*" or precarious workers joined the homeless camp community in several public parks in Osaka City and they started an annual cultural festival that functioned as people's media in the literal sense, as it mediated a sense of solidarity between generational and social divides evinced in the 1992 Osaka Riot.

In fact, by this time, most Japanese youths found themselves in undeniably precarious situation, with at least one-third of them being irregular, temporary, or casual workers. Unemployment became generalized, and the long-term depression, which occurred even before the world economic crisis at the end of 2008, pushed some of the poor youths to a kind of invisible homelessness, which was reported as the emergence of "netcafe refugees" or cyber-homeless who do not own or rent any accommodation, have no permanent address, and sleep in twenty-four–hour cafes. This invisibility—in contrast to the mediated visibility of street homelessness—signified the permeation of precarious labor throughout society, including the apparatus of cognitive capitalism. Inspired by EuroMayDay parades, which mobilized West European precarious workers from 5,000 to 300,000 in the span of the first five years of the new millennium, "precariat" became a popular word in Japan after the spring issue of the magazine *Impaction* featured it in 2006 and initiated a new trend of *freeters*" mayday activities. Given that serious precarity lies in its invisibility and silence, the question as to whether the precariat can rebuild their own identity arises. One major vehicle for such class self-definition appears to be their media activities, such as the aforementioned festivals and cultural practices that, despite the experience of neoliberal dislocation and poverty, enable them to live collectively as poetry readers, cardboard artists, painters, or indymedia writers in their lifelong midnight hour, or "night of labor" in the sense rediscovered by Jacques Rancière's 1981 *Nights of Labor: The Workers" Dream in Nineteenth Century* (in many ways a major French historiographical pendant to Thompson's *Making*), completely independent or autonomous from the wage or money economy.

Like the 1990 Kamagasaki Riot, the 1992 Los Angeles Rebellion originated in the abuse of police power in the broader context of generalized poverty and unemployment in the inner city. But, as in the previous cycle of rioting in the two regions, the difference lay in the respective structure of the urban labor market. In Kamagasaki, as is evident in the Suzuki-gumi struggle and the police collusion with organized crime which the 1990 riot exposed, *yakuza* or gangs have been long institutionalized as recruiters of cheap, precarious labor in Japan, while youth gangs in South Central L.A. have been more readily an organic component of the urban underclass, functioning variously in different historical periods as informal self-defense groups against white supremacist violence, rank-and-file source of democratic community organizing, and agents of illegal private capital that, with its unregulated drug dealing and internecine violence, absorbed the mass supply of young unemployed labor created by capital flight and deindustrialization. It was at the height of this last historical moment that the 1992 L.A. Rebellion happened, producing in its wake an unprecedented truce between the Blood and the Crips—which, however, failed to turn into a viable political project in the manner of the Panthers a generation earlier and eventually faded away. Here we see further evidence of "class struggle without class" in its negative aspect: not only is the class identity of industrial working class unable to be revived but even the lumpen-proletarian subject is barely conceivable. This is true not only of the Los Angeles and Osaka slums but the "global informal working class (overlapping with but non-identical to the slum population," as Mike Davis points out:

> Politically, the informal sector, in the absence of enforced labor rights, is a semifeudal realm of kickbacks, bribes, tribal loyalties, and ethnic exclusion. A place on the pavement, the rental of a rickshaw, a day's labor on a construction site, or a domestic's reference to a new employer: all of these require patronage or membership in some closed network, often an ethnic militia or secret gang. Whereas traditional formal industries such as textiles in India or oil in the Middle East tended to foster interethnic solidarity through unions and radical political parties, the rise of the unprotected informal sector has too infrequently gone hand in hand with exacerbated ethnoreligious differentiation and sectarian violence. (Davis 2006b: 185)

At the same time, like the slender shoots of reinvented commoning that Osaka's homeless collective life on the streets and young precariat's media activism exemplify, powerful community projects among the urban poor have also developed after the L.A. Rebellion, including the Bus Riders" Union that fights against the gentrification of the means of transportation, L.A. Community Action Network that defends the homeless" human right to housing and freedom from police brutality in Skid Row, and Koreatown Immigrant Workers Alliance (established a month prior to the L.A. Riots) that organizes Korean and Latino immigrant workers.

But, as important and productive as these various forms of urban working-class activism are in defending basic human rights to subsistence, housing, and mobility, their resources are too limited and effects too marginal to constitute or imply the formation of a singular class identity, which persistently eludes coherent definition in our era of seemingly permanent late capitalist crisis. This is not necessarily a lamentable fact. Two years after the L.A. and Osaka Riots, which dissolved even the centrality of the lumpen-proletariat or *romusha* as a revolutionary subject, the Zapatista uprising in

Chiapas decentered the city once and for all as a primary site of anti-capitalist insurrection. For not only did the Zapatista struggle rise out of indigenous rural communities, it refused either to valorize the country as a revolutionary counterpoint to the city or to smash the state and seize its power in the fashion of the classical vanguardist guerrilla army. Instead it succeeded in creating a globally resonant, radical democratic voice that become a fundamental source for the anti-globalization movement, whose class composition is no more singularly proletarian than the recent widespread municipal rebellions across the world. As one of the coincidental echoes of anti-globalization struggle and urban rioting, in June 2008 the protest action against the physical abuse of a worker in the police department prompted the so-called "twenty-fourth" Kamagasaki Riot on the same day that the G8 financial meeting was taking place in Osaka. The riot was one of the most radical actions in Japan against global capital and the ostentatious festival of its representatives, who were retooling the failed neoliberal global framework for managing the persistent, if not permanent, capitalist crisis of command over labor. As the twenty-fourth Kamagasaki Riot had fused protest against police brutality and dissent against global finance capital, David Harvey declared in the same year that the "global struggle, predominantly with finance capital" revolves around the city and how "[o]ne step towards unifying these struggles is to adopt the right to the city as both working slogan and political ideal, precisely because it focuses on the question of who commands the necessary connection between urbanization and surplus production and use," concluding euphorically that "Lefebvre was right to insist that the revolution has to be urban, in the broadest sense of that term, or nothing at all" (Harvey 2008).

While Harvey's revival of Henri Lefebvre's quintessential phrase "the right to the city" seems to have come at a historically opportune moment, soon followed by urban insurrections all over the world, from Syntagma Square and Occupy Wall Street in 2011 to Istanbul's Taksim Square and Brazilian V for Vinegar Movement in 2013, we should approach its ideological assumptions with a grain of historically retrospective caution. As with Lefebvre's same-titled essay that situated the end of classical humanism with the 1870–71 Franco-Prussian War, Harvey's major historical referent is the Paris Commune (reflected most obviously in the collection *Paris, Capital of Modernity*). But neither the hundred years following the Commune which Lefebvre was reviewing nor the subsequent forty years that Harvey has lived through—and that coincides with our chronology—indicates that the city will be the ultimate arbiter of future revolutions. Even as Lefebvre was invoking the "right to the city" against the "pseudo-right" to "nature," which consumer capitalism was engineering through its leisure industry and urban planning, the world had already witnessed the concatenation of agrarian revolutions, or "peasant wars" in Eric Wolf's phrase, in delinking former Western imperialist colonies in Africa, Asia, the Caribbean, and Latin America toward independence and relativizing the classical Marxist notion of the urban proletariat as the vanguard of modern revolution.

In modern history the city has been a physical figure of bourgeois class power, from the walled enclaves of the early modern burghers to the mercantile town of Osaka and postmodern metropolis of Los Angeles. It signified freedom but in a very restrictive sense, as a leading social historian of the era reminds us:

> Freedom to the capitalist meant freedom from the restriction on commerce, markets, and production that characterized medieval city. Freedom also meant freedom of movement. This entailed a contradiction, however. The principle of movement was opposed by the principle of enclosure. Individual units were enclosed, especially production, discipline, punishment, docks, even streets while thoroughfares, canals, and later railroads could hasten the movement of commodities. Just as some walls come down, others go up. (Linebaugh 2013: 3)

Indeed, as we have seen in our brief comparative sketch, the urban riots of the 1960s and 1970s opened up the walls of enclosure—which also affects the ontological definition of social class—that the narrowly defined urban industrial workers accepted in their Keynesian capitalist bargain, selling the birthright of their horizontal solidarity and unequivocal autonomy for the mess of job security in alienated wage-labor and business union representation. They did not so much confirm the city as a privileged site of revolutionary struggle as erase its geographic and conceptual borders, whether drawn by capitalist planners or orthodox Marxists. When Malcolm X, former factory worker, street hustler, and prison inmate, in 1963 looked to the American, Chinese, and Algerian revolutions and affirmed the necessity of land struggle in his speech to the grassroots ("Revolution is based on land. Land is the basis of all independence. Land is the basis of freedom, justice, and equality"), he was in effect rejecting the narrow concept of urban revolution that limited itself to the bourgeois right of citizenship and franchise. This implied a revolutionary return to the etymological root of "culture," in seizing the land and cultivating it in common.

Moreover, contemporary urban reality has made the classical notion of the autonomous city virtually unsustainable. While concurring with Jacques Donzelot's analysis that "the city is being destroyed according to the three tendencies of gentrification/relegation/peri-urbanisation," we must also consider "the conduct of defending such a matter as the spirit of the city while neglecting polarization[2] and the relationship of the three tendencies . . . which may be understandable in a critical scholarship that makes urban policy its object of study—as a conservative attitude lacking somewhat in self-reflection or lacking sufficient despair" (Sakurada 2013: 360). Any meaningful radical rethinking of the "right to the city" must, therefore, ask with sufficient despair in the face of urban wastelands and heterogenous class struggles in which, to recast Yeats's famous poem, the industrial working class's hegemony and autonomous metropolitan "centre cannot hold" anymore and "anarchy is loosed upon the world": "What is the city, and whose right?" That would go a long way in redefining the "city," along with "culture," in the explicit context of class antagonism and reveal them as linguistic indices that register the varying degrees and intensities of class struggle.

NOTES

1. According to Edward Fowler, *anko* comes from "*ankō* or "angler fish," that is, one who idly awaits a job—typically dock work—to snap up" (Fowler 1996: 9).
2. The "polarization" here refers to a quote from Deleuze and Guattari's *A Thousand Plateaus*, which Donzelot cites to buttress "the horizontal institution of the city, as opposed to the state institution that presupposes the vertical system of bureaucracy" in defending the spirit of the city as not yet dead. But the original quote—"The town exists only as a function of circulation, and of circuits. . . . It effects a polarization of matter, inert, living or human; its causes the *phylum*, the flow to pas through specific places, along horizontal lines. It is a phenomenon of *transconsistency*, a *network*, because it is fundamentally in contact with other towns"—presents urban space as an "apparatus of polarization" that "invents the idea of the *magistrature*, which is very different from the State *civil-service sector*" but whose "civil violence" is comparable (Deleuze and Guattari 2005: 432–33; Sakurada 2013: 359–60).

BIBLIOGRAPHY

Abu-Lughod, Janet and Richard Hay (eds.) (1979), *Third World Urbanization*, New York: Methuen.

Asante, Molefi Kete and Stephen Robb (eds.) (1971), *The Voice of Black Rhetoric: Selections*, Boston: Allyn and Bacon.

Biko, Steve (1987), *I Write What I Like: A Selection of His Writings*, Oxford: Heinemann Publishers.

Camp, Jordan T. and Christina Heatherton (eds.) (2012), *Freedom Now!: Struggles for the Human Rights to Housing in LA and Beyond*, Los Angeles: Freedom Books.

Davis, Mike (2006a), *The City of Quartz: Excavating the Future in Los Angeles*, London: Verso.

———. (2006b), *The Planet of Slums*, London: Verso.

Deleuze, Gilles and Felix Guattari (2005), *A Thousand Plateaus: Capitalism and Schizophrenia* (trans. Brian Massumi), Minneapolis: University of Minnesota Press.

Eagleton, Terry (2000), *The Idea of Culture*, Oxford: Blackwell Publishing.

Fowler, Edward (1996), *San'ya Blues: Laboring Life in Contemporary Tokyo*, Ithaca: Cornell University Press.

Funamoto, Shuji (1985), *Damatte notare jinuna Funamoto Shuji ikoshu* [*Don't Die on the Street in Silence: Funamoto Shuji's Posthumous Work*], Tokyo: Renga-shobo-shinsha.

Glaberman, Martin (1973), *Punching Out*, Detroit: Bewick Editions.

Glass, Ruth (1964), "Introduction," in *London: Aspects of Change*, Center for Urban Studies (ed.), London: MacGibbon and Kee, pp. xiii–xlii.

Gorz, Andre (1982), *Farewell to the Working Class: An Essay on Post-Industrial Socialism*, (trans. Michael Sonenscher), London: Pluto Press.

Hall, Stuart and Tony Jefferson (eds.) (1976) *Resistance Through Rituals: Youth Subcultures in Post-War Britain*, London: Hutchinson.

238   *Manuel Yang, Takeshi Haraguchi, and Kazuya Sakurada*

Haraguchi, Takeshi, Nanami Inada, Tatsuya Shirahase and Takaaki Hirakawa (eds.) (2011), *Kamagasaki no susume [Recommending Kamagasaki]*, Kyoto: Rakuhoku-shuppan.
Haraguchi, Takeshi (2011), *"Chimei naki yoseba: toshi-saihen to homuresu"* ("Nameless *Yoseba*: Reorganizing the City and the Homeless"), in *Rodo saishin 4: shuen-rodoryoku no ido to hensei [Reviewing Labor 4: Movement and Formation of Marginal Labor Power]*, A. Nishizawa (ed.), Tokyo: Otsuki-shoten, pp. 157–200.
———. (2012), *"Oka no bodo, umi no sutoraiki"* ["Riot on Land, Strike on the Sea"], *Gendai-shiso [Contemporary Thought]*, 40: 6, pp. 196–209.
Harvey, David (2008), "The Right to the City," *New Left Review*, II: 53, http://newleftreview.org/II/53/david-harvey-the-right-to-the-city
Heatherton, Christina (ed.) (2011), *Downtown Blues: A Skid Row Reader*, Los Angeles: Freedom Now Books.
Industrial Workers of the World (1905), "Preamble to the IWW Constitution," http://www.iww.org/culture/official/preamble.shtml
Lefebvre, Henri (1996), "The Right to the City," in *Writings on Cities*, E. Kofman and E. Lebas (eds.), Oxford: Blackwell Publishing, pp. 63–181.
Linebaugh, Peter (2013), "The City and the Commons: A Story for our Times," paper delivered on 6 May at Museo Nacional Centro de Arte Reina Sofia: Madrid.
Marable, Manning and Leith Mullings (1999), *Let Nobody Turn Us Around: Voices of Resistance, Reform, and Renewal*, Lanham, MD: Rowman and Littlefield Publishers.
Sakai, Takashi (2011), *Tsutenkaku: shin nihon shihon-shugi hattatsushi [Tsutenkaku: A New History of Japanese Capitalist Development]*, Tokyo: Seidosha.
Sakurada, Kazuya (2012), *"Posutomodan toshi ni okeru yuibutsu-ron no shigaku-shiron"* ["An Essay on Materialist Poetics in the Post-modern City"], *Gendai-shiso (La revue de la pensée d'aujourd'hui)*, 40: 6, pp. 210–19.
———. (2013), *"Posutomodan toshi ni okeru kikai-jou bunseki no tame ni"* ["Towards a Mechanic Analysis on the Post-modern city"], *Seizongaku [Ars Vivendi]* 6, pp. 354–63.
Smith, Neil (1996), *The New Urban Frontier: Gentrification and the Revanchist City*, New York: Routledge.
Terashima, Tamao (1975a), *"News sun-hyo"* ["A Brief Comment on the News"], *Asahi Janarau [Asahi Journal]*, 8/29.
———. (1975b), *"Romusha tosei no koto"* ["On *Drifting Life of Romusha*"], *Romusha tosei*, 10.
———. (n.d., ca. 1973), *Kamagasaki bodo ryakushi [An Abbreviated History of Kamagasaki Riots]*, unpublished mss.
Thompson, E. P. (1978), "Eighteenth-Century English Society: Class Struggle without Class?" *Social History*, 3: 2, pp. 133–65.
———. (1991), *Customs in Common*, London: Penguin Books.
Thompson, Edward Palmer (1966), *The Making of the English Working Class*, New York: Vintage Books.
Weir, Stan (2004), *Singlejack Solidarity*, Minneapolis: Minnesota University Press.
Williams, Raymond (1973) "Base and Superstructure in Marxist Cultural Theory," *New Left Review* I: 82
———. (1983), *Keywords: A Vocabulary of Culture and Society*, Revised Edition, New York: Oxford University Press.

Index

Adlard, Mark, 138
Adler, Max, 161, 165, 170, 172, 179
adolescence. *See Barrio*
Adorno, Theodor, 67, 195
advertising, 11, 64, 66, 96, 114, 115, 172
AFL-CIO, 220
agriculture, 114, 151, 195–197, 200,
    203–204, 205, 206, 221. *See also* rural
Aguado, Txetxu, 51
Alexandria, 205
Ali, Muhammed, 203–204
alienation, xix, xx, 43, 56, 63, 65, 66,
    67–70, 71, 72–73, 75, 76, 77, 79, 80,
    81–84, 95, 101, 108, 149, 163, 169,
    171, 174, 181, 198. *See also*
    disalienation
Almodóvar, Pedro, 26, 27, 28
Alvarado Rubio, Mario, 114
anarchist/anarchism, 104–105, 107, 237
anti-communism, 119, 221. *See also*
    communist/communism; socialist/
    socialism
Antonioni, Michelangelo, 54
Aragon, Louis, 98
Arbenz, Jacobo, 114, 119, 128
architecture, xv, 5, 7, 8, 10, 11, 13, 14–15,
    50–51, 76, 96, 116, 140, 144, 148, 160,
    163, 164, 165, 176, 203. *See also* built
    environment; Ehn, Carl; Le Corbusier;
    urban planning
Arévalo, Juan José, 119, 128, 132n8

Aristotle, 196
art/arts, xi, xiv, xv–xvi, xvii–xviii, xix, xx,
    7, 8, 25, 26, 44, 45, 56, 69, 74, 77, 94,
    97, 103, 119, 123, 144, 154, 160, 169;
    art of rent, xv. *See also* architecture;
    avant-garde; Dada; books (pop-up);
    film; *La antena* (radio in); music;
    novels; painting; photography; poetry;
    Surrealist/Surrealism; television; texts/
    textual representation; theater; world
    literature
avant-garde, 45, 94–98, 108
Axelrod, Jeremiah B. C., 138, 144

Badiou, Alain, 181
Balzac, Honoré de, 25
Bachelard, Gaston, 51
Ballard, J. G., 137, 139, 140, 145–151,
    154; biographies of, 139; *Concrete
    Island*, 145; *Crash*, 139, 145; interview
    with, 146; *Empire of the Sun*, 139;
    High-Rise, 137, 140, 145–151
banks/banking, 4, 91, 92, 143, 204, 205;
    Interamerican Development Bank
    (IDB), 122. *See also* economy
Barcelona, 45, 46
Barrio, 23, 25, 26, 27, 28–35
Barthes, Roland, 77
Basilica of the Sacred Heart, 25
Bauer, Otto, 160–164, 167, 169–173, 176,
    181–182

239

Notes on Contributors

Malcolm Alan Compitello is professor of Spanish and head of the Department of Spanish and Portuguese at the University of Arizona. He is the author of four books: *Ordering the Evidence: Volverás a Región and Civil War Fiction*; *Critical Approaches to the Writing of Juan Benet*; *Rewriting the Good Fight*; and *De Fortunata a la M: 40: Un siglo de cultura urbana en Madrid*. His essays on contemporary Spanish narrative, film, and Cultural Studies have appeared in numerous professional journals and in volumes published here and in Spain and he is currently completing *From the Reina Sofía to Lavapiés: Urban and Cultural Change in Madrid's City Center*, a book on the relationship between the urban process in Madrid and its manifestation in cultural imaginaries of novelists and filmmakers. Recently, his research has expanded to include a consideration of virtual recreations of real spaces and their implications on the pedagogical exchange and research about space, place, and culture. Professor Compitello is the Executive Editor of the *Arizona Journal of Hispanic Cultural Studies*. A collection of essays honoring his accomplishments—*Capital Inscriptions: Essays on Hispanic Literature, Film and Urban Space in Honor of Malcolm Alan Compitello*—was recently published.

Kimberly DeFazio is assistant professor at the University of Wisconsin-La Crosse and author of *City of the Senses: Urban Culture and Urban Space* (2011). Her essays have appeared in such journals as *Textual Practice* and *Nature, Society and Thought* as well as in the collection *Confronting Universalities: Aesthetics and Politics Under the Sign of Globalisation* (2011). One of her essays on the city and class has been translated into Swedish ('Transnational urbanism ouch capitalist crave') in the journal of cultural theory *Fronesis*.

Brecht De Smet obtained his PhD in Political Sciences at Ghent University, Belgium and works as a post-doctoral research assistant and lecturer at the Conflict and Development Department, Ghent University. He also obtained a Masters degree in History, and a Masters degree in Eastern Languages and Cultures: Arabic and Akkadian at Ghent University. Since 2008 De Smet is investigating political and economic protest movements in contemporary Egypt. He has done extensive fieldwork, doing interviews and participative observation, with labor militants and political activists in particular. De Smet has presented his research in international seminars such as the Middle East Studies Association (USA) and Historical Materialism (GB) conferences. He has published in international peer-reviewed journals about the Egyptian workers' movement, the 25 January Revolution, Nasserism, Marxist political theory and philosophy, and is looking forward to the publication of his book by Brill about Gramsci, Vygotsky, and the Egyptian uprising (2014).

Benjamin Fraser is associate professor of Spanish Film and Cultural Studies at the College of Charleston. He is the executive editor of the *Journal of Urban Cultural Studies*, the managing editor of the *Arizona Journal of Hispanic Cultural Studies* and an associate editor of *Hispania*. He has published over sixty articles—in journals such as *Environment and Planning D: Soceiety and Space, Social and Cultural Geography, Studies in Hispanic Cinemas*, the *Journal of Spanish Cultural Studies*, and *Revista Iberoamericana*—as well as numerous monographs and edited volumes. Among the latter are *Henri Lefebvre and the Spanish Urban Experience: Reading the Mobile City* (2011), *Trains, Culture and Mobility: Riding the Rails* (2012), *Trains, Literature and Culture: Reading/Writing the Rails* (2012), *Understanding Juan Benet: New Perspectives* (2013), and *Disability Studies and Spanish Culture* (2013). His current book projects are titled *Antonio López García's Everyday Urban Worlds: A Philosophy of Painting* and *Toward an Urban Cultural Studies: Henri Lefebvre and the Humanities*.

Takeshi Haraguchi is an associate professor in the Department of Geography at Kobe University. From the dual methodological perspective of fieldwork and urban theory, he studies the social geography of contemporary cities. In his fieldwork, he has aimed at clarifying social/spatial exclusion and recording the dynamics of social movements on the basis of research in the post-war history of Osaka's Kamagasaki—renowned as a day laborers' district, waterfront, and homeless community. In the area of urban theory, he analyzes the contemporary reality of gentrification and privatization of public space, with the aid of Henri Lefebvre and David Harvey's spatial theories. He is the co-author of *Kamagasaki no susume* (*Recommending Kamagasaki*) and the Japanese translator of Neil Smith's *The New Urban Frontier: Gen-*

trification and the Revanchist City. His writings have appeared in such collections and periodicals as *Rodo-saishin* (*Labor Review*) 4, *Homeless Studies: Reality of Exclusion and Subsumption, Geographical Review of Japan, Gendai-shiso* (*Contemporary Thought*), and *Japanese Journal of Human Geography.* He is currently collaborating with Kazuya Sakurada on the working-class history of shipbuilding.

Jeff Hicks is a PhD candidate at the University of California, Riverside whose interests include science fiction and fantasy, dystopian literature, and cult film. He has published reviews in *Science Fiction Studies* and *Science Fiction Film and Television,* and is the co-author of the *Oxford Bibliographies Online* entry for the film *Blade Runner* and the chapter "Urban Dystopias" in the *Cambridge Companion to the City in Literature.* He is also the founding editor of *The Eaton Journal of Archival Research in Science Fiction.* He is currently researching the ways in which twentieth-century literature and film have responded to the explosion of urban populations and the geographic territory of urban areas.

Marc James Léger is an independent scholar living in Montreal. He has published essays in critical cultural theory in such places as *Afterimage, Art Journal, C Magazine, Canadian Journal of Film Studies, Creative Industries Journal, Etc, FUSE, Inter, Left Curve, Parachute, RACAR,* and *Third Text.* He is editor of the collected writings and interviews of Bruce Barber in *Performance, [Performance] and Performers* (2007) as well as Barber, *Littoral Art and Communicative Action* (2013). He is also editor of *Culture and Contestation in the New Century* (2011) and of the forthcoming *The Idea of the Avant Garde—And What It Means Today,* and is author of *Brave New Avant Garde* (2012) and *The Neoliberal Undead: Essays on Contemporary Art and Politics* (2013). He is presently working on a book of essays on film titled *Drive In Cinema.*

Andy Merrifield is a fellow at Murray Edwards College, University of Cambridge, and author of numerous books, including *Metromarxism* (2002), *Dialectical Urbanism* (2002), *Henri Lefebvre* (2006), *Magical Marxism* (2011), *The Politics of the Encounter* (2013), and *The New Urban Question* (2014).

Les Roberts is a lecturer in the Department of Communication and Media at the University of Liverpool, UK. His research interests and practice fall within the areas of urban cultural studies, cultural memory, and digital spatial humanities. His work explores the intersection between space, place, mobility, and memory with a particular focus on film and popular music cultures. He is author of *Film, Mobility and Urban Space: A Cinematic Geography of*

Liverpool (2012), editor of *Mapping Cultures: Place, Practice and Performance* (2012), and co-editor of *Locating the Moving Image: New Approaches to Film and Place* (2013), *Liminal Landscapes: Travel, Experience and Spaces In-between* (2012), and *The City and the Moving Image: Urban Projections* (2010).

Kazuya Sakurada is a lecturer (nontenured) at Urban Research Plaza of Osaka City University who focuses on sociology of unemployment and research methodology. He has written a number of essays on contemporary arts, jobless/homeless, and precarity, in addition to editing and co-authoring magazines and books, including *VOL lexicon*. His practical work as a researcher involves social statistics, documentation and data archiving, distribution of computing based on Unix tools, and project organizing in media, arts, and academics, while his theoretical work revolves around the study of Italian post-Operaismo. Currently, he is translating Franco Berardi's monograph on Félix Guattari into Japanese and also, with Takeshi Haraguchi, investigating the labor history of shipbuilding industries, in collaboration with a global research project hosted by the International Institute of Social History in Amsterdam.

Cayley Sorochan is a doctoral candidate in Communication Studies at McGill University. Her current research is concerned with the ideological function of "participation" in online culture, political organization, and consumer capitalism. She has published essays in *TOPIA: Canadian Journal of Cultural Studies, Reviews in Cultural Theory, Seachange Journal*, and co-edited a special supplement on the 2012 Quebec Student Strike for *Theory and Event*. Her wider research interests include psychoanalytic approaches to political subjectivity, the politics of space, networked performance, spectatorship, and mobile/social networking technologies.

Jelle Versieren obtained his Master's degree in History at Ghent University and is working on a PhD dissertation in Early Modern History at the University of Antwerp for the Centre for Urban History on guild craftsmen and wage workers in the economic transition of capitalism in the Low Countries. This dissertation focuses on the formation and development of modern labor concepts, the disappearance of precapitalist corporative institutions, the making of the early factory system, and the historical processes between technology and social relations of production. He has also published on the history of economic thought, value theory, Marxist philosophy and theoretical humanities, and the history of the Belgian labor movement.

Heather Vrana is an assistant professor of History at Southern Connecticut State University. A forthcoming book, *Do Not Tempt Us!: Guatemalan Uni-*

versity Students and the State, 1944–Present further explores the volatile relationship between Guatemalan university students and the government mentioned in this volume. A more detailed discussion of students' political funerals may be found in a *Radical History Review* Vol. 114 article entitled, 'Revolutionary Transubstantiation in "The Republic of Students": Death Commemoration in Urban Guatemala from 1977 to the Present.' Additional research interests include disability, race, medicine, and production in the making of modern Central America and intellectual histories of student movements throughout the Spanish-speaking world.

Manuel Yang has taught history at the University of Toledo, Monroe County Community College, Lourdes College, and Bowling Green State University. His most recent writings have appeared in *Reconstruction, Gendai shiso* (*Contemporary Thought*), *Rekishi toshite no 3.11* (*History as 3.11*), *Hibaku-shakai nenpo* (*Annual Report on Radioactive Society*), and J-Fissures. He is currently writing a book on the Japanese thinker and poet Yoshimoto Takaaki, a travelogue on the hydrangea revolution, and a comparative history of the New Left, as well as co-translating Mike Davis's *Late Victorian Holocausts* into Japanese. He lives in the San Gabriel Valley.